These wise and experienced authors know that truly effective discipline is all about education, not punishment. This well-organized and beautifully written book shows parents how they can employ plenty of common sense and a lot of love to teach their children invaluable life lessons that will enable them to become thoughtful, responsible, caring citizens of the world.
—Dr. Michael Meyerhoff, Ed.D., Executive Director, The Education for Parenthood Information Center

This is the most important book you can buy for your family—now and for the future.
—Victoria Moran, author of *Creating a Charmed Life*

The best book I have read to teach appropriate behavior and to encourage kind, resilient, and caring children.
—Nicole Wise, coauthor of *The Over-Scheduled Child: Avoiding the Hyper-Parenting Trap*, and mother of four

By following the suggestions in this simple, easy-to-read book, you are building a foundation of peace, love, empathy, and self-control in your children's lives. You will be forever grateful.
—Wally Amos, author of *The Cookie Never Crumbles: Inspirational Recipes for Everyday Living*

This book should be required reading for any parent who wants to react to preschooler conflicts calmly and nonviolently. This invaluable guide is a treasury of practical principles and concrete strategies for answering the universal childrearing challenges parents face every day.

—Linda Lantieri, coauthor of *Waging Peace in Our Schools*, and Founding Director of the Resolving Conflict Creatively Program of Educators for Social Responsibility

If all parents could follow the path outlined in this book, wars would be reduced to a memory of madness from a long time ago. I'd like to thank the authors for writing a book that helps parents answer the question, "What part can I play in trying to make sure that my children grow up to be confident, productive, happy people with their self-esteem intact?"

—Peter Yarrow, member of Peter, Paul, and Mary, and founder of Operation Respect: Don't Laugh at Me

DISCIPLINE

without

SHOUTING
or SPANKING

**Practical Solutions to the Most Common
Preschool Behavior Problems**

Jerry Wyckoff, Ph.D.
Barbara C. Unell

Meadowbrook Press
Distributed by Simon & Schuster
New York

Library of Congress Cataloging-in-Publication Data
Wyckoff, Jerry, 1935–
    Discipline without shouting or spanking: practical solutions to the
    most common preschool behavior problems / Jerry Wyckoff, Barbara C.
    Unell.
        p. cm.
    Includes bibliographical references and index.
    ISBN 0-88166-410-3 (Meadowbrook) ISBN 0-7432-2854-5 (Simon &
    Schuster)
        1. Discipline of children—Handbooks, manuals, etc I. Unell, Barbara
    C., 1951– II. Title.

    HQ770.4 .W93 2002
    649.64—dc21

                                                        2002020182

Editorial Director: Christine Zuchora-Walske
Editor: Joseph Gredler
Proofreader: Megan McGinnis
Production Manager: Paul Woods
Desktop Publishing: Danielle White, Mark Jacobson
Cover Photo: Tony Garcia, SuperStock
Index: Beverlee Day

© 1984, 2002 by Jerry Wyckoff and Barbara Unell

Published by: Meadowbrook Press
                 5451 Smetana Drive
                 Minnetonka, MN 55343

www.meadowbrookpress.com

BOOK TRADE DISTRIBUTION by Simon & Schuster, a division of Simon and Schuster, Inc., 1230 Avenue of the Americas, New York, New York 10020

07 08 09 10 9 8 7   10 9 8 7

Printed in the United States of America

Dedication

This book is dedicated to our adult children,
Christopher Wyckoff, Allison Wyckoff,
Justin Unell, and Amy Unell,
for their unsolicited and priceless
contributions to this book.

Acknowledgments

We would like to thank all the parents and other caregivers who continue to reinforce our belief that disciplining without shouting or spanking will always be the kindest and most effective way to teach children how to become self-sufficient, empathetic, responsible, self-controlled people.

We would also like to thank Bruce Lansky for his continued confidence in this book over the past two decades. Our thoughtful, dedicated editor, Joseph Gredler, has been our able steward during the revision and expansion of *Discipline without Shouting or Spanking*, which has been a reliable and trustworthy road map for hundreds of thousands of parents. We are grateful to Meadowbrook Press for the opportunity to help a new generation of parents discipline their children in loving, practical ways.

Contents

Preface

If you are a parent, recognize that it is the most important calling and rewarding challenge you have. What you do every day, what you say and how you act, will do more to shape the future of America than any other factor.

—*Marion Wright Edelman*

All children—especially preschoolers—create discipline problems, no matter how "perfect" the children or parents might be. Both well-adjusted and not-so-well-adjusted children of every socioeconomic background have needs and wants, as do their parents. Problems arise when the needs and wants of parents and children don't fit together like pieces of a puzzle.

The occasionally overwhelming problems of parenting can often be minimized when parents learn how to adjust their responses according to their preschoolers' needs. This book offers practical remedies for the common behavioral problems of preschoolers—remedies that parents and caregivers can apply in the heat of conflicts that arise during the course of normal family life.

Our intent is to show parents how to react to discipline problems in calm, consistent, and effective ways—without shouting or spanking. We want to help parents become "disciplined parents" who can control themselves when their children are losing control. By maintaining self-control, parents can avoid the dangers of using violence in any form, either inflicted or threatened. Shouting and spanking are forms of violence that teach children that inflicting fear and pain on others is a way to control their behavior.

The approach we take in this book—discipline as *teaching* rather than punishing—mirrors that of our original edition and combines the best of our forty collective years of professional and parental experience. We have studied and taught developmental and child psychology at the university level; served on the psychology staff of a state hospital for children; worked as a psychologist in a major suburban school district; founded five national parenting publications; conducted numerous parent groups, national seminars, and workshops; consulted with school districts and mental health centers; written extensively about parenting for radio, magazines, and newspapers, as well as the internet and other media; and raised a total of four children.

Our problem-solving principles and discipline strategies are based on behavioral psychology, which studies the behavior of children in "real" settings—homes, schools, and playgrounds. Since the publication of the first edition of *Discipline without Shouting or Spanking* in 1984, new behavioral issues have emerged. We have addressed these issues in this new edition.

- The relationship between violence in the home and violence at school.
- The link between playing with imaginary or toy guns as a preschooler and using guns in school and elsewhere.
- The spanking debate: Is moderate spanking harmful?
- The influence of electronic media (computers, internet, TV, electronic games) on behavior.
- The concern about the diagnosis of hyperactivity or Attention Deficit Hyperactivity Disorder (ADHD).
- The long-term causes and consequences of childhood obesity.
- The challenge of discipline for single parents.
- The crucial role parents play in building and maintaining empathy in children.

We have designed this book, like the original edition, to be a handy reference guide for parents and other caregivers—a first-aid handbook for managing misbehavior. We recognize parents' need for brevity, immediacy, and practicality. We offer advice on how to prevent misbehavior problems from occurring and how to solve them when they happen. We also include "case histories" that illustrate how a number of fictionalized families have used the strategies to handle real problems.

Who Is a Preschooler?

We use the term *preschool years* to describe the awesome, metamorphic days and nights during which a one-year-old child seems to suddenly become a five-year-old miniature adult. Generally speaking, *preschooler* refers to a child who hasn't reached school age (kindergarten or first grade) and includes toddlers but not infants. Newborn babies and children under one year old are unique creatures primarily governed by needs (food, sleep, and human contact) that are generally met through physical and emotional nurturing. Preschoolers' needs, on the other hand, often require psychological strategies. For this reason, this book focuses on post-infancy children whose normal development creates behavioral problems that force parents and other caregivers to adopt civilizing strategies in order to give children the tools they need to become happy, healthy human beings. The central work that is done during the preschool years is the teaching and civilizing that prepares children for formal schooling. (See "The Transition to Elementary School for You and Your Child" on page 9.)

Note: Please read "Milestones of Development" (pages 10–11) and "The Differences between Boys and Girls" (pages 8–9) before applying the do's and don'ts in each chapter. Doing so will help you understand the general behavioral characteristics of one- to five-year-olds as well as the influence of brain structure, body chemistry, and hormones on boy-girl behavioral dissimilarities. Understanding preschooler development will help prevent you from mistaking certain behaviors as abnormal or from erroneously blaming yourself for causing your child's misbehavior. For example, in order to understand the motivations behind your two-year-old's prolific use of *no,* it helps to know that negativism is a normal part of a two-year-old's behavior. To understand why boys are generally more aggressive during their tantrums than girls, it helps to know something about biological differences between the sexes.

Introduction

The preschool years are the prime physical, emotional, and intellectual learning years of life. At their best, preschoolers are curious, inventive, eager, and independent. At their worst, they are obstinate, inhibited, and clinging. Both their chameleonlike personalities and their inability to use adult logic make them tough customers for those selling life's behavior lessons. Preschoolers live in a world that is challenging to them as well as to their parents, and teaching preschoolers—which is what disciplining really is—is sometimes like working with fertile ground and sometimes like hitting your head against a brick wall.

This should not be especially surprising. Parents and their preschoolers are usually at least twenty years apart in age and light-years apart in experience, reasoning ability, and the capacity for self-control. They also have different ideas, feelings, expectations, rules, beliefs, and values about themselves, each other, and the world. For example, children are born not knowing that it isn't acceptable to write on walls. They will only learn the desirable ways of expressing their artistic talents if their parents consistently teach them where they can write, praise them when they follow directions, and outline the consequences of breaking the rule.

At the same time, children have their own needs, desires, and feelings, most of which they cannot articulate very well. Throughout their first five years, they struggle to become independent human beings and rebel against being "raised" by older people.

The ultimate goals that parents have for their preschoolers are the immediate goals they have for themselves: self-control and self-sufficiency. It's important for parents to understand that they operate on a timetable that's different from their children's and that each child's ability to learn is unique. This understanding helps parents use empathy, trust, and respect as the foundation for healthy family communication.

The number one task facing parents of preschoolers is teaching them appropriate behavior *on a level they can understand*. When dealing with their children's temper tantrums, for example, parents are not only attempting to restore calm and order to their household, they're also trying to teach their children how to handle frustration and anger in a more appropriate way. Parents must model the kind of behavior they want to teach. They must also communicate their values in ways that make the values as important for their children as they are for themselves.

Building Emotionally Strong Children

Children who believe they are the masters of their fate, who feel they belong, and who feel competent are more likely to become strong, resilient children and adults. This fact of life is as true today as it was in 1984 when the first edition of *Discipline without Shouting or Spanking* was published. In this book and also in *How to Discipline Your Six to Twelve Year Old…Without Losing Your Mind* (Doubleday, 1991), we help you understand that children thrive in a climate in which parents:

- accept children's inborn personality and temperament;
- help them develop a sense of responsibility for their actions;
- create a loving and safe environment built on mutual trust;
- teach them decision-making and problem-solving skills;
- show them how to handle mistakes as challenges rather than as disasters.

Parenthood Is Naturally Problematic

Because childhood is naturally full of problems and conflicts, parents need to ask themselves a number of questions before labeling any of their children's behaviors a "problem."

How often does a certain kind of misbehavior occur?

And how intense is it? For example, if your child becomes angry easily, anger may be his natural reaction to disappointment. However, if he becomes so angry that he risks injuring himself or others, you need to find a way to at least reduce the intensity of his anger.

Do I tolerate my child's misbehavior?

Your biases, needs, or rules may allow you to tolerate or even find amusing some behaviors other parents find intolerable. Asking yourself "What will the neighbors think?" moves the problem outside the family. A parent who accepts what a child does at home may realize that other parents will not approve of it. The parent may then decide to do something about the misbehavior.

A child's behavior becomes an issue or a problem from the parents' point of view or from the point of view of other parents. Children, on the other hand, do not see their behavior as a problem; they simply have not yet learned more appropriate or self-controlled ways of seeking satisfaction.

In order to adequately manage the problems of their children's behavior, parents *themselves* need to become more disciplined (where *discipline* is defined as a teaching-learning process that leads to orderliness and self-control). Parental behavior must change before their children's behavior is most likely to change, and parents must become disciplined parents before their children will most likely become self-disciplined.

Discipline Issues for Single Parents

Parenting a young child alone is a very difficult job for even the most skilled parent. Not only is parenting a twenty-four-hour, seven-days-a-week job that requires infinite patience, it's also designed to be a team effort. In order to build independent, self-sufficient, loving, empathetic children, it's best for parents to work together to plan strategies, share duties, and decide on rules. But that's not always possible.

Instead of focusing on trying to control what the parent who lives in another house or even in another state does or doesn't do, each parent is best advised to develop the most efficient discipline plan that teaches responsible behaviors, encourages positive attitudes, and provides emotional strength. As with all parents, a single parent also needs to develop a support system with preschool, daycare, babysitters, and extended family at its core.

The ABCs of Disciplined Parenting

Over forty years of behavioral research and experience, drawn from theory and based on working with thousands of families, have taught us that it's important for practical as well as philosophical reasons to separate a child from her behavior when dealing with behavior problems. Calling a child who leaves her toys out a "slob" won't get the toys picked up or teach neat behavior. It may only affect the child by contributing to an unhealthy self-image and possibly becoming a self-fulfilling prophecy. It's best for the child's self-esteem to concentrate on specific, constructive ways of changing the behavior. Based on this principle, here are our ABCs:

Decide on the specific behavior you would like to change.

If you focus on specifics rather than abstracts, you'll manage better. For example, don't tell your child to be neat; explain that you want her to pick up her blocks before she goes out to play.

Praise your child's behavior.

Don't praise your child, but rather praise what she is *doing*. For example, instead of saying, "You're a good girl for sitting quietly," say, "It's good you're sitting quietly." Focus your praise or disapproval on your child's behavior, because that is what you're interested in managing.

Continue the praise as long as the new behavior needs that support.

Praising the appropriate things your child does reminds her of your expectations and reinforces your model of good behavior. Praise motivates your child to continue behaving appropriately.

Try to avoid power struggles with your children.

Using a technique like Beat-the-Clock (page 12) when you want your children to get ready for bed faster, for example, will help you reduce parent-child conflict because you're transferring authority to a neutral figure: a timer.

Be there.

This does not mean that parents must be with their children every minute of every day, but it does mean that children need fairly constant supervision. If parents do not pay close attention to their children, many behavior problems will go unnoticed and uncorrected.

Avoid being a historian.

Leave bad behavior to history and don't keep bringing it up. If your child makes an error, constantly reminding her of it will only lead to resentment and increase the likelihood of bad behavior. What's done is done. Working toward a better future makes more sense than dwelling on the past. Reminding your children of their errors only reminds them of what *not* to do; it doesn't show them what to do.

Spanking and Shouting Are Counterproductive

The principles outlined in this book represent what we as parents *should* do when we're confronted with our children's misbehavior. What we *often* do, however, is shout at or spank our children, especially if we're tired or distracted or frustrated by their failure to obey us. Shouting and spanking are quite natural responses to misbehavior—especially continued misbehavior—but they're also quite counterproductive. They *never* teach appropriate behavior, which is the number one task of parenting. In fact, they teach just the opposite:

- How to shout
- How to hit
- How to be sneaky
- How to fear
- How to be ashamed
- How to take anger out on others

All degrees of shouting and spanking—light, moderate, occasional, rarely, always—give children the wrong kind of attention. If it's the only kind they're given, they may misbehave just to get noticed. Also, parents don't always know if spanking works because they don't actually observe its effect on a child's behavior over time. Spanking as punishment simply drives bad behavior underground: It stops the behavior from happening in front of parents, but it doesn't stop it altogether. In fact, children become experts at not getting caught. Parents may even say, "Don't let me catch you doing that again!"

In the hierarchy of moral development, as defined by Lawrence Kohlberg, the lowest level is "following rules only to avoid punishment." The highest level is "following rules because they are right and good."[1] When parents spank their children for misbehavior, they stop their children at the lowest level of moral development. The children are interested in avoiding the punishment, not in doing what is good or right.

Spanking is also often the earliest experience a child has with violence. Children learn to behave in violent ways through adult example— a compelling reason to avoid spanking, particularly with the increased exposure children have to violence in the media. (See pages 101–105.) It's difficult to justify the admonition "Don't hit!" while you're hitting your child for hitting.

Children see the world in concrete terms. When they see that it's permissible for adults to hit children, they assume it must be permissible for children to hit adults or other children. Hitting begets hitting—as well as anger, revenge, and the breakdown of communication between parents and their children.

The *primary* message given when parents shout or spank is that adults are bigger, stronger, and more powerful than children and can inflict fear and pain if displeased. The resulting sense of being a victim and being powerless in the face of greater size and strength creates fear and anxiety in children, and ultimately the desire to use violence themselves when upset.

No positive consequences result from spanking. In fact, the link between the victimization of children and their subsequent anger-management problems, as discussed in the work of Jay Barrish and others,[2] further underscores the argument for creating a zero-tolerance policy regarding spanking in your home, at daycare, in preschool, and in other settings. However, creating a zero-tolerance policy should not result in criminal penalties for spanking. Instead, this policy should be a statement of your own beliefs that discipline should be a teaching system that builds appropriate behavior.

The Learned Nature of Violence

Much research has been done to identify the causes of violent behavior in children and adults. Although the results are still somewhat controversial, Dr. Lonnie Athens' work, as cited in Richard Rhodes' book *Why They Kill*,[3] presents strong evidence regarding the development of violent adults.

Dr. Athens conducted in-depth interviews with people who were imprisoned for violent behavior. The interviews revealed that children who are frequently abused, threatened with abuse, or who witness others being abused are at very high risk for learning that violence is a way to solve problems, get what they want, or protect themselves from a perceived threat. When violence accomplishes these goals, children gain reputations as "nobody messes with me" kind of people. They get glory from infamy, and violence becomes a way of life. We believe that it's vitally important for every caregiver of every child to be aware of these dangerous consequences of the use of violence in any form, either threatened or actually inflicted on a child or other person. When caregivers understand this risk, we believe they will refuse to support spanking as a discipline option.

The Importance of Empathy in Discipline

Empathy is the ability to identify with and understand another's situation, feelings, and motives. All children are born with the capacity to be empathetic. Research indicates that this ability varies from child to child as they grow, and that girls have a greater capacity than boys to read emotions. Nevertheless, by two years of age, both boys and girls are able to understand others' feelings. By four years of age, children have the ability to comprehend the reasons for others' feelings. However, if empathy is to grow and flourish, parents must nurture its development.

The most important factor in building and maintaining empathy in children is respecting their individuality by modeling empathy, understanding, and caring—regardless of how difficult a child's behavior may be to manage. For example, by beginning your response to inappropriate behavior with the statement "I'm sorry you chose to do that…," you're showing your child that you care about his feelings and have empathy for his being in the "hot seat." In addition, parents can develop their children's potential to be empathetic by pointing out the impact of their behavior on others.

Conversely, the use of shouting or spanking to manage children's behavior erodes their ability to be empathetic. When we react with anger to children's behavior, we teach them to act without considering another person's feelings—a consequence we need to avoid. Studies by JoAnn Robinson, Ph.D., of the University of Colorado,[4] support this truth. She reported that greater maternal warmth is associated with increases in children's empathy during the second year of life, but children whose mothers control them with anger show decreases in empathy. Without empathy, it's nearly impossible for children to learn to share toys, play well with others, avoid angry and violent reactions to adversity, and take personal responsibility for their actions.

Using the positive teaching strategies outlined in this book will not only help keep *your* empathy quotient high, it will also help develop your children's potential to become empathetic, loving, caring adults.

The Role of Self-Talk

We encourage parents to use what we call *self-talk* to help them avoid falling into the habit of saying irrational things to themselves. *Self-talk* is best defined as what people say to themselves that governs their behavior. For example, if a parent says, "I can't stand it when my child whines!" then that parent's level of tolerance for the whining will be greatly diminished. However, if that parent says, "I don't like it when my child whines, but I can survive it," then not only will that parent be able to tolerate the whining longer, he or she will also be more likely to plan effective ways of changing the behavior.

Self-talk should be used to set ourselves up for success rather than failure. What we say to ourselves constitutes the most important messages we receive, so self-talk is a great tool for parents of preschoolers. If parents can calm themselves in times of stress by using helpful self-talk, then they will be more likely to follow through with reasonable and responsible actions.

Sometimes parents sabotage themselves with self-talk that encourages them to "follow the crowd." For example, if your child's friend's parents let your child use a bed as a trampoline, you may feel pressured to do the same by telling yourself you won't fit into the "good-parent club" if you don't. This peer-pressure self-talk can be harmless: You buy a certain kind of peanut butter because other parents buy it. However, it can also be dangerous if it leads you to shout at or spank your child because other moms and dads do. Instead of following the crowd, we encourage you to follow your heart, your common sense, and your knowledge of the most effective and caring ways of raising responsible, self-sufficient, and empathetic children.

The Differences between Boys and Girls

To better understand your preschooler's behavior, it's helpful to understand the differences between boys and girls. This information can help you distinguish between normal behaviors and those that need to be addressed as discipline issues. Knowing the natural differences between boys and girls can also help you avoid comparing your different-sex children. (See also "Milestones of Development" on pages 10–11 for more information on preschooler development.)

Research has shown that boys and girls differ in brain structure, body chemistry, and hormones, and that these differences strongly influence boy-girl behavioral dissimilarities. For example, boys' brains develop more slowly than girls'. In boys, the left half of the brain, which controls thinking, develops more slowly than the right half, which controls spatial relationships. As a result, the connection between the two hemispheres is not as fully formed in boys, who generally enjoy greater ability in math and reasoning, but lesser ability in language and reading.

Girls' brains develop more evenly, giving them the ability to use both hemispheres for such activities as reading and emotional awareness. The female brain is at work most of the time, allowing girls to be more skilled at multi-tasking. Girls' brains also secrete more serotonin, a neurotransmitter that inhibits aggression.

On the other hand, boys' brains secrete more testosterone, a hormone that drives aggression. As a result, boys tend to seek instant gratification (eating quickly, jumping from activity to activity), to move quickly to problem-solving (even in highly emotional situations), and to engage in activities that create tension (sports, contests, and games). These tendencies allow boys to release pent-up energy.

Other common differences* between boys and girls include the following:

- Boys prefer to focus on a single task, and they react more aggressively to interruptions.
- Girls' motor activities peak less quickly, are less vigorous, and last longer.
- Boys create and play games that fill larger spaces, and they need to be outside more.
- Girls' attention to objects is less fleeting and less active.
- Girls rely more on their five senses.

- Boys do better with visual information presented to the left eye, which feeds the right hemisphere.
- By age five, girls are six months ahead of boys in general development.
- Boys who see themselves as physically strong will seek rough and tumble play.
- Boys who feel safe and competent will seek independence earlier than girls.

*These differences are broad generalizations based on the vast amount of research on the development of boys and girls. Individual children may vary from these tendencies.

The Transition to Elementary School for You and Your Child

One- to five-year-olds are referred to as *preschoolers* because this is the stage in which they become self-disciplined or "civilized" by the pre-educational process that prepares them to function in the organized and regimented world of elementary school. So who does this civilizing? Parents, childcare providers, preschool teachers, coaches, friends, extended family members, neighbors, and other adults play important roles in teaching preschoolers such virtues as empathy, patience, self-control, responsibility, respect, cooperation, courage, courtesy, perseverance, and honesty.[5]

A steady moral compass of virtues will guide children on their journey from being "little" preschoolers to "big" elementary schoolers. It's crucial for parents to carefully select their preschoolers' first teachers based on their ability to teach these virtues. Children must learn to play cooperatively and to become increasingly self-sufficient when they are separated from their moms and dads for greater amounts of time. The preschool years are the foundation for children's learning readiness.

In our book *The Eight Seasons of Parenthood* (Times Books, 2000), we describe how preschoolers' behaviors force parents to assume the identity of "Family Managers" when teaching their children appropriate behaviors. As children change from being helpless, horizontal human beings to upright, mobile, do-it-myselfers, parents move from managing their children's lives to becoming organizational wizards who juggle working, cooking, cleaning, driving, and playing—all while being their children's first and most important teachers. Becoming a mother or father is so much more than giving birth to a child. It's a developmental process that continues for the rest of a parent's life.

Milestones of Development

The following chart describes some of the milestones parents can expect their one- to five-year-olds to reach during their preschool years. These milestones are presented according to the age at which they usually occur. Since each child develops on an individual timetable, a particular child may be ahead of, on, or behind the statistical average. Consult your child's health-care professional if your child is consistently delayed in reaching milestones or if you're concerned about other aspects of your child's development.

Age	Milestones
1–2 Years	• Explores his environment; gets into things • Takes one long nap a day • Plays alone for short periods of time • Explores his body
2–3 Years	• Runs, climbs, pushes, pulls; is very active • Legs appear knock-kneed • Feeds himself with fingers, spoon, and cup • Can remove some of his clothing • Explores his genitalia • Sleeps less, wakes easily • Likes routines • Becomes upset if his mother is away overnight • Wants to do things himself • Is balky and indecisive; changes his mind • Has flashes of temper; changes his moods often • Imitates adults • Plays beside but not with children his own age • Is not yet able to share, wait, take turns, give in • Likes water play • Prolongs the good-night ritual • Uses single words, short sentences • Is often negative; says "No" • Understands more than he can say
3–4 Years	• Runs, jumps, and climbs • Feeds himself; drinks neatly from a cup • Carries things without spilling • Can help dress and undress himself • May not sleep at naptime, but plays quietly

- Is responsive to adults; wants approval
- Is sensitive to expressions of disapproval
- Cooperates; likes to run simple errands
- Is at a "Me, too!" stage; wants to be included
- Is curious about things and people
- Is imaginative; may fear the dark, animals
- May have an imaginary companion
- May get out of bed at night
- Is talkative; uses short sentences
- Can wait his turn; has a little patience
- Can take some responsibility, such as putting away toys
- Plays well alone, but group play can be stormy
- Is attached to parent of opposite sex
- Is jealous, especially of a new baby
- Demonstrates guilt feelings
- Releases emotional insecurity by whining, crying, requesting reassurance of love
- Releases tension by thumbsucking, nail biting

4–5 Years
- Continues to gain weight and height
- Continues to gain coordination
- Has good eating, sleeping, and elimination habits
- Is very active
- Starts things, but doesn't necessarily finish them
- Is bossy, boastful
- Plays with others, but is self-assertive
- Has short-lived quarrels
- Speaks clearly; is a great talker
- Tells stories; exaggerates
- Uses toilet words in a silly way
- Makes up meaningless words with lots of syllables
- Laughs, giggles
- Dawdles
- Washes when told
- Is at the "How?" and "Why?" stage
- Demonstrates dependence on peers

Discipline Dictionary

The following terms are defined according to how they are used in this book:

Beat-the-Clock

A motivational technique that uses your child's competitive nature to encourage her to complete tasks on your timetable. Here's how it works: Set a timer for the amount of time you want to allow your child to complete a task. Ask, "Can you finish before the timer rings?" Since children love to win, this allows them to win a race against time. More importantly, your child completes the task in a timely fashion without a power struggle. Our forty years of working with thousands of children and families have shown that Beat-the-Clock reduces parent-child conflicts because it transfers authority to a neutral figure: a timer.

Grandma's Rule

A contractual arrangement that follows the pattern "When you have done X (what the parent wants the child to do), then you may do Y (what the child wants to do)." Grandma's Rule is best stated in the positive rather than the negative. Never substitute "if" for "when." This encourages a child to ask, "What if I don't do X?" Grandma's Rule, which is derived from the axiom "When you work, you eat," has a powerful effect on behavior because it sets up established reinforcers (rewards, positive consequences) for appropriate behavior.

Neutral Time

Time that's free from conflict, such as the time after a tantrum is finished and your child is playing calmly. Neutral time is the best time for teaching new behavior because your child is calm and receptive to learning.

Praise

To verbally recognize a behavior you want to reinforce. Praise should always describe the behavior and not the child. For example, say, "Good eating," not "Good girl for eating." When you say, "Good girl for eating," you're doing something you don't want to do: connecting a child's worth to her behavior. You don't want to teach a child that as long as she's behaving appropriately, she's a good person—but should she make a mistake, she becomes a bad girl. We believe that children are inherently good. Their behavior is what parents are judging and striving to change for the better.

Reprimand

A short statement that includes the following: (1) a command to stop the behavior, (2) a reason why the behavior should stop, and (3) an alternative to the behavior. For example, you might say to your child, "Stop hitting. Hitting hurts people. Ask your friend nicely to give you the toy."

Rule

A predetermined behavioral expectation that includes a stated outcome and consequences. For example, one of your rules might be "We put our dirty clothes in the hamper when we take them off so we can keep our house neat and so we won't have to pick up stuff all the time. And for remembering the rule, you won't have to practice putting your dirty clothes in the hamper." Establishing and enforcing rules is an effective problem-solving technique. Our years of working with children and families have shown that children will behave more appropriately when their world has clear boundaries and when they can anticipate the consequences of their behavior.

Time Out

To take a child out of a situation for a set period of time, usually because of inappropriate behavior. A typical Time Out involves taking your child to a chair or room, setting a timer for a certain length of time (approximately one minute for each year of age, up to five minutes), and telling her she must stay there until the timer rings. If she leaves Time Out before the timer rings, reset the timer and tell her she has to stay there until the timer rings. Repeat the process until she stays in Time Out for the designated time. One of the benefits of Time Out is that it separates you from your child when tempers are flaring, giving you and your child the opportunity to regain self-control.

Using This Book

To use this book most effectively, think of each "What to Do" suggestion as a remedy for a certain behavior problem. Judge for yourself the seriousness of the problem, then begin with the least severe first-aid measure. The guiding principle for changing children's behavior is "Try the mildest strategy first." This usually means showing your child what to do and encouraging him to do it. If that doesn't work, try the next mildest strategy and proceed from there until you find something that works. It's equally important to know what *not* to do in a behavioral crisis, so pay special attention to the "What Not to Do" suggestions listed in each section. These will help you prevent certain behavior problems from recurring or becoming more severe.

Because parents and children are individuals, certain words and actions as applied in specific situations in this book will feel more natural to some than to others. Change a word or two if the exact language doesn't flow comfortably from your mouth. One- to five-year-olds are acutely aware of and sensitive to the feelings and subtle reactions of their parents. Make what you say and do believable to your children, and they will more readily accept your discipline.

The remedies in this book are designed to show your child the kind of respect you would give others in your home. Your children learn to be respectful by being treated respectfully. Treat your child as if he were a guest in your house. This does not mean your child shouldn't follow the rules; it means he should be taught in a kind and respectful way how to follow the rules.

Since 1984, this book has been the discipline framework for hundreds of thousands of parents and childcare providers. We are honored to be such an important part of the beginning chapter in families' lives. Their journey is your journey, our journey, as we nurture preschool-aged children.

Aggressive Behavior

Like bulls in china shops, many energetic preschoolers hurl toys or their bodies at the nearest targets when frustrated, angry, or rambunctious. Why? Because the little dynamos are not able to reason or compromise, and throwing books or toys doesn't seem any different from tossing balls. Tame your child's aggressive behavior by first explaining that hitting, biting, throwing, and teasing are unacceptable. Then show and tell (even your one-year-old) the kind of behavior you want your child to exhibit: kissing, hugging, talking, and so on. Also, explain why these actions are acceptable. Make sure to strictly and consistently enforce the rules in order to guide your child on the path toward appropriate behavior.

Note: If your child's aggressive behavior is a regular feature of her daily play and is disruptive to friends, family, and yourself, seek professional help to find out what may be causing this behavior.

Preventing the Problem

Closely supervise your child's play.
To prevent your child from learning aggressive behavior from her peers, monitor how she and her friends interact with each other and how they care for their toys. Don't let aggressive behavior cause injury or damage. Also, treat your child's friends' misbehavior as you would your child's.

Don't model aggressive behavior.
Treat your things they way you'd like your children to treat theirs. For example, hitting or throwing things when you're angry shows your child how to be aggressive when she's mad.

Explain why biting and hitting are unacceptable.
To help your child understand just how unpleasant aggressive behavior is for both sides, explain how biting and hitting make the victim feel.

Solving the Problem

What to Do

Tell your child what to do besides hit.

When aggressive behavior starts, tell your child things to do besides hit when she's feeling upset. For example, tell her she may ask for help or say, "I'm not playing anymore," or she may simply leave the playgroup. Ask her to practice these lines five times until she's familiar with the words and how to use them.

Compliment getting along.

Explain what you mean by *getting along* by telling your child you appreciate her behavior when she shares, takes turns, asks for help, and so on. For example, say, "Good sharing with your friends, honey." Always be specific about what you're praising. The more you praise your child's behavior, the more it will be repeated.

Use reprimands.

Reprimanding your child helps her understand why you disapprove of her behavior. It also shows that you respect your child's ability to understand your reasons. The three parts of an effective reprimand for hitting, for example, include telling your child to stop ("Stop hitting!"), explaining why you disapprove ("Hitting hurts people!"), and suggesting an acceptable alternative to hitting ("When you're angry, just leave the group."). If your child continues to be aggressive, repeat the reprimand and include a Time Out to reinforce your message.

Forget the incident when it's over.

Reminding your child of her previous aggressions doesn't teach her acceptable behavior. On the contrary, it reminds her of how she could be aggressive again.

What Not to Do

Don't use aggression to stop aggression.

Hitting your child only gives her permission to hit others in similar circumstances.

Don't let off steam when your child does.

Getting angry when your child hits, for example, only proves to your child that she can use aggression to get power over you.

Mike the Biter

At twenty-two months of age, Mike Morgan became known as the neighborhood biter, having had lots of practice on his two older brothers, who teased him mercilessly. Mrs. Morgan threatened her youngest child in order to stop his aggressiveness. "If you don't stop biting people, Mikey, I'm going to spank you." But she knew she never intended to back up her threat.

Mike's three- and five-year-old brothers' teasing didn't seem to bother their mother. In fact, her family joked frequently about lots of things, and she considered the older boys' making fun of Mikey all in the spirit of not taking yourself too seriously. Her husband didn't agree. "Think how all that teasing must make Mike feel," he said one day.

Though she didn't want to admit it, Mrs. Morgan had never thought about this problem from Mike's point of view—that he got back at his brothers by biting because he couldn't match their verbal attacks. She decided to teach all three boys that biting, hitting, teasing, and throwing things would not be tolerated. She believed that this was the only way to teach the older boys to model good behavior and to teach Mike to make better choices about how to get attention.

The next day, Mike began to bite his brothers after they called him "little Oscar the Grouch." Mrs. Morgan reprimanded Mike first. "Stop biting, Mikey. Biting hurts people. We bite apples, not people." She also reprimanded Mike's brothers. "Stop teasing. We do not tease people. It hurts their feelings."

But the reprimands didn't stop the boys' verbal and physical attacks. So Mrs. Morgan said, "I'm sorry you're still biting and teasing each other. Time Out!" The three boys were then directed to separate chairs and told to think about what happened and to think about ways in which they could avoid having it happen again.

As Mrs. Morgan became consistent in her discipline, and as she praised any getting along the boys did within the home, the Morgan boys learned what to expect from fighting and from being friendly. Mike began to bite less, since he didn't have to tolerate his brothers' teasing, and the older boys learned that teasing was hurtful.

Behaving Shyly

Imagine seeing your neighbor at the supermarket as you're happily shopping with your three-year-old son. Suddenly, he clutches your leg and won't answer your neighbor's simple greeting, "How are you, Sam?" You're surprised at this odd behavior and ask your son, "What's the problem? You love Kathy!"

You're not alone. Millions of parents are confused by their children's "freezing up" when confronted with questions. While some children approach the world with unbridled curiosity, others keep tight rein on their inquisitiveness, choosing to "look before they leap." Both tendencies are considered normal, each reflecting an innate style.

In other words, shyness is not a problem in and of itself. However, it becomes a problem when a child's shyness becomes so powerful that it prevents him from making friends or participating in social activities away from home, such as going to a birthday party or the library. Teaching social skills and role-playing various social situations will help preschoolers reduce their shyness and increase their self-confidence.

Preventing the Problem

Develop realistic expectations and goals.

How you expect your child to act around other people may not be realistic given his developmental stage. For example, if your two-year-old isn't ready to go to a birthday party, forcing him to go will only create more fear about future social events. Preschoolers overcome their shyness as they gain experience interacting with others. However, don't expect changes overnight.

Accept your child's shyness.

Children are born with different temperaments: Some are friendly and outgoing, some are cautious and shy, and some bounce back and forth between the two. Instead of sending your shy child the message that something's wrong with him because he doesn't act according to your expectations, accept his shyness as part of his unique temperament.

Compliment your child.

When your child makes a comment during a conversation, pay him a compliment. For example, say, "I like what you said about the puppy, Stevie. He does have an unusual white paw."

Be a good role model.

Give your child plenty of opportunities to watch you interact with people in social situations. Also, role-play different scenarios with your child, teaching him what to say in certain situations. For example, say, "When people ask me how I feel, I usually say, 'Fine. How are you?'"

Solving the Problem

What to Do

Provide an environment that's free from blame and shame.

When your child feels he can make mistakes without being blamed or shamed, he can more easily give up his shy ways. If your child spills his milk, say, "That's no big deal. Here, we can clean it up together."

Practice responding to questions.

If your child shifts into shy mode, he's probably telling you he needs to be taught how to answer questions. Practice with him while you're riding in the car or playing in the bathtub. For example, say, "When somebody says, 'What's your name?' say, 'Stevie.' That way they'll know who you are. Now, let's practice. When I say, 'What's your name?' what do you say?" Practice with your child several times each day until "Stevie" is the automatic response.

Practice with family and friends.

Provide your child opportunities to participate in conversations. For example, say, "What do you think about having pizza for dinner tonight?" or, "Tell Johnny about your trip to the zoo today."

Seek professional help if necessary.

If shyness is interfering with your child's happiness, if it keeps him from participating in appropriate activities, and if it seems to be making him miserable, you should seek help from a qualified professional.

What Not to Do

Don't humiliate or punish.

Even though you may feel embarrassed by your child's shyness, punishing or humiliating him will further discourage him from becoming socially confident. Apologizing for his behavior by telling others he's "your shy child" or he "doesn't speak" will only deepen his fear of others.

Don't beg.

Although you may be sorely tempted to beg your child to "answer the nice lady," doing so will give your child's reticence considerable power and will encourage more refusals in the future.

Don't label.

Making excuses to family and friends by saying your child is "shy" creates a self-fulfilling prophecy he has to live up to. It also discourages him from trying to behave differently in the future.

Getting to Know Eduardo

Eduardo Bartone had been a shy baby who would turn his face away from strangers or bury his head in his mother's shoulder when strangers were around. His dad, Miguel, had also been shy as a child. Eduardo's Grandma Leona said that no one outside the family heard Miguel talk until he was almost a teenager.

Eduardo's mother, Maria, had hoped that Eduardo would outgrow his shyness. But at five years old, "Timido" Eduardo, as she called him, showed no signs of becoming more outgoing. Miguel understood his son and the pain he felt when he was confronted with talking to strangers.

So Miguel worked out a plan to help his son. First he engaged him in conversation by asking lots of questions that Eduardo had to answer with more than a yes or no. Miguel asked his son, "What did you have for lunch today?" or, "What games did you play at preschool today?" When Eduardo answered with more than one or two words, Miguel would say, "Eduardo, I'm glad you told me about that," or, "That was a really interesting story about playing airplane on the playground."

Miguel also had Eduardo practice greeting people. The two would pretend they were meeting on the street, and Eduardo would say, "Hello, how are you?" Miguel would answer, "Fine, thank you. And you?" Then they would both laugh. Eventually, Eduardo began to relax more around people he didn't know well, and family and friends started to comment on how polite he was becoming.

Eduardo's mom and dad were happy for him. They had expected him to follow Miguel's timid path, and they were thrilled to see him coming out of his shell. They pledged to each other that they would never again put a label on their son.

Being a Couch Potato

In today's world of high-tech, low-energy toys and games, your child can easily let her fingers—not her legs—do the walking. However, young children need physical activity to develop their muscles and minds. Resist the urge to buy yourself some free time by constantly plunking your preschooler in front of an electronic babysitter. Parent-approved computer and video games and educational television programs can be constructive teaching tools. However, if used excessively, they can lay the foundation for an unhealthy, sedentary lifestyle.

Preventing the Problem

Turn off the TV.

The American Academy of Pediatrics recommends that parents restrict the amount of children's television viewing to less than two hours per day. Limiting television viewing and other "couch" activities encourages children's creativity and reduces aggressiveness.

Get moving!

Physical activities stimulate the heads and hearts of both children and parents. Playing jumping jacks, galloping horses, and other fun physical games tones your toddlers' muscles and also tires the little ones out so they sleep more soundly.

Cultivate creativity.

Instead of letting your preschoolers become passive media sponges, focus their attention on building forts, inventing games, drawing pictures, creating collages, and doing other creative activities to keep their growing minds and bodies active.

Solving the Problem

What to Do

Set time limits on using electronic media.

To avoid habitual media overindulgence, set a timer to tell your child when it's time to click the off button, and praise her when she turns to more physical activities. Say, "I'm glad you turned off the TV and chose to play school. What are you teaching this morning?"

Show your children how to be active.

Children are professional imitators, so showing them how to stay active means staying active yourself. If they see you cooking, cleaning, washing, writing, exercising, visiting with friends, paying bills, working outside, and playing with them, they'll be encouraged to use their time interacting with their world instead of watching TV.

Praise activity.

When your children are engaged in active play, point out their healthy behavior by saying, "Swinging is fun, and it helps your body and mind grow healthy and strong."

What Not to Do

Don't use the TV to buy child-free time.

Telling your child to "go watch TV and stay out of the kitchen while I'm fixing dinner" only encourages her to be a couch potato. Instead of banishing your child from the kitchen, introduce her to the world of broiling, baking, and boiling by asking her to do age-appropriate tasks such as washing the potatoes or tearing up the lettuce.

Don't reward with food.

Help your child learn that food is to be used for nourishment, not as a reward for good behavior or as something to soothe a broken heart. Keep your praise food-free, so that your giving food is not confused with giving approval or love.

Don't allow eating in front of the TV.

Linking watching TV with snacking can cause couch potatoes to "fluff up" in an unhealthy manner! Moreover, when your child eats while watching TV, she isn't able to focus properly on either activity, and she misses the value of each.

A Weighty Problem

Latisha Johnson's favorite pastime was watching television, but a close second was playing video games on the family computer. The fact that she was occupied for hours was both good and bad for her mother, Janelle. The good news? Janelle could make dinner after work without interruptions because Latisha would race for her beloved electronic toys as soon as she got home from daycare. The bad news? Latisha's massive doses of media were becoming hazardous to her health.

Not only did the four-year-old love watching TV, she also loved eating while watching. She begged Janelle to buy all the junk food advertised on TV, and Janelle, hating to upset her daughter, obliged. However, Janelle started to feel guilty when the pediatrician mentioned how much weight Latisha had gained since her last checkup.

Unfortunately, Latisha wasn't the only one who loved TV and junk food. Anthony, Latisha's dad, was an inveterate "couch potato." He came home from work and plunked himself on the sofa, where he watched ball game after ball game. Anthony understood the problem his daughter was developing because he knew how hard it was to get a belt buckled around his ever-growing middle.

One night at dinner, Janelle said, "Latisha, sweetheart, your dad and I think that we all watch too much TV around here, so we've made three new rules. First, we're going to allow only one hour of TV each day, and we'll decide as a family what to watch. Second, the computer will be used for only one hour each day. Third, we'll eat in the kitchen or dining room, and we won't have TV on during that time."

"But I like TV!" Latisha whined. "What can I do if I can't watch TV or play games on the computer?"

"I have an idea," Anthony said. "Let's make up our own television shows. We'll get costumes, imagine stories, and become actors."

"Oh, yes!" Latisha said excitedly. So that night they rummaged through the house gathering old clothes for costumes and designing a set in the basement. They worked so hard that Latisha was exhausted when she went to bed that night. Every week after that she invited her preschool friends over to play "TV Show" in the basement.

Janelle not only saw her plump little girl begin to slim down, she also noticed how creative Latisha was becoming in so many different ways. Latisha was also becoming more interested in being read to at bedtime, instead of insisting that they watch TV together before she went to sleep. The family's creative play was the perfect diet for Anthony, too. His middle started firming up when he started hosting an exercise class for their home "TV Show."

Although Janelle had lost her free time to family time, she realized that the change was good for everyone. She knew that the rewards of talking, laughing, loving, and growing closer far outweighed the sacrifice.

Clinging to Parents

The image of a preschooler clutching his mother's skirt, hanging on for dear life while she tries to cook or walk out the door, is not make-believe for many parents. It's a real and emotionally draining part of everyday life. Though it may be tough, resist the temptation to constantly attend to your clinging vine as you go about your day. If you want (or need) to leave your child with a babysitter, firmly and lovingly reassure him by telling him that you're proud of him for staying with the sitter and that you will return. Tell him in a sincere voice that you're happy he has the chance to play with the babysitter. Your positive attitude will be contagious (as would a negative one). You'll also be a good model for feeling okay about being separated and having a good time with other people. Provide lots of hugs and kisses during neutral times, to prevent him from feeling ignored and needing to cling to you to get attention. Clinging, unlike hugging, is an urgent demand for immediate attention.

Preventing the Problem

Practice leaving your child with a sitter.

To get your child used to the idea that you may not always be around, practice leaving him occasionally for short periods of time (a few hours) early in his life. These breaks are healthy for both parents and children.

Tell your child what you'll both be doing in your absence.

Telling your child what you'll be doing while you're gone gives him a good example to follow when you ask him to talk about his day's activities. Describe what he'll be doing and where you'll be while you're away, so he won't worry about his fate or yours. For example, say, "Laura will fix your dinner, read you a story, and tuck you into bed. Your daddy and I are going out to dinner, and we'll be back at eleven o'clock tonight." Or say, "I need to cook dinner now. When I've done that and you've played with Play-Doh, then we can read a story together."

Play Peek-a-Boo.

This simple game gets your child used to the idea that things (and you) go away and, more importantly, come back. Toddlers and preschoolers play Peek-a-Boo in a variety of ways: by hiding behind their hands or some object, by watching others hide behind their hands or some object, and (for two- to five-year-olds) by engaging in a more physically active game of Hide-and-Seek.

Reassure your child that you'll be coming back.

Don't forget to tell him that you'll be returning, and prove to him you're as good as your word by coming back when you said you would.

Create special "sitter" activities.

"Activity treats" help your child look forward to staying with a sitter instead of being upset by your absence. Set aside special videos, finger-paints, games, storybooks, and so on that only come out with a sitter.

Prepare your child for the separation.

Tell your child that you'll be leaving and plant the suggestion that he can cope while you're gone. For example, say, "You're getting to be such a big boy. I know you'll be fine while I'm gone." If you surprise him by leaving without warning, he may always wonder when you're going to disappear suddenly again.

Solving the Problem

What to Do

Prepare yourself for noise when you separate and your child doesn't like it.

Remember that the noise will eventually subside when your child learns the valuable lesson that he can survive without you for a brief time. Tell yourself, "He's crying because he loves me. But he needs to learn that although I can't always play with him and I occasionally go away, I'll always come back."

Praise your child for handling a separation well.

Make your child proud of his ability to play by himself. For example, say, "I'm so proud of you for entertaining yourself while I clean the oven." This will further reinforce his self-confidence and independence, which will benefit both of you.

Use the whining chair (pages 147–149).

Let your child know that it's okay for him not to like your being busy or leaving, even for short periods of time. However, make it clear that his whining disturbs others. For example, say, "I'm sorry you don't like my having to cook dinner now. Go to the whining chair until you can play without whining." Let a whining child whine—away from you.

Recognize that your child needs time away from you.

Breaks from constant companionship are necessary for children and parents. So keep your daily routine, even if your child protests your doing something besides playing with him or fusses when you occasionally leave him with a babysitter.

Start separations slowly.

If your child demands too much of your time from age one and up, play Beat-the-Clock. Give him five minutes of your time and five minutes to play by himself. Keep increasing the play-by-himself time for each five minutes of time spent with you, until he can play by himself for one hour.

What Not to Do

Don't get upset when your child clings.

Tell yourself your child prefers your company to anything in the whole world.

Don't punish your child for clinging.

Instead, follow the steps outlined above to teach him how to separate.

Don't give mixed messages.

Don't tell your child to go away while you're holding, patting, or stroking him. This will confuse him about whether to stay or go.

Don't make sickness a convenient way to get special attention.

Don't make being sick more fun than being well by letting your sick child do things that are normally unacceptable. Sickness should be dealt with in a matter-of-fact way with few changes in routine.

"Don't Leave Me!"

Natalie and Rick Gordon loved the party circuit so much that when their four-year-old son, Tyler, clutched both their jackets in horror when a babysitter arrived, both parents discounted his feelings. "Oh come on, Tyler, honey, don't be a baby! We love you. It's silly for you to feel bad. We go out every Saturday."

    But Tyler wasn't comforted. He screamed at the top of his lungs, "Don't go! Don't leave! Take me!" His clinging persisted, and the Gordons couldn't understand what they were doing wrong to make their son "punish" them whenever they wanted to leave the house. They asked themselves, "Does he hate us that much, to embarrass us in front of the babysitter and stain our party clothes with sticky fingers?"

    The Gordons eventually related their frustration to their friends, the Reillys, who tried to reassure them by explaining that Tyler clung to them because he loved them, not because he hated them. The Reillys also related how they had helped their daughter adjust to their absence.

    The Gordons tried the Reillys' strategy the following Saturday night. Before leaving, they prepared Tyler for their upcoming departure by saying, "You're such a big boy, now. You'll have fun playing with Laura while we're at the movies. We'll be back after you're in bed, but we'll be here in the morning when you wake up. Laura will make you popcorn in our new popcorn maker, she'll read you a story, and then you'll go to bed. Have fun!" They didn't drag out their exit with tearful hugs, and they left Tyler while he was only whimpering.

    After this apparent success, they began to praise Tyler about how quiet he was being during their explanation of where they were going, what they were planning to do, and how long they'd be gone. Whenever they got a good report from the babysitter, they'd let Tyler know how proud they were of him for playing nicely while they were gone. "Thanks for being so calm and for helping Laura make the krispy treats last night," they'd say with a hug.

    The Gordons were also patient. They knew they might have to wait several weeks before being able to leave to the sounds of happy feet instead of stomping and wailing. But in the meantime, they stopped verbally attacking Tyler for any "babyish" behavior, and they reduced his crying by ignoring it.

Dawdling

Because time has no meaning to a child under six years old, hurrying has no great advantages. Disguise urging your child to "come on" or "please hurry" by running races with her or by giving her chances to run to your arms. Turn instructions into fun, not frustrating orders. Let your child feel she's in control of how slow or fast she does things, so she won't need to dawdle to exert influence over the pace of events.

Preventing the Problem

Try to be an on-time person.

Tuning in to being on time helps your child understand the importance of meeting time goals and builds empathy for others. Saying "We must hurry to get ready so we can be at preschool on time and not keep your teacher waiting" motivates your child to move more quickly and makes the connection between being on time and the impact of lateness on others.

Try to allow lead time.

If you're in a hurry, waiting for your preschool tortoise may lead you to lose your cool and be that much later. Make every effort to allow enough time to get ready for outings, understanding that dawdling is a typical response to movement by someone who doesn't understand what hurrying means and is a full-time world investigator.

Establish and maintain a schedule.

Since a child needs routine and consistency in her daily life and tends to dawdle more when her routine is broken, establish time limits and a regular pattern of eating, playing, bathing, and sleeping, to familiarize her with the time frame on which you want her to operate.

Solving the Problem

What to Do

Make it easy for your child to move at your pace.

Ask motivating questions and play simple games to disguise hurrying. For example, encourage your child to get ready by having her guess what

Grandma has at her house. Or, ask your child to run to your arms if you want her to hurry along the path to your car.

Play Beat-the-Clock.

Children always move more quickly while trying to beat a timer (a neutral authority) than while trying to do what you ask. Say, "Let's see if you can get dressed before the timer rings."

Offer incentives for speed.

For example, say, "When you beat the timer, then you may play for ten minutes before we leave for school." This lets your child see for herself that good things come to those who stay on a schedule.

Reward movement as well as results.

Motivate your child to complete a task by encouraging her along the way. For example, say, "I like the way you're getting dressed so quickly," rather than waiting until she's done and only saying, "Thank you for getting dressed."

Use manual guidance.

You may need to physically guide your child through the task at hand (getting in the car, getting dressed, and so on) to teach her that the world goes on regardless of her agenda at the moment.

Use Grandma's Rule.

If your child is dawdling because she wants to do something while you want her to do something else, use Grandma's Rule. For example, say, "When you've finished getting dressed, then you may play with your train."

What Not to Do

Don't lose control.

If you're in a hurry and your child is not, don't slow both of you down even more by giving her attention for dawdling (nagging or screaming at her to get going, for example). Getting angry will only encourage your child's easygoing pace.

Don't nag.

Nagging your child to hurry up when she's dawdling only gives her attention for *not* moving. Disguise a hurry-up technique by turning it into a game.

Don't dawdle yourself.

Getting your child ready to go somewhere only to have her wait for you tells her that you don't really mean what you say. Don't announce that you're ready to go to Grandma's house, for example, when you're not.

Dawdling Allison

Three-year-old Allison had a knack for noticing blades of grass or toying with her shoestrings instead of doing what was necessary at the moment. Grandma Harris, her daily babysitter, felt bad about having to get angry and nearly drag her granddaughter to the preschool door. "Hurry! Stop dawdling!" she would command, but Allison was oblivious to any encouragement to do things faster than she wanted.

Feeling helpless, angry, and resentful toward her favorite granddaughter, Grandma Harris finally told her daughter that she could no longer care for Allison. Mrs. Smith advised her mother to praise Allison's attempts at not dawdling and to ignore her when she dawdled. Mrs. Smith also encouraged her mother to offer Allison rewards for hurrying, something that came naturally to Grandma Harris, who enjoyed bringing her grandchildren presents.

"I'm glad you're getting to the door ahead of me today," Grandma Harris said to Allison as she walked toward preschool more quickly than usual. When Allison slowed to her normal pace as they neared the school, Grandma Harris decided to encourage her instead of complaining about her dawdling. "When you've scurried up the walkway toward the preschool before I can count to five, I'll give you that comb you saw in my purse." Allison hustled as if she'd never dawdled in her life.

Grandma Harris followed through with the comb and saw for herself the impact that rewards had on getting her granddaughter to do what she wanted her to do. Allison still had to be coaxed into dressing on her grandmother's timetable, but Grandma Harris began to enjoy her grandchild again, and she felt more in control of the time frame in which they would both operate.

Demanding Freedom

Immersed in pushing their way out into the world, preschoolers may need to be pulled back to safety because they're not as self-sufficient, self-reliant, and self-controlled as they think. As your one-year-old grows, your apron strings will gradually stretch to accommodate him. However, let him go only as far as you know is safe. Get to know your child's limits by testing his maturity and responsibility before making the mistake of allowing more freedom than he can safely handle. Allow him freedoms that are commensurate with his abilities, and give him frequent opportunities to reinforce your belief that he's mature enough to handle those freedoms.

Preventing the Problem

Establish limits and communicate them clearly.

Your child needs to know his limits before he can be expected to do what you want him to do. Even a one-year-old should be told what's "legal," to prevent as many "illegal" actions as possible.

Let your child know when he can cross the boundaries.

Reduce the attraction of certain no-no's by showing and telling your young adventurer how he can do what he wants without getting in trouble for it. For example, say, "You can cross the street, but you must hold my hand."

Allow as much freedom as your child shows he can safely handle.

If your child shows he is responsible within the limits, extend them a little. Let him know why they've changed, to help him feel good about his ability to follow directions and be responsible enough to earn freedom. Say, "Because you always tell me before you go to your friend's house next door, you can now go up the street, too. Always ask me before you go, of course."

Solving the Problem

What to Do

Offer rewards for staying within limits.

Encourage your child to stay within the limits by rewarding him for doing so. Say, "I'm happy you stayed at the swing set instead of going into the neighbor's yard. Now you may swing for three more minutes."

Establish consequences for not respecting limits.

Teach your child that not heeding your limits brings his fun to a stop. Say, "I'm sorry you left the yard. Now you must stay in the house." Or, "I'm sorry you crossed the street. Now you must stay in the backyard."

Be consistent.

Make sure you enforce the consequences every time your child breaks a rule. This teaches him you mean what you say. It also helps him feel more secure about his actions when he's away from you, because he'll clearly know what you expect him to do.

What Not to Do

Don't spank your child for going into the street.

Spanking encourages your child to hide from you while doing what you punished him for. Children who sneak into the street are in great danger, of course, so don't add to the problem by making them want to do it on the sly.

Ashley on Her Own

Five-year-old Ashley Hamilton was the most popular little girl on Twelfth Street, a situation that also caused her behavior to be the biggest problem in the Hamilton family. At breakfast one morning, Ashley told her mother, "Today, I'm going to walk to school with Susie, then I'm going to Donna's house after lunch, and then I'm going to play dolls with Maria." When her mother told Ashley she couldn't go anywhere anytime she pleased, Ashley pleaded, "Why? Why not? I'm going anyway! You can't stop me!"

These kinds of rebellious statements encouraged angry name-calling episodes between Ashley and her parents, who couldn't decide where freedom should be given and boundaries drawn to protect their "baby" from dangers she wasn't old enough to handle. Because Ashley was constantly getting invitations, the Hamiltons couldn't ignore the problem of deciding where and when she could go.

They decided to establish rules that could be changed depending on how Ashley managed her freedom and responsibility. The Hamiltons clearly explained these rules to Ashley, who was more than happy to learn how to get more freedom.

One of the things Ashley needed to learn was how to cross the street. So Mrs. Hamilton took her to the curb and began teaching her street-crossing behavior: how to stop at the curb, look to the left, look to the right, and not only look but see. Mrs. Hamilton asked Ashley to describe what she saw to the left and right.

When Mrs. Hamilton was sure the street was clear, she instructed her daughter to cross the street only when holding her hand. They crossed the street together, looking left and right and describing what they saw. Mrs. Hamilton praised her daughter for following directions perfectly. After ten practices, Mrs. Hamilton said, "Ashley, let me watch you cross the street on your own."

When Ashley demonstrated that she could follow directions on her own, Mrs. Hamilton announced the new rule: "You may cross the street to go to your friend's house, but you must come tell me first. I will come with you to watch you."

Mrs. Hamilton thought this compromise was a lot of work, but she realized that the only way she would feel comfortable loosening her apron strings was if she knew her daughter could handle the responsibilities that freedom required. Establishing and practicing the conditions of freedom allowed everyone to feel safe, secure, and satisfied with the limits and expectations.

Demanding to Do Things Themselves

"Me do it!" is one of the lines parents of preschoolers can expect to hear starting around a child's second birthday. This declaration of independence provides a golden opportunity for parents to allow their young try-it-alls to perfect their skills, as long as household rules aren't broken. Parents should remind themselves of their ultimate goal: to produce self-confident and self-sufficient children. So dig deep for extra patience as you bear with your child's mistakes, and balance the need to get chores done against the importance of teaching your preschoolers important living skills.

Preventing the Problem

Don't assume your child can't do something.

Keep track of your child's changing levels of expertise. Make sure you've given her a chance to try something before doing it for her, so you don't underestimate her current ability.

Buy clothing your child can manage.

Buy clothes that easily go up and down for your child in potty training, for example. Buy shirts that will go over her head and not get stuck on her shoulders when she puts on her clothes.

Store clothing in coordinated, accessible units.

Help your child develop an eye for coordination by sorting her clothes. Make them accessible by putting them in bins or drawers she can easily reach.

Prevent frustration.

Try to make tasks as easy for your child to accomplish as possible. Undo the snaps on her pants or start the zipper on her coat, for example, before you let her finish the job.

Solving the Problem

What to Do

Play Beat-the-Clock.

Tell your child how much time you have for a certain activity, so she won't think it's her inability to do something that makes you take over the job. Set a timer for the number of minutes you want to allow for the task, and say, "Let's see if we can get dressed before the timer rings." This helps your child learn a sense of being on time, and it reduces the power struggle between you and your child because you're not telling her to do something, the timer is. If you're in a hurry and must finish a task your child has started, explain the circumstances before taking over, to prevent your child from thinking it was her inability that made you take over.

Suggest cooperation and sharing.

Because your child doesn't understand why she can't do something, and she doesn't realize that she'll be able to do it eventually, suggest sharing a job by having her do what she can while you do the rest. For example, when tying shoes for a one-year-old, say, "Why don't you hold your sock while I'll put on your shoe." Whenever possible, let your child accomplish some portion of the task instead of merely watching you and feeling inadequate.

Make effort count.

As your child's first and most important teacher, you can encourage her to attempt various tasks. Teach her the axiom that "practice makes perfect" by saying, for example, "I like the way you tried to braid your hair. That was a great try. You can try again later, too." Or praise your child's attempt at putting on her shoes, even if she does it incorrectly.

Remain as calm and patient as you can.

If your child wants to do everything ("*I'll* put on my shorts," "*I'll* open the door," "*Me* close the drawer,"), remember that she's asserting her independence, not her obstinacy. Since you want her to learn to do things by herself, let her try. Avoid getting upset when things aren't done as quickly or precisely as you'd like. Instead, take delight in the fact that your child is taking the first step toward being self-sufficient and be proud of her for taking the initiative.

Allow as much independence as possible.

Let your child do as much by herself as she can, so frustration doesn't replace her innate curiosity. While tying her shoe, for example, don't insist on keeping her other shoe away from her fidgety fingers if she wants to hold it. She can hand it to you when you're finished with the first.

Ask your child to do things; don't demand.

To make your preschooler more likely to ask for things nicely, show her how to make requests politely. Say, "When you ask me nicely, I'll let you do X." Then explain what you mean by *nicely*. For example, tell your child to say, "Please, may I get a fork?" when she wants a fork.

What Not to Do

Don't punish your child's mistakes.

There are bound to be a few mishaps along the way, so be patient. If your child tries to pour the milk herself and accidentally spills it, help her do so more carefully the next time. Don't expect success right away.

Don't criticize your child's effort.

Avoid pointing out your child's mistakes. If she puts her sock on inside out, for example, simply say, "Let's put the smooth side of the sock inside next to your foot, okay?"

Don't feel rejected.

Don't feel hurt because your child doesn't appreciate your help. She's trying to do things on her own, and your help may be perceived as an obstacle. If she says, "Let me open the door," let her do it. She knows you can do things faster and with less effort, but she wants and needs to develop her skills. Appreciate her efforts to do things on her own.

Independent Jasmine

During the first three years of Jasmine Manning's life, her mother did everything for her. Now "Miss Independence" wanted her mother to do nothing for her, a personality change that was confusing and frustrating for Mrs. Manning. "I can't stand waiting for you, Jasmine!" Mrs. Manning would say when they were late for preschool and Jasmine would insist on putting her coat on by herself. "You're not old enough to do that by yourself."

The waves of demanding and refusing to comply began to subside when Mrs. Manning realized that the problem was causing her to dislike Jasmine and her desire to do things herself. One morning while Jasmine was dressing to go outside, Mrs. Manning noticed Jasmine putting on her coat perfectly for the first time. "That's great the way you put on your coat," Mrs. Manning said. "You're really hurrying to get ready for school! I'm so proud of you!" Jasmine let her mother finish the zipper without putting up a fight, something that hadn't happened in weeks.

As they rode to school, Mrs. Manning realized how independent her daughter was becoming. Jasmine's preschool teacher also noticed how she wanted to answer questions and be "the helper" without being told. Mrs. Manning decided she would try to adjust to Jasmine's overwhelming desire to be self-sufficient.

The next day, Jasmine wanted to set the table by herself, as usual. Instead of sending her the message that she couldn't do the job, Mrs. Manning tried to encourage Jasmine's independence while meeting her own agenda: getting the table set in short order. She announced, "Jasmine, you can set the table yourself until the timer rings. When it goes off, it's time for me to help you."

Jasmine wasn't eager for her mother's assistance, but she loved the idea of beating the timer. She was extra proud of herself for completing the job before the bell sounded. Jasmine's mother was proud, too. "That's great the way you set the table by yourself," she remarked while silently shifting the spoons to their place beside, not inside, the bowls.

Mrs. Manning continued to praise her daughter's efforts toward independence. She also made it as easy as possible for Jasmine to complete her tasks, and they began to work together to finish jobs when necessary.

Destroying Property

The line between destructive and creative play is not drawn for preschoolers until parents etch it in stone for them. So before your child reaches his first birthday, draw the line by telling (and showing) him what he can and cannot paint, tear up, or take apart. This will prevent your budding artist from doing unintentional damage to his and others' property. Consistently teach your child to be proud of and to care for his things, and let his creative juices flow in appropriate ways such as on drawing paper (not wallpaper) or with a take-apart play phone (not your real phone).

Preventing the Problem

Provide toys that are strong enough to be investigated but not destroyed.

It's natural for preschoolers to try to take apart and put together toys that lend themselves to this kind of activity (as well as ones that don't). In order to stimulate the kind of creative play you want to encourage, fill your child's play area with toys he can *do* something with (like stacking toys, push-button games, and so on) instead of ones that just sit there (like stuffed animals).

Give him plenty of things to wear and tear.

Provide lots of old clothes and materials for papier-mâché, dress-up, painting, or other activities, so your preschooler won't substitute new or valuable items for his play projects.

Communicate specific rules about caring for and playing with toys.

Young children don't innately know the value of things or how to play with everything appropriately, so teach them, for example, to use crayons on coloring books instead of newspapers and novels. Say, "Your coloring book is the only thing you can color on with crayons. Nothing else is for crayons." With regard to other destructive behavior, say, "Books are not for tearing. If you want to tear, ask me and I'll give you something." Or, "This wax apple does not come apart and cannot be eaten like a real one. If you'd like to eat an apple, please ask me and I'll give you one."

Supervise your child's play and be consistent.

Don't confuse your child and make him test the legal waters over and over by letting him destroy something he shouldn't. He won't know what to expect and won't understand when you destroy his fun by reprimanding him for a no-no that was formerly a yes-yes.

Remind him about caring.

Increase your chances of keeping destruction to a minimum by letting your child know when he's taking wonderful care of his toys. This reminds him of the rule, helps him feel good about himself, and makes him proud of his possessions.

Solving the Problem

What to Do

Overcorrect the mess.

If your child is over two years old, teach him to take care of his things by having him help clean up the messes he makes. For example, if he writes on the wall, he must clean up not only the writing but all the walls in the room. This overcorrection of the problem gives your child a sense of ownership and caring. (It also teaches him how to clean walls!)

Use reprimands.

If your child is under two years old, briefly reprimand him (tell him what he did wrong, why it was wrong, and what he should have done instead) to help him understand why he's been taken away from his fun.

Put your child in Time Out.

If you've given your child a reprimand and he destroys property again, repeat the reprimand and put him in Time Out.

What Not to Do

Don't overreact.

If your child breaks something, don't throw a tantrum yourself. Your anger communicates the idea that you care more for your things than your child. Make sure your degree of disappointment over something being destroyed isn't out of proportion to what happened.

Don't overly punish.

Just because your child damaged something valuable to you doesn't give you permission to damage your child. Rather than putting him in jail, put the valuable item away until he's old enough to understand the value.

Tim the Terror

Walt and Becky Brady knew they had a destructive three-year-old long before the preschool teacher called them in for a conference. They could have bent the teacher's ear with tales of purple crayon on the yellow dining-room wallpaper and mosaics made out of pages from hardcover books.

When the Bradys arrived home from their conference, the babysitter reported that Tim had drawn on the tile floor with his crayons. "When are you going to stop all this destruction, Tim?" Mr. Brady screamed as he spanked his son and sent him to his room. A little later the Bradys discovered that Tim had torn up three of his picture books while he was in his room.

The Bradys decided to change their approach. Instead of threatening or spanking Tim, they required him to make amends for his destructive behavior. The next time they found Tim tearing a page from a book, they said, "Now you have to fix this book, Tim." They took him by the hand to the tape drawer and helped him tear off the appropriate amount of tape to repair the book.

Tim not only had to fix books, he had to wash walls, scrape crayon off the tiles, and tape cards that he ripped. An interesting thing happened: Tim seldom repeated a destructive behavior once he fixed the damage.

Each time something was damaged, Mr. and Mrs. Brady explained what Tim was allowed to tear and what he was not allowed to tear. The Bradys also encouraged Tim to be as responsible for his possessions as his parents were for theirs. Eventually Tim began to embrace this responsibility. He beamed with pride when his parents praised him for caring for his books, toys, and stuffed animals in a responsible way. And he was quick to make amends whenever he slipped back into his old destructive habits.

As Tim's behavior became less destructive, his parents still didn't expect him to care for his toys as they did their adult toys, but they were careful to model neat behavior so Tim could see that they practiced what they preached about respecting property.

Fighting Cleanup Routines

From a no-more-tears shampoo to disposable diapers, products abound to make bathing, diapering, and shampooing as palatable as possible to preschoolers and their parents. It's expected and even predicted (as these manufacturers know) that preschoolers will find cleanup routines distasteful, so don't feel alone as you persevere with rinsing and soaking. Try to make the cleanup tasks less tedious by diverting your child's attention (sing songs, tell stories) and praising any cooperation (even handing you the soap).

Note: Distinguish between products that irritate your child physically (burns her eyes) as opposed to mentally (all soaps are undesirable) by carefully evaluating her protests. Most parents can tell the difference between distress cries and those that are motivated by anger, frustration, or the desire for attention. Distress cries don't change in tone or duration when parents or other distractions intrude. Other cries generally occur in short bursts interrupted by pauses during which the child listens for a reaction from parents or other caretakers. If necessary, switch from products that irritate your child physically to those that are professionally recommended.

Preventing the Problem

Compromise on cleanup times and places.

Try to make compromises with your child about issues like where you diaper her (on the couch, standing up) or when you wash her hair. Be flexible so your child will not miss a favorite activity just to get her hair washed or miss an episode of a parent-approved television program just to have her diaper changed.

Involve your child in the process.

Help your child play a part in the cleanup or diapering routine. Ask her to bring you things she can carry (according to her age, skill level, and ability to follow directions). Let her pick a favorite toy or towel, for example, to give her a feeling of control over the bathtime routine.

Prepare your child for the cleanup event.

Give your child some warning before a bath, for example, to make the transition from playtime to bathtime less abrupt. Say, "When the timer rings, it will be time for the tub," or, "In a few minutes, we will change your diaper," or, "When we finish this book, it will be time for your bath."

Gather materials before starting.

If your child is too young to help you prepare, make sure you get things ready before beginning the cleanup. This helps avoid unnecessary delays and minimizes frustrations on both ends.

Develop a positive attitude.

Your child will pick up on the dread in your voice if you announce bathtime like it's a prison sentence. If you sound worried or anxious, you're telling her it must be as horrible as she thought. Your attitude is contagious, so make it one that you want imitated.

Solving the Problem

What to Do

Remain calm and ignore the noise.

A calm mood is contagious when dealing with your upset child. If you don't pay attention to the noise, she'll learn that noise has no power over you, which is what she wants when she's resisting your cleaning her up. Say to yourself, "I know my child needs to be diapered. If I don't pay attention to her noise, I'll get this done faster and more effectively."

Have fun in the process.

Distract your child by talking, playing, reciting nursery rhymes, or singing. Say, "Let's sing 'Old MacDonald,'" or, "I'll bet you can't catch this boat and make it dive into the water." Make it a monologue if your child is too young to participate verbally.

Encourage your child to help and shower her with praise.

Ask your child to wash her own tummy, rub on the soap, or open the diaper (if time permits) to give her a feeling of controlling and participating in her personal hygiene. Even the slightest sign of cooperation is a signal for praise. Lather on the words of encouragement. The more your child gets attention for acting as you'd prefer, the more she'll repeat the action to get your strokes. Say, "I really like how you put that shampoo on your hair," or, "That's great the way you're sitting up in the tub," or, "Thanks for lying down so nicely while I diaper you."

Exercise Grandma's Rule.

Let your child know that when she's done something you want her to do (take a bath), she can do something she wants to do (read a story). Say, "When your bath is over, then we'll have a story," or, "When we're finished, then you can play."

Persist in the task at hand.

Despite the kicking, screaming, and yelling, be determined to finish the cleanup process. The more your child sees that yelling isn't going to prevent you from washing away the dirt, the more she'll understand that you'll get the job done faster if she takes the path of least resistance.

Compliment your child when you're done.

Tell your child how delightful she looks and smells. Ask her to go look in the mirror. This will remind her why she needs to have a bath or her diaper changed. Learning to take pride in her appearance will help her make cleanliness a priority.

What Not to Do

Don't demand cooperation.

Just because you demand that your child gets diapered doesn't mean she's going to lie still while you do it. Acting rough and tough only teaches her to be rough and tough, too.

Don't make cleanup painful.

Try to make cleanup as comfortable as possible for your child. Provide towels she can use to wipe her eyes, make the bath water temperature just right, wrap her in a robe after you're done, and so on.

Don't avoid cleanup.

Just because your child resists doesn't mean you should back down. Resistance to cleanup can be overcome by persistence, practice, and patience.

Oceans of Fun

Carol and Phil Porter bathed and shampooed their two-year-old daughter, Lauren, just as they thought most parents they knew did. But they feared something was wrong with Lauren when she screamed and fought her way through these normal cleanup routines. The Porters never experienced this problem with their other daughter, Elizabeth, and none of their friends ever complained about it.

The Porters talked to their pediatrician, who assured them that the soaps, water, and towels were not harmful or irritating. Mr. Porter thought stricter discipline was needed, but they eventually agreed that the best approach was to make cleanup more appetizing to Lauren. The only water-related activity Lauren enjoyed was swimming in the Pacific Ocean during summer vacation. So the Porters decided to call bathtime Oceans of Fun.

That evening they set a timer to ring when it was time to get in the "ocean." During trips to California, they always set a timer to signal when they could go in the real ocean, because Lauren was always begging to get in the water. They hoped this technique would prove helpful at home in Minneapolis, too. "When the timer rings, it will be time to play Oceans of Fun," Mrs. Porter told Lauren. "Let's finish this book while we're waiting."

When the timer rang, Lauren and her mother gathered towels and soap, and Lauren excitedly asked questions about the new game. Lauren smiled with delight as her mom led her to the bathroom where she found the bluest "ocean" she'd ever seen (the result of blue bubble bath) and jaunty boats cruising around a toy ship holding a container of soap (toys Mrs. Porter bought to add to the experience).

Lauren jumped in without a push or an invitation and began playing with the "ocean" toys. Her mother started singing a song about a tugboat, and she gave Lauren a palmful of shampoo to wash her own hair for the first time. The cleanup continued without yelling or screaming—and just a little too much splashing. Mrs. Porter began bathing Lauren in the "ocean" at least once a day, to give her opportunities to learn how to splash less, wash herself more carefully, and enjoy the experience.

Getting into Things

Just getting into first gear in their first year, one-year-olds feel the joy of exploration from their toes to their teeth. They don't automatically know what's off-limits and what isn't, but by two and older they're able to make the distinction once you've set them straight. While restricting the adventures of your little explorers, keep in mind the balance you're trying to strike between letting normal, healthy curiosity be expressed and teaching what behavior is and isn't appropriate.

Preventing the Problem

Childproof your home or apartment.

Keeping doors closed, stairways blocked, cabinets locked, and dangerous areas fenced off will reduce the number of times you have to say no to your child. Children under three years old are busy establishing their independence and making their mark on the world, and they can't understand why they can't go wherever they want. Establishing physical limitations will help you avoid unnecessary confrontations. (See Appendix I.)

Decide what's off-limits.

Decide what your child's boundaries will be and communicate this information early and often. For example, say, "You may play in the living room or in the kitchen, but not in Daddy's office."

Put away valuable items you don't want broken.

A one-, two-, or three-year-old will not understand the difference between an expensive vase and a plastic one. Play it safe by removing valuable items until your little one won't grab for everything despite being told not to.

Teach your child how and when he can go into off-limits areas.

Explain to your child the acceptable ways of playing in off-limits areas. Never allowing him to go into a room or across the street, for example, makes him want to do it even more. Say, "You can go into Mommy's office, but only with Mommy or another adult."

Solving the Problem

What to Do

Use reprimands.

Consistently reprimand your child for a repeated offense, to teach him you mean what you say. Say, "Stop going into that room! I'm sorry you were playing in here. You know this is off-limits. I'd like you to ask Mommy to come with you if you want to go into this room."

Put your child in Time Out.

If your child climbs on the kitchen table repeatedly (and if that's a no-no), reprimand him again and put him in Time Out to reinforce the message.

Compliment your child when he follows the rules.

Tell your child how proud you are of him for remembering not to do certain things. Giving him that compliment will reward his desirable behavior with attention, which will encourage him to do the right thing again. Say, "How nice of you to play in here where you're supposed to," or, "Thanks for not climbing on the coffee table."

Teach your child to touch with his eyes, not his hands.

Tell your child that he may look at a piece of jewelry, for example, with his eyes but not with his hands. This allows him the freedom to explore the item in a limited, controlled way.

What Not to Do

Don't leave guns or knives where children can reach them.

No matter how much safety training children receive, the allure of weapons is too great to resist. Keep all guns locked up, each with its own approved trigger lock, and lock up the ammunition in a separate place that is inaccessible to children. Also, keep *all* knives locked away in a childproof place. It's always better to be safe than sorry.

Don't make no-no's more inviting by getting upset.

If you become angry when your child breaks a rule, he'll see that he can get your attention from misbehavior, and he'll be encouraged to get into trouble more often.

Don't overly punish.

Rather than punishing your child for being naturally curious and getting into things, teach him how to use his curiosity safely—a skill that will serve him well his entire lifetime. Instead of trying to stamp out inappropriate behavior, emphasize the positive.

"Do Not Touch!"

"Curiosity killed the cat" was the line Mrs. Stein remembered her mother saying to her when she climbed on off-limits counters as a youngster. Now she found her fifteen-month-old son, Sam, exploring forbidden lamps and plants. She knew he wasn't being intentionally bad; he was behaving like a normal child. But Mrs. Stein didn't think her reactions to his curiosity seemed normal or showed much self-discipline. "No! Do not touch!" she would shout, slapping her son's hands or spanking him whenever he got into things he knew were no-no's.

Mrs. Stein eventually realized that Sam was only learning to avoid the penalty for getting caught by committing his "crimes" behind her back. So she decided to lock up things she didn't want him to touch, to put breakable items out of reach, and to keep an eye on him as much as possible.

"Touch with your eyes, not your hands," she said to him one particularly active morning when he had started taking everything out of a jewelry box she had forgotten to put on the top shelf. She removed the box and guided her son back to the kitchen where they both had a good time taking the pots and pans out of the cabinet. They also played with the key and lock box and several other toys that provided stimulation for his imagination and curiosity—toys that were appropriate for his age and appropriate for him to take apart and try to destroy.

Once the dangerous and expensive things were removed from Sam's reach and replaced with things he could play with safely, the Steins began having a more pleasant household. Though Mrs. Stein knew she would have to continue monitoring her son's curiosity, she let him have more freedom than before since her house was more childproofed.

One day Sam demonstrated that he was learning the rules when he pointed to a sack of flour he knew was off-limits and said, "No! Mommy's! Do not touch!" To reward his good behavior, Mrs. Stein gave him a sealed box of rice, which he loved to shake like a rattle.

Getting Out of Bed at Night

Children under six years old are famous for piping up with late-night requests for books, kisses, milk, or getting in bed with their parents. Remember that your child's need for sleep is very important. She probably wants those ten books and four drinks to keep you near her, so teach her that going to sleep will bring you back to her bedside faster than demanding attention.

Note: If you're not sure whether your child needs something or merely wants your attention (if she's not talking yet or if she cries out instead of asking for something), go check on her. If all is medically sound, give her a quick kiss and hug (thirty seconds maximum) and make your exit. Tell her firmly and lovingly that it's time for sleep, not play.

Preventing the Problem

Discuss bedtime rules at a nonbedtime time.

Set limits for how many drinks of water or trips to the toilet your child may have at bedtime. Tell her these rules at a neutral time, so she's aware of what you expect her to do when bedtime comes. Say, "You can take two books to bed and have one drink, and I'll tell you two stories before you hit the sack." If your child likes to get in bed with you, decide before she arrives whether your rules allow that. It's up to parents to decide whether they want their children in their bed.

Promise rewards for following the rules.

Make your child aware that following the rules, not breaking them, will bring her rewards. Say, "When you've stayed in your bed all night (if that's your rule), then you may choose your favorite story to read in the morning." Rewards could include special breakfasts, trips to the park, favorite games, or anything else you know is enjoyable for your child.

Reinforce the idea of going back to sleep.

Remind your child of bedtime rules as you put her in bed, to strengthen her memory of previous discussions.

Solving the Problem

What to Do

Follow through with consequences for breaking the rules.

Make breaking the rules more trouble than it's worth. For example, if your child breaks a rule by asking for more than two drinks, go to her bedside and say, "I'm sorry you got out of bed and broke the two-drink rule. Now you must have your door closed, as we said" (if that's what you said you would do if she asked for more drinks of water).

Stand firm with your rules.

Enforce the rule every time your child breaks it, to teach her that you mean what you say. For example, when you put your child back in her bed after she gets in bed with you (in violation of your rule), say, "I'm sorry that you got in bed with us. Remember the rule: Everyone sleeps in her own bed. I love you. See you in the morning."

Follow through with rewards.

Teach your child to trust you by always making good on your promises of rewards for following the rules.

What Not to Do

Don't neglect to enforce the rules.

Once you've set the rules, don't change them unless you discuss this first with your child. Every time you neglect to consistently enforce the rules, your child learns to keep trying to get what she wants, even though you've said no.

Don't give in to noise.

If your child screams because you enforced a rule about going to sleep, remind yourself that she's learning an important health lesson: Nighttime is for sleeping. Time how long your child cries, and chart the progress you're making in getting her not to resist sleep. If you don't respond to the noise, the crying time should gradually decrease and eventually disappear.

Don't use threats and fear.

Threats such as, "If you get out of bed, the lizards will get you," or, "If you do that one more time, I'm going to whip you," will only increase the problem. Unless you back them up, threats are meaningless noises. Fear may keep your child in bed, but the fear may grow until your child becomes afraid of many things.

Don't talk to your child from a distance.

Yelling threats and rules from another room teaches your child to yell, and it tells her you don't care enough to talk to her face to face.

Jennifer's Midnight Ramblings

Two-and-a-half-year-old Jennifer Long had been sleeping through the night since she was six months old. For the past month, however, she had been sleeping only a few hours before waking up her parents with screams of "Mommy! Daddy!" At first, Jennifer's parents would race to see what was wrong with their daughter, only to find her begging for drinks of water one night, an extra hug the next, and bathroom visits on other evenings.

After several weeks of these interruptions, Jennifer's weary parents decided to put a stop to these requests. "If you don't stay in bed, you're going to be punished, young lady," they commanded. Then they returned to their bed, only to hear their daughter padding down the stairs toward their room. They tried spanking Jennifer firmly and telling her to "Get in bed or else!" but their heavy hand seemed to carry little weight.

The Longs kept telling themselves that Jennifer's waking up in the middle of the night was natural; everyone went through periods of shallow and deep sleep. But they also knew that their daughter could choose to go back to sleep instead of calling out to them. They also felt confident in their ability to distinguish between a genuine distress call (an intense and uninterrupted cry) and one that merely sought their attention (short bursts of crying).

To solve the problem, they offered Jennifer more attention for staying in bed. "When you stay in bed without calling out to us," they explained as they tucked her in bed the next night, "you'll have your favorite surprise at breakfast in the morning. When you call out in the middle of the night, we'll close your door, you'll have to stay in bed, and you'll have no surprise." They made sure they stated the new rule in plain terms their daughter could understand.

That night, Jennifer called out for her mother: "I want a drink!" But her mother followed through with her promise to close Jennifer's door and not answer her cries. "I'm sorry you didn't go back to sleep, Jennifer," Mrs. Long said. "Now we'll have to close your door. I'll see you in the morning."

After three nights of closed doors and interrupted sleep for all the Longs, Jennifer learned that calling out did not bring her parents to her bedside and that staying quiet and in bed all night made the promised surprises materialize in the morning. The Longs were finally able to get some uninterrupted sleep, and Jennifer found that their praise for sleeping through the night made her feel grown-up and important—an extra reward.

"Hyper" Activity

"John's so hyper!" his grandmother exclaimed after two hours of grueling babysitting with her young grandson. "He wouldn't sit down once…not even to eat!" John's mother had heard the term *hyper* used before to describe her son, and she had even used it herself. But when her mother started complaining about John's behavior, John's mother asked herself, "Is John a normal, busy two-year-old, or is he hyperactive?"

To be clinically diagnosed as hyperactive, a child must fidget frequently, leave his seat, run or climb excessively, have problems playing quietly, be constantly on the go, or be overly talkative. He blurts out answers before the question is completed, has trouble waiting in lines or taking turns, and interrupts or intrudes on others. Because these behaviors often describe the average preschooler, it's very difficult to attach the label of hyperactive to a little whirling dervish. Clinical tests must be done for a proper diagnosis, but even these may not be definitive for preschoolers. If you see four of the above symptoms in your child daily for at least six months, a professional trained in diagnosing hyperactivity can help you understand the difference between a "hyper" active child and a hyperactive child, and he or she can help you manage the behavior of both.

Note: Hyperactivity is considered part of a larger disorder commonly referred to as Attention Deficit Hyperactivity Disorder (ADHD), which comes in three forms: ADHD, predominantly inattentive type; ADHD, predominantly hyperactive/impulsive type; and ADHD, predominantly combined type. All forms of ADHD are difficult to diagnose before children enter formal schooling at about age five, when they're first required to sit and pay attention for longer periods of time, to work while remaining seated, and to memorize material that they'll be tested on later. (See Appendix II.)

Preventing the Problem

Suggest quiet activities.

If your child regularly runs instead of walks and screams instead of talks, introduce calm activities to slow his breakneck speed. For example, play a quiet game, read to him, or have a tiptoe-and-whisper time to teach him that slow and calm is a refreshing change of pace.

Watch your own activity level.

Does hyperactivity run in families? Research has shown that when a parent is diagnosed with hyperactivity, it's highly likely that his or her child will be, too. Look at your own life: Do you ever sit down? Do you talk fast? Is your pace always rushed? If you're a high-energy, always-on-the-go person whose "hyper" activity doesn't get in the way of your success and happiness, then your child may simply have your inborn temperament. Since young children are such great imitators, slowing down your activity level will show your preschooler how to savor the moment.

Avoid "hyper" active TV.

When your child is in constant motion, his entertainment shouldn't be. Wild and crazy television programs model behavior you don't want him to emulate. Turn off the TV to turn off at least one source of noise and "hyper" activity you don't need around the house. Instead, play quiet restful music and encourage TV with a softer tone.

Solving the Problem

What to Do

Practice slowing down.

Give your child opportunities to practice walking—not running—from point A to point B. Say, "Show me how to walk from the kitchen to the family room. I know you can do it. When you walk instead of run, you keep yourself safe." Gradually increase the number of practice walks to a maximum of ten each practice session.

Provide a variety of activities.

Born-to-be-busy children flit like summer houseflies from one activity to another and have trouble staying in one place. Give your "hyper" active child a cafeteria of choices by saying, "You can color on your drawing table, play with clay in the kitchen, or play with your building blocks. I'll set the timer, and you can do one activity until the timer rings. Then you can choose something else if you want." Providing many options lets your child fulfill his need to be busy without driving you to distraction.

Exercise.

Your high-energy child needs constructive outlets in which to satisfy his need to be on the go. Let him run in the park or in your yard whenever you can, or make sure his preschool or daycare provider gives him some running time. Although it may be tempting to sign him up for the neighborhood sports team that all his buddies are on, beware of starting your preschooler too early in sports that can injure his growing body or cause him to burn out before he's ten. Young children need the freedom to rev up their newly charged engines without being corralled in an organized, competitive setting.

Teach relaxation.

When your child learns to relax his body, his motor slows down and he feels less frantic. Help him avoid constantly pushing to do more, faster, sooner by keeping your voice soft and soothing, by rubbing his back, and by talking to him about how calm and relaxed his body feels.

Seek help.

If your child's "hyper" activity endangers his health, alienates others, and jeopardizes his learning, consult a trained professional to determine the cause of his above-average activity level. (See Appendix II.)

What Not to Do

Don't punish.

When your "hyper" active child accidentally collides with your most precious vase, take a deep breath and say, "I'm sorry you chose to run instead of walk. Now you have to practice walking in the house, so I'll know you can do it. Then we'll clean up the mess." In this way, you reach your ultimate goals of teaching your child to walk instead of run, to respect property, and to be responsible for his actions.

Don't ground.

Your busy child needs daily opportunities to play in the great outdoors, so grounding him to the house or his room can cause two problems: (1) His "hyper" activity will swell to explosive levels, and (2) he will only learn to be hyper in the house instead of outside.

Don't rely on medication alone.

Relying on medication alone won't teach your child self-control. Get a thorough evaluation from a professional experienced in assessing "hyper" active children before you decide what behavioral tools and medication are necessary for your child's well-being.

Wild about Ethan

When Jane and Russell Anderson attended Ethan's teacher conference at preschool, they weren't at all surprised at Miss Sharon's comment that their five-year-old son was very active. "He even kept me awake at night when I was pregnant with him, he was so restless and busy," Jane told her. "When Russell is out of town, I let Ethan sleep with me, and it's the same thing. I don't get much sleep because he's so restless. He never walks; he runs. He's just like his dad." Jane put her hand on Russell's knee, which had been in constant motion since he first sat down for the conference.

"Yeah, I was a hyper kid," Russell grinned. "Mom had to go to school lots to bail me out because I was always in trouble for being out of my seat, talking, or doing something stupid. I had to take medication to calm down. Do you think Ethan needs medication?"

"Well, it's not such a big problem in school now, so I don't think medication is called for. But it would be good to keep an eye on him," Miss Sharon told them. "When he's in kindergarten next year, you should work closely with his teacher to see if something more needs to be done. In the meantime, here's a list of things you can do to try to slow him down a bit, as well as the best places you can go for a full evaluation. We believe that children should have a thorough evaluation before starting any kind of medication."

Jane and Russell took the list home and began working with Ethan. Several times a day, they had quiet time during which they read stories or relaxed. At first, Ethan couldn't sit still for more than fifty or sixty seconds, but gradually he began to sit for ten minutes at a time. They also cut out most of the TV Ethan liked to watch and imitate—from wrestling mayhem to martial arts—after his teacher suggested limiting his exposure to such frantic fare. His mom and dad also made a new household rule: "When you're in the house, you must walk. Running is for outside." To teach him the rule, they had Ethan practice navigating the house by walking. This was new to Ethan.

"But what if I'm in a hurry! Why can't I run if I want to?" Ethan whined. Jane smiled inside at Ethan's question. She remembered having to help Russell learn how to slow down after he knocked over a lamp one night trying to get to the kitchen and back before the television commercial was over.

"Because it's against the rule to run in the house," she answered. "Running is for outside where you have lots of room to run and won't bang into the furniture."

Jane also started doing simple relaxation exercises with Ethan at bedtime. She rubbed his back while softly saying, "You're feeling quiet and relaxed. Your feet feel heavy and relaxed, your legs, your tummy, your back, your arms and hands, all feel relaxed and comfortable. Your whole body is relaxed and warm. Your mind is quiet, and you're comfortable and still. Now, Ethan my love, think of being in your bed all quiet and snuggly while you're feeling so calm and quiet."

Ethan gradually became calmer and quieter and somewhat less active. It wasn't always easy for him to keep his body quiet, but he worked at it with his parents and his teacher, which helped prepare him for making a smooth transition to the less active world of the "big school."

Interacting with Strangers

"**D**on't take candy from strangers" is an admonition millions of parents of preschoolers dish out to their young ones. The warning is valid. Children need to learn how to behave with strangers, just as they need to learn how to interact with family, friends, and acquaintances. When you're with your child, minimize her fear of strangers by teaching her how to be friendly to people she doesn't know. At the same time, teach her what to do when approached by a stranger when you're not there. Both you and your child will feel more secure knowing that she understands what to do when you're there and when you're not.

Preventing the Problem

Establish the rules.

Let your child know your rules about interacting with strangers. A basic rule could be, "When I'm with you, you can be friendly and talk to strangers. But when I'm not with you, don't talk to strangers. If a stranger asks you to go with him or tries to give you anything, say, 'No,' and run to the nearest house and ring the doorbell."

Practice following the rules.

Pretend you're a stranger and ask your child to follow your rules concerning strangers. Rehearse several different scenarios, making sure she knows how you want her to respond.

Don't frighten your child.

Instilling fear of strangers only breeds confusion and doesn't teach your child what to do. She needs to know how to think on her feet when strangers invade her privacy. Being fearful will destroy her ability to behave rationally.

Solving the Problem

What to Do

Remind your child of the rule by praising correct behavior.

If your child says hello to a stranger while you're present, show your approval by saying, "I'm so glad you're being friendly. Now tell me the rule about behaving with strangers when I'm not with you." Then praise your child for remembering the rule.

Encourage your child to be friendly.

Friendly children tend to be more readily accepted by others as they go through life, so teaching friendliness is important. However, it's also important to explain to young and older children how to be friendly and keep themselves safe. For example, suggesting that your child say hello to strangers when you're with her encourages her to be friendly. But not allowing her to say anything to strangers when you're not with her helps keeps her safe.

Set stranger boundaries.

It's impossible for children to quickly distinguish between potentially dangerous strangers and ones who are harmless. That's why you have to establish a rule about how to interact with strangers when you're not present. Explain to your child that being friendly with strangers, whether you're there or not, never includes taking offers of candy, gifts, rides, or helping them find lost pets.

What Not to Do

Don't instill fear of people.

To help your child avoid the danger of being molested, teach her your rules about dealing with strangers. However, don't teach her to fear people. Fear only inhibits correct decision making, regardless of age.

Don't worry about your child bothering others by being friendly.

Even if strangers don't acknowledge the greeting, it's good for your child to offer salutations at appropriate times and places.

Keeping Kevin Safe

"How can we teach our three-and-a-half-year-old son to be friendly, yet keep him safe when we're not around?" This was the challenge Mr. and Mrs. Docking faced in trying to solve the problem of their overly friendly son, Kevin. "Some day someone might take advantage of your friendliness," they explained to Kevin, "so do not talk to strangers."

Kevin followed their orders so intently that he became terrified of strangers and began to throw tantrums every time his parents took him to the shopping center or grocery store. He didn't want to see strangers, he explained to his mother, because they were so mean and dangerous that he couldn't even say hello to them.

The Dockings were frustrated to see their well-intentioned instructions backfire this way. They finally realized that Kevin didn't understand the difference between saying hello, which they wanted to encourage when they were with him, and saying hello or going with strangers or taking things from them, which they wanted to prevent when they weren't with him. Kevin didn't understand because the Dockings had not given him the chance to understand.

"Strangers may hurt you if you go places with them or take things from them," Mrs. Docking told her son. "The new rule is that you can talk to anyone you want when I'm with you. But if I'm not with you and someone offers you something or wants you to go somewhere with him, ignore the person and go to the nearest house or nearest adult in a store." The Dockings practiced this rule by taking Kevin to a shopping center and rehearsing his actions while his mother played the "stranger."

Mrs. Docking reminded her son of the rule on a weekly basis, until it became a habit for him. To reinforce the lesson, Mrs. Docking practiced saying hello to others, too. Kevin noticed this and praised her for it, just as she had praised him for following the rule.

The Dockings' concern for Kevin's safety never completely disappeared. They had Kevin practice stranger safety from time to time, to convince themselves that he understood and remembered this potentially life-saving behavior.

Interrupting

Because a preschooler's most priceless possession is his parents' attention, he'll try anything to get it back when the telephone, doorbell, or another person takes it away. Limit the tricks your child tries to play to get your undivided attention by providing him with special playthings reserved for those times when you're chatting with the competition. This will keep your child busy without you, while you're busy without him.

Preventing the Problem

Limit the length of your conversations.

Your child has a limited ability to delay gratification, so keep your conversations short while your child is nearby, unoccupied, and wanting your attention.

Practice "play" telephone.

Teach your child what you mean by *not interrupting* by practicing with two play phones—one for you and one for him. Tell him, "This is how I talk on the phone, and this is how you play while I'm on the phone." Then let your child pretend to talk on the phone while you play without interrupting him. This shows him what he can do instead of interrupting you.

Set up activities for telephone playtime.

Gather special toys and materials in a drawer near the phone. (Let children over two years old choose their materials). Have your child play with those toys while you're on the phone. To further reduce the likelihood of his interrupting you, periodically give him attention by smiling and telling him how nicely he's playing. Some materials require adult supervision (fingerpaints, watercolors, Play-Doh, shaving cream, and magic markers, for example), so make them available to your preschooler only when you're able to watch him carefully. Make sure the phone toys match your child's skill level, to reduce the possibility of his needing to interrupt you for help.

Solving the Problem

What to Do

Praise nice playing and not interrupting.

If your child is getting attention (smiles, praise, and so on) for playing and not interrupting, he'll be less inclined to barge in on your conversation. Excuse yourself momentarily from your conversation and say to your child, "Thanks for playing so nicely with your toys. I'm so proud of you for having fun on your own."

Whenever possible, involve your child in your conversation.

When a friend visits, try to include your child in your conversation. This will reduce the possibility of his interrupting you to get attention.

What Not to Do

Don't get angry and yell at your child for interrupting.

Yelling at your child about any behavior only encourages him to yell.

Don't interrupt people, especially your child.

Even if your child is a constant chatterbox, show him you practice what you preach by not interrupting him while he's talking.

Use Grandma's Rule.

Use a timer to let your child know that you'll soon be all his again. He can earn your attention and have fun at the same time. Tell him, "When you've played with your toys for two minutes and the timer rings, I'll be through talking on the phone and I'll play with you."

Reprimand and use Time Out.

Use a reprimand such as, "Stop interrupting. I cannot talk to my friend while I'm being interrupted. Instead of interrupting, please play with your cars." If your child continues to interrupt, use Time Out to remove him from the possibility of getting attention for interrupting. Say, "I'm sorry that you're continuing to interrupt. Time out."

"Not Now, Lin!"

Whenever Mrs. Wilkens talked on the phone, her three-year-old daughter, Lin, interrupted the conversation with requests for drinks of apple juice or toys from the "high place." She also asked questions like, "Where are we going today?" Although Mrs. Wilkens wanted to answer, she tried to explain calmly at each interruption, "Sweetheart, Mommy is on the phone. Please don't interrupt." But Lin continued to interrupt.

So one day Mrs. Wilkens started screaming, "Don't interrupt me! You're a bad girl!" She also gave her daughter a swift swat on the bottom to shut her up. Not only did the swat not shut Lin up, it angered her into crying and screaming so loudly that her mother couldn't continue her conversation. The more her mother screamed, the more Lin interrupted—a cause-and-effect situation that Mrs. Wilkens finally understood and decided to reverse. She would now give her daughter attention for not interrupting instead of interrupting.

The next morning, Sally called Mrs. Wilkens for their regular Monday morning chat. But Mrs. Wilkens told her that she couldn't talk because she was playing with the children. As she was explaining this to her friend, she noticed how Lin had begun playing with the toys Mrs. Wilkens had gathered around the phone. "Thanks for not interrupting!" she said to Lin, giving her a big hug.

When she got off the phone, Mrs. Wilkens again praised Lin, "Thanks for not interrupting me while I told Sally about our dinner tonight. She wanted a recipe for meat loaf. These markers are here for you to play with, if you want, while I talk on the phone." The toys were especially fascinating to Lin because they were called "telephone" toys—ones she was allowed to play with only when her mother was on the phone.

The next time the phone rang, both Lin and her mother smiled with anticipation. "Lin, the phone is ringing. Let's play with the telephone toys." Lin ran to get the markers. While talking on the phone, Mrs. Wilkens watched Lin carefully and encouraged her uninterruptive behavior with an occasional, "Nice playing."

Jealousy

Toddlers and preschoolers believe they should get undivided attention whenever they order it because they live at the center of their universe. This self-centered view of life is the source of sibling rivalry and jealousy. When the attention they demand isn't there because it's being given to a new baby, another sibling, or even a spouse, preschoolers often morph into green-eyed monsters. Smitten with jealousy, they sulk, sabotage, scream, or solicit more attention by hitting their siblings, breaking toys, throwing tantrums, and so on. Justified or not, your child's jealousy can tear your heart out. Interpret her jealous behavior as a teachable moment by giving her both the attention she needs and the opportunity to be helpful. (See "Sibling Rivalry" on pages 118–121 for additional insights into problems involving jealousy.)

Preventing the Problem

Keep your child involved.

While you're changing the baby, for example, enlist your child's help by asking her to get a new diaper, hold the lotion, or entertain the baby. If your preschooler becomes jealous while you're hugging your hubby, a bigger hug to include her can put the wind back into her sails.

Praise sharing.

When your child accepts your attention being directed elsewhere, point out her willingness to share by saying, "That was so nice of you to share me with the baby. Thanks for being so generous."

Help your child feel special.

To keep the green-eyed monster at bay, allow an older sibling to help open the baby's gifts and show them to the baby. Encouraging friends and relatives to bring gifts for both children helps keep the older child feeling special.

Solving the Problem

What to Do

Show empathy.

When jealousy flares, tell your child you understand how she feels by saying, "I know you don't like it when I have to take care of the baby, but I think you can handle it. After you play with your building blocks until I'm through, then I'll play with you."

Provide alternative activities.

Understand that your child gets jealous because she feels left-out when you and your spouse want some time together. Give your child something constructive to do until you're ready to give her your undivided attention. Say, "Daddy and I want to talk for a while. You can play with your toys until the timer rings. Then you can talk to me if you want."

Monitor your time.

To a child, love is spelled T-I-M-E. Consider how much time you spend with your child reading stories, answering questions, sharing meals, playing games, and so on. When your child feels secure in your love, her jealousy meter stays low because she knows she's your number one priority. Tell her "I love you" many times each day. Strengthen your bond with each of your children by making special play dates for just the two of you so each child feels valued and important.

Turn jealousy into helpfulness.

A young child wants her world to exist for her alone, but she also wants to be independent. She needs to learn that independence comes at a price: She has to give up having her parents' undivided attention to gain a sense of control and self-determination. By teaching toddlers and preschoolers to be helpful toward siblings and others when feeling left-out and jealous, you're helping them turn negative behavior into something positive and praiseworthy. Say, "I know you want me to play with you now, but first I have to take your brother to soccer practice. Come help me put the oranges in the sack so the boys will have a treat. You can have one, too."

What Not to Do

Don't compare your child to siblings or others.

Saying, "I wish you could be as helpful as your little brother," or, "Why can't you be as sweet as your big sister?" only tells your child that she's not living up to who you want her to be. To children, that translates into not being as lovable as other family members, which is a sure-fire way to stir up the green-eyed monster.

Don't punish.

When your child gets out of sorts because she wants your undivided attention, punishing her for being upset will only increase her sense of alienation. Instead, show her how she can better cope with not getting the attention she wants when she wants it. Say, "I'm sorry you're so upset because I can't play right now. Let's make a deal. I'll play with your baby sister for a while, and when the timer rings, I'll read your book to you. Next time, we'll switch, and you can go first."

Green-Eyed Jana

Jana Goodman was really excited when she learned that she was going to have a baby brother or sister. She loved the idea of having a new playmate, which seemed to her like a new toy. Her parents, Sam and Christine Goodman, were convinced that Jana wouldn't have any problems accepting the new baby. But were they in for a surprise!

Everything went well the first few days after Baby Jay was brought home, because Grammy was there and Jana got lots of attention. Jana told her mom and dad that she thought Baby Jay looked funny, didn't smell very good sometimes, and wasn't able to play with her like she wanted. But she reassured her mom by saying, "I guess it's okay if he stays. Let's keep him for a while."

However, when Grammy left to go back home—a thousand miles away—Jana realized that her mom had to spend way too much time taking care of Baby Jay. Jana decided she needed to reassert herself as the "number one kid" in her house.

She tried whining for a while, but that didn't make her mom leave Baby Jay and come play with her. Then she tried sulking, but nobody seemed to pay any attention to that, either. So she started refusing to do what her mom and dad asked, like putting away her toys or brushing her teeth. Her mom was exasperated by this change of attitude and said, "Jana, what's gotten into you? It's Time Out for you, little missy."

When Sam came home that evening and heard what Jana had done, his first response was, "Oh yes, the green-eyed monster has come to visit. Your mother warned us this might happen."

So the Goodmans developed a plan to involve Jana in caring for Baby Jay. She became Mommy's Little Helper and was eager to assist when Baby Jay was being changed or fed. She even held the storybook so Christine could read to her while feeding Baby Jay. When Grammy came to visit, she brought Jana a little gift as well as one for Baby Jay. Jana got to open Baby Jay's gift so she could show him what Grammy brought. Grammy also spent plenty of time with Jana so she didn't feel so left-out when Grammy was holding Baby Jay.

Like a miracle, green-eyed Jana became a much more pleasant child to have around. The Goodmans knew that their empathy for Jana helped her accept the new family member and the important responsibility of being a big sister.

Lying

Toddlers and preschoolers live in an interesting world where fantasy and reality mix. They enjoy cartoons, pretend play, Santa Claus, wicked witches, flying capes, make-believe on demand, and so on. Their storytelling often reveals hidden fears. For example, "Mommy, there's a monster in my room! Come save me!" may be your child's way of telling you he's afraid of the dark. Toddlers and preschoolers can be convinced of almost anything. If they want to believe something badly enough, they can convince themselves of the truth in even the biggest lie.

Lying signals another step toward independence, as fledglings stretch their wings and push away from parental control. So what's a parent to do? Your job is to understand the flavor of the lie and sell your child on the benefits of telling the truth. Knowing that the truth is important to you will make being honest more important to your child.

Preventing the Problem

Reinforce telling the truth.

Offer praise when you know you're hearing the truth, whether it's about something bad that happened or something good. This helps the under-six set begin to understand the difference between what's true and what's not.

Tell the truth.

When your preschooler asks for a cookie right before dinner, you might be tempted to say, "We don't have any cookies," instead of telling him the truth, which is, "I don't want you to eat a cookie before dinner." By lying to him, you're telling him that it's okay to lie when he wants to get out of doing something unpleasant. He knows where the cookies are, so don't pretend he doesn't. Say, "I know you want a cookie now, but when you've eaten your dinner, you can pick one out yourself."

Learn the flavors of lying.

Lying comes in a variety of flavors. Plain old vanilla is the one we all know so well: lying to stay out of trouble. "I didn't take the last cookie" is a good example. A more pungent flavor is lying to get out of doing something you don't want to do. For example, your child might say, "Sure,

Mommy, I brushed my teeth," when he hasn't. And then there's the ever popular, extrasmooth lying that gets whipped up when children try to impress others with comments like, "I have *three* horses that I get to ride every day. So there!"

Be empathetic.

Understand the flavor of lying your child is using and respond accordingly. For example, when your child tells you that he didn't mark his bedroom wall with crayons even though you know he did, tell him, "I understand that you don't want to be punished, but I'm more disappointed that you chose to lie rather than tell the truth. You can always tell me the truth so we can fix the problem together." Your child will feel more comfortable facing the music and telling the truth when he knows you'll be sensitive to his feelings.

Look for honesty.

Look for people and events that demonstrate honesty and truth. Point these out to your preschooler to reinforce your message that being honest is important.

Solving the Problem

What to Do

Show how lying hurts.

When your child is caught in a lie, explain to him how it hurts him as well as you. "I'm sorry you chose not to tell the truth. It makes me feel sad that I can't trust what you say. Let's work on telling the truth so I can believe what you tell me is true."

Explain the difference between lying and telling the truth.

Preschoolers don't always know that what they're saying is a lie because it might seem like the truth to them. Help your child understand the difference between reality and fantasy by saying, "I know you want your friend to like you, but telling him that you have 101 dalmatians living at your house isn't truthful. The truth is that you'd *like* to have all those dogs, but you only have one dog named Molly. She's a really nice dog, and you love her a lot."

Help your child accept responsibility.

When you send your son to do a chore such as putting the toys away in his room, he might lie to get out of doing the job by telling you that he already did it. Say, "I'm so glad you did what I asked. I'll go see what a great job you did." If your son says, "Oh no, Mommy, not yet," you can be reasonably sure he's avoided his responsibility. Check it out! If you discover that he lied, say, "I'm sorry you chose to lie about doing what I asked. I know you didn't want to put all those toys away and didn't want me to be disappointed, but doing what I ask and telling the truth are important. Now let's go get the job done. I'll watch while you pick up."

Practice telling the truth.

When your child lies to you, he's letting you know he needs practice telling the truth. Say, "I'm sorry you didn't tell me the truth when I asked you if you had turned off the TV. Let's practice telling the truth. I want you to say, 'Yes, Mommy, I'll turn off the TV when this show is over.' Now let's try it."

Play make-believe with your child.

To help your child understand the difference between truth and fiction, set aside time for him to make up stories. Then contrast this make-believe time with truth time in which he's asked to tell the truth about what happened. When your child tells you something you know isn't true, say, "That's an interesting make-believe story you just told me. Now tell me a true story about what really happened."

What Not to Do

Don't test your child's honesty.

If you know your child has done something wrong, asking him a question to which you already know the answer forces him into a dilemma: tell the truth and get punished, or lie and maybe get away with it. Don't make him choose.

Don't punish.

When you catch your child telling a lie in order to stay out of trouble, don't punish him for doing so. Instead, teach him how to accept responsibility for making a mistake and to fix the problem it caused. For example, say, "I'm sorry the wall has marks on it. Now we're going to have to learn about taking care of walls. Let's get the cleaning stuff and start cleaning. I'll get the cleaner while you get the paper towels. See? Telling me the truth lets us fix the problem."

Don't lie.

Avoid exaggerating or making up stories to impress people, avoid consequences, or get out of doing what you don't want to do.

Don't overreact.

Even if you've said a hundred times that you can't stand a liar, going ballistic when your child lies only forces him to avoid telling the truth in order to keep you from being mad.

Don't label your child a "liar."

Don't make lying a self-fulfilling prophecy. A child who's called a "liar" will believe that what he does is what he is. Your child isn't what he does. You might not love his behavior, but you'll always love him unconditionally.

Don't take lying personally.

Little Danny isn't telling you an exaggerated version of his morning at daycare just to make you crazy. He may actually believe that the classroom's pet snake got out of its cage because he was so scared that it would. Listen to his story and tell him, "That's an interesting story, sweetheart. I'm sure having the snake loose in the room would be really scary. Do you want me to talk to Miss Laura about keeping the snake safely locked up in its cage?"

"Don't You Lie to Me!"

Although Larry Kirk had just turned four years old, his parents had already tagged him as a "liar." He'd come home from preschool and tell Julie, his mother, the most fantastic stories about how somebody broke into his school and held everyone hostage, or how his teacher had been told she couldn't work there anymore, or how his friend, Adam, had brought his pony to school. Every day it was something new, and Julie was becoming afraid that Larry's fantasies were getting out of hand.

Lawrence, Larry's dad, had also heard Larry's tall tales. He had recently confronted his son about some juice that had been spilled in the kitchen, and the answer he got astonished him. Larry tried to convince his dad that someone broke into the house to steal stuff and must have spilled the juice on the floor. "But son, it's the same grape juice that you have in your cup right now. How do you explain that? Now don't you lie to me!" When Larry didn't have an answer, he was put in Time Out.

Julie and Lawrence realized that this consequence would not teach their son to tell the truth, because the more they put him in Time Out, the more he lied. He even tried to lie his way out of Time Out.

Julie and Lawrence loved their son and needed to help him understand that they would love him no matter what happened. They also knew that their son didn't have to lie to impress them or to stay out of trouble, but they weren't sure if he knew that. When they thought about how the world must seem to little children—a confusing blend of fantasy and reality—the Kirks understood that they could help their son by teaching him the difference between truth and fiction.

"Tell me about school today," Julie said when Larry got into the car after preschool the next day.

"Well, today was real neat because the football team that plays in the stadium came and showed us how to play football, but Josh got hurt and they had to take him to the hospital in an ambulance..." Larry began, but Julie stopped him.

"Wow!" she exclaimed. "That must have been exciting. Is this what you wanted to happen today at school, or did this really happen?"

"Well..." Larry answered, "I wished it happened. Then school would have been more exciting."

"Larry, your story was very interesting, but I really want to know the truth. You don't have to make up things about school so I'll think your day was exciting. You can tell me about the games you played, who sat next to you at snack time, what Miss Sharon talked about, and all sorts of things that I'd like to hear about. I have an idea. You like to make up stories, so let's have story time when you can make up stories, and then let's have truth time when you can report what actually happened during your day."

Larry got into the habit of saying, "Story time, Mom." Then he'd launch into a fantastic tale about his day at school, and they'd both laugh. Julie would rave about how much she enjoyed story time.

"Now it's truth time, Larry," his mom would say, and he'd report on the more mundane events of the day. Julie would tell Larry how much she loved his truth-time tales, too. Lawrence and Julie accomplished two goals: They taught their son lessons in honesty, and they taught him how important telling the truth was to them.

Messiness

Little people make big messes, and unfortunately for orderly parents, small children are almost always oblivious to their self-made clutter. Knowing that your child isn't deliberately messy but simply unaware of the need to clean up after herself, teach her (the younger the better) that messes don't disappear magically—the mess maker (with helpers) cleans them up. Share this fact of life with your child, but don't expect perfection in her following the rule. Encourage rather than demand neatness by praising the slightest attempt your child makes at playing the cleanup game.

Preventing the Problem

Clean as you go.
Show your child how to put away her toys immediately after she's done playing, to limit clutter as she bounces from plaything to plaything. Help her pick up the picking-up habit early in life, to encourage her to be a neater child and, later, a more organized adult.

Show her how to clean up her mess.
Provide appropriately sized boxes and cans in which your child can store her toys and other playthings. Show her how to fit her things inside the containers and where they go when they're filled. This way she'll know exactly what you mean when you ask her to put something away or clean something up.

Be as specific as you can.
Instead of asking your child to clean up her room, tell her exactly what you'd like her to do. For example, say, "Let's put the pegs in the bucket and the blocks in the box." Make it as simple as possible for your child to follow your instructions.

Provide adequate cleanup supplies.
Don't expect your child to know what to use to clean up her mess by herself. For example, give her the right cloth to wash off the table. Make sure to praise all her cleanup efforts after you've given her the tools of the trade.

Confine messy activities to a safe place.

Avoid potential catastrophes by letting your child play with messy materials (fingerpaints, clay, markers, crayons, and so on) in appropriate places. Don't expect her to know not to destroy the living-room carpet when you've let her fingerpaint in there.

Solving the Problem

What to Do

Use Grandma's Rule.

If your child refuses to clean up a mess she's made, make her fun dependent on doing the job you've requested. For example, say, "Yes, I know you don't want to pick up your blocks. But when you've picked them up, then you may go outside to play." Remember that a child one year old or older can help clean up in small ways. She needs to try her best at whatever level she can, slowly building up to more difficult tasks.

Work together.

Sometimes the cleanup job is too big for a young child's muscles or hands. Join in the work to encourage sharing and cooperation—two lessons you want your child to learn as a preschooler. Seeing Mom or Dad clean up makes the activity that much more inviting.

Play Beat-the-Clock.

When your child is trying to beat the timer, picking up toys is a fun game instead of an arduous task. Join in the fun by saying, "When you've picked up the toys before the timer rings, you can take out another toy." When your child is successful at beating the clock, praise her accomplishment and follow through on your promise.

Praise your child's cleanup effort.

Encourage your child to clean up after herself by using a powerful motivator—praise! Comment on the great job she's doing putting away her crayons, for example. Say, "I'm really glad you put that red crayon in the basket. Thanks for helping clean up your room."

What Not to Do

Don't expect perfection.

Your child hasn't had much time to practice cleaning up after herself, so don't expect her job to be perfect. The fact that she's trying means she's learning how to do it. She'll improve over time.

Don't punish messiness.

Your child cannot yet understand the value of neatness and doesn't have the physical maturity to stay tidy, so punishing her for being messy will not teach her the cleanup skills she needs to learn.

Don't expect preschoolers to dress themselves for a mess.

Your child doesn't understand the value of nice clothing, so provide her with old clothes (and put them on inside out, if you want) before allowing her to play with messy materials.

Multiple Messes

As parents, John and Mandy Wareman were getting used to everything but the messes their five-year-old twins, Leah and Hannah, made almost daily. "Good children always put away their toys," Mrs. Wareman told them, trying to convince the girls not to leave their toys in the living room when they were done playing. When that didn't work, she began spanking her daughters and putting them in their rooms when they didn't clean up their mess. But that punishment seemed to punish only her, because the girls created additional messes while in their rooms.

Mrs. Wareman finally saw a way to solve the problem when she realized how much her children liked to play outside on their new swing set. She decided to turn that activity into a privilege that had to be earned. One day the girls wanted to go outside instead of cleaning up the pegs and the kitchen set they had been playing with. Mrs. Wareman said, "Here's the new rule, girls. I know you want to go outside, but when you've picked up your kitchen set, Leah, and your pegs, Hannah, then you can play on the swing set. I will help."

The two girls looked at each other. They didn't want to pick up their toys, but they really wanted to play on the swing set. Mrs. Wareman began helping put the pegs in the jar to make sure that Hannah knew what clean up the pegs meant. Mrs. Wareman also opened up the bag so Leah could deposit the kitchen utensils in their proper place, leaving no doubt about what cleaning up the kitchen set *meant.*

As the girls began cleaning up, Mrs. Wareman let them know how happy she was with their efforts. "Thanks for cleaning up. You're doing a great job filling that jar with pegs. I sure like the way that kitchen set fits into that tiny bag." She hugged each girl with genuine pride, and soon both children spilled out the door, leaving their mother to fix lunch instead of clean up after them.

For many weeks, the girls needed to be offered rewards for cleaning up, but they finally learned that putting away one toy before taking out another made the cleanup process quicker and also brought great compliments from Mom.

Name-Calling

Blossoming preschool linguists test the power of name-calling to let the world know that they're the boss and can talk like it. By calling people names, your child is testing the strength of words as well as the reactions they get. If you react calmly when he calls you a name, you'll teach him that name-calling will not achieve his desired effect. Explain that he should also react calmly when he's called a name. He'll realize that the name-calling game isn't much fun when played by only one.

Preventing the Problem

Watch your nicknames.

Avoid calling your child nicknames you wouldn't want him to call someone else. There's a big difference between "You little devil" and "You little doll."

Teach your child to respond calmly to name-calling.

Suggest appropriate ways for your child to react when he's the victim of name-calling. Encourage him to avoid getting angry. Say, "When your friend calls you a bad name, tell him calmly that you can't play with him when he calls you names."

Decide what's a bad name and what isn't.

Make sure you've educated your child about "illegal" names before expecting him to know what they are.

Solving the Problem

What to Do

Put your child in Time Out.

For example, say, "When you do things that aren't acceptable, you lose your chances for playing. I'm sorry you called your sister a bad name. Time out."

Wear out the name.

For some preschoolers, repeating a name takes away its power. Put your child in a chair and have him repeat the word without stopping (one minute for each year of age). If he refuses to do so (many preschoolers do), simply have him sit there until he starts, no matter how long it takes. When he's done, focus on teaching him appropriate things to say.

Notice nice talk.

Praise your child when he's using appropriate language instead of name-calling, to help him distinguish between what's acceptable and what's not.

Be consistent.

Every time your child is the name-caller, use the same response to teach him that name-calling is never acceptable. Say, "I'm sorry you called your friend a name. Now you'll have to go to Time Out," or, "Now you must wear out the word."

What Not to Do

Don't be a name-caller.

Because being called names is so irritating, it's easy to shout back at your child the same hurtful words he says to you. Saying something like, "You dummy! You should know better than to call people names," gives your preschooler permission to use the names you used. Instead, channel your anger into an explanation of how and why you feel upset. Your child will learn when his words make you unhappy and how you'd like him to behave when he feels like name-calling.

Don't use severe punishment for name-calling.

If you severely punish your child for name-calling, he'll only learn to avoid the behavior when you're within earshot. Instead of learning that name-calling is wrong, he'll learn that he needs to avoid getting caught. Punished behavior does not go away; it just goes out of sight.

"That's Not Nice!"

Max and Suzanne Glass were shocked when they first heard their precious four-year-old daughter, Sarah, call her friends "dummy," "jerk," and "dog poo poo." They had never used these words around the house, so they couldn't understand where Sarah had picked them up, and they didn't know what to do about it.

"Don't call people names, Sarah! That's not nice!" they would say every time their daughter used an offending word, but this had little effect. In fact,

Sarah soon began calling her parents names, which caused them to spank her. But even this didn't stop the name-calling.

Finally, Mrs. Glass tried a different strategy. She began to supervise her daughter's play more closely, to notice when Sarah played well with others and when she didn't. "How nicely you girls are getting along," Mrs. Glass pointed out when Sarah and her cousin, Maria, were dressing their baby dolls. But when Maria tried to take Sarah's doll for a ride in the blue car, Sarah yelled, "You dummy, Maria, you know that's my car."

Mrs. Glass immediately separated the girls. "I'm sorry you called your cousin a 'dummy,'" she told Sarah. "Time out." After four minutes in the Time Out chair, Sarah learned that her mother meant business. Playtime would be halted and Sarah would be put in Time Out if she called anyone names. Sarah started to learn that name-calling was hurtful, and the behavior began to disappear.

Not Following Directions

Preschoolers love to test whether their parents' warnings will be enforced, how far rules can be stretched, and how closely directions must be followed. Give your child consistent results for her research on the adult world. Prove to your child that you mean what you say so she'll feel more secure about what she can expect from other adults. Your making and enforcing rules may seem dictatorial to your child, but despite her protests she will feel more secure knowing that limits are set and rules are defined as she moves from a little to a big person's world.

Preventing the Problem

Learn how many directions your child can follow at once.

Your preschooler will only be able to remember and follow a certain number of directions, depending on her developmental stage. To find out your child's limit, give one simple direction, then two, then three. For example, for three directions say, "Please pick up the book, put it on the table, and come sit by me." If all three are followed in the proper order, you'll know your child can remember three directions. Identify her limit and wait until she's older before giving her more complicated directions.

Let your preschooler do as many things by herself as possible.

Because she wants to follow the beat of her own drum and have total control over her life, your preschooler will fight for the chance to make choices. Whenever possible, give her the opportunity to develop her decision-making skills and increase her self-confidence. The more control she feels she has, the less likely she'll be to reject taking directions from someone else.

Avoid unnecessary rules.

Analyze a rule's importance before you etch it in stone. Your preschooler needs as much freedom as possible to develop her independence.

Solving the Problem

What to Do

Give simple, clear directions.

Be as specific as possible about what you want your child to do, to make it easier for her to follow your directions. Make suggestions but try not to criticize what she's done. For example, say, "Please pick up your toys now and put them in the box," rather than, "Why don't you ever remember to pick up your toys and put them away on your own?"

Praise following directions.

Reward your child for following your directions by praising her job well done. You can also show her how to appreciate someone's effort by saying, "Thank you for doing what I asked you to do."

Use countdown.

Make the rule that your child must start a task by the count of five, for example, to ease her into the idea of leaving her fun for something you want her to do. Say, "Please pick up your toys now. Five-four-three-two-one." Thank her for starting to clean up so quickly, if she does.

Praise your child's progress.

Be a cheerleader as your child takes steps toward completing your requested task. For example, say, "That's great the way you're getting up and starting to put those toys away."

Use Grandma's Rule.

Children are more likely to follow directions when they know they can do what they want to do after a task is completed. For example, say, "When you've picked up the books, you may turn on the television," or, "When you've washed your hands, we will have lunch."

Practice following directions.

If your child is not following your directions, find out whether she's unable or unwilling by walking her through the task. Guide her manually and praise her progress along the way. If you discover she can do the task but simply refuses to do so, say, "I'm sorry you aren't following directions. Now we have to practice." Practice five times, then give her the opportunity to follow the directions on her own. If she still refuses, say, "It looks like we need more practice. When you finish practicing, then you may play with your toys."

What Not to Do

Don't back down if your child resists.

Say to yourself, "I know my child doesn't want to do as I say, but I'm more experienced and know what's best for her. I need to teach her by giving her clear directions so she can eventually do things herself."

Don't punish your child for not following directions.

Teaching your child how to do something, instead of punishing her for not doing it, avoids damaging her self-esteem and doesn't put attention on her failure to follow directions.

"Do What You're Told!"

Four-and-a-half-year-old Eric Jackson knew his alphabet and his numbers, and he was even starting to sound out words in his favorite books. The one thing he couldn't do was the one thing his mother wanted most: follow her directions.

On a daily basis, Eric's mother would give him simple directions like, "Eric, please pick up your toys and then put your dirty clothes in the hamper," or, "Come sit here on the couch and put on your boots." Eric would get about halfway through the first task, then he'd lose track of what he was supposed to be doing and wander off to investigate a toy truck or to see what his brother was doing.

"How many times do I have to tell you what to do?" his frustrated mother would yell. "You never listen to me! You never understand what I tell you!" she would continue, giving him a swift spanking for not complying with her wishes.

This continued until one day Eric shouted back, "I can't do what you want!" His mother actually heard what he said and took it seriously. She decided to try limiting her directions to one simple command, to see if Eric could do that.

"Eric, please bring me your boots," she asked simply. Eric marched right over to his blue and white boots and brought them to his mother, who clapped her hands with delight. "Thanks so much for doing what I asked!" A while later, she asked Eric to go get his coat on. When Eric fulfilled her request, she again followed up with praise for his effort.

Eric's mother was delighted that she could stop threatening and screaming at her son. She realized that listening to Eric's feelings was crucial to their getting along. She slowly increased the number of directions she gave her son, waiting until he was able to do two at a time before giving him three at a time. Her clear language and use of Grandma's Rule helped her win the war against not following directions.

Not Sharing

Mine is the buzzword preschoolers use to remind each other (and adults) of their territorial rights. Despite the wars this four-letter word incites in households with children under five years old, possessiveness will unfortunately not disappear until children are developmentally ready to let it go (between three and four years old). Help lay the groundwork for peace by consistently teaching your preschooler the give-and-take rules of the world. Enforce these sharing rules at home, but be patient. Don't expect them to be righteously followed until you see your child sharing without your intervention—the glorious sign that he's ready to broaden his boundaries.

Preventing the Problem

Make sure some toys belong strictly to your child.

Before preschoolers can let go of the word *mine* and all the things attached to it, they must be given the chance to possess things. Put away your child's favorite toys or blankets when visitors come over to play so he won't be forced to share them.

Point out how you and your friends share.

Show your child that he isn't the only one in the world expected to share his things. Give examples at neutral (nonsharing) times of how you and your friends share things. Say, "Mary borrowed my cookbook today," or, "Charlie borrowed my lawnmower."

Point out what sharing means and how much you like it.

Tell your child how nicely he's sharing whenever he's allowing another person to hold or play with his toys. For example, say, "I like the way you're sharing by letting your friend have that toy for a minute."

Put labels on similar toys (for twins or children close in age).

Make sure you don't confuse your son's teddy bear with his sister's or brother's, if they're the same. Label each one with a nametag or piece of thread to help your children feel confident in their ownership.

Set up sharing rules.

Before friends come over to play, let your child know what's expected of him at group sharing times. For example, say, "If you put a toy down, anyone may play with it. If you have it in your hands, you may keep it."

Understand that your child may share better at a friend's house.

Your child may be less aggressive about ownership when he's not defending his own territory.

Remember that sharing is a developmental task.

Learning to share is an accomplishment that cannot be rushed. Usually at three to four years of age, your child will begin sharing things without being reminded.

Solving the Problem

What to Do

Supervise one- and two-year-olds' play.

Because children younger than three years old cannot be expected to share, stay close by while they're playing, to help resolve sharing conflicts they're too young to handle without assistance.

Set the timer.

When two children are calling a toy "mine," show how the give-and-take of sharing works. Tell one child that you'll be setting the timer, and when the timer rings, the other child can have the toy. Keep using the timer until they've grown tired of the toy.

Put toys in Time Out.

If a toy is creating a problem because one child won't share, put the toy in Time Out to remove it from the situation. If the toy is out of reach, it can't cause any trouble. Say, "This toy is causing a problem. It must go into Time Out." If the children keep fighting over the toy after it's been brought out, keep removing it to make the point that not sharing a toy means no one gets to play with it.

What Not to Do

Don't get upset.

Remember that your child will learn the rule about sharing when he's developmentally ready, not when you force him to do so. When you see your child sharing, you'll know he's ready!

Don't punish for occasionally not sharing.

If your child occasionally has trouble sharing, remove the offending toy rather than punish your child. This puts the blame on the toy, not the child.

Learning to Share

Three-year-old Cody Smith knew what the word sharing *meant; it meant that he couldn't sit and hold as many toys as he wanted when his friend, Jim, came over to play. "You* must *share!" Cody's mother told her son after another day of Cody clutching his toys and saying "Mine" whenever his mother said, "Now, Cody, let's share."*

One day Mrs. Smith screamed, "I'm going to give all your toys to poor children who will appreciate them," as she spanked Cody into tearfully giving up his toys. That night after Cody was tucked in bed, Mrs. Smith told her husband, "Cody just doesn't know how *to share." This simple statement shed new light on the problem. The Smiths realized that they needed to teach* Cody what *sharing* meant.

The next time Cody's cousins came over, Mrs. Smith took him aside for a talk. "Cody, here's the new sharing rule. Anyone can play with anything in this house as long as another person is not holding it. If you or Mike or Mary is holding a toy, no one can take it away. Each of you may play with only one toy at a time." Mrs. Smith also told Cody that he could put away one favorite toy, which could belong to him and him alone.

The next few hours were tense for Mrs. Smith, but Cody seemed to be more relaxed. He began by holding only one toy and letting his cousins have their pick of the lot in the toy box. "I'm so proud of you for sharing," his watchful mother praised him as she oversaw the operation.

When she ventured off to fix lunch, the familiar "Mine" cry brought her back to the playroom. The new "burp-itself" doll was being pulled limb from limb by Mary and Cody. "This toy is causing trouble," Mrs. Smith stated matter-of-factly. "It must go to Time Out." The children stared in disbelief as they watched poor Betsy sitting in the Time Out chair looking as lonely as a misbehaved pooch. After two minutes, Mrs. Smith returned the toy to the children, who had long since forgotten about it and were busy playing with blocks.

As the weeks went by, the children played side by side with fewer Time Outs needed to restore peace, particularly since Cody was more open to letting "his" toys be "their" toys during the play period.

Not Wanting to Eat

Parents often find themselves pushing their on-the-go preschoolers to eat, since many children under six are too busy investigating their world to take much time out for food. If the temptation to force food on your child seems overwhelming, try giving her more attention for eating (even the smallest pea!) than for not eating.

Note: Preschoolers are notorious for their occasional bouts of not wanting to eat; don't mistake these for illness. However, get professional help if you feel your child is physically ill and can't eat.

Preventing the Problem

Don't skip meals yourself.
Skipping meals yourself gives your child the idea that not eating is okay for her, since it's okay for you.

Don't emphasize a big tummy or idolize a bone-thin physique.
Even a three-year-old can become irrationally weight conscious if you show her how to be obsessed with her body.

Learn the appropriate amount of food for your child's age and weight.
Growth rate, activity level, and physical size determine how many servings from the five food groups (milk, meat, vegetable, grain, and fruit) a child needs each day. Consult your child's health-care provider for answers to specific nutrition questions about your child. For more information about recommended guidelines for one- to five-year-olds, consult the National Dairy Council's website at www.nutritionexplorations.org.

Solving the Problem

What to Do

Encourage less food, more often.
Get your child's system in the habit of eating meals at particular times during the day. However, your child's stomach isn't as large as yours, so it can't

hold enough food to last four or more hours between meals. Let your child eat as often as she likes, but only the right foods for good nutrition. For example, say, "Whenever you're hungry, let me know, and you can have celery with peanut butter or an apple with cheese." Make sure you can follow through with your suggestions, based on what foods are available and what time a bigger meal is coming.

Let your child choose foods.

Occasionally let your child choose her between-meal snack or lunch food (with your supervision). If she feels she has some control over what she's eating, she may be more excited about food. Offer her only two choices at a time, so she doesn't become overwhelmed with the decision-making process, and praise her choice with comments like, "I'm glad you chose that orange. It's really a delicious snack."

Provide variety and balance.

Children need to learn about proper diet, which involves a wide range of foods. Expose your child to the various tastes, textures, colors, and aromas of nutritious foods. Remember that preschoolers' tastes often change overnight, so expect your child to turn down a food today that was a favorite last week.

Let nature take its course.

A normal, healthy child will naturally select a balanced diet over a week's time, which pediatricians say will keep her adequately nourished. Keep a mental note of what your child has eaten from Monday through Sunday—not from sunup to sundown—before becoming alarmed that she's undernourished.

Catch your child with a mouthful.

Give your child encouragement when she downs a spoonful of nutritious food, to teach her that eating will bring her as much attention as not eating. Praise good eating habits by saying, "That's great the way you put that meat loaf in your mouth all by yourself," or, "I'm glad you like the rolls we have today."

Establish regular mealtimes.

Because your child is not on the same eating schedule as you, she may often want to play outside or finish block building when your mealtime arrives. She may need to be trained to switch to your schedule for sitting together. Do this *not* by forcing your child to eat a lot of food, but by setting a timer for the length of time she must remain at the table, eating or not. Say, "The timer will tell us when dinner is over. The rule is that you must stay at the table until the timer rings. Tell me when you're done eating, and I'll remove your plate." Let children under three stay at the table a shorter time (not more than five minutes) than four- or five-year-olds (not more than ten minutes). Identify the times when your child seems to get hungry, to learn what kind of hunger clock she's on (which you could switch to, if possible).

What Not to Do

Don't offer food rewards for eating.

Keep food in its proper perspective. Food is meant to provide nourishment, not to symbolize praise. Instead of offering your child ice cream for eating her vegetables, say, "Since you ate your green beans so nicely, you can go outside after dinner."

Don't bribe or beg.

When your child is not eating, don't bribe or beg her to clean her plate. This makes noneating a game to get your attention, which gives your child a feeling of power over you.

Don't get upset when your child won't eat.

Giving her attention for not eating makes not eating much more interesting to your child than eating.

Don't overreact.

Downplay the attention you give to your child's not wanting to eat so eating time does not become a battleground on which you wage power struggles.

"I Won't Eat!"

When John Rowland turned four years old, his appetite dropped to zero. His parents didn't know why and neither did his pediatrician, who checked him over physically at the insistence of John's fretful mother. One night, after Mrs. Rowland had begged him to eat just one pea, John threw a vehement tantrum, pushed his plate off the table, and shouted, "No, I won't eat!"

Mr. Rowland decided he had let his wife handle the situation too long. "Now, Johnny, listen to me. If you don't take a bite of macaroni, you'll have to leave the table," he threatened, firmly letting his son know the rule of the moment. He never guessed that Johnny would take him up on the offer and get down from his chair. "Johnny Rowland, you will not get down from this table! You will stay and eat your dinner if you have to sit here all night!" Mr. Rowland yelled, changing the rules and thoroughly confusing his son.

Later that night, after they had kissed and hugged their son and put him to bed, the Rowlands decided that something different had to be done—they did not want to spank and yell at their little boy for not eating. They wanted to turn mealtime back into what it used to be: a time for food and fun exchanges of stories, songs, and the events of the day.

The next night at dinner, they shifted their attention away from food and pretended to ignore John's lack of appetite. "Tell me about how you were the helper at preschool today," Johnny's mother began (with all the sincerity and calmness she could muster) as she passed the broccoli to her husband. John perked up as he told the story of how he was chosen to hold the flag. In between his excited explanations, he just happened to swallow a forkful of mashed potatoes.

"That was so nice of you to be such a good helper today," Mrs. Rowland complimented her son. "I'm glad you like the mashed potatoes, too," she added. The Rowlands continued their meal but refrained from pushing their son to try a few more potatoes.

The next morning John's parents discussed the evening's success and decided to continue what they were doing. They also remembered what John's doctor had said: "John may eat only small amounts, judging from his normal but slight body size, and he may eat those more than three times a day, as many people do."

Dinnertime became less of a daytime preoccupation for Mrs. Rowland. She began creating fun carrot-stick boats and cheese-and-raisin faces for John to eat throughout the day. John developed a whole new interest in eating more during the day, though he still only took a few mouthfuls at dinner. But the Rowlands appreciated those minutes John did spend eating, and they let their son dictate when he was and wasn't hungry.

Overeating

The appetite of many preschoolers can be as endless as that of the famous Cookie Monster on *Sesame Street*. Like the puppet hero, your child may not be aware of why he wants more food than he needs. But *you* need to understand his motivation in order to get his eating habits back on track. Because overeating is a symptom of a problem, not the problem itself, try to discover the reasons behind your child's seemingly bottomless pit. Possible explanations include habit, boredom, mimicry, or the desire for attention. Help him find ways to satisfy his needs and wants without overeating.

Note: Get professional help if your child is a consistent overeater. Avoid diets that are not medically supervised.

Preventing the Problem

Model a healthy attitude toward food.

Your relationship with food is contagious. When you complain about dieting or being too fat, for example, your child learns that food has power beyond making him healthy. Food becomes the enemy to defend against, lest he lose control and pig out on a forbidden chocolate cake. Since moderation is the key to health, moderate your talk as well as your behavior. Eating disorders in young children have become more prevalent, due in part to our dieting-obsessed culture.

Become well versed in what's appropriate for your child.

Growth rate, activity level, and physical size determine how many servings from the five food groups (milk, meat, vegetable, grain, fruit) a child needs each day. Consult your child's health-care provider for answers to specific nutrition questions about your child. For more information about recommended guidelines for one- to five-year-olds, consult the National Dairy Council's website at www.nutritionexplorations.org.

Serve healthy foods.

Keep both high-calorie and empty-calorie foods out of your overeater's reach so he won't be tempted to grab for them.

Check your child's diet.

Since your preschooler is too young to know what he should and shouldn't eat, it's up to you to establish healthy eating habits—the earlier the better. Foods high in fat and sugar should be replaced with those high in protein, vitamins, and minerals, to offer a balance of nutritious calories in a day.

Teach when, how, and where eating is allowed.

Restrict eating to the kitchen and dining room only. Slow down the eating pace and insist that food be eaten from a plate or bowl, instead of directly from the refrigerator. Taking more time between mouthfuls allows our brains to get the message that we're full *before* we've eaten more than we need. (This process takes about twenty minutes.)

Solving the Problem

What to Do

Provide pleasurable activities other than eating.

Get to know what your child likes to do besides eat, and suggest these activities after he's eaten enough to satisfy his hunger. Show him how delicious things other than food can be.

Keep food in perspective.

Don't offer food as a present or reward, to avoid teaching your child that eating means more than satisfying hunger.

Provide nutritious between-meal snacks.

A well-timed snack can prevent your child from getting overhungry and gorging at mealtime when it finally arrives.

Watch when your child overeats.

Try to discover why your child overeats by seeing if he turns to food when he's bored, mad, sad, watching others eat, or wanting attention from you. Help him resolve his feelings in noneating ways like talking or playing. Communicate with him about trouble spots in his life so he won't be tempted to make food a problem solver.

Control your own eating habits.

If parents snack on empty-calorie junk foods all day, their children will be inclined to do the same.

Praise wise food selections.

You can mold your child's food preferences by your tone of voice and by encouraging foods you want him to favor. Whenever your child picks up an orange instead of a piece of chocolate, say, "That's a great choice you made for a snack. I'm glad you're taking care of yourself so well by eating yummy treats like oranges."

Encourage exercise.

Overweight children often don't eat any more than normal-weight children; they just don't burn enough calories off through exercise. If you live in a cold climate, suggest physical activities to play inside in the winter, like dancing or jumping rope. In the summer, activities such as swimming, walking, baseball, and swinging are not only good for your child's physical development, they also relieve tension, give him fresh air, and build coordination and strength. Your participation will make exercise even more fun for your child.

Communicate with your child.

Make sure the encouragement you give your child to eat all his peas isn't the only encouragement you ever give him. Praise his artwork, the clothes he's chosen, the way he's cleaned up his toys, and so on to give him attention for things other than eating and overeating.

What Not to Do

Don't give in to his desire to overeat.

Just because your child wants more food doesn't mean he needs it, but don't make him feel guilty for wanting more by making fun of him and calling him "Little piggy," for example. To learn healthy portion sizes, consult the National Dairy Council's website at www.nutritionexplorations.org or ask your child's doctor for a nutrition plan. After you're sure your child has had enough, briefly explain why he shouldn't have more, because he's too young to tell himself the reason.

Don't give treats when your child is upset.

Your child may begin to associate food with emotional rather than physical nourishment if you consistently offer treats to ease his pain.

Don't consistently allow food while you're watching TV.

Avoid teaching your child to associate food with TV. Because television advertising bombards your child with food messages, it's also a good idea to limit his television viewing time.

Don't give junk foods as snacks.

What you allow for snacks and meals is what your child will expect. Food preferences are learned, not inborn.

Don't make fun of your child if he's overweight.

Making fun of your child only compounds the problem by adding to his guilt and shame.

"No More Cookies!"

Two-and-a-half-year-old Rosa Hanlon was getting a reputation at preschool and family functions for being a "walking bottomless pit." If food was in sight, Rosa ate it. She never seemed to be full.

"No, you can't have another cookie, Rosa!" Mrs. Hanlon would scream every time she caught her daughter with her hand in the cookie jar. "You've had enough cookies to last your lifetime!" But neither angry outbursts nor the threat of taking away her tricycle lessened Rosa's desire to finish every morsel in a box or on a plate.

Mrs. Hanlon decided to consult her pediatrician to learn how to change Rosa's eating habits. The doctor provided a nutrition plan and recipe suggestions specifically tailored for Rosa. The next day, Rosa asked for another helping of oatmeal after eating the suggested amount, but Mrs. Hanlon finally had an answer that wasn't angry or insulting: "I'm glad you liked the oatmeal, Rosa. We can have some more tomorrow morning. Let's go read that new book now."

Knowing that the amount she had given Rosa was nutritionally adequate made it easier for Mrs. Hanlon to stand firm when Rosa begged for more oatmeal. It was also easier for Mrs. Hanlon to plan each meal, because she knew what amounts were enough to nourish her daughter.

The Hanlons also reduced their steady supply of cookies, so Rosa started to try new foods that were tasty and more nutritious. Mrs. Hanlon praised Rosa every time she chose a healthy food. "That's great the way you picked an orange for a snack instead of cookies."

Rosa started to hear fewer comments about being a bottomless pit, and she received lots of hugs and compliments for eating fruit instead of fudge. Not only were her parents delighted to share exercise and fun with her, but Rosa seemed to have more fun with her friends and teachers, too.

Overusing *No*

No ranks as the most-likely-to-be-used word by toddlers because it's the most-likely-to-be-used word by parents. Toddlers are famous for getting into, on top of, and underneath things they shouldn't, and parents are famous for saying, "No! Don't touch!" "No! Don't open!" "No! Don't do that!" The best way to reduce the frequency of your toddler's use of *no* is by limiting her opportunities. Do this by avoiding yes-no questions and by not always taking her literally when she says no to every request.

Preventing the Problem

Get to know your child's personality.

If you're familiar with your child's needs and wants, you'll know when her *no* means no and when it really means yes or something else.

Think before saying "no."

Avoid telling your child "no" when you don't really care whether she does something or not.

Limit yes-no questions.

Avoid questions your child can answer with "No." For example, ask her *how much* juice she wants, not whether she wants some. If you want her to get in the car, don't say, "Do you want to get in the car?" Say, "We're getting in the car now," and do it!

Change your *no* to something else.

For example, say, "Stop," instead of, "No," when your child is doing something you don't want her to do.

Redirect your child's behavior.

Because you usually want your child to stop a behavior when you say "No" to her, teach another behavior to replace the one you want stopped. During a neutral time, take your child's hand and say, "Come here, please." Practice five times a day, slowly increasing the distance your child is away from you when you say, "Come here, please," until she can come to you from across the room or across the shopping center.

Solving the Problem

What to Do

Ignore your child's *no.*

If you're not sure what she means by *no*, assume she really means *yes*. For example, if she doesn't want the juice she just said "No" to, she won't take it. Eventually you'll know when she really means *no*.

Give more attention for *yes* than *no.*

Your child will learn how to say yes if nodding her head or saying "Yes" makes you smile and praise her. React positively by saying something like, "How nice of you to say 'Yes,'" or, "I'm really glad you said 'Yes' when your aunt asked you that question."

Teach your child how to say "Yes."

Children over three can learn to say "Yes" if they're shown how to do it. Tell your child that you want her to say "Yes." When she does, praise her with words like, "It's nice to hear you say 'Yes,'" or, "I really like the way you said 'Yes.'" Then say, "I'm going to ask you to do something for me and I want you to say 'Yes' before I can count to five." If she says it, tell her what a great *yes* that was. Practice this five times for five days and you'll be in for a more positive-sounding child.

Let your child say "No."

Even though she must still do what you want (or need) her to do, your child is entitled to say "No." When you want her to do something but she has said "No," explain the situation to her. For example, say, "I know you don't want to pick up your crayons, but when you've done what I asked you to do, then you may do what you want to do." This lets your child know that you've heard what she's said and are taking her feelings into consideration—but you're still the boss.

What Not to Do

Don't laugh or encourage the use of *no.*

Laughing or calling attention to your child's overuse of the word only encourages her to use it more to get your reaction.

Don't get angry.

Remember that the "no" stage is normal in your developing preschooler and will soon pass. Getting angry will be interpreted as giving your child attention for saying "No," and attention and power are just what she wants.

Negative Nathan

Twenty-month-old Nathan Shelby's favorite word to say was his parents' least favorite word to hear: no. Because little Nate used that word to answer every question asked of him, his parents started to wonder about his mental powers. "Can't you say anything besides no?" they'd ask their son, only to get his usual response.

So the Shelbys tried to reduce the number of times they used the word during the day, to see if that would have an effect on Nathan's vocabulary. Instead of saying, "No, not now," whenever Nate demanded a cookie, they said, "Yes, you may have a cookie when you've eaten your dinner." While they were still, in effect, saying no, Nate didn't react negatively in return. Instead, he took his parents up on their promise and got his cookie immediately after dinner.

As his parents traded in their no's for yes's, Nate started to increase his use of yes, a word that was immediately met with smiles, hugs, and compliments from his delighted parents. "Thanks for saying 'Yes' when I asked you if you wanted to take a bath," his mother would say. They were delighted that their son was decreasing his no's in direct proportion to how much praise he got for saying yes.

The Shelbys also tried to limit the number of yes-no questions they asked Nate. Instead of asking him if he wanted something to drink with his dinner, they said, "Do you want apple juice or milk?" Nate would happily make a choice between the two. Their efforts were painless ways to manage their son's negativism, and they soon found their household taking on a more positive tone.

Playing with Food

Take a one-, two-, or three-year-old, mix her with food she doesn't want to eat, and—presto!—you have an instant mess on your hands, her hands, and probably the floor and table, too. When your child starts playing with her food instead of putting it in her mouth, it usually means she's finished eating, whether she can say the words or not. Consistently take her food away as soon as it becomes a weapon or a toy, even if she's still hungry. This will teach her that food is meant to be eaten, not played with.

Preventing the Problem

Don't play with food yourself.
If you flip peas with your fork, even unconsciously, your child will assume that she can do it, too.

Plan food your child likes to eat.
To reduce the likelihood of a mess, cut her food into bite-size pieces that are easily handled and chewed.

Keep bowls of food out of reach.
Steer playful preschoolers away from the temptation to stir and pour just for fun.

Teach your child table manners at a noneating, neutral time.
Your child needs to know what you expect of her in restaurants and at home, because she didn't come built-in with table manners! It's best to teach her when you're not actually sitting down to dinner. For example, have frequent "tea parties" where you show her how to use her spoon, keep food on her tray, keep her hands out of her food, tell you when she's done, and so on. For a child under two, say, "Say, 'I'm done,' and then you can get down and play." For your three-, four-, or five-year-old, say, "When the timer rings, you can leave the table. Tell me when you're finished and I'll take your plate."

Talk to your child at the table.
If you make conversation with her, she won't find other ways to get your attention, like playing with food.

Solving the Problem
What to Do

Compliment proper eating habits.
Anytime your child is *not* playing with her food at the table, tell her you like how well she's eating. Say, for example, "That's great the way you're using your fork for those peas," or, "Thanks for twisting that spaghetti around your fork as I showed you."

Make playing with food unappetizing.
If your child breaks an eating rule you've previously discussed, tell her what the consequences are, to prove to her that playing with food is unacceptable. For example, say, "I'm sorry that you stuck your hands into your mashed potatoes. Now dinner is over."

Ask whether your child is done when she starts playing with her food.
Don't immediately assume that your child is being devilish. Ask her why she's dissecting her meat loaf, for example, to give her a chance to explain herself (if she's verbal).

What Not to Do

Don't lose your cool.
Though you may be disgusted and angry at your child for wasting her food, your anger may be the spice she wants with her meal. Your preschooler thrives on having the power to affect the world (for better and worse). Don't let playing with food become a way of getting attention. Ignore any nondestructive food play that you feel comfortable accepting at the table.

Don't give in.
If your child has to pay the price for playing with food, don't give in and remove the cost, even if she's screaming about how high it is. Teach your child you mean what you say every time you make a rule.

Dinnertime Disasters

Dinnertime at the Langners' looked more like art class than mealtime, since three-year-old Nick had begun smearing food around his plate and spitting out what didn't tickle his taste buds. His parents, who were disgusted with their son's wasteful games, tried to stop him by screaming, "Don't play with your food!"

Even after his mother threatened, "If you do that with your peas one more time, I'll take you down from the table," Nick tried to flip one more pea into his glass of milk. Spanking didn't bring any results either. Nick continued to eat only a few bites, after which he began feeding his frankfurters and beans to the nearby plants.

So the Langners decided to anticipate when Nick would be full. They noticed when his playful eyes and hands started to find new things to do with his French fries and green beans, and they quickly removed his plate. Nick's mother also spent a few minutes during the day teaching her son to say, "Through now," which he could use to signal when he was done eating.

Both of Nick's parents were relieved after experiencing three straight weeks without any food "art" at the table. But then Nick decided to try his hand at smearing creamed corn on the tablecloth. Fortunately, they had decided what the rule would be for slip-ups, and they calmly explained it to Nick. "Whenever you make a mess, you must clean it up." Instead of yelling at Nick, they calmly demonstrated the process.

Nick didn't get any attention for having to clean up his mess by himself, and it took only three wipe-up nights for him to start saying, "Through now." Those words worked like magic, he discovered, and he appreciated the hugs and kisses from his parents, who would say, "Thanks for saying, 'Through now,' Nick. I know you're done with your dinner and now you may go play with your trucks."

The whole family seemed relieved that more time was spent talking about how nice Nick was eating instead of how destructive he was with his food. Dinners with their son were shorter but sweeter than ever before.

Pretending to Use Weapons

Many moms and dads lament the fact that little boys, in particular, love to turn every object they touch into a weapon, from baseball bats to carrots, often imitating what they see on TV (with boys being more affected by violent TV than girls).[1] Young children do not process information the same way as adults, nor do they have the tools to evaluate what they see.

It has been reported that preschoolers who were given guns and other violent toys to play with acted more aggressively than preschoolers who only watched a television program with violent content.[2] But studies have shown that by the age of three, children will imitate someone on TV as readily as they will a real person.[3] The results of the studies on the effects of viewing television violence are consistent: Children learn how to be aggressive in new ways and draw conclusions about whether being aggressive will bring them rewards.

Those children who see television characters getting what they want by using weapons are more likely to imitate those acts themselves. If parents ignore or approve of their children's use of weapons or exhibit violent behavior themselves, they serve as role models for their children. On the other hand, parents who show their children how to solve problems nonviolently and who consistently praise their children for finding peaceful solutions to conflicts show their children how to be less aggressive.[4]

So when your preschooler makes pretend guns out of French fries, don't panic, but don't ignore his imaginative play either. Instead, teach the important lesson that even pretending to physically hurt people can hurt their feelings. Keep in mind that the behavior of the adults closest to a child encourages him to be kind or cruel. Watch what you do and say—and how "explosively" you act—in order to help curb your child's appetite for violent play.

Preventing the Problem

Make caring a household rule.
When your child behaves aggressively, make a rule that tells him what is or isn't allowed regarding pretending to use toys in violent ways. For

example, say, "The rule is we treat people nicely to show them that we care. Pointing guns, even pretend ones, is against our rules because it hurts people's feelings and makes them afraid."

Think before speaking.

Use words and a tone of voice that you wouldn't mind your child repeating. For example, when he breaks a rule, instead of threatening (even in jest) to "knock his head off if he doesn't stop," calmly say, "I'm sorry you decided not to follow the rule about pretending to use a gun. The rule is, 'We treat each other nicely and don't ever hurt or pretend to hurt anyone.'"

Model kindness.

You are your child's first and most important role model. When you listen to, hug, apologize to, and respect your child, he will learn to behave in kind.

Learn to control your anger.

What causes children to "go off" is the same thing that causes adults to explode: anger over something beyond their control. Tell yourself you *hope* you get a raise, *hope* the traffic is light, *hope* your favorite dress still fits, and so on. But if none of these wishes comes true, don't have a meltdown. By keeping your cool, you set a powerful example for your child of maintaining self-control when things don't go your way.

Solving the Problem

What to Do

Teach empathy.

When your child pretends to attack another person with a toy gun or other object, consider this a teachable moment. Ask him to think about how it would feel to be shot by a pretend gun. Say, "Guns can hurt people. How would you feel if someone acted as if he were going to shoot you? I wouldn't want to scare or hurt anyone. I hope you wouldn't want to, either."

Encourage cooperative play.

Children who learn to enjoy building things, sharing with others, and engaging in supervised social activities will have less opportunity to resort to violent games for entertainment. Praise your preschooler when he's getting along with others while playing, so he knows you approve of his playing nicely. Say, "I like the way you're getting along and being kind to each other by sharing toys."

Restrict violent TV and video/computer games.

It's well documented that preschoolers like to imitate what they see. Many children have been victimized by kung fu kicks being tried out by playmates. In one Canadian study, children were found to be significantly more aggressive two years after TV was first introduced to their town.[5] Strong identification with a violent television character and believing that the television situation is realistic are both associated with greater aggressiveness.[6]

You need to know what your child is watching and what games he's playing. Reduce the amount of violent content your child is exposed to by making a rule about what he can watch or what games he can play as well as how long he can watch or play. Put yourself in charge of the television remote control and the computer power switch, to keep violence out of your home and out of your child's imagination.

When your child watches TV, watch with him.

Studies have shown that when an adult watches TV with a child and comments on the action, children remember more and are more likely to imitate what they've seen.[7] Because watching TV with an adult may actually intensify the positive (or negative) effect of the content on children, it's imperative that you select only nonviolent shows for your child's viewing and discuss the content with him. Your child should not watch with you if you're watching violent TV.

Teach your child to make amends.

When an overly exuberant tot tries to "shoot" a sibling or playmate with a ruler, for example, take away the "weapon" and say, "Guns hurt people. The rule is that we treat each other kindly and never even pretend to hurt another person. We don't hurt people; we love people. Please tell Sam you're sorry for pointing a gun at him." When your child follows your directions, say, "Thank you for being Sam's friend. I like the way you're showing him you care about him."

Teach your child to compromise.

Help your child learn to be fair when resolving disputes. When you see him threatening to hit his friend for taking his toy, for example, say, "Let's think about what else you could do when your friend takes your toy and you want it back. You could get the timer and set it like I do so your friend can play with the toy for a while and then you can play with it. That way both of you get to play with it and have fun."

What Not to Do

Don't hit!

No matter how tempting it is to spank a child to "smack some sense into him" or "teach him a lesson," resist the urge. Although you may be angry and scared when your child crosses the street without your permission, spanking him for doing so sends him a mixed message: It's okay for me to hit you, but not for you to hit me or anyone else. Practice what you preach. Spanking teaches him it's okay to hurt people to get them to do what you want. Even the occasional swat on the behind sends the hurtful message that if you're bigger and stronger, it's okay to hit to make a point.

Avoid overreacting.

When your child pretends to shoot his little brother with his pencil, for example, remain calm. Instead of simply forbidding the behavior, take advantage of a teachable moment by saying, "I'm sorry you broke the rule about treating people kindly. Tell me the rule and show me how you can treat your brother kindly now."

Don't threaten.

Threatening to hit your child with a wooden spoon when he's pretending to hit his sister with his stuffed animal only teaches him to fear your presence. To your child, a threat is an empty promise and an example of how adults don't keep their word. Instead of threatening a violent consequence such as, "I'll give you a spanking if I see you pretending to shoot your brother with that empty paper towel roll again," simply say, "I'm sorry you chose to break our rule about pretending to hurt someone. Now I want you to think about how scared you'd feel if somebody pointed a gun at you."

"Killer" Kyle

No matter what he got his hands on, three-year-old Kyle Liggett made it into a gun, knife, or sword. Then he shot, stabbed, or slashed away at any "bad guys" who were around. Kyle's mother, Diane, was beside herself. She was convinced that if she didn't bring play weapons into the house, her son wouldn't play so violently. Gary, Kyle's dad, only laughed about her fears. "Oh, Diane, boys will be boys. Why, I had toy guns when I was a kid, and you don't see me going around acting like I'm going to shoot people."

"But he makes a weapon out of everything," Diane lamented. "Today at

lunch, he bit his peanut butter and jelly sandwich into a gun and pretended he was shooting it at me. It was scary to see the mean look on his face as he was pointing the 'gun' at me."

"You should spank him when he does that," Gary responded. "That'd teach him not to point even a pretend gun at anybody."

"I'm not going to spank him," said Diane indignantly. "It doesn't make any sense to hurt him to try to teach him not to hurt people. I was talking to Amy, Josh's mom, and she said that they got Josh to think about how others feel when a gun's pointed at them. She also made a rule that all kung fu cartoons and other violent stuff on TV were not welcome in their home. The TV went off whenever Josh chose that kind of garbage. She told me he got the message."

"Well, let's try the same thing," Gary suggested. "By the way, I just thought about something else I should stop doing. You know how I'm always saying stuff like, 'If you do that once more, I'll rip your arm off!' I guess that sends Kyle the message that if a person is mad at someone, it's okay to hurt them."

Over the next few weeks, Kyle's parents squelched their violent messages. Instead of threatening him when he played pretend "shoot-'em-up," they said things like, "I'm sorry you're choosing to point guns at people. Guns can kill, and pointing guns at people scares them. Let's play school with that ruler instead of pretending to hurt somebody with it. Put the ruler on this paper and see what a straight line you can draw with your crayons."

"It's amazing," Diane told Gary. "I've been catching Kyle every time he uses a pretend gun and showing him something else to do with it. Now he's saying, 'Mommy doesn't like this TV,' whenever he sees somebody hurting someone on TV."

Gary laughed and said, "I overheard Kyle playing with Josh, and they started to pretend they were shooting each other when Kyle said, 'That's not nice to point guns at people. It hurts their feelings. Let's play with my trucks and stuff.'"

Kyle wasn't allowed to pretend to shoot someone at home, nor was he allowed to do so at preschool, church, or anywhere else. Although the Liggetts didn't believe that Kyle truly wanted to hurt someone, they knew that others might not be so sure of his motives. Sadly, children using violence against each other was not just pretend anymore. They wanted Kyle to understand that life is precious and it's wrong to hurt people, a message they hoped every child would be fortunate enough to hear from a loving parent.

Resisting Bedtime

Active, energetic preschoolers often do anything to avoid sleep. They turn bedtime or naptime into chase time, crying time, or finding-another-book-to-read time to postpone the dreaded bed. No matter what your child may think about the right time to sleep, stand firm with the time *you* have chosen. However, help your child gradually wind down instead of requiring him to turn off his motor instantly.

Note: Since your child's need for sleep changes as he gets older, you may need to let him stay up later or shorten his nap as he grows. Children (even ones in the same family) require different amounts of sleep. Your two-year-old may not need the same amount of sleep his older brother did when he was two.

Preventing the Problem

Establish a bedtime routine.
End the day or begin a nap with a special feeling between you and your child by reciting a poem or story as a regular part of the going-to-bed routine. Make the event special so it's something he can look forward to. Try reciting, "Night night, sleep tight, don't let the bedbugs bite," or have a talk about the day's events, even if it's a one-sided conversation.

Make exercise a daily habit.
Make sure your child gets plenty of exercise during the day, to help his body tell his mind that going to bed is a good idea.

Maintain a fairly regular nap schedule.
Don't let your child put off napping until late afternoon or evening, and then expect him to go to sleep at eight o'clock. Put him down for naps early enough in the day to make sure he's tired at bedtime.

Spend time together before bed.
Play with your child before bedtime arrives, to prevent him from fighting bedtime just to get your attention.

Keep bedtime consistent.

Determine how much sleep your child needs by noticing how he acts when he's taken a nap and when he hasn't, and when he's gone to bed at nine o'clock versus seven o'clock. Establish a consistent sleep schedule that meets his needs, and adjust it as he gets older.

Solving the Problem

What to Do

Use a timer to manage the bedtime routine.

An hour before bedtime (or naptime), set the timer for five minutes and announce that the timer will tell your child when it's time to start getting ready for bed. This avoids surprises and allows him to anticipate the upcoming events. When the timer rings, say, "The timer says it's time to start getting ready for bed. Let's take a bath and get into our pajamas." Then reset the timer for about fifteen minutes and say, "Let's see if we can beat the timer getting ready." This gives you the opportunity to praise your child's efforts at getting himself through the basic bedtime routine.

Make sure you allow enough time for him to get the job done. When the routine is finished, reset the timer for the remainder of the hour you set aside and announce, "You beat the timer. Now you get to stay up and play until the timer rings again and tells us that it's time to get into bed. Now, let's set the timer for brushing our teeth, getting a drink, and going potty (if he's old enough)." The timer routine helps you and your child make a game instead of a struggle out of bedtime.

Follow the same rituals regardless of time.

Even if bedtime has been delayed for some reason, go through the same rituals to help your child learn what's expected of him when it comes to going to bed. Don't point out how late he's stayed up. Quicken the pace by helping him get pajamas on and get a drink, and set the timer for shorter intervals. But don't omit any steps.

Maintain the same order of events.

Since preschoolers find comfort in consistency, have your child bathe, brush his teeth, and put on his pajamas in the same order every night. Ask him to name the next step in the routine, to make a game out of getting ready for bed and to help him feel as if he's calling the shots.

Offer rewards for going to bed.

Greet your child upon waking with the good news that going to bed nicely is worthwhile. Say, "Because you got in bed so nicely, I'll read you an extra story."

What Not to Do

Don't let your child control bedtime.

Stick with your chosen bedtime despite your child's resistance. Remember that you know why your child doesn't want to go to bed—and why he should. Say to yourself, "He's only crying because he doesn't want to end his playtime, but I know he'll play happier later if he sleeps now."

Don't threaten or spank.

Threatening or spanking your child to get him into bed can cause nightmares and fears, not to mention making you feel upset and guilty when the behavior persists. Punishing a child doesn't teach him appropriate behavior. Instead, focus on using a timer as a neutral authority to determine when bedtime arrives.

Don't be a historian.

Saying, for example, "Because you didn't go to bed on time last night, you don't get to watch TV this morning," doesn't teach your child how to get into bed on time. Focus on the future instead of the past.

Bedtime at Ben's

Evenings at the Shores' house meant one thing: a tearful battle of wills between three-year-old Ben and his father when the younger Shore's bedtime was announced. "I'm not tired! I don't want to go to bed! I want to stay up!" Ben would plead each night as his angry father dragged him to bed.

"I know you don't want to go to bed," his father would reply, "but you will do what I say, and I say it's bedtime!" Forcing his son to go to bed upset Mr. Shore as much as it did Ben. Even though Mr. Shore believed he should be boss, he knew there had to be a way to avoid the battles and Ben's crying himself to sleep.

The next night, Mr. Shore decided to control himself and let something else—the kitchen timer—control bedtime. An hour before Ben's bedtime, he set the timer for five minutes. "It's time to start getting ready for bed," Mr. Shore explained to his curious son. "When you get yourself ready for bed before the timer rings, we'll set the timer again and you can stay up and play until it rings."

Ben raced around and got ready for bed before the timer rang. As promised, Mr. Shore reset the timer, then read Ben his favorite animal tales and sang some new sleepytime songs until the timer rang again almost an hour later. "It's time for bed, right?" Ben announced, acting delighted to have this game all figured out.

"That's right! I'm so proud of you for remembering the new rule," his dad replied.

As the two journeyed up to bed, Mr. Shore once again told his son how proud he was of his getting himself ready for bed. Using the timer to control bedtime routines helped them enjoy a painless evening for the first time in months. After several weeks of following this routine, going to bed never became something to look forward to, but it was far from a struggle for Ben and his dad.

Resisting Car Seats

Car seats and seat belts are the number one enemy of millions of freedom-loving preschoolers. These adventurous spirits don't understand why they must be strapped down, but they *can* understand the rule that the car doesn't move until the belts are on or they're strapped in their car seats. Ensure your child's safety every time she gets in a car by enforcing the belts-on rule. The seat-belt habit will become second nature to your child—a passenger today and a driver tomorrow—if you're not wishy-washy about this life-or-death rule.

Every state now requires that infants and children be buckled up when riding in a motor vehicle. Approved car seats and seat belts have weight and age specifications to make car travel as safe as possible for your child. Infants should be placed in rear-facing seats until they're at least one year old *and* weigh at least twenty pounds. As children outgrow their infant car seats, they move to forward-facing seats, convertible seats, and eventually booster seats, depending on their age and weight.

The leading cause of death in children is trauma from automobile accidents. Children who are not buckled up will continue to travel forward if the car stops suddenly. They will hit anything in their path—the dashboard, the windshield, or the back of the front seat—with an impact equivalent to a one-story drop for each ten miles per hour the car is traveling. Even though the dashboard and back of the front seat are padded, the impact of a crash at fifty-five miles per hour can do considerable damage to small bodies. This trauma can be prevented by making sure children are properly restrained. *Never* compromise the rule about being buckled up, or you may be compromising your child's life.

Note: The infant death rate can be reduced by almost three quarters and the injury rate for one- to four-year-olds can by lowered by fifty percent by using properly installed car seats. For more information on car seats, check the American Academy of Pediatrics website at www.aap.org or call 800-433-9016.

Preventing the Problem

Give your child room to breathe.

Make sure she has room to move her hands and legs and still be safely buckled up.

Make a rule that the car will not move unless everyone is buckled up.

If you enforce this rule from the beginning, your child will become accustomed to the idea of sitting in a car seat and eventually wearing a seat belt.

Make your child proud to be safe.

Tell your child why she's graduating to a bigger car seat or using only a seat belt, to make her proud of being strapped in. For example, say, "You're getting to be so grown-up. Here's your new safety seat for the car!"

Don't complain about having to wear a seat belt.

Casually telling your spouse or friend that you hate wearing a seat belt gives your child a reason to resist her belt, too.

Conduct a training program.

Let your child know how you expect her to act in a car. Take short drives around the neighborhood with one parent or friend driving and the other praising your child for sitting nicely in her car seat. Say, "You're sitting in your car seat so nicely today," or, "Nice sitting," while patting and stroking her.

Solving the Problem

What to Do

Buckle yourself up.

Make sure to wear your seat belt and point out how your child is wearing one, too, to make her feel she's not alone in her temporary confinement. If you don't wear a seat belt, your child will not understand why she has to.

Praise staying in the seat belt.

If you ignore your child while she's riding nicely, she may look for ways to get your attention, including trying to get out of her car seat or seat belt. Keep your child out of trouble in the car by talking to her and playing word games, as well as by praising how nicely she's sitting.

Be consistent.

Stop the car as quickly and safely as possible every time your child gets out of her car seat or seat belt, to teach her that the rule will be enforced. Say, "The car will move again only when you're back in your car seat [or seat belt], so you will be safe."

Divert your child's attention.

Try activities such as number games, word games, Peek-a-Boo, singing songs, and so on, so your child won't try to get out of her seat because she needs something to do.

What Not to Do

Don't attend to your child's defiant behavior, unless she unfastens her seat belt or gets out of her car seat.

Not giving attention to your child's crying or whining while she's belted in helps her see that there's no benefit in protesting the seat-belt rule. Say to yourself, "I know my child is safer in her car seat and will only fight it temporarily. Her safety is my responsibility and I am fulfilling it by enforcing the seat-belt rule."

Unbuckled Jacob

Stephen Brenner loved to take his four-year-old son, Jacob, on errands with him, until his son figured out how to get his father's undivided attention by unbuckling his seat belt and jumping around in the back seat. "Don't you ever undo that belt again, young man!" Mr. Brenner ordered when he saw that his son had gotten free.

Simply demanding that Jacob stay put didn't solve the problem, however, so Mr. Brenner decided that harsher, more physical punishment was necessary. Though he had never spanked his son before, he gave him a swift swat on his bottom whenever he found him roaming unbuckled in the back seat.

To accomplish the spanking, Mr. Brenner had to stop the car. Every time he did that, Jacob would scramble back to his seat and fasten his belt to avoid being walloped. So Mr. Brenner decided that instead of spanking Jacob, he would stop the car and refuse to continue until Jacob's belt was buckled. Mr. Brenner knew that Jacob wasn't patient enough to sit for very long, even if he didn't really want to go where they were going.

Mr. Brenner tried this new method the next time they were on their way to the park. When Jacob unbuckled himself, Mr. Brenner stopped the car. "We can go to the park when you're back in your seat and buckled up," Mr. Brenner explained. "It's not safe for you to be unbuckled." Mr. Brenner crossed his fingers, hoping that Jacob would get back in his seat, since Mr. Brenner knew Jacob was eager to get to the park. Jacob cooperated.

A few miles from home, Jacob unbuckled himself again, and Mr. Brenner stopped the car. He didn't spank his son; he simply repeated the rule. "The car will not move unless you're back in your car seat." Jacob returned to his seat and calmly buckled himself in. Mr. Brenner told him, "Thanks for getting back in your seat," and they drove home without incident.

That didn't end the problem, however. The next time Jacob released himself, Mr. Brenner was so angry he was tempted to yell and scream again, but he stuck to his new method. He also began to include Jacob in conversations and to praise his safe behavior. Soon after, Mr. Brenner was once again enjoying his outings with his son, assured that they were traveling safely.

Resisting Change

"**N**o! *Mommy* do it!" your son shrieks as your husband tries to give him a bath, a job he says is "*Mommy's.*" Change can be hard for people, but it's particularly difficult for the under-six set. It's even more trying for children born with a temperament that wants *everything* to be routine and predictable. Preschoolers haven't had much experience adjusting to change, so when you ask your little guy to get ready to leave when he's immersed in playing with a friend, he's likely to have a meltdown. Finding security in predictable sameness is common in little people, but sometimes the need for security borders on absolute inflexibility. Help reticent children learn how to go with the flow, to increase their chances of rolling with the punches as they grow.

Preventing the Problem

Provide a mistake-friendly environment.

By sending your child a no-big-deal message when he makes a mistake, you help him learn that no one's perfect. This lesson will serve him well as he gets experience bouncing back from a problem. Say, "I'm sorry you spilled your milk. Let's see how we can clean it up. Everyone has accidents."

Teach decision-making skills.

Your child wants to feel as if he's the master of his fate, so allow him to make simple decisions. Choosing between two cereals, two pairs of socks, and two games to play, for example, gives him a sense of control over his world.

Respect your child's individuality.

You may have made friends with change long ago, but your child might have a more difficult time because his temperament might be different. Understand that each child has a unique temperament, even within the same family. Avoid saying, "Don't be like that!" when your child's inflexible feathers are ruffled. Instead, say, "I know it's hard for you to change babysitters. But you can handle it. It'll be okay."

Remind children that they belong.

We all want to feel that we fit in with a particular group. So frequently tell your child that he's a valued member of your family, and encourage his participation by asking him to help out around the house. Say, "Thanks for picking up your toys and putting them away. You're helping our home look nice and neat."

Solving the Problem

What to Do

Build resilience.

Resilient children look at change as a challenge to be overcome. On the other hand, inflexible children resist change as much as possible. Telling your child he *gets* to do something rather than *has* to do it will transform his feelings of fear and loss of control into feelings of excitement. Help him build this framework for change by saying, for example, "You get to have a new babysitter tonight. She's going to be lots of fun. Isn't it exciting getting to know someone new?"

Teach your child how to handle change.

Children who are shown how to deal with change are more prepared to meet the challenge. For example, say, "This new shirt is very nice. Not getting to wear your old blue one is no big deal. You'll feel so good wearing your new yellow one today."

Set goals for accepting change.

Children feel more in control of their destiny if they have ample time to think about and prepare themselves for change. You can help your child accept change more readily by having him set goals for handling change. For example, say, "We're going to the zoo with your class tomorrow. It'll be fun. Let's set a goal of having a good time at the zoo." Then periodically remind him of the goal and have him repeat it to you. Ask him, "What's your goal about going to the zoo?" When he says, "I'm going to the zoo to have fun," say, "That's right, you're going to the zoo to have a good time."

Teach problem solving.

When children are confronted with change and don't know what to do, giving them limited choices helps them see their options. For example, say, "I know you don't want to move into the big bed. Let's think about what we can do to make it easier. Maybe you could take your teddy bear into the big bed with you, and he'll keep you company while you're there."

What Not to Do

Don't meet resistance with anger.

Children who are upset by change need lots of support and empathy to reduce their anxiety. Getting angry with your child for being inflexible only increases his sense of helplessness.

Don't overreact to mistakes.

Getting upset when your child tracks dirt into the house tells him he isn't loveable if he makes mistakes, which (because he's a preschooler) he'll probably do many times a day. Treat mistakes as no big deal. Show him how to correct his behavior by treating mistakes as teachable—not terrorizing—moments. Say, "Please get the paper towels so we can clean this up. When we work together, we can have it cleaned up in no time."

The Cup and Bowl Caper

Julia Bardwell was only two-and-a-half-years old, but she had a mind of her own that belied her years. She knew what she wanted and how she wanted it, and her parents, Dena and Jim, knew better than to go against her wishes. If it wasn't a fight over using the blue cup instead of the yellow one at breakfast, it was a war over wearing something other than her green shorts and pink T-shirt. When confronted with change, Julia would first resist, then scream, and finally melt into an inconsolable, tearful tirade.

Dena and Jim wanted to help Julia become more resilient. Jim knew that setting goals at work helped him stay focused and not get distracted by his anxiety over getting everything done. He thought that Julia might be able to see beyond her fear of change if she had a goal to think about.

Dena and Jim decided that Julia's first goal would focus on her steadfast refusal to use different dishes at breakfast. When she could learn to be more flexible by using different dishes, they were hopeful she'd be able to be less rigid in dealing with other changes. So they began by talking to Julia about getting a new cup and bowl set for breakfast, one they let her pick out herself.

That night Dena said, "Julia, lets set a goal for tomorrow morning. I think it would be a good idea for your goal to be having fun using your new cup and bowl when you have breakfa..." Julia looked at her mother and nodded, but Dena wasn't sure the idea of a goal had sunk in. A few minutes later, Dena said, "Julia, remember your goal for tomorrow morning? You're going to have fun using your new cup and bowl."

This time Julia answered, "Yeah, I 'member." The Bardwells repeated this reminder several more times that evening. They even made an occasional trip to the kitchen to look at the cup and bowl sitting all shiny and new on the counter.

At breakfast the next morning, Julia eagerly headed for the table saying, "Where's my new cup and bowl?" Dena and Jim knew they were onto something. They could help Julia accept change by helping her look forward to it. After a few days with the new cup and bowl, Dena and Jim said, "Julia, let's use the old blue cup and bowl at breakfast tomorrow."

"No!" Julia cried. "The new cup and bowl! I want the new cup and bowl!"

Dena and Jim didn't say anything about her digging in her heels like they had in the past. Instead, they decided to help her set a new goal. That evening Dena said, "Julia, let's set a new goal for breakfast tomorrow. I'd like your new goal to be using the old blue cup and bowl." Later that evening, Dena said, "Julia, what's the new goal for breakfast tomorrow?"

Julia thought for a minute and said, "The blue cup and bowl?"

"That's right," Dena said. "We're going to use the blue ones tomorrow. I'm glad you remembered the new goal."

Although Dena and Jim weren't sure this little exercise would pay off, they were delighted when Julia started treating it like a game and actually looked forward to the new goal for the day. They knew that Julia could ease into change as long as she was prepared for it. They now had a plan that made the whole family happy. Their perseverance had paid off.

Sibling Rivalry

Tattling on brothers and sisters and hating a new sibling from the first day he invades the family are just two examples of how sibling rivalry wreaks havoc on family relationships. Because preschoolers are constantly flapping their wings of independence and importance, they often fight with their siblings for space, time, and the number one position in their most important world: their family. Though sibling rivalry is part of human nature, its frequency can be decreased by showing each of your preschoolers that she's special. To keep sibling rivalry to a manageable minimum, teach your children that getting along gives them what they want: attention and privileges.

Preventing the Problem

Prepare your child before the new baby arrives.

Discuss with your first child (if she's over one year old) how she'll be included in the life of the new baby. Tell her what the new family routine will be and how she'll be expected to help out. This will help her feel that she's an important part of loving and caring for her younger sister or brother.

Play with your older child whether your baby is asleep or awake.

To decrease the sibling rivalry associated with a new baby, make sure you play with your older child when your new baby is awake as well as asleep. This will prevent your older child from concluding that you only give her attention when the baby's out of sight. Spending time with your older child no matter what the baby is doing makes your older child think, "I get Mom's attention when the baby's here as well as gone. That baby's not so bad after all!"

Make realistic getting-along goals.

Don't expect your child to smother the new baby with as much tenderness as you do. She may be older than the baby, but she still needs lots of individual attention.

Plan time alone with each of your children.

Even if you have half a dozen preschoolers to attend to, try to plan time alone with each of them (a bath, a walk, or a trip to the grocery store, for example). This will help focus your attention on each child's needs, and it will keep you informed about feelings and problems that may not surface amid the roar of the crowd at home.

Make individual brag boards (for parents of twins or children close in age).

Display each child's creativity in her own special place, to reassure each child that her efforts merit individual attention.

Solving the Problem

What to Do

Let a timer manage taking turns.

When your children are fighting for your undivided attention, let the timer determine each child's turn. This teaches your children about sharing, and it lets each child know she'll have a turn being your number one object of attention.

Offer alternatives to fighting.

Allowing fighting to flare up and burn out of control doesn't teach your children how to get along. Instead of allowing battles to be fought, give your children a choice: They can either get along or not get along. Say, "You may get along with each other and continue to play, or not get along and be separated in Time Out." Let them get in the habit of making choices, to give them a feeling of control over their lives and to help them learn to make decisions on their own.

Define *getting along*.

Be specific when praising your children for playing nicely together, to make sure they know what you mean by *getting along*. Say, "That's great the way you're sharing and playing together so nicely. I really like how you're getting along so well. It makes playing together fun."

What Not to Do

Don't respond to tattling.

Children tattle on each other as a way of enhancing their position with their parents. Stop this game of one-upmanship by saying, "I'm sorry you aren't getting along," and by pretending that the tattling didn't occur. Even if a dangerous activity has been reported, you can stop the activity and still ignore the tattling.

Don't set up one child to tattle on another.

Asking your older son to come tell you when his baby sister is doing something wrong is not a good way to teach your children how to get along without tattling.

Don't get upset when your children don't love each other all the time.

Children cannot live in the same home without *some* rivalry going on. It's human nature. Keep friction to a minimum by rewarding getting along and by not allowing the rivalry to escalate to fighting.

Don't hold grudges.

After the dispute has been settled, don't remind your children that they used to be enemies. Start over with a clean slate and help them do the same.

Starr Wars

The constant warfare between four-year-old Jason Starr and his two-year-old sister, Julie, made their parents wonder why they ever had children. The kids obviously didn't appreciate the sacrifices their parents made to buy them nice clothes, new toys, and good food.

Biting and teasing were Jason's favorite ways of letting his sister "have it" when he thought she was taking too much of his parents' time and attention. Physical punishment obviously wasn't working, since Jason seemed to want to get yelled at and walloped whenever he started hurting his sister.

The only time Mrs. Starr ever noticed her son being nice to his sister was when he helped her across an icy patch on the driveway. Mrs. Starr was so grateful for the bit of decency that she told her son, "That's great the way you helped your sister. I'm really proud of you." The Starrs decided to encourage more random acts of kindness by dishing out compliments when their children got along and by enforcing a new rule when their children began to fight.

They got the chance to put their new policy into practice later that day when a battle over blocks broke out after they got home from a shopping trip. Mrs. Starr had no idea who started the argument, but she told her children, "You have a choice now, kids. Since I don't know who took the toy from whom, you can get along like you did in the car today, or you can be separated in Time Out."

Both children ignored Mrs. Starr's statement and continued to play tug of war with the blocks. So she followed through with her promise. "You've both chosen to take a Time Out."

Julie and Jason screamed their way through most of Time Out, but after quieting down and being allowed to get up from their chairs, they had different looks on their faces for the rest of the day. They began to act like comrades rather than enemies, and Mrs. Starr was delighted that she had not lost her temper when her children had.

The Starrs continued to praise getting along. They put less emphasis on any fighting they noticed, and they consistently used Time Out to separate the children and reinforce the consequence of choosing to fight.

Taking Things

Since everything in the world belongs to a preschooler until someone tells him differently, it's never too early to teach him not to take things from others unless you approve it. Parents provide consciences for their children until they develop their own. So every time your child takes things that aren't his, enforce the consequences that will help him develop a sense of right and wrong.

Preventing the Problem

Make rules.

Encourage your child to let you know when he wants things by teaching him how to ask for them. Decide what may and may not be taken from public places or others' homes, and let your child know your expectations. A basic rule might be, "You must always ask me if you can have something before you pick it up."

Solving the Problem

What to Do

Explain how to get things without stealing.

Your child doesn't understand why he can't take things when he wants them. Make him aware of correct and incorrect behavior by saying, "You must ask me for a piece of gum before picking up the pack. If I say yes, you may pick it up and hold it until we pay for it."

Explain what *stealing* means.

Make sure your child understands the difference between borrowing and stealing (and the results of each), to make sure he knows what you mean when you say, "You must not steal." Stealing is taking something without permission; borrowing is asking for and getting permission before taking something.

Have your child pay for stealing.

To help him realize the cost of stealing, have your child work off the theft by doing odd jobs around the house or by giving up one of his prized possessions. Say, for example, "I'm sorry you took something that didn't belong to you. Because you did that, you must give up something that does belong to you." The possession he gives up could be used several months later as a reward for good behavior.

Make children return stolen objects.
Teach your child that he cannot keep something he's stolen. Enforce the rule that he must return it himself (with your help, if necessary).

Enforce Time Out.
When your child takes something that doesn't belong to him, let him know that he must be isolated from people and activities because he broke the rule. Say, "I'm sorry you took something that wasn't yours. Time out."

What Not to Do

Don't be a historian.
Don't remind your child about a stealing incident. Bringing up the past will only remind him of wrong behavior and won't teach him how to avoid the mistake in the future.

Don't label your child.
Don't call your child a "thief," because he will behave according to how he's labeled.

Don't ask your child whether he's stolen something.
Asking only encourages lying. He'll say to himself, "I know I'll get punished. Why not lie to avoid the pain?"

Don't hesitate to search your child.
If you suspect your child has stolen something, verify it by searching him. If you discover he did steal, make sure to enforce the consequences. For example, say, "I'm sorry you took something that didn't belong to you. Now you must pay for it."

The Short Shoplifter

Sandy and Doug Berkley had never broken the law and gone to jail, and they didn't want their four-year-old son, Scott, to get locked up either. But if he continued to steal gum, candy, toys, and other objects that caught his fancy while shopping with his parents, they wondered if he'd have a future outside of prison.

"Don't you know that stealing is wrong?" Mrs. Berkley would scream at her son when she'd catch him red-handed. She also tried slapping his hand and telling him he was a bad boy, but that didn't do any good, either. She became afraid to do errands with her son, dreading both the embarrassment of his behavior and how she would feel when she punished him.

Scott was totally oblivious to the reasons why stealing was forbidden. He didn't understand why it wasn't fun to take things that didn't belong to him. So the Berkleys decided to explain the situation in terms he could understand.

"Scott, you cannot take things that you do not pay for," Mr. Berkley began. "You must ask me for a pack of gum. If I say yes, you may pick up the pack and hold it until we pay for it. Let's practice." Scott was delighted to oblige because now when he asked for gum, as the rule stated, his mother and father complimented him for following the rules and paid for the gum.

But the Berkleys didn't always say yes to Scott's request. So when Scott tried to get by with taking a candy bar without first asking his mother to pay for it, Mrs. Berkley enforced her second rule by making him pay for the wrongdoing. "Because you took this candy bar," she told her son as they walked back into the store, "you will have to give up the toy candy bar that's in your grocery store at home."

Despite Scott's protests, Mrs. Berkley did take away his beloved toy. "To earn the toy back," she explained, "you have to follow the rules by asking first and by not taking what is not paid for."

After several weeks of praising Scott for following the rules, Mrs. Berkley gave him his toy candy bar back, and both parents began to feel more secure about their frisky little son's future.

Talking Back

When backtalk (sarcasm, sassy retorts, and unkind remarks) spews forth from your preschooler's previously angelic mouth, you become painfully aware of her ability to mimic words (good and bad) and control her world with them. Like other forms of language, backtalk can only be learned by exposure to it. So limit your child's opportunities to hear unpleasant words. Monitor television viewing, your own language, and that of friends and family.

Preventing the Problem

Talk to your child the way you want her to talk to you.

Teach your child how to use language you want to hear. Say "Thank you," "Please," "I'm sorry," and other polite phrases. Have your child practice using the words you've modeled. Remember that preschoolers are the world's greatest imitators.

Decide what constitutes backtalk.

In order to react fairly to your child's increasingly diversified verbal behavior, you need to determine whether your child is talking back or doing something else. For example, sarcasm, name-calling, shouting answers, and defiant refusals are backtalk. Simple refusals like "I don't *want* to" are whining. Questions like "Do I have to?" are expressions of opinion. Make sure your child understands what you mean by *backtalk*.

Monitor friends, media, and your own speech.

Limit your child's exposure to backtalk by keeping tabs on what words slip through your lips. Also monitor friends, peers, family members, and television characters. What goes in preschoolers' ears comes out preschoolers' mouths.

Solving the Problem

What to Do

Wear out the word.

Overusing a word reduces its power. Therefore, help your child grow tired of using an offensive word by having her repeat it (one minute for each year of age). Say, "I'm sorry you said that word. I'll set the timer. You must say the word until the timer rings. When it rings, you can stop saying the word." After the word is worn out, she'll be less likely to use it in the heat of the moment.

Ignore the backtalk.

Try to pay as little attention to inoffensive backtalk as you can. Pretending the event didn't occur takes away the backtalker's power over you. The game isn't much fun to play without the anticipated payoff of your reaction.

Compliment nice talk.

Let your child know what kind of talk you prefer by pointing out when she's using desirable language. Say, "I like it when you answer me kindly when I ask you a question, just as we practiced. That makes me feel good."

What Not to Do

Don't play a power game.

Since you know that backtalk is one way your child tries to get power over you, don't use backtalk yourself. She may find fun ways of entertaining herself by seeing how she can get you mad or get your attention by using backtalk, which you don't want to encourage.

Don't teach backtalk.

Shouting answers back at your child only shows her how to use backtalk. Although it's hard not to yell when you're being yelled at, teach your child how to be respectful by being respectful to her. Be polite to your child, as if she were a guest in your home.

Don't punish backtalk.

Backtalk is, at worst, annoying. No evidence supports the belief that we make children respectful by punishing them for disrespect. Only fear is taught through punishment—not respect.

Carlos' Backtalk

Whenever Mrs. Martinez would ask her four-year-old son, Carlos, to do anything like clean up his toys or put away the peanut butter, Carlos would shout, "No! I don't like you! I'm not going to!" Carlos became so experienced at backtalk and verbal abuse that whenever he was asked any kind of question, he would angrily shout back his answer, as if he had forgotten how to answer someone politely.

"No child of mine is going to talk like that!" Mr. Martinez would shout back at his son. Unfortunately, Mr. Martinez's backtalk would cause an even greater uproar in the family. Once the Martinezes realized their sarcasm and shouting were teaching their son this kind of behavior, they tried hard to react calmly to Carlos' backtalk and to praise his pleasant responses.

One day they asked Carlos to put his toys back in his toy box. When he calmly said, "Okay," they responded by saying, "That's really great the way you answered so pleasantly."

It wasn't hard for the Martinezes to control their anger. As Carlos' yelling and sassy talk became less frequent, they usually pretended they didn't hear it. But when Carlos kept saying "Idiot" over and over, trying hard to get some attention, the Martinezes decided to have Carlos wear out the word.

"Say the word idiot for four minutes," they instructed Carlos. Their son repeated the word for two minutes and then couldn't say it anymore. Much to the delight of his parents, it was the last time he said the word.

Temper Tantrums

Millions of normal, lovable preschoolers throw temper tantrums as their way of coping with frustration or anger, or of telling the world they're the boss. Tantrums can become less frequent and even be prevented by not giving the performer an audience and by not giving in to his demands. Though you may want to give in or crawl under the nearest checkout counter when your child throws a tantrum in public, be patient until he's finished and praise his gaining control after he's calm.

Note: Common, periodic crying is not a temper tantrum and needs to be treated differently. Get professional help if your child has more than two to three temper tantrums per day.

Preventing the Problem

Teach your child how to handle frustration and anger.

Show your child how adults like you can find other ways of coping besides yelling and screaming. When you burn the casserole, for instance, instead of throwing the burned pot into the garbage, say, "I'm upset now, honey, but I can handle it. I'm going to figure out how to solve this mess by seeing what else I can fix for dinner." Regardless of the situation, teach your child to look at the choices he has to solve his problems instead of getting violent about them.

Praise coping.

Catch your child being good. For example, praise his asking you to help him put together a complicated puzzle that might otherwise frustrate him. Say, "I'm so glad you asked for my help instead of getting mad at the puzzle." Helping your child handle his frustration and anger calmly helps him feel good about himself. You'll find him repeating a problem-solving technique when he knows he'll get praised for it. Tell him you understand his frustration by saying, "I know how you feel when things get tough, and I'm really proud of you for being able to solve the problem calmly."

Don't let playtime always mean alone time.

Pay attention to your child when he's playing appropriately with his toys, so he doesn't have to resort to inappropriate play to get your attention.

Don't wait for an invitation.

If you spot trouble brewing in your child's play or eating activities, don't let it simmer too long. When you see that the situation is difficult or frustrating for him, say, "I bet this puzzle piece goes here," or, "Let's do it this way." Show him how to work the toy or eat the food, and then let *him* complete the task so he feels good about his ability to let others help.

Solving the Problem

What to Do

Ignore your child's tantrum.

Do nothing for, with, or to your child during his performance. Teach him that a temper tantrum is not the way to get your attention or get his demands met. But how do you ignore a tornado tearing through your living room? Walk away from him during his tantrum, turn your back on him, put him in his room, or isolate yourself. If he's being destructive or dangerous to himself or others in public, put him in a confined place where he's safe. Don't even look his way during this isolation. Though it's tough to turn away, try to busy yourself in another room of the house or with another activity in public.

Try to stand firm.

Despite the power of your child's screaming and pounding, make sure you maintain self-control by holding tight to your rule. Tell yourself silently that it's important for your child to learn that he can't have everything he wants when he wants it. Your child is learning to be realistic, and you're learning to be consistent and to give him boundaries for acceptable and unacceptable behavior.

Remain as calm as you can.

Say to yourself, "This is not a big deal. If I can stay in control of myself, I can better teach my child to control himself. He's just trying to upset me so he can have what he wants." Keeping calm while ignoring his tantrum is the best model for him when he's upset.

Praise your child.

After the fire of a temper tantrum is reduced to smoldering ashes, immediately praise your child for regaining self-control, and get both of you involved in a favorite game or activity that isn't frustrating for him or you. Say, "I'm glad you're feeling better now. I love you, but I don't like screaming or yelling." Since this is your only reference to the tantrum, it will help him know that it was the tantrum you were ignoring, not him.

Explain rule changes.

If you and your child are at the store and he asks you to buy a toy that was off-limits before, you can change your mind—but change your message, too. Say, "Remember when we were here before and you threw a tantrum? When you behave nicely by staying close to me, I've decided that you can have the toy." This will help him understand that it wasn't the tantrum that changed your mind; you're buying the toy for another reason. If you like, tell him why you've changed your mind, particularly if it includes praise for his good behavior.

What Not to Do

Don't reason or explain during the tantrum.

Trying to reason your child out of his tantrum *during* the tantrum is wasted breath. He doesn't care. He's in the middle of a show and he's the star. Any discussion at this time only encourages the tantrum, because it gives him the audience he wants.

Don't throw a tantrum yourself.

Say to yourself, "Why do I need to act crazy? I know that when I said no, I said it for a reason." Losing your cool only encourages your child to keep the heat on, and it shows him that he doesn't need to learn self-control.

Don't belittle your child.

Just because your child has a temper tantrum doesn't mean he's a bad person. Don't say, "Bad boy! Aren't you ashamed of yourself?" Your child will lose respect for himself and feel that he didn't deserve what he wanted anyway.

Don't be a historian.

Don't remind your child of his tantrum later that day. This only gives more attention to the behavior and increases the chances of his having another tantrum, just to be the center of your conversation.

Don't make your child pay for the tantrum.

Having nothing to do with him after it's over will only cause him to have more tantrums to try to get your attention. Don't send him the message that he's unloved and unwanted just because his behavior was.

Tantrum Time

Donald and Mary MacLean were worried about their two-year-old daughter, Amy, who would get a bad attack of "temper tantrumitis" every time her request for a cookie before dinner was refused. When her parents said, "No," she would scream, "Yes!" pull on her father's pant leg, and jump up and down on the kitchen floor until both she and her distraught parents were so exhausted that they finally gave in.

In frustration, the MacLeans wondered what they were doing wrong. Was there something terribly wrong with saying no to Amy's demands? It finally occurred to them that Amy's tantrums were more frequent when they said no to her. They also realized that giving in to Amy's uncontrollable desire for a cookie before dinner only encouraged her bad behavior.

The next time Amy had a tantrum, they were ready with a new strategy. Instead of saying, "No," Mary said matter-of-factly, "Amy, I know you want a cookie, but you won't get one until you're quiet and have finished your dinner."

Amy didn't stop her tantrum, so her parents simply walked away, leaving her with no audience for her big scene. Although it was hard to stay away from their screaming child, the MacLeans waited until their daughter was quiet before entering the kitchen. Without any physical or verbal attention, Amy had eventually stopped wailing and was waiting to see if her parents would practice what they preached.

Her father appeared, wearing a smile, and said, "Amy, I know you want that cookie now, but when you've eaten your dinner and we're ready for dessert, then you may have the cookie. I'm glad you're not screaming and yelling now. It's nice to see you controlling yourself." Amy quietly went to dinner and, as promised, received her cookie when she was finished eating.

The MacLeans complimented themselves later that night on the self-control they had exhibited in not giving in to Amy's tantrum. Although they were tempted later on to give in, they continued to remove themselves from their daughter when she had a tantrum, and they praised her any time she reacted calmly when something was denied her. The frequency of Amy's tantrums diminished to the point that Amy would cry from time to time when she was disappointed, but she wouldn't have the explosive scenes she often had in the past.

Toileting Accidents

Toilet training is the first major battle of wills between parents and preschoolers. The war breaks out when parents ask their independence-loving offspring to give up something that is second nature to them and to begin doing something that is new and often undesirable. To most children, what is desirable about toilet training is pleasing their parents. So foster the least accident-prone toilet training possible by putting more attention on what your child *should* do (keep her pants dry, go to the bathroom in the potty) than on what she shouldn't do (go potty in her pants). Help your child feel proud of herself while you lessen the likelihood that she will have an accident just to get your attention and reaction.

Note: If your child is having continuous toileting accidents after the age of four, consult a medical professional. This chapter does not discuss bedwetting because many preschoolers are simply not developmentally able to stay dry all night. Many authorities believe that after age six, bedwetting may be considered a problem that requires professional help.

Preventing the Problem

Look for signs of readiness (usually around two years of age).

The generally accepted signs of readiness include a child's awareness of the fact that she's urinating or defecating (or is about to do so); more regular and predictable elimination patterns; the ability to pull her pants down and climb on the toilet (and do the opposite); the ability to understand toileting terminology and follow simple directions; an interest in toileting; and a general dislike of having a soiled diaper.

Don't train too early.

Early training simply teaches children to depend more on their parents than on their own ability to manage toileting. Children who are forced to learn before they're ready take longer to master toileting.

Model correct potty behavior.

Familiarize your child with the potty and how it's used by showing her how you go to the bathroom (and how she can when she's ready).

Make it as convenient as possible for your child to use the potty when she needs to go.

Keep the potty chair in the kitchen, for example, during toilet training. Take the potty with you in the early stages, to help your child feel comfortable about pottying outside the home.

Choose a toilet training procedure and stick with it.

Many resources (books, tapes, and videos) are available to help you toilet train your child. Find one that feels comfortable to you and consistently follow through with the recommended methods. Consistency and patience are the keys to success!

Solving the Problem

What to Do

Reward being dry as well as correct toileting.

Teach your child to keep herself dry by telling her how good staying dry is. This increases her awareness of what you want her to do (stay dry). About every fifteen minutes say to your child, "Check your pants. Are they dry?" This gives her the responsibility of checking her dryness, which makes her feel more in control of the process. If she's dry, tell her you're glad. Say, "How nice that you're staying dry."

Remind your child of the rule for going potty in wrong places.

Many preschoolers occasionally go to the bathroom in an inappropriate place (outside, for example). When your child has that experience, remind her that the rule is, "You're supposed to potty in the potty. Let's practice." Then proceed with practicing correct pottying procedures.

React calmly to accidents.

If your child is wet, say, "I'm sorry that you're wet. Now we need to practice staying dry." Then practice ten times going to the toilet from various parts of the house. (Pants down, sit on the toilet, pants up. Then repeat these steps in the next part of the house.) In practice it's not necessary for your child to urinate or have a bowel movement, but only to go through correct toileting motions.

Use Grandma's Rule in public.

When your child wants to go only in *her* potty when you're in a public place, try Grandma's Rule. Say, "We need to keep dry. One potty is the same as another. We can't use your potty because it's not here. When you've used this potty, we can go on a trip to the zoo." If you prefer, take your child's potty with you.

What Not to Do

Don't punish toileting accidents.

Punishment only gives your child attention for toileting in her pants (or another wrong place). It doesn't teach how to stay dry.

Don't ask the wrong question.

Saying "Check your pants" increases your child's awareness and puts her in charge. It's a good substitute for "Do you need to go potty?" which is generally answered with a "No." Help your child feel responsible for checking her dry-wet condition and doing something about it.

Kelly's "Accidents"

As soon as preschool let out for the summer, three-and-a-half-year-old Kelly Winter started to lose more than her knowledge of numbers and letters. Her occasional toileting accidents signaled that she was waiting too long before heading for the bathroom. Mrs. Winter watched her "dance" as she worked hard to avoid going to the bathroom.

Kelly discovered that she could relieve the physical pressure of having to go by releasing only a small amount of urine into her pants. When her mother would scold and spank her for wetting her pants, Kelly would point out how she wet "just a little." Mrs. Winter realized that Kelly wanted some attention for her accidents. Why else would she point out that she was wet "just a little"?

After analyzing the situation, Mr. and Mrs. Winter decided to reinstate the routine they had used to toilet train their daughter the previous year, and they began praising Kelly's dry pants instead of getting upset when she had wet ones. "Check your pants, Kelly. Are they dry?" Mrs. Winter said the next morning after breakfast. She was as delighted as Kelly when her daughter happily replied, "Yes!" with a big grin.

"Thanks for keeping yourself dry, honey," Mrs. Winter said, giving her daughter a hug at the same time. "Let's keep them dry all day!"

After a few days of periodically asking Kelly to check her pants (Kelly always found herself dry), Mrs. Winter thought her problem was behind her—until the very next day when Kelly was wet again. "Let's practice ten times going to the potty," she told her glum-looking daughter, who seemed very disappointed that her mother was not praising her as she did when her pants were dry.

Kelly soon learned that it was easier to go to the potty and get the praise for dry pants than it was to practice ten times. She continued to follow through with keeping her pants dry for several months.

Mr. and Mrs. Winter praised Kelly and occasionally reminded her during the next year. They kept in mind that Kelly had to firmly reestablish the right way of toileting, something her parents would rather help her do instead of become angry and frustrated when she soiled her pants.

Traveling Problems

For most adults, vacation traveling is a change of pace, scenery, and routine when cares of home are abandoned for the free and easy life. For many preschoolers, however, traveling is anything but vacation. Young ones thrive on the sense of security offered by familiar toys, beds, and foods, so try to prevent needing another vacation away from your child by making sure your preschooler knows that some of his favorite things (toys, blankets, clothes) will be near and that he'll be included in the fun. The comforts of home are often absent when you're traveling, so teach your child how to cope with change and how to enjoy new experiences—two tasks made easier if you have a happy, interested pupil who feels secure in his new surroundings.

Note: Remember that children who are not buckled in safely will create a dangerous distraction for the driver. If the car stops suddenly, they will continue to travel forward at the same rate of speed the car was going. They will hit anything in their path—the dashboard, the windshield, or the back of the front seat—with an impact equivalent to a one-story drop onto concrete for each ten miles per hour the car is traveling. Even though the dashboard and back of the front seat may be padded, hitting them from three to seven stories up (the impact you would have at speeds ranging from thirty to seventy miles per hour) could still be fatal. In addition, young children should *never* ride in the front seat of the car, even if restrained in car seats or seat belts. Always buckle them safely in the back seat in approved safety seats or booster seats. (See pages 110–113 for more on car seat safety.)

Preventing the Problem

Check the car seat or seat restraints before traveling.

The safety measures you take before leaving will determine how relaxed you are with your children when you finally depart. Don't wait until the last minute to find out you must delay your trip because you lack an essential item: the safety seat.

Practice the rule.

Before you and your child leave on a long-distance car trip, take a few dry runs so your child can graduate from basic training to the real thing. Praise proper sitting in the car seat or seat belts during practice time, to show your child that staying in his car seat produces rewards.

Make car rules.

Institute the rule that the car moves only when everyone is buckled in. Say, "I'm sorry your belt is not buckled. The car can't move until you're safely buckled in." Be prepared to wait until the passengers comply with your rule before you go.

Provide appropriate play materials.

Make sure you pack toys that are harmless to clothing and upholstery. Crayons are okay, but felt-tip pens are discouraged because they may permanently mark clothing and upholstery. If you're taking public transportation, provide activities that are quiet, usable in controlled spaces, and capable of holding your child's attention for long periods of time.

Familiarize your child with your travel plans.

Discuss your travel plans with your child so he'll know how long you'll be gone, what will happen to his room while you're away, and when you'll return. Show him maps and photos of your destination. Talk to him about the people, scenery, and events you'll experience. Share personal stories and souvenirs from previous visits to the destination. If your child is anxious about going to an unknown place, compare the destination to one he's familiar with.

Personally involve your child traveler.

Allow your child to participate in the preparation and execution of the trip. Enlist his help in packing his clothing, selecting carryon toys, carrying a tote bag, staying close in the terminal, and so on.

Establish rules of conduct for traveling.

Before you leave, explain to your child any special rules of the road. For example, you might establish a noise rule, an exploring rule, a pool rule, and a restaurant rule for stops along the way.

Solving the Problem

What to Do

Praise good behavior.

Frequently praise good behavior and provide rewards for staying in car seats. For example, say, "I like the way you're looking at all the trees and houses. It's really a pretty day. We can get out soon and play in the park because you've been sitting in your car seat so nicely."

Stop the car if your child gets out of his car seat or unbuckles his safety belt.

Make sure your child realizes that your car seat rule will be strictly enforced, and that the consequences will be the same every time the rule is violated.

Play car games.

Count objects, recognize colors, look for animals, and so on, to keep your child entertained. Make a list of fun things to do before you leave home. Switch games as needed, to maintain your child's (and your) interest.

Make frequent rest stops.

Your restless preschooler is usually happiest when he's mobile. Restraining him for hours in a car, plane, or train does not suit his adventurous spirit. Give him time to let off steam in a roadside park or rest stop, or you'll find him rebelling when you least desire it.

Monitor snacks on long trips.

Highly sugared or carbonated foods may not only increase a child's activity level, they may also increase the chance of nausea. Stick to protein snacks or lightly salted ones to keep him healthy and happy.

Use Grandma's Rule.

Let your child know that good behavior on trips brings rewards. For example, if your child has been whining about getting a drink, say, "When you've sat in your seat and talked with us without whining, then we'll stop and get something to drink."

What Not to Do

Don't let young children sit in the front seat.

No matter how much they fuss and beg to sit next to mommy or daddy in the front seat, young children should never be allowed to sit there, even on the shortest of trips. The safest place for preschoolers is buckled safely in a car seat or booster seat in the back, regardless of the type of air bag.

Don't make promises you may not fulfill.

Don't be too specific about what your child will see on your travels, because he might hold you to it. For example, if you say you'll see a bear in Yellowstone Park and you don't, you might hear whining such as, "But you *promised* I'd see a bear," when you leave the park.

Car Wars

Jerry and Andrea Sterling wanted to take their children on a vacation that was just like the vacations they had each enjoyed when they were young. But traveling with three-year-old Tracy and five-year-old Travis was more like punishment than a joy ride.

The back seat of the car became a fighting zone, and the children's screaming frequently led to threats and spanking. But punishment didn't seem to help. The Sterlings, who often felt just as angry after the punishment as they did before, felt nearly hopeless about finding a solution to their traveling problems.

Eventually they decided to develop new rules for traveling. They found some toys that their kids could play with without supervision; they explained the new policy for car trips; and they tested the rules on ordinary trips to the grocery store, park, and friends' homes. "Kids," they began, "we're going to the grocery store. When you've sat in your car seats and talked with us nicely all the way there, you can each pick out your favorite kind of juice."

The Sterlings praised their kids for initially following the rule. "Thanks for being so quiet. I really like the way you're not whining and hurting each other." But ultimately the plan failed and the kids didn't get a treat. However, it only took two more tests for the children to behave kindly toward each other and follow the car rules during the entire time in the car. They received praise for their efforts, and they were rewarded for their good behavior.

Two weeks later, the Sterling family began its two-hour trek to Grandma's, the longest trip in the car since the practice sessions had begun. The children knew what was expected of them and what rewards were available along the way and at their destination. This made going over the river and through the woods a lot more fun for everyone.

Wandering Away in Public

Curious preschoolers make mental lists of what to see and do at shopping centers, grocery stores, and so on, just like their parents. Preschoolers think their lists take priority, and chaos breaks out when their lists don't match their parents'. Your child's safety takes precedence over her curiosity in dangerous situations (getting in the way of cars, pedestrians, or grocery carts, for example), so enforce your rules about public behavior despite her protests. Make staying close in public a habit for your child until you can rely on her to know what is and isn't dangerous—a distinction she'll have learned from you.

Note: To foster your child's staying close in public, your emphasis must be on preventing any wandering. Once your child has left your side in public, the only thing to do is find her and prevent her from wandering away again.

Preventing the Problem

Establish rules for behaving in public.
At a neutral time (before or long after she misbehaves), let your child know what you expect of her in public. Say, "When we're in the store, you must stay within one arm's length from me."

Practice ahead of time.
Practice before leaving the house, so your child knows how to follow your rules. Say, "We're going to try staying within an arm's length of each other. Let's see how long you can stay close." After she does it, say, "Good staying close. Thanks for not moving away from me."

Teach your child to come to you.
During a neutral time, take your child's hand and say, "Come here, please." When she comes to you, give her a hug and say, "Thank you for coming." Practice five times a day, gradually increasing the distance your child is away from you before saying, "Come here, please," until she can come to you from across the room or across the store.

Praise staying close.

Make it worth your child's while to stay close by praising her every time she does. Say, "Good staying close," or, "You're being such a good shopper by staying close to me."

Involve your child in shopping.

Let your child hold a package or push the stroller, if she's able. This will make her feel like an important part of the shopping trip, and she'll be less tempted to roam.

Change your rule as your child changes.

As your child matures and becomes able to walk away briefly and come right back to your side in a public place like a shopping center, for example, you might change your rule and allow her to do that. Tell her why you're giving her more freedom. Knowing that she's earned more independence by good behavior in public will help her realize that following the rules is rewarded.

Be firm and consistent.

Don't change your public behavior rules without first telling your child. Being firm and consistent will give your child a sense of security. Your restrictions may occasionally produce some yelling and screaming, but the safety net you provide will help her feel protected in strange territory.

Solving the Problem

What to Do

Use reprimands and Time Out.

Reprimanding your child for not staying close in public will teach her what behavior you expect and what will happen if she doesn't follow your rule. When you see her not staying close, say, "Please stay close. You're supposed to stay with me. Staying close to me keeps you safe." If she repeatedly breaks your rule, restate the reprimand and put her in Time Out in a nearby chair while you stay with her.

What Not to Do

Don't let your child dictate your agenda.

Don't threaten to go home if your child doesn't stay close. Going home may be just what she wants, so she might wander away to get it.

Don't take your child shopping for longer than she can tolerate.

Some preschoolers can follow staying-close rules for longer periods of time than others. Get to know your child. One hour may be her limit, so consider that before leaving home.

Staying Put

Mr. and Mrs. Brody could not comfortably take their four-year-old son, Matthew, to a shopping center or grocery store anymore. He was always wandering out of sight as soon as his parents turned their backs. "Stay here! Never run away while we're shopping!" Mrs. Brody screamed at her son the last time he disappeared under a lingerie rack at the department store.

Her order proved ineffective. As they left the store and strolled down the mall, Matthew ran toward a shop window, pointed upward, and screamed, "Look at that train! Look at that train!" The shop window was almost out of hearing range, which caused Mrs. Brody to panic.

She realized that some rules needed to be established to prevent her son from disappearing while she did her holiday shopping. The next morning, she explained the new rule to her son before they went to the grocery store, because the grocery store was his favorite place to race from aisle to aisle. "Matthew, you must stay within arm's length of me while we're shopping," she began. "As long as you stay that close, you may look at things with your eyes, not with your hands."

During their trial run, Matthew was out of sight in minutes. "Remember the rule," Mrs. Brody told him when she finally caught up with him in Aisle 3 and pulled him close to her. "You're supposed to stay within an arm's length of me. Staying close to me keeps you safe."

Matthew acted like he didn't hear what she was saying, taking off toward his beloved granola bars. Mrs. Brody, boiling inside but cool on the surface, told herself that the rules were new. Like all new rules, they'd need practice before they'd be followed perfectly. "You're supposed to stay with me because staying close keeps you safe," she repeated. Then she walked him to the quiet corner by the produce and turned her back on him while staying near.

Matthew glared at his mother in protest, yelling, "No! I want to play. I don't like you!" Embarrassed but unflinching, Mrs. Brody ignored his outburst. She decided that if a reprimand didn't solve the problem, she'd put her son in Time Out to help him learn the rule.

At the end of three minutes (which seemed like three hours to Mrs. Brody), she greeted Matthew with a smile and reviewed the rule as they finished shopping. Whenever Matthew stayed within arm's length, Mrs. Brody praised him. "Thanks for staying close, honey. I'm really glad we're shopping together." They began talking about cereals and planning which ones to buy for breakfast that week.

Mrs. Brody consistently reminded him of the rule over the next few weeks, but she rarely had to use Time Out because they were having so much fun enjoying the new closeness between them.

Wanting Their Own Way

Because patience is not an innate virtue, young children must be taught the art of waiting for what they want. Because *you* are more experienced in knowing what's best for your preschooler, you're more qualified to control when he can do what he wants to do and what conditions must be met before he does it. Explain these conditions clearly. For example, say, "I know you want to eat the cake batter, but you don't need it now. When you wait until it's baked, it will turn into more cake for you to eat."

Also, show him how having patience pays off in your life, too. Say, for instance, "I know it's unpleasant for me to wait to buy the new dining-room furniture I want, but I know that if I work hard at saving money, I'll be able to buy it soon." Your child is just discovering that the world will not always revolve around his desires. It's not too soon for him to start learning how to cope with this often frustrating fact of life.

Preventing the Problem

Provide a menu of activities from which your child may choose.

Set up conditions that must be satisfied before your child gets his own way, and provide him with suggestions for activities he can do while he's waiting for what he wants. For example, say, "When you've played with the pegs for five minutes, then we'll go to Grandma's."

Solving the Problem

What to Do

Encourage patience.

Reward even the slightest sign of patience by telling your child how glad you are he waited. Define *patience* if you think he might not be familiar with the word. For example, say, "You're being so patient by waiting calmly for your drink until I clean the sink. That shows me how grown-up you are." This teaches your child that he *does* have the ability to put off his wants, even though he doesn't know it yet. It also helps him feel good about himself, because you feel good about his behavior.

Remain as calm as you can.
If your child protests waiting or not having things his own way, remind yourself that he's learning a valuable lesson for living: the art of patience. By seeing you be patient, he'll soon learn that demanding doesn't get his wants satisfied as quickly as getting the job done.

Use Grandma's Rule.
If your child is screaming, "Go! Go! Go to the park!" simply state the conditions he must meet in order to satisfy his wants. Be positive. For example, say, "When you've put the books back on the bookshelf, we'll go to the park."

Avoid a flat "No."
Whenever it's possible and safe, tell your child how he can have his own way. Avoid making him feel that his desires will never be satisfied. For example, say, "When you've washed your hands, then you may have an apple." Sometimes, of course, you need to say no to your child (when he wants to play with your lawnmower, for instance). At those times, try to offer alternative playthings to satisfy his wishes and to foster a sense of compromise and flexibility.

What Not to Do

Don't demand that your child do something "now."
Demanding that your child immediately do what you want contradicts the lesson you're trying to teach. If you don't want him to demand instant results, don't do it yourself.

Don't reward impatience.
Don't give in to your child's desires every time he wants his own way. Although it may be tempting to do so in order to avoid a battle or a tantrum, constantly giving in only reinforces his impatient behavior and fails to teach him patience.

Make sure your child knows it's not his demanding that got his wants fulfilled.
Though your child may moan and groan throughout the waiting time, make sure he knows that you're getting in the car because you're ready

and your jobs are done, not because he wailed his way out the door. Say, "I've finished washing the dishes. Now we can go."

"I Want It Now!"

"Drink now!" two-year-old Emily Randolph wailed every time she was thirsty. When she saw her mother giving a bottle to her new baby brother, Justin, she wanted one, too—immediately.

"No, I'm busy. You'll just have to wait!" her mother responded, growing impatient with her daughter for not understanding that babies don't know how to wait for what they want.

Emily made so many demands to be held or given toys or drinks that Mrs. Randolph began to dread the moment when Emily would enter the room while her mother was busy with anything, especially taking care of Justin. When Emily began taking food, drinks, toys, and blankets away from Justin, saying that they were "mine," Mrs. Randolph realized that she needed to fix the problem. She declared a new rule, called Grandma's Rule, and explained it to Emily: "When you do what I ask you to do, then you may do what you want to do. This is the new rule."

That afternoon, Emily insisted on having a drink only ten minutes after the last one. Mrs. Randolph stated firmly, "When you put your shoes on, then you may have some apple juice." Emily was used to hearing, "No," and then throwing a tantrum until her mother gave in, so she ignored the new rule and continued to plead, "I'm thirsty!"

Not only did her tantrum not bring a drink, it caused Mrs. Randolph to ignore Emily completely. The frustrated girl finally put on her shoes to see if that would bring her the attention (and drink) she wanted, since screaming had not. She was surprised and delighted when it did.

Emily quickly learned that her mother meant what she said, because she never strayed from enforcing Grandma's Rule. When Emily fulfilled her part of the bargain, Mrs. Randolph praised her accomplishments with comments like, "I'm so glad you cleared the dishes from the table. You can go outside now."

Mrs. Randolph's admiration was sincere. Emily appreciated it and became more responsive to her mother's rules, which Mrs. Randolph tried to limit whenever possible. As the family learned to work together to satisfy everyone's needs, they grew to enjoy living with—not in spite of—each other.

Whining

Just as adults occasionally find themselves in a bad mood for no apparent reason, preschoolers are sometimes whiny and cranky even though their physical needs have been met. This behavior is usually the result of your child wanting attention or wanting her own way. Though it may be hard to do, ignoring the whining does help wind it down. Your child will soon learn an important rule: Asking nicely speaks louder than being cranky and noncommunicative.

Preventing the Problem

Catch 'em being pleasant.
When your child is not whining, tell her how much you like being with her. Your attention teaches her the rewards of a positive attitude.

Keep her needs met.
Make sure your child eats, bathes, dresses, sleeps, and gets plenty of hugs on a regular basis, to prevent her from becoming cranky because she's wet, hungry, overtired, or too upset to tell you her feelings without whining.

Solving the Problem

What to Do

Define *whining*.
Make sure your child knows exactly what you mean by *whining*. Then explain how you'd like her to ask for something or tell you what she wants without whining. For example, say, "When you ask nicely, I'll give you some apple juice. Here's how I'd like you to ask: 'Mommy [or Daddy], may I please have some apple juice?'" If your child isn't talking yet, show her how to indicate what she wants by using actions or gestures. Let her practice requesting things pleasantly at least five times. Make sure you fulfill her request, to prove your point that asking nicely gets results.

Create a "whining place," if necessary.
If your child's whining continues even after you've taught her how to express her wants nicely, let her know that she has the right to have

feelings and frustrations that only whining can relieve. Tell her that she can whine as much as she wants, but that she must do it in the "whining place," an area designated for whining. Let her know that you'd rather not be around a whiner who can't tell you what she wants, and when she's done whining she can come out. Say, "I'm sorry you're so upset. You can go to the whining place and come back when you're feeling better."

Ignore your child's whining.

Because your child's whining is so nerve-racking, you can easily pay more attention to her when she's whining than when she's quiet, even though that attention is not affection. After you've put her in the whining chair and given her the go-ahead to get the frustration out of her system, put on headphones or do something else to help yourself ignore the whining until it's over.

Point out nonwhining times.

To show your child the vivid contrast between how you react when she does and doesn't whine, immediately praise her quieting down by saying, "You're being so pleasant! Let's go get a toy!" or, "I haven't heard you whine for the longest time!" or, "Thanks for not whining!"

What Not to Do

Don't give in to the whining.

If you give your whining child attention by getting upset or giving her what she's whining for, you're teaching her that whining is the way to get what she wants.

Don't whine yourself.

Adult complaining may sound like whining to a child. If you're doing it, your preschooler may think it's okay for her. If you're in a bad mood, don't get angry with your child because you're angry with the world. Simply tell her that you're feeling out of sorts; don't whine about it.

Don't get angry with your child.

Don't get angry with your child because she's having an "off" day. She'll not only mistake your outbursts for attention, she'll feel a sense of power over you because she's made you mad. She may continue to whine just to show you she's the boss.

Don't punish your child for whining.

The old retort "I'll give you something to really whine about" only creates conflict between you and your child. It tells her that it's never okay to whine, which makes her feel guilty for having disgruntled feelings. Allow whining with restrictions, because whining may be the only way your child can vent frustrations at the time.

Remember, this won't last forever.

Your child may be having a bad day or going through a period when nothing seems to please her, so she may spend more time whining until she gets back in sync with her world. Tell yourself, "This too shall pass," while you try to lift her spirits by praising her good behavior.

The Whining Chair

From the moment three-year-old Aisha Gonzalez woke up in the morning until she closed her eyes at night, she was a constant whirlwind of whining. "Mommy, I wanna eat! Mommy, what's on TV? Mommy, where are we going? Mommy, pick me up!"

Mrs. Gonzalez tried to ignore her daughter's noisemaking, but she frequently gave in to Aisha's demands in order to get her to be quiet. But the whining and whimpering started to grate on Mrs. Gonzalez's nerves until one day she screamed, "Aisha, stop that stupid whining. You sound horrible!"

Yelling at Aisha only increased her whining, so Mrs. Gonzalez decided she'd have to use a different method. She decided to try a variation of Time Out, a technique she'd used whenever her daughter misbehaved.

"This is the whining chair," she told Aisha the next morning after she began her regular whining routine. "I'm sorry you're whining now. You must sit here until you're finished whining. When you're done, you can get up and we'll play with your dolls." She placed her daughter in the chair she had selected for this purpose. Then she walked away, making sure she wasn't around to give her daughter any attention. When she heard the whining stop, she returned to her daughter and praised her. "Oh, I love the way you're not whining. Let's go play."

When Mrs. Gonzalez realized her daughter was going to the whining chair nearly ten times a day, she decided to take the next step and teach Aisha how to stop herself from being put in the whining chair. "When you ask me nicely, I'll give you a drink," she explained. Then she taught Aisha how to ask nicely: "Please, Mom, may I have a drink?"

Her daughter practiced these instructions whenever she wanted something she had previously whined for. Though Aisha's whining never completely disappeared (she still whined on her "off" days), Mrs. Gonzalez became much happier with her relationship with her daughter.

Appendix I: Childproofing Checklist

Alarming statistics show that accidents are the number one cause of death in young children. Most accidents occur as a result of children's normal, healthy curiosity. Chances of getting hurt increase as children creep, crawl, walk, climb, and explore. The following checklist identifies steps parents should take to prevent home accidents:

- Always keep guns and knives locked safely away from children. Each gun should have its own trigger lock, and ammunition should be locked in a separate location out of reach of little hands.
- Install childproof latches on all cabinets and drawers that contain dangerous objects.
- Crawl through the house on your hands and knees to spot enticing hazards to be remedied.
- Plug empty electrical outlets with plastic plugs designed for this purpose.
- Remove unused extension cords.
- Move large pieces of furniture in front of electrical outlets that have cords plugged in them, or install protective outlet coverings that prevent a child from unplugging the cord.
- If small tables or other furnishings are not sturdy or have sharp corners, put them away until your child is older, or install protective coverings around sharp edges.
- Large pieces of furniture that a child can climb and tip over should be safely secured to a nearby wall.
- Place dangerous household substances, such as detergents, cleaning fluids, razor blades, matches, and medicines, well out of reach in a locked cabinet.
- Install a proper screen on a fireplace.
- Always use a correct car seat in your automobile.
- Regularly check toys for sharp edges or small broken pieces.
- Check the floor for small objects that your child could swallow or choke on.
- Put a gate on a stairway to prevent unsupervised play on the stairs.
- Never leave your baby unattended on a changing table, in the bathtub, on a couch, on your bed, in an infant seat or highchair, on the floor, or in a car.
- Have syrup of ipecac on hand to induce vomiting in case your child swallows a noncorrosive poison.

- Place small, fragile tabletop items out of your child's reach.
- Keep the door to the bathroom closed at all times. Use a childproof doorknob cover if your child knows how to turn the doorknob.
- Install safety latches on toilet lids.
- Keep plastic bags and small objects (pins, buttons, nuts, hard candy, money) out of reach at all times.
- Make sure toys, furniture, and walls are finished in lead-free paint. Check labels to make sure toys are nontoxic.
- Teach the word *hot* as early as you can. Keep your child away from the hot oven, iron, vent, fireplace, wood stove, barbecue grill, cigarettes, cigarette lighter, and hot teacups and coffee cups.
- Always turn pot handles inward when cooking, and remove gas knobs on the stove when not in use.
- Install safety latches for stand-alone freezers and oven doors, if they don't have locks.
- Always raise crib sides in the up position when your baby (even a tiny infant) is in the crib.
- Do not hang a tablecloth off a table when your small child is close by.
- Never tie toys to a crib or playpen. Your baby could strangle on the string. Also, never attach a pacifier to a string that could get wrapped around your baby's neck.

Appendix II: Is My Child Hyperactive?

If you suspect your child is hyperactive, the following guidelines will help you know what to expect when his behavior is evaluated. Only a detailed picture of your child and how he navigates his world can lead to an appropriate diagnosis and effective treatment plan. When conducting a thorough evaluation, a trained mental health professional (psychologist, social worker, psychiatrist) will gather information in the following areas:

A. Family history, including:
1. Your child's developmental, school, and treatment history
2. Your family's psychiatric history
3. All previous diagnostic screenings done on your child
4. Behavior checklists completed by parents, teachers, and so on
5. Your child's social functioning at home, in the neighborhood, and at school
6. How your family understands and reacts to your child's behavior
7. Your child's sleep patterns
8. Your child's diet and allergies
9. An analysis of the factors related to your child's behavior, including:
    a. How your child interacts with his mother, father, siblings, peers, teachers, coaches, and so on
    b. How your child reacts at home, in school, at social gatherings, in the neighborhood, and so on
    c. How your child reacts to reading, writing, homework, video games, getting dressed, and so on
    d. How your child behaves early in the morning, after school, during meals, when he's bored, at bedtime, and so on

B. An interview with your child to gather the following information:
1. His understanding of and thoughts about his problems
2. His general emotional functioning

C. An analysis of your child's behavior in school, including:
1. Teacher-completed behavior checklists
2. Teachers' understanding of and reaction to your child's behavior
3. Classroom observation of your child across several tasks and settings

D. Formal testing to evaluate the following:
1. General cognitive functioning
2. Achievement skills
3. Attention to task
4. Language processing
5. Sensory-motor skills

References

Introduction

1. Lawrence Kohlberg, "Moral Stages and Moralization: The Cognitive-Developmental Approach," in T. Lickona (ed.), *Moral Development and Behavior*, Holt, Rinehart, and Winston (1976).

2. Harriet H. Barrish, Ph.D., and I. J. Barrish, Ph.D., *Managing Parental Anger*, Overland Press (1985).

3. Richard Rhodes, *Why They Kill: The Discoveries of a Maverick Criminologist*, Alfred A. Knopf (1999).

4. Beth Azar, "Defining the Trait That Makes Us Human," *APA Monitor*, Vol. 28, No. 11 (November 1997).

5. Barbara Unell and Jerry Wyckoff, *20 Teachable Virtues*, Perigee Books (1995).

Pretending to Use Weapons

1. M. M. Lefkowitz, L. D. Eron, L. D. Walder, and L. R. Huesmann, *Growing Up to Be Violent*, Pergamon Press (1977).

2. R. Potts, A. C. Houston, and J. C. Wright, "The Effects of Television for and Violent Content on Boys' Attention and Social Behavior," *Journal of Experimental Child Psychology*, 41 (1986): 1–17.

3. R. B. McCall, R. D. Parke, and R. D. Kavanaugh, "Imitation of Live and Televised Models by Children One to Three Years of Age," *Monographs of the Society for Research in Child Development*, 42, Serial No. 173 (1977).

4. D. Singer and J. Singer, "Family Experiences and Television Viewing As Predictors of Children's Imagination, Restlessness, and Aggression," *Journal of Social Issues*, 42 (1986): 107–24.

5. L. A. Joy, M. M. Kimball, and M. L. Zabrack, "Television and Children's Aggressive Behaviour," in T. T. Williams (ed.), *The Impact of Television: A Natural Experiment in Three Communities*, Academic Press (1986).

6. L. R. Huesmann, "Psychological Processes Promoting the Relation between Exposure to Media Violence and Aggressive Behavior by the Viewer," *Journal of Social Issues*, 42 (1986): 125–39.

7. J. E. Grusec, "Effects of Co-Observer Evaluations of Imitation: A Developmental Toleration of Real-Life Aggression?" *Developmental Psychology*, 10 (1973): 418–21.

Index

lying and, 68
teaching, violence and, 102
Exercise
   bedtime resistance and, 106
   hyperactivity and, 54
   overeating and, 93
Exploring, 46–48

F

Fear of strangers, 57, 58
Following directions, 79–82
Food
   eating too much, 91–94
   on long trips, 138
   not wanting to eat, 87–90
   playing with, 98–100
   rewarding with, 23
   television and, 23
Freedom, demanding, 32–34
Friendliness, 58

G

Games and activities
   car, 138
   for clinging to parents, 25–26
   creative, 22
   for dawdling, 29–30
   for experiencing jealousy, 64
   hyperactivity and, 52–53
   physical, 22, 23
   while waiting, 144
   See also Play; Toys
Getting along
   defining for child, 119
   praising, 16, 102, 120, 121
Getting into things, 46–48
Getting out of bed at night, 49–51
Girl-boy differences, 8–9
Grandma's Rule
   for cleaning up, 73
   for cleanup (hygienic) routine, 44
   for dawdling, 30
   defined, 13
   for following directions, 80
   for interrupting, 61
   for toilet training, 133–34
   for travel behavior, 138
   for wanting their own way, 145, 146
Grounding, 54

Guns, keeping locked up, 47
   See also Weapons

H

Hitting, 15, 16
   See also Spanking
Hyperactivity, 52–56, 152–53

I

Independence
   demanding, 35–38
   helping with siblings and, 64
   taking directions from others and, 79
Interrupting, 60–62

J

Jealousy, 63–66

K

Kindness, modeling, 102
Knives, keeping locked up, 47
Kohlberg, Lawrence, 5

L

Labels
   liar, 70
   shy, 20, 21
   thief, 123
Language
   backtalk, 125–27
   name-calling, 76–78
Limits
   establishing, 32
   physical, 46
   rewards/consequences for, 33
Lying, 67–71

M

Make amends, teaching child to, 103
Make-believe play, 69
Medication, 54
Messiness, 72–75
"Mine," 83
Mistakes
   criticism and punishment for, 37
   resistance to change and, 114

N

Name-calling, 76–78

Nap schedule, 106
Neutral time, 12
Nicknames, 76
Night wandering, 49–51
"No," overusing, 95–97

O

Objects
    destroying, 39–41
    taking from others, 122

P

Parents
    activity levels of, 53
    assessing problems of child, 2–3
    clinging to, 25–28
    goals of, 1–2
    self-talk by, 7
    See also Role modeling
Patience
    assertion of child's independence
        and, 36
    teaching to child, 144–46
Peek-a-Boo, 25–26
People, other
    aggressive behavior toward, 15–17
    interacting with strangers, 57–59
    name-calling, 76–78
    shyness with, 18–21
    taking things from, 122–24
    teaching nonviolence towards, 102,
        103
    See also Siblings
Play
    destructive, 39–41
    make-believe, and lying, 69, 71
    outdoor, 54
    while on the telephone, 60
    with play weapons, 101–2, 103, 104–5
    See also Games and activities; Toys
Playing with food, 98–100
Practice
    car behavior, 111, 137
    following directions, 80
    overcoming shyness with, 19
    public behavior, 140
Praise, 3–4
    for active play, 23
    for cleanup efforts, 73

for cooperative play, 102
for coping efforts, 128
for correct behavior with strangers,
    58
for correct toileting, 133, 134–35
defined, 12
for efforts at independence, 36
for following directions, 80, 91
for food selections, 93
food-free, 23
for getting along with others, 16, 58,
    120, 121
for handling separation well, 26
for not dawdling, 30
for not interrupting, 61, 62
for regaining control during temper
    tantrums, 129–30
for saying "Yes," 96
for sharing, 63
shyness and, 19
for staying close to you in public, 141
for staying in safety belt, 111
for telling the truth, 67
for using nice talk, 77
while traveling, 138
See also Complimenting; Rewards
Preschoolers
    boy-girl differences in, 8–9
    characteristics of, 1
    defined, viii–ix
    milestones of development in, 10–11
    transition to elementary school, 9
Problem solving, teaching, 115
Property, destroying, 39–41
Public, wandering away in, 140–43
Punishment
    for backtalk, 126
    hyperactivity and, 54
    for lying, 69
    for name-calling, 77
    for shyness, 20

Q

Questions
    limiting yes-no, 95, 97
    practicing responses to, with child, 19

R

Relaxation, hyperactivity and, 54, 56

Busy Books

Each busy book contains 365 activities (one for each day of the year) for your children using items found around the home. The books offer parents and child-care providers fun reading, math, and science activities that will stimulate a child's natural curiosity. They also provide great activities for indoor play during even the longest stretches of bad weather! All three books show you how to save money by making your own paints, play dough, craft clays, glue, paste, and other arts-and-crafts supplies.

Toddler's Busy Book

Preschooler's Busy Book

Children's Busy Book

✦ *Preschooler Play & Learn*

Child-development expert Penny Warner offers 150 ideas for games and activities that will provide hours of developmental learning opportunities, including bulleted lists of skills that your preschooler is learning, step-by-step instructions for each game and activity, and illustrations demonstrating how to play many of the games.

✦ *Practical Parenting Tips*

The number-one selling collection of helpful hints for parents with babies and small children, containing 1,001 parent-tested tips for dealing with diaper rash, nighttime crying, toilet training, temper tantrums, traveling with tots, and lots more. Parents will save time, trouble, and money.

✦ *Healthy Food for Healthy Kids*

A practical guide to selecting and preparing healthy meals for kids and teaching healthy attitudes toward food. More than just a cookbook, this is a user-friendly book with real-world advice for parents who want their children to eat better.

✦ *When You Were a Baby*

This one-of-a-kind baby record book is designed with a die-cut hole that enables parents to prominently feature baby's photograph on every page. Baby's photo will be featured in illustrations showing crawling, first bath, first word, and more.

✦ *When You Were One*

Following the tremendous success of *When You Were a Baby,* Amanda Haley introduces the second book in her delightful record book series.

Now parents can record their child's second year in this beautifully illustrated keepsake.

✦ *When I Grow Up*

This is a book that you "write" with your child. Record his or her thoughts on future careers. A die-cut hole prominently features your child's photo on every page.

Also from Meadowbrook Press

✦ *Feed Me I'm Yours*
Parents love this easy-to-use, economical guide to making baby and toddler food at home. More than 200 recipes cover everything a parent needs to know about teething foods, nutritious snacks, and quick, pleasing lunches.

✦ *Parent-Tested Ways to Grow Your Child's Confidence*
With 150 tested ideas designed to enhance your child's self-confidence, you'll discover great ways to share enjoyable moments together, teach important skills, celebrate special occasions, encourage creativity, and recognize achievements.

✦ *What Do You Know about Manners?*
A book about manners that kids will enjoy reading? Absolutely—and parents will love it, too! Filled with fun, imaginative ways to fine-tune a child's manners, presented in a humorous format with over 100 quiz items and illustrations.

✦ *How to Read Your Child Like a Book*
This book helps parents interpret their child's behavior by teaching parents what their child is thinking. Dr. Lynn Weiss, a nationally recognized expert on child development, explains 50 different behaviors of children from birth to age 6. You will gain new insight into such behaviors as boundary testing, irritability, selfishness, and temper tantrums.

We offer many more titles written to delight, inform, and entertain.
To order books with a credit card or browse our full
selection of titles, visit our web site at:

www.meadowbrookpress.com

or call toll-free to place an order, request a free catalog, or ask a question:

1-800-338-2232

Meadowbrook Press • 5451 Smetana Drive • Minnetonka, MN • 55343

101 WAYS

TO HELP BIRDS

101 WAYS TO HELP BIRDS

LAURA ERICKSON

Illustrations by Roger Hall

STACKPOLE
BOOKS

Published by
STACKPOLE BOOKS
5067 Ritter Rd.
Mechanicsburg, PA 17055
www.stackpolebooks.com

Printed in the United States of America

10 9 8 7 6 5 4 3 2 1

First edition

Cover design by Wendy Reynolds
Cover photograph of Magnolia Warbler by Tom Vezo

Library of Congress Cataloging-in-Publication Data

Erickson, Laura, 1951–
    101 ways to help birds / Laura Erickson ; Illustrations by Roger Hall.
      p. cm.
    ISBN-13: 978-0-8117-3302-1
    1. Birds—Conservation. 2. Gardening to attract birds. I. Title: One hundred one ways to help birds. II. Title.

QL676.5.E75 2006
639.9'78—dc22

2006000682

This book is dedicated to the memory of Rachel Carson, who understood that the future of humans and birds is inextricably intertwined. We're all in this together.

CONTENTS

ACKNOWLEDGMENTS

I GOT THE IDEA FOR THIS BOOK WHILE DRIVING HOME FROM THE Midwest Birding Symposium in September 2003. I'd left the symposium charged with energy thanks to the many organizers and participants, especially Alicia Craig, Kenn Kaufman, Don and Lillian Stokes, Ron Windingstad, and Ric Zarwell. The inspiring work of a great many people kept me going when learning more about the issues facing birds and humans grew oppressive—I can't even begin to list the many names of those working tirelessly in ornithology and conservation who have unknowingly given me greater understanding and inspiration. They strengthened this work through their own contributions to books, magazines, journals, listservs, and Web sites.

Many friends and conservationists gave me specific and substantive help with the book. I'm afraid I'll leave out important contributions since so very many people helped, but I am grateful to Mark Alt, Paul Baicich, Val Cunningham, Noel Cutright, Robert DeCandido, Scott Diehl, Melissa Driscoll, Rob Fergus, Joel Geier, Marge Gibson, Karen Etter Hale, Carrol Henderson, Bob Holtz, Paul Kerlinger, Daniel Klem, David B. Marshall, William Mueller, Bruce Newhouse, Holly Peirson, Heather Ray, Tom Schultz, Tom Stehn, Tim Tuominen, Jim Williams, and Steve Wilson. I am sure there are others who deserve credit; I apologize for being so absent-minded. I'm also grateful to my agent, Julie Mayo, who has the practical gene that I lack, and to Mark Allison, Chris Chappell, and Ken Krawchuk at Stackpole, who have been such a pleasure to work with. Despite the help of so many, I'm stubborn enough that any mistakes that may remain are entirely my responsibility.

My husband Russ has put up with my eccentricities and monomaniacal focus with good humor and sweetness. My children never made me feel guilty for not being like other kids' mothers. These past two years I've been more out of it than usual, and they've supported my work with grace and understanding.

I owe a special debt of gratitude to my dear professor, Gary Duke, whose warmth and generosity in sharing his expertise in avian physiology, and whose faith in me, have enriched my life even though I never did finish my Ph.D. As he noted, I probably didn't want to be referred to as "Dr. Laura" anyway. But it was one of the most inspiring and fulfilling experiences of my life to have worked with him.

Why Help Birds?

BIRDS ARE IN TROUBLE. HOW CAN THAT POSSIBLY BE TRUE WHEN gulls and crows, pigeons and geese, blackbirds and sparrows are everywhere? Those birds have adapted to living in urban and suburban habitats or agricultural monocultures. Our burgeoning population and increased demand for gigantic homes and huge manicured lawns encroach on more and more natural habitat while providing the perfect environment for those animals that share our fondness for grain, ornamental plants, turf grass, and forests cut on short rotation cycles.

But a great many birds, including familiar and beloved songbirds such as bobolinks, meadowlarks, tanagers, and orioles, require natural habitats. These are the species that are in trouble. Compare today's satellite images of just about any place on earth with those taken only a few decades ago to see how much we humans have changed the face of the natural world. How can birds that require relatively wild conditions be expected to maintain steady numbers as so much of their habitat disappears? Dr. Sidney Gauthreaux of Clemson University, analyzing bird migration patterns by radar, found that major migration movements of birds over the Gulf of Mexico had declined by 50 percent in just two decades. Studies by the National Audubon Society indicate that fully 25 percent of American bird species are declining significantly. In just the past three years, seabirds have been dying and suffering reproduction crashes at unprecedented levels.

But in a world where human beings are suffering from poverty, hunger, disease, war, terrorism, and natural disasters, isn't it misguided to spend time and energy trying to help birds? What does that say about our priorities?

Birds are an Essential Part of Our Lives, History, and Culture

In my own life, wild birds have provided a refuge from childhood terrors and adult pressures, to say nothing of delight and fun. They've provided intellectual pleasure, giving me insight into the sciences of taxonomy, ecology, ethology, physiology, and anatomy, as well as geography, history, art, literature, and etymology. Birds have given me, an avid birder, an outlet for my classifying, listing, and organizing side, yet they've also given me aesthetic and sentimental joy. In other words, they've given me infinite riches for my human heart, soul, mind, and spirit.

But I'm far from the only human being whose life has been enriched by birds. Thomas Jefferson loved birds, mentioning them in detail in his correspondence and his *Notes on the State of Virginia*. He specifically charged Lewis and Clark with studying and collecting as many birds as possible on their expedition. Henry David Thoreau and Emily Dickinson fed their backyard birds. During World War II, Franklin Roosevelt found solace in a birding excursion he took one morning during spring migration. Even the Bible makes mention of birds. In Genesis, Noah sent out a dove to see if the waters had receded after the flood. When the dove brought back an olive branch, Noah was assured that never again would God visit such a flood upon the earth. And in Luke 12:6, Jesus said, "Are not five sparrows sold for two pence? And not one of them is forgotten in the sight of God."

One woman told me about her husband who had suffered a stroke, leaving his arms and legs paralyzed. He became discouraged and clinically depressed; the only thing that lightened his spirits was seeing his backyard birds. My friend would push him in his wheelchair out on their deck, where he'd sit for hours, entertained by birds. He had poor eyesight, so to bring them closer, she began putting mealworms into his paralyzed hands. Wrens, nuthatches, and chickadees quickly started coming to him for treats, and months later, the very first sensation he felt was a chickadee alighting on his finger.

On the day after September 11, 2001, when the entire nation was grieving and in shock, and people in the airline industry were particularly hard hit from losing so many of their own, my phone rang and the caller identified himself as the manager of an airline maintenance base. His voice was shaking as he asked, "Are you the Laura Erickson who takes care of birds?" I'd let my bird rehabilitation license expire a few years earlier, but I was too numb and confused to explain, so I just answered, "Yes." He told me that a group of people had rescued an injured pigeon being attacked by crows in the parking lot. He said, "I know a lot of people don't think much of pigeons, but can you please come and help?"

When I arrived, several men and women stood around the box containing the pigeon, their eyes filled with sadness and hope. Over a bird? The day before, those gleaming twin towers in New York City had collapsed before the nation's eyes, and thousands of human beings were suddenly dead. These people at the maintenance base had watched their TVs like we all did, powerless to do anything. Now one little pigeon needed help, and suddenly there was something that they could do to make the world a little less cruel and unfathomable.

As the producer of a radio program, I've received hundreds of phone calls and letters from people telling me their own personal stories about birds. I've heard from hunters who've had lovely or fascinating bird encounters while sitting in their deer stands. And a man in northern Canada called to tell me about his wife's fight with cancer. The thing that got her out of bed every morning in those final months was the thought of seeing the chickadees at her feeders.

Anne Frank wrote in her diary from her dark hiding place, "The best remedy for those who are afraid, lonely or unhappy is to go outside, somewhere where they can be quiet, alone with the heavens, nature and God. Because only then does one feel that all is as it should be and that God wishes to see people happy, amidst the simple beauty of nature. As long as this exists, and it certainly always will, I know that then there will always be comfort for every sorrow, whatever the circumstances may be. And I firmly believe that nature brings solace in all troubles."

Helping birds helps human beings.

Birds are Environmental Indicators

Birds provide humans with incalculable environmental benefits. Songbirds eat a tremendous, unquantifiable amount of insect pests in our forests, prairies, cities, and towns and on our farms. Raptors and shrikes eat huge numbers of rodent pests. And hummingbirds pollinate many plants.

Perhaps equally important, birds are environmental indicators. When I was a little girl, my grandpa had pet canaries, and I remember sitting on his lap, his cheek warm against mine, as he told stories about how canaries had saved people's lives. Miners brought canaries just like my grandpa's down into the mines with them. The miners often grew attached to the little birds, but the reason they kept them was to detect poisonous gases underground that have no odor. Like all birds, canaries have a much faster metabolic rate than humans do, so they react more quickly to a wide range of poisons, from carbon monoxide to pesticides. When a canary suddenly keeled over, the miners knew that they had to get out in a hurry. In the same way, when something bad happens to birds in the natural world, we, too, may be in danger.

Of course, other wildlife also reacts to environmental problems. For example, salamanders are far more vulnerable to acid rain than many birds seem to be. So why focus so much attention on birds?

Of all wildlife, birds are the easiest for us to keep track of, so it's relatively easy to notice when a bird population changes. Birds and humans both rely on sight and hearing over other senses, and we produce visual and auditory signals in similar wavelengths. And more birds are active in the daylight compared with mammals, reptiles, or amphibians, so we notice birds far more easily than we notice salamanders, for instance. Avian territorial singing makes census work for many species a straightforward matter of careful listening and recording, even in the densest forests or deepest grasslands. With regular censuses, we can detect changes in bird populations much more quickly and accurately than we can detect changes in the populations of most other wildlife, and we can quickly discover and react to what is happening, helping not only the birds but also the plants and other animals that associate with them in their habitat. It may seem trivial and unnecessary to protect a single species, such as the Spotted Owl, until one realizes that this species is near the top of the food chain in a specific habitat made up of a great many plants and animals. If something is happening to make the owl decline, clearly something is happening to the northwestern forest ecosystem that may be harder to detect.

There is a huge variety of wild birds—more than 900 species have been recorded in the continental United States, Canada, and our offshore waters. Some, such as common pigeons, crows, and gulls, can survive in a wide range of conditions; these are called generalists. Others that have very specific needs are called specialists. The Yellow-rumped Warbler, a generalist, thrives over a vast range in many habitats, but Kirtland's Warbler, a specialist, nests only on sandy, well-drained soil beneath young jack pines in north-central Michigan. Kirtland's Warblers can use a given stand of trees only until the sheltering bottom branches fall off. Then, until fire regenerates the habitat in that area, the warblers must go elsewhere. Barred Owls, generalists, can survive in woodlands young and old, but closely related Spotted Owls, specialists, require ancient growth. Protecting a single endangered bird can also protect dozens or even hundreds of other plants and animals sharing the same ecosystem.

Noticing when birds succumb to various pollutants helps protect us, too. DDT was banned when scientists, such as Dr. George Wallace at Michigan State University, traced huge songbird die-offs to the pesticide, which is stored in fatty tissues. During migration and the breeding season, when fat reserves are quickly metabolized, thousands, perhaps millions, of migratory songbirds were killed outright. Scientists also discovered that Bald Eagles and Peregrine Falcons, which don't expend significantly more energy during migration than during day-to-day activities, were no longer successfully reproducing because DDT caused eggshell thinning. It took less than two decades of DDT use in the United States to completely wipe out Peregrine Falcons east of the Rocky Mountains and to decimate Bald Eagles and Osprey because of this eggshell thinning.

At the same time that the Nixon administration was banning DDT in 1972, we were discovering that human babies were ingesting this toxin in their mothers' milk, which had worked its way up the food chain after being applied in the outside environment. It wasn't until 2002 that analyses of blood samples collected and preserved in the 1960s established that DDT in the serum of pregnant women caused low birth weight and premature births. DDT may control the spread of dangerous pathogens when it is applied to the upper walls and ceilings of houses where malaria and other mosquito-borne diseases are prevalent, but when applied to crops, wetlands, residential areas, and other outdoor places, it remains in lethal form in soil, groundwater, and surface water for years, advancing up the food chain until it reaches our own tissues. Ironically, malaria became more, not less, prevalent in most areas where DDT was sprayed outdoors. Mosquitoes, with their short life cycle, can quickly build up a resistance to pesticides, necessitating higher and higher dosages to keep their populations in check. Predatory insects such as dragonflies (which eat mosquitoes) have much longer life spans and lower reproductive rates, making them more vulnerable to pesticides. Thus, pesticides harm an effective and safe mosquito control even as the chemicals themselves become less effective.

When any bird species declines, we know that something it needs is gone or that something bad is happening that may negatively affect humans too.

Protecting Birds and Their Habitats Is a Sound Investment

We set aside land in the national parks and national wildlife refuges as an investment in the future. As our population mushrooms, these green spaces become more precious, not only for birds but for all of us who live on this planet. In 1872, the year Congress proclaimed Yellowstone the first national park, the entire U.S. population was 38 million, and Yellowstone had 300 visitors. Now, as our national population approaches 300 million, 3 million visitors crowd into Yellowstone each year. In other words, as the human population has grown by one order of magnitude, the number of visitors to national parks has grown by four orders of magnitude. Clearly, parks and wildlife refuges provide increasingly important refuges for humans too.

But protecting and acquiring new wild areas can help more than animals and vacationers. Excess rainwater is far more easily absorbed in wetlands than on concrete. Healthy trees and other plants produce oxygen for all of us to breathe. Clean water and air are essential for our very survival. Healthy forests also provide lumber, paper, and even pharmaceuticals. For example, one of the most effective treatments for ovarian and breast cancers, Taxol, is a drug derived from the bark of the Pacific yew tree, a slow-growing understory tree found in the virgin rain forests of the Pacific Northwest. The more high-quality habitats we keep healthy, the easier it will be for us to continue to thrive, even as our population swells and our country becomes increasingly urbanized.

The Clean Water Act, Clean Air Act, and Endangered Species Act were all signed into law during the Nixon administration, which also established the Environmental Protection Agency. It took a horrifying event such as a stretch of the Cuyahoga River in Cleveland bursting into flame in June 1969 for the national will to finally override powerful corporate interests that had a vested financial interest in dumping their wastes into our lakes, rivers, streams, and atmosphere. A river afire is national news. *Time* magazine described the Cuyahoga in August 1969:

> Some river! Chocolate-brown, oily, bubbling with subsurface gases, it oozes rather than flows. "Anyone who falls into the Cuya-

hoga does not drown," Cleveland's citizens joke grimly. "He decays." The Federal Water Pollution Control Administration dryly notes, "The lower Cuyahoga has no visible life, not even low forms such as leeches and sludge worms that usually thrive on wastes."

Conditions such as this finally roused the sleeping public, and the Nixon administration had no choice but to respond. Some three decades later, the majority of Americans have forgotten just how bad things can become in short order when industry is unregulated or regulations are not strictly enforced. We citizens must remain vigilant and continue to demand critical environmental safeguards. Our own lives and health, as well as the lives of birds, are at stake.

I sometimes read articles by financial investment advisers who suggest, quite sensibly, that the point of investing is to end up with more money for our future needs and to bequeath to our children and grandchildren. Isn't that the attitude we need to adopt toward the environment? We need to keep growing our habitat holdings, growing or at least maintaining the number of species with healthy populations, and growing the cleanliness of our air, water, and soil for our own future protection and for our children and grandchildren.

When my daughter Katie was five years old, I took her to the Bell Museum of Natural History. Her eyes grew big as she looked at the lovely display cases of Passenger Pigeons, so rosy and blue. These "blue meteors" had once filled the skies as the most abundant land bird on the planet. Katie had just started her own bird list and told me that she couldn't wait to see a "real Passenger Pigeon" and add it to her list. I gently explained that the Passenger Pigeon was gone—extinct—and she broke down sobbing in the museum, quaking with sorrow and outrage that people had killed every one.

The story of the Passenger Pigeon is, of course, more complicated than that. Huge flocks lived and wandered and bred together, females apparently ovulating and laying their single eggs in synchrony. Then, as soon as the babies were able to fly, they all left the breeding area en masse. When over-hunting decimated flocks, the remaining birds apparently lacked some critical social stimuli necessary for breeding. Back in the early 1800s, John James Audubon warned that the species couldn't sustain such heavy hunting for long, but even he continued to shoot them, and the general public simply did not heed the warning. Thus we, supposedly the wisest species on the planet, squandered this magnificent and unique national treasure, one that had provided abundant natural food for us humans as well as for Peregrine Falcons.

Since Katie was born in 1983, we've lost the Dusky Seaside Sparrow forever, Bachman's Warbler has been declared officially extinct, and the Ivory-billed Woodpecker hangs on by a gossamer thread. How many extinct bird species preserved in a museum will Katie show her own children one day? And how will she explain to my grandchildren that it was my generation who squandered their inheritance?

Human Population Growth Is the Biggest Threat to Birds

Wouldn't it be lovely if there were just a few simple problems that could be easily solved to save birds? Unfortunately, the single biggest threat to birds is a monumental one: human population growth. According to the National Audubon Society's Population and Habitat Campaign:

> During the last 100 years, the world's population has quadrupled even as per capita consumption of natural resources has skyrocketed. At current birth rates, world population could double in the next 60 years. Even with rapidly declining birth rates, the population of the world is expected to increase by 50 percent in the next 50 years. To put it another way, the world will add more people in the next 50 years than existed in the world in 1950.
>
> While fertility has fallen in many countries and regions, demographic momentum means we are now adding a near-record number of people to the world's population every year. At present fertility rates, world population could double from 6 billion to 12 billion people by 2060.
>
> As the population of the world has risen from 1.5 billion people in 1900 to over 6.2 billion people today, forests have fallen to farms and freeways at breathtaking speed. As forests have become fragmented, wetlands drained, and coastal areas developed, many migrant song bird species have experienced rapid population declines.

Even a cursory glance at the satellite images in the United Nations Environment Program's massive 2005 book *One Planet Many People: Atlas of Our Changing Environment* shows the dramatic and often destructive changes that the increasing mass of human beings has made to our planet.

Except for limiting the size of our own families and supporting the efforts of national and international organizations to educate people and provide family planning services, there isn't much we can do as individuals to deal with this staggering issue—the root of most environmental issues and the most critical problem facing birds. But tackling many of the offshoot problems can help birds as well as our own species as we work out ways to improve the standard of living for humans throughout the world for generations to come.

Picture windows kill as many as a billion birds in the United States every year. House cats running loose kill hundreds of millions. Habitat loss eliminates even greater numbers. Lighted tall buildings and communication towers, pesticides, mercury and other toxins, acid rain, automobiles—the list of things that kill massive numbers of birds goes on and on. So many things are hurting birds right now that their situation is comparable to that of a person suffering from an autoimmune disease. For example, a patient with AIDS could die from Kaposi's sarcoma, a cold, or even an infected toe. Once the immune system is compromised, all manner of things can be lethal. Although some conservation issues are much larger than others, they're all important, and none should be ignored. Every action we take that helps a little is better than doing nothing at all. It is better to light a single candle than to curse the darkness. Of course, the more we do to help birds, the better, but even small steps move us forward. Still, it will take a concerted effort on all fronts to minimize the massive extinctions we face in the twenty-first century.

We All Have a Job to Do

Many of us love birds for the fun and diversion they provide us, and few of us have expertise in conservation or much stomach for politics. We have so many other responsibilities and pressures in this modern age. Why should we have to assume the burdens of conservation on top of all that?

When I made the decision to have children, it was because I wanted the fun and satisfaction of motherhood—songs and bedtime stories, smiles and giggling, birthday parties and Christmas traditions. Now that my children are in college, I take deep pleasure in their adventures and accomplishments. But suppose I'd wanted children for all the pleasure they provide yet refused to do the work involved in raising them. People may avoid some of the burdens of parenthood by hiring nannies or babysitters. They're like those of us who contribute money to conservation organizations to do the work for us. If done conscientiously, we can fulfill many of our obligations this way, but we still bear great responsibilities.

Birds are in trouble, and we who love them are obliged to do something about it. *To love* is an active verb. If God truly notices the fall of a single sparrow, surely he noted the death of an entire race when the Dusky Seaside Sparrow became extinct. In the Bible, God charged Noah with saving every species. According to the Religious Campaign for Forest Conservation:

> For reasons rooted in the moral principles of Judaism and Christianity, for reasons of sound science untainted by commercial manipulation, and for reasons dealing with our human responsibility to provide a healthy world for future generations, we see ourselves as morally bound to work for the protection and preservation of the forests and wilderness as crucial elements of the planet's life support system. We do this as our obedience to God and our service to humanity and particularly the children of today and tomorrow.

Yes, we owe it to our fellow human beings, to future generations whose survival and quality of life will depend on the environment we bequeath to them, and to God himself to protect these irreplaceable treasures.

I wish it were an easy matter to "save birds." Unfortunately, some of the problems they face are extremely complex, and figuring out the best ways to deal with them will take ingenuity as well as passion and commitment. Is it too late? Is it childish or naive to hope that we can actually make a difference? Margaret Mead wrote, "Never doubt that a small group of thoughtful, committed citizens can change the world. Indeed, it is the only thing that ever has."

It's time to roll up our sleeves and get to work.

PART I

HELPING BIRDS AT HOME

1

In the Kitchen

THE WAY TO A BIRD'S HEART MAY NOT BE THROUGH OUR STOMACHS, but our eating practices directly affect bird populations. The more aware we are of how our shopping habits and diet affect birds, the better their prospects are.

1 Wake up with bird-friendly coffee

Coffee comes from a shrub, *Coffea arabica,* that is related to gardenias and is native to the forest understory of East Africa. In dollar value, according to the Smithsonian Migratory Bird Center, coffee is second only to petroleum as the most important legal export commodity in the world. The United States consumes about one-third of the world's coffee. Although coffee originated in Africa, more than two-thirds is currently produced in the Caribbean and Latin America.

Wild, natural coffee plants require shade to grow. In the American tropics, coffee was traditionally grown in the understory of rain forests. Natural diversity, along with the trees' biochemical defenses against at least some of the insects and fungi that thrive in such a wet environment, helped minimize the pests that can easily destroy monocultures, so traditional coffee growers had few problems with disease or insects. The shade trees not only protected the coffee plants from too much rain and sun but also provided organic matter for natural mulch, reducing the need for fertilizer, protecting the soil from erosion, and contributing important nutrients to the soil. And these traditional coffee plantations, because they preserved or at least supported natural forest diversity, provided food and habitat for many birds, both tropical residents and neotropical migrants. In areas of the tropics that had been heavily deforested, shade-grown coffee plantations were often the last refuge for forest-adapted plants and animals. Today, shade coffee, especially organic shade coffee, is grown primarily on small family-owned farms. Many experts and coffee connoisseurs believe that shade-grown coffee tastes better than sun-grown coffee. Shade coffee beans ripen more slowly, giving them more time to develop their full taste. And many of the shade-grown cultivars are "heirloom" varieties of the original coffee strains from Ethiopia.

Unfortunately, the huge economic value of coffee has led to more intensive growing techniques. Some "shade-grown" coffee is actually grown on plantations where the natural vegetation has been cleared away and the coffee planted in rows under screening, keeping out natural vegetation and birds and other wildlife that depend on it. People have also developed coffee cultivars that can be grown in the sun, planted like corn-fields. Either way, plantation owners grow more coffee per acre, but at the cost of heavy use of fertilizers, pesticides, and irrigation; the rapid depletion and erosion of the soil; and the loss of many natural plants and animals. Some sun-grown coffee in Costa Rica and Brazil is organic, meaning that no pesticides are used to grow it, but even organic sun-grown coffee plantations destroy valuable tropical habitat and drastically reduce the number of species that can survive in the area.

Interestingly, the huge amount of transpiration from tropical plants produces much of the rain and clouds in tropical forests. Cutting rain forest for any monoculture actually alters the local climate, reducing the natural rainfall and cloud cover. The continuing use of irrigation, chemical fertilizers, and pesticides makes these intensive plantations impractical except for large landowners and corporations that can afford to move on when one area becomes too depleted and damaged to support coffee growth. And without the variety of tropical trees and bromeliads to hold and slowly release what rain does fall, it takes many, many years for natural forest regeneration once a coffee plantation is abandoned.

Natural shade-grown coffee farms are diverse enough to sustain about two-thirds of the natural bird species found in the rain forest, whereas monoculture coffee plantations support barely one-tenth of the natural bird population. Buying organic shade-grown coffee helps tropical birds, helps the many U.S. and Canadian birds that winter in the tropics, and helps small farmers earn a living.

Since either shade- or sun-grown coffee can be grown on monoculture plantations, how can we know whether the coffee we buy is truly bird friendly? The Smithsonian Migratory Bird Center has established criteria

Cerulean Warbler

for the best coffee-growing techniques for supporting bird populations. Coffee carrying its "Bird Friendly" logo is certified as shade grown and organic by an independent third-party inspector using the Smithsonian's criteria. The National Audubon Society, American Birding Association, and Rainforest Alliance also sell organic shade-grown coffees that support bird populations. At the very least, coffee marked "fair trade" is more likely to be grown in sustainable ways by family farmers.

Whenever you order coffee at a coffee shop or restaurant, ask whether the coffee is organic and shade grown. Wait staff and managers probably won't know what you're talking about, and people working at gourmet coffee shops are usually unfamiliar with how damaging coffee plantations are for birds. So be prepared to explain the importance of the issue in a simple, clear way. The more demand there is for bird-safe coffee, the more likely these establishments are to start offering it and encouraging growers to change their agricultural techniques. Encourage those at your workplace, church, and other organizations or clubs to serve coffee with the Smithsonian "Bird Friendly" logo. It costs a little more than most coffees, so perhaps you can make a contribution to help defray the cost and demonstrate how important this issue is.

2 Eat lower on the food chain, and especially eat less beef

Cattle, pork, and poultry production harms the environment because of habitat destruction and loss, pesticide use, heavy water demand, disease, manure runoff into lakes and streams, and hormones and antibiotics working their way into natural systems. It requires far more acres to produce the same number of calories of meat than of vegetables or grains. And intensive "factory farms," where animals are overcrowded and stressed, can become hotbeds of disease and are a primary source of bird flu (which might more appropriately be called "overcrowded poultry flu"), salmonella, conjunctivitis, and other disease organisms. Meat production in particular causes a huge array of serious problems for birds.

Habitat destruction. Grazing cattle can degrade natural grassland habitat, especially when too many cattle are grown per acre. Overgrazing in the American West has destroyed a great deal of valuable habitat, causing population crashes among Sage Grouse and other species. Forested habitat, especially in the tropics, is destroyed by cutting and burning to provide more farmland for beef and the crops used for cattle feed. About 57 percent of U.S. corn production, 45 million acres, is used for livestock feed. An additional 60 million acres are used to grow hay crops. That's more than 100 million acres—larger than the state of California—devoted to nothing but meat.

Disease organisms. Antibiotics are used to stimulate livestock growth as well as for disease control. According to the Centers for Disease Control and Prevention, more than 50 million pounds of antibiotics are produced in the United States each year. The Union of Concerned Scientists, which advocates against the overuse of antibiotics, says that 70 percent of the total antibiotic use in the United States is for livestock. But the more antibiotics are used, the more rapidly pathogens develop resistance to them, rendering the antibiotics less potent for treating or curing diseases. According to a November 3, 2001, *New York Times* editorial by Ellen Silbergeld and Polly Walker:

> Cipro, despite its current fame for preventing and treating anthrax, is in danger of becoming a casualty of what might be called the post-antibiotic age. Bayer, the maker of Cipro, also sells a chemically similar drug called Baytril, which is used in large-scale poultry production worldwide. The widespread use of Baytril in chickens has already been shown to decrease Cipro's effectiveness in humans for some types of infections.
>
> Bacteria have always adapted to our new drugs faster and more efficiently than we can adapt to their genetic changes. Through prudent use, we can preserve the effectiveness of our drugs for use in treating human disease while we search nature and chemistry for new defenses. Yet we are now squandering this precious resource by using powerful antibiotics carelessly for livestock and poultry— mostly for nontherapeutic reasons.

Tragically, more and more bacteria are becoming resistant not only to one antibiotic but to many. Antibiotic-resistant bacteria may transfer resistance genes to other bacteria, and these resistant bacteria can be transferred between animals and between animals and people.

Consumers who are aware of this problem can encourage farmers or even pressure the government to minimize the use of antibiotics, especially for nontherapeutic reasons such as growth promotion. If we can find out where meat comes from and refuse to buy from companies that overcrowd their livestock or poultry or use antibiotics to promote rapid growth, we can protect both ourselves and wildlife from the spread of more virulent diseases.

Antibiotics aside, growing any livestock in overcrowded conditions allows disease organisms to flourish. Mycoplasmal conjunctivitis *(Mycoplasma gallisepticum)*, which has taken a huge toll on the eastern population of House Finches, may have originated on high-production turkey farms. Bird flu reaches humans via unsanitary, overcrowded poultry, not through wild birds. Mad cow disease is also linked to factory farming; cattle acquire the disease by eating commercial feed that contains the ground-up parts of infected animals.

Hormones. When hormones are added to cattle feed to increase meat or milk production, they may work their way not only into our bodies when we consume the products but also into our water, affecting birds, frogs, and other wildlife.

Water shortages. Livestock and poultry raised in confined spaces require a lot of water, mostly drawn from groundwater supplies. According to David Pimentel, professor of ecology in Cornell University's College of Agriculture and Life Sciences, "Producing a pound of animal protein requires, on average, about 100 times more water than producing a pound of vegetable protein." He noted that raising grain-fed beef takes 100,000 liters of water for every kilogram of food produced. Raising broiler chickens takes 3,500 liters of water to make a kilogram of meat. In comparison, soybean production uses 2,000 liters per kilogram of food produced; rice, 1,912; wheat, 900; and potatoes, 500. "Water shortages already are severe in the western and southern United States, and the situation is quickly becoming worse because of a rapidly growing U.S. population that requires more water for all of its needs, especially agriculture," Pimentel observed.

Genetically modified crops. More and more grain produced for livestock and poultry feed is genetically modified. Some genetic modifications render these crops toxic to butterfly larvae and other useful insects that feed birds; others make them resistant to pesticides so that farmers can increase the amount of herbicides they apply to their fields. Either way, genetically modified crops are fostering the evolution of resistant weeds and pests, which may ultimately lead to a vicious circle of even heavier pesticide applications. Also, genetically modified crops "spill over," cross-pollinating other crops. The Union of Concerned Scientists produced a report, *Gone to Seed,* that confirms the difficulty of preventing cross-pollination from genetically engineered crops that are grown in large quantities. According

Burrowing Owl

to analyses by two independent laboratories, five out of six samples of corn, soy, and cotton seeds certified as pure enough for commercial grade contained traces of genetically engineered DNA. The report warns that if the rules for segregating genetically engineered crops are not tightened as the number of engineered varieties grows, the entire U.S. food supply will soon be contaminated.

Fossil fuel use. Meat production requires fossil fuels to power tractors and harvesting equipment on grain fields, to transport animals to slaughterhouses and the market, and for refrigeration. Tracking the production of meat from the feed trough to the dinner table, David Pimentel found that broiler chickens represented the most efficient use of fossil fuel and beef the least efficient. Chicken production consumes energy in a 4:1 ratio to protein output; for beef cattle production, the ratio of energy input to protein output is 54:1. Lamb meat production is nearly as inefficient at 50:1, according to Pimentel's analysis of U.S. Department of Agriculture statistics. Other ratios are 13:1 for turkey meat, 14:1 for milk protein, 17:1 for pork, and 26:1 for eggs.

Pesticide toxicity. The American Bird Conservancy estimates that at least 672 million birds are directly exposed to pesticides on farms each year, and 10 percent of these, or roughly 67 million birds, die. According to the U.S. Fish and Wildlife Service, approximately fifty pesticides currently used in the United States have caused bird die-offs. Pesticide use is particularly heavy in corn production, and much corn is grown for cattle feed.

Mowing of nestlings. Many farmers now cut hay three times a season and begin cutting earlier, while many ground-nesting grassland birds are still nesting. Cutting hay (much of it for cattle feed), especially before the Fourth of July, may kill up to a million birds a year.

Soil erosion. Livestock is directly or indirectly responsible for much of the soil erosion in the United States. Pimentel found that on lands where feed grain is produced, soil loss averages 13 tons per hectare per year. Pasturelands are eroding at a slower pace, averaging 6 tons per hectare per year. However, erosion may exceed 100 tons on severely overgrazed pastures, and 54 percent of U.S. pastureland is being overgrazed.

Some beef production methods cause less harm than others. Melissa Driscoll, a University of Minnesota researcher, studies the effects of grazing practices on grassland birds and their reproductive success. She writes:

In my neck of the woods, less than 1 percent of original native prairie areas remain for grassland birds to nest in. Instead, they depend on pastures and hayfields to nest and raise their young. In large part because U.S. farm policy supports the corn and soybean market with price subsidies, most beef and dairy cattle in Minnesota are fed grain in feedlots and huge dairy barns. The pastures that could be providing habitat for declining grassland birds (such as Eastern and Western Meadowlarks, Upland Sandpipers, Bobolinks, and Henslow's Sparrows) as well as feeding cattle are plowed and turned into corn and soybean fields. Any person who eats beef or drinks milk can help protect habitat for grassland birds (and other creatures) by buying grass-fed beef, and milk from grazing cows. Farmers who depend on forage for their livelihood (and understand the long-term consequences of overgrazing) practice methods of grazing that support good nesting habitat. Pastures also prevent nutrient runoff and protect soil from erosion.

Farmers who cut pastures with scythes rather than tractors, identify where nests are located and leave a buffer zone as they cut, or wait until after the Fourth of July for their first cutting can minimize the numbers of birds killed.

It's hard to be sure what agricultural practices were used to produce a fast-food hamburger or even most meat we buy in grocery stores. The more we can curb our appetite for meat, the more we protect our own health as well as birds. But we don't need to be vegetarians to help birds when we eat. We help birds every time we buy meat marked "organic," "free range," or "grass fed" rather than feedlot or "corn fed." Buying locally grown meat minimizes the amount of fossil fuels used in transport and refrigeration, too.

3 Buy groceries with bird conservation in mind

Many other foods we buy are produced in bird-unfriendly ways. For example, most fruits and vegetables and virtually all the grains used to make cereals, breads, and flour are produced in monocultures using environmentally damaging farming methods such as irrigation, fertilizers, and pesticides. Jeff Pentel, who ran a bird-feeding store in Bozeman, Montana, during the 1990s, told me that his customers often reported dead and dying robins after crop dusters flew over potato fields. Agriculture and grazing often provide opportunities for invasive weeds to plague an area, spilling over into the more natural surroundings. Cheatgrass has taken over rangeland in the West, reducing the amount of sage grass and in turn contributing to a huge reduction in the population of Greater Sage Grouse.

Small family farms traditionally maintained fencerows and other remnants of natural habitat. But now many crops are grown intensively in monocultures, destroying even the smallest remnants of natural habitat. Growing sugar involves pesticides and heavy irrigation as well as habitat disruption. Sugarcane fields have encroached on the Florida Everglades, causing devastating and lasting damage to this fragile and important national treasure. Orange groves, tea plantations, and corn, wheat, and soybean fields are also proliferating. As the human population grows, more of the earth is converted to agricultural uses to feed people.

Some methods of agriculture are far more sustainable over the long term than others. The increasingly intensive agricultural practices of corporate farms are much more damaging than the practices of many family farms. Because of legal requirements, any food labeled "organic" must have been grown without pesticides or manufactured fertilizers and is generally more bird-friendly compared with other foods. But it can be tricky to identify which products were produced in ways that are safe for birds. Here are some foods with serious implications for birds.

Fish and seafood. Consumers should demand that the fish sold in grocery stores bear labels indicating how much mercury it contains. Only if consumers are aware of mercury levels will they start calling for power companies, other corporations, and the government to reduce mercury emissions and clean up after themselves. Refusing to buy fish with high levels of mercury also encourages the fishing, food processing, and retailing industries to put pressure on the government to set strict limits for mercury emissions and to enforce those limits. This not only protects human health; it also protects the eagles, osprey, herons, and other birds that share our appetite for fish.

Ocean fish are caught in ways that kill many seabirds each year. According to the American Bird Conservancy:

> Hundreds of thousands of albatrosses and other seabirds are being killed each year by the fleets of longline fishing vessels which now crisscross the world's oceans. The longliners set lines up to 60 miles long and may use up to 30,000 baited hooks on each set to

catch tuna, swordfish, cod, halibut, Patagonian toothfish (Chilean sea bass), and other fish. While the longlines are being set behind the fishing boats, albatrosses and other seabirds grab the bait and become impaled on the barbed hooks, either caught by their bills, or hooked into their bodies or wings. Dragged under the surface, the birds are unable to free themselves and drown. Data show that this mortality is having a significant impact on populations, with many species showing rapid recent declines. Scientists now fear that unless action is taken, many seabird species will become extinct.

Although longlining is increasing, an alternative does exist. According to the American Bird Conservancy:

> Bird-scaring or "tori" lines (*tori* meaning bird in Japanese) have been shown to virtually eliminate seabird mortality caused by longlines. They were first developed by Japanese bluefin tuna fishermen who recognized that keeping birds off bait was in their own economic interest, as leaving more bait for fish increases the chances of success. The tori lines are mounted on poles at the stern of the boat, and are connected to a floating buoy that is dragged behind the vessel. Colored streamers are attached to the lines, and these flap erratically in the wind above the area where the bait enters the water. When the longlines are properly weighted, they sink immediately behind the boat and the flapping streamers scare the birds away. By the time the baited hooks are beyond the streamer zone, they have already sunk below the depth where they can be reached by most seabirds. In Hawaii, where lines are set at shallower depths than in Alaska, regulations are in place that require thawing the bait so it sinks more quickly, dyeing bait blue so it is less visible to birds, adding weights so the lines sink more quickly, setting lines at night when fewer birds are feeding, and strategically discharging offal during line setting, so that birds are attracted away from the boat's stern where the lines are set (or not discharging offal at all, so fewer birds are attracted to the boat). These measures also have been shown to be effective means of reducing seabird mortality.

But how are consumers to know whether the fish or seafood they buy was captured in a bird-safe manner? Until informative labeling becomes mandatory, you can carry a "Pocket Seafood Selector," offered for free on the Web sites of several environmental organizations, that can help you make quick decisions in restaurants or grocery stores.

Corn. Corn is one of the most pesticide-intensive of all crops. In the same way that pathogens can develop resistance to antibiotics, insects can develop resistance to pesticides. Intensive and prolonged use of any insecticide creates a high selection pressure for pests that are resistant to the pesticide. Thus, insects may rapidly become resistant, leading to the use of even more pesticides. Sometimes, in secondary outbreaks, the pests come back much stronger than those in the original infestation, due to both their own increased resistance and the loss of natural predators. And with just about all pesticides, there is a serious risk of toxicity or deleterious health effects in nontarget species, including humans.

One form of genetically modified corn was developed to limit the need for broad-spectrum insecticides. "Btk corn" includes genetic material from a naturally occurring soil bacterium, *Bacillus thuringiensis,* which produces a protein that kills the larvae of butterflies and moths. The intended target of this "built-in pesticide" was the European corn borer, a caterpillar that not only damages corn directly but also indirectly fosters fungal growth in the damaged corn. The whole point of developing Btk corn was to reduce the dependence on dangerous insecticides and fungicides, and indeed, Btk cornfields are safer for birds than are other nonorganic cornfields. Unfortunately, nontarget insects, including monarch butterflies, that feed on Btk corn or on the leaves of nearby plants where the corn pollen collects can be killed too, although almost certainly fewer than are killed when a cornfield is sprayed with insecticides.

However, the contamination of nongenetically modified crops and even naturally occurring plants by genetically modified pollen may present a long-term danger for birds and for us. A 2004 University of Wisconsin study found that "genetically modified crops can spread artificially inserted genes to similar wild plants despite attempts at containing them." "These [genes] could escape from our ability to control them effectively," according to wildlife ecology professor Stanley Temple. "Extremely valuable gene pools could change in a way that might result in a loss of genetic variation . . . and lead to [extinctions]." The article continued, "Another possible result of escaping transgenes is an increase in the tenacity of wild plants considered weeds, because they would share the same resistance to pests, herbicides and unfavorable climates that crops containing the genes have." Of course, a resistance to caterpillars would also make them more likely to kill beneficial butterflies and moths, including those species that provide an important food source for birds.

Obviously, the situation is nuanced and complex. How are consumers supposed to make wise decisions about which corn and other field crops to buy? Right now, there is no way to tell from a label whether the product was treated with pesticides, genetically modified, or grown in an environmentally sensitive area, unless it is clearly labeled "organic." And even if such important data were included on labels, it still wouldn't be easy to make the wisest and most bird-friendly choice when buying groceries. But the more information we have about the environmental implications of the foods we eat, and the more we keep abreast of new information, the better decisions we can make. Meanwhile, reducing our use of corn oil and corn syrup and of the products that contain them is a start.

Chocolate. Chocolate comes from a small tree of the tropical rain forest interior, *Theobroma cacao*. Chocolate production isn't as big an industry as coffee production, but many of the same concerns about damage to the rain forest exist. Searching for organic chocolate produced in sustainable ways helps both tropical birds and our own neotropical migrants. The Rainforest Alliance certifies chocolate grown using environmentally friendly, sustainable methods.

Tea. Tea, like coffee, is grown on huge plantations in tropical areas. Although tea is grown mostly in Asia, where it doesn't affect North American birds, it poses the same risks to Asian birds, other wildlife, and plants as coffee plantations do in the Americas. Some companies work harder than others to ensure that tea is grown in a sustainable, environmentally friendly way. But unlike coffee, it isn't easy to identify bird-friendly teas yet. Doing research on the Internet about your favorite brands of tea and other products may help you discover which companies are more likely to be using sustainable or even organic agricultural methods.

Sugar. Sugarcane and sugar beets are both grown intensively, often requiring heavy irrigation and pesticides. Processing these crops into sugar also causes problems, including excessively rich discharge that contributes to the eutrophication of waterways. Like just about everything, sugar is not a substance to be wasted.

In the final analysis, until food is accurately labeled, buying locally produced, organic groceries is better for ourselves, for birds, and for the environment.

4 Compost as much kitchen waste as possible

As increasing numbers of people put greater pressure on municipal sewer systems, nutrient loads on water supplies become increasingly dangerous, ultimately contributing to dead zones in the ocean and to eutrophication of fresh water, both of which degrade water quality for many aquatic organisms and the birds that depend on them. When we dispose of food wastes in the garbage, they add to the nutrients seeping into groundwater or running off into lakes, rivers, ponds, and streams from the landfill. Garbage disposals contribute not only to nutrient loads but also to wastewater; in addition, grease, oil, peanut butter, and other items may harden in the drain or in the sewage system.

It's better to put greasy food garbage in a container (cardboard juice boxes and milk cartons work well) to dispose of it in the garbage. Also, wrap and dispose of bones, cheese, eggs, and other animal products in the garbage. To minimize food waste, as well as to minimize your contribution to the problems associated with food production, don't prepare more food than will actually be eaten.

Composting discarded vegetable items and eggshells provides a wonderful resource for improving your backyard soil while minimizing your contribution to environmental problems. The simplest compost pile can be a pile of leaves, grass clippings, and kitchen waste (use only plant waste and eggshells—not meat, eggs, cheese, and the like) in an unobtrusive corner of the yard. If you want to accelerate the composting process, mix "greens" (grass clippings, vegetable peelings, coffee, and eggshells) and "browns" (dried leaves or cow or horse manure). Because dogs and cats eat meat, their waste shouldn't be composted; dispose of it in the garbage, flush it, or bury it.

Select a shady spot for your compost pile, where runoff is unlikely. Compost piles set too close to storm sewers or on hills can cause nutrients to run off.

5 Recycle plastic six-pack rings, aluminum cans, and plastic bags

Occasionally, plastic six-pack rings from beer and soda cans ensnare or entangle birds at landfills and other places. Once, while birding along the Rio Grande in Texas, I spotted an Anhinga in the river with a plastic six-pack ring in a chokehold around its throat. The bird looked sick and distressed; its throat, swollen above the ring, was probably filled with decaying fish that the bird had caught but couldn't swallow and couldn't spit out. The poor creature was swimming too far out for me to even try to catch it, and no one in the group knew where to find a rehabber.

It's unlikely that a person dropped the six-pack ring at the river. Someone probably removed it from a six-pack at home and threw it in the wastebasket. After the garbage reached the landfill, it became lethal. Perhaps a crow looking for nesting material carried it off and dropped it; perhaps the wind blew it into the water. But somehow the Anhinga thrust its narrow beak and head into it and couldn't get it out again. I also saw a Ring-billed Gull with a six-pack ring stuck around its neck at a Wisconsin landfill.

Metal rings and lids from cans can also be picked up by birds, harming them. In April 2004, a yearling Whooping Crane from the Whooping Crane Eastern Partnership's reintroduction program was almost killed when it inserted its bill into the ragged top of an aluminum can that cut into its lower mandible; luckily, its blood-clotted wounds appeared clean when the can was removed. Ironically, the can clearly bore the words, "Dispose of properly." It's unlikely that this fate befalls many birds, but even a single Whooping Crane hurt in this senseless way is one too many. Aluminum cans should always be crushed and recycled.

Plastic grocery bags can also harm birds. The "Save Our Seabirds" Web site has a photo of a Brown Pelican trapped in a plastic bag. Again, the best way to dispose of these is to recycle them. It's not a bad idea to tie plastic bags in knots before recycling. That way, if they do end up getting blown out of a recycling bin, they won't billow up and pose a danger.

Although the cases we see are dramatic and distressing, the problems associated with six-pack rings, pop-top aluminum rings, and plastic bags are fairly insignificant compared with other issues. But why risk hurting even one bird when the solution is so simple?

2

AROUND THE HOUSE

THE HOUSES WE LIVE IN HAVE A DIRECT IMPACT (SOMETIMES LITER-
ally) on our local birds. Being aware of how house location and design
and home furnishings can affect birds allows us to make wise decisions
about our own quality of life while protecting the birds we love.

6 Make your windows safer for birds

People have known that windows can kill birds since at least
1832; that's the earliest published account I could find of a bird
hitting a window in North America, written by Thomas Nuttall in *A Man-
ual of the Ornithology of the United States and of Canada*. He described a
Sharp-shinned Hawk that, while pursuing prey, flew through two panes of
greenhouse glass and was killed by a third. Most home owners have had at
least one experience with a bird kill at a window, and for decades, various
ornithological museums have been adding window-killed specimens to
their bird collections. In fact, more birds are killed each year from striking
windows than from any other direct cause of death, and the problem is
growing as window sizes increase and houses get larger.

When a bird strikes a window, sometimes it flies off immediately or
shortly thereafter, but many of these injured birds have fractured their beaks,
suffered hairline skull fractures, or developed hematomas or other serious
injuries that will kill them within hours or days. Birds that hit windows are
often picked up by predators that have learned to associate the familiar
"thud" with an easy meal. In 2004 I was sitting at a window when a Yellow-rumped Warbler struck it; within two seconds a Blue Jay flew in and
picked up the stunned little bird. Research indicates that at least half of all
birds that hit windows end up dying, either directly from trauma, from predation or accidents that occur while the bird is stunned, or later from inter-

nal injuries. When I was rehabilitating wild birds, several people brought me woodpeckers that they thought were going to be fine because the birds seemed alert and could move their wings, but on examination, I discovered that they were paralyzed, incapable of any controlled movement whatsoever; these birds always died.

Window strikes may happen only once or twice a year at some windows, while other windows may kill hundreds of birds annually, particularly during migration or when birds are concentrated at feeding stations. Multiply this by all the windows in America, and the problem becomes staggering, especially as average house and window sizes increase. Dr. Daniel Klem Jr., an ornithologist at Muhlenberg College, states, "Glass is ubiquitous and it's indiscriminate, killing the fit and the unfit." After decades of research, Klem estimated that collisions with glass kill 100 million to 1 billion birds in the United States every year; he believes that the upper limit of this estimate is conservative and that only habitat destruction is responsible for the loss of more birds.

Until Klem started researching the magnitude of the problem, ornithologists and conservationists focused on other issues that were considered more important to bird conservation. Now, as researchers gather more data about the extent of this problem and search for viable solutions, perhaps we can envision a day when all new windows will be made from more bird-safe technologies.

Klem has been researching different ways of manufacturing glass to make it more visible to birds. Glass etched with closely spaced dots or other patterns may help birds see it without detracting from a window's aesthetic qualities. Angling windows downward, so that they reflect ground rather than sky, can help, but it's difficult and expensive to change already constructed windows, and no windows currently manufactured have casings designed for this. But Klem seems hopeful: "The heart of this is to get a piece of glass that will solve this problem. We can't say that we have that yet. But I'm more encouraged than ever that we can come up with a solution that will stop this senseless slaughter of wildlife." Developing bird-safe glass will take time and money, and only when consumers start demanding it will manufacturers go to the trouble of funding studies and changing their manufacturing practices.

Meanwhile, while we wait for more permanent solutions, we have to figure out how to minimize the death toll at our own windows. The windows on single-family dwellings kill mainly feeder visitors, other resident backyard birds, and, during migration, ovenbirds, cuckoos, and other low-flying migrants that are passing through. Whether the glass is clear or reflective, birds simply don't see it.

Klem discovered that the distance between feeders and a window is directly related to the number of feeder birds killed at that window. Feeders placed directly on the window glass or within three feet of it are significantly safer than those placed farther away. Birds at window feeders are more likely to see the glass, and even if they don't, when they take off from a window feeder they aren't going at top speed for at least a few wing beats. When feeders are farther away but still close enough to the windows for us to enjoy watching the birds (within about thirty feet), window kills are inevitable.

Besides placing feeders right outside windows, what else can we do to reduce or eliminate kills?

Absorb the impact. Put something outside the window glass that will absorb the impact when birds do hit it. A window screen or netting works very well if it's set three or four inches from the glass and is taut enough to actually "catch" a bird and bounce it off, like a trampoline, before the bird reaches the glass.

Make the glass more visible. The following things can help birds see windows (listed roughly from most to least effective):

- One-way transparent film that permits people on the inside to see out but appears opaque on the outside. The best product currently available is CollidEscape, marketed by Large Format Digital. This prevents birds from both colliding into the glass and fighting their reflections. Part of the purchase price supports the Fatal Light Awareness Program.
- Vertical exterior tape strips, set no more than four inches apart on the glass.
- External shutters that are kept closed when you're not taking advantage of the light or the view.
- External sun shades or awnings, to reduce reflections of the sky.
- Windows angled downward. This is possible only on houses under construction or when putting in new windows, but kills are reduced when the glass reflects the ground rather than the sky and trees.
- Interior vertical blinds with the slats half open.
- Soap on the outside of the window.
- Decals, sun catchers, Mylar strips, or other objects on the outer surface of the glass. These should be set close enough that an open adult handprint can't fit between them.

During migration, and particularly on foggy nights, when nocturnal migrants are disoriented, birds are drawn to lights on tall buildings jutting into their migration pathway. Once in the lighted area, they mill about, striking one another, the windows, or the building itself. Volunteers for the Fatal Light Awareness Program (the pioneering organization with regard to this issue), Lights Out Chicago, and other groups monitor kills at lighted high-rise buildings. These organizations provide educational programs to encourage owners and residents of tall buildings to turn off unnecessary lights and close drapes or blinds at night, especially during migration, to minimize the death rate. Research by Dr. Robert DeCandido and Deborah Allen is currently being done at the Empire State Building in New York to evaluate bird collision patterns in the vicinity of large lighted buildings so that these structures, romantically called "the nearest thing to heaven," stop dispatching birds to heaven before their time.

7 Know what to do when a bird hits your window

If a bird slams into your window and isn't moving or is fluttering helplessly, what should you do? Is it best to leave the bird alone or to interfere?

If an injured bird is lying on its back, it may go into what seems to be a hypnotic state and simply be unable to balance or right itself. If you don't help, it may die unnecessarily. But how do you help? First, protect yourself. Most songbirds, even chickadees, can pack a wallop with their beaks but are usually harmless while in a dazed state. However, the talons on even a semi-conscious hawk can cause serious injuries. Wear thick leather gloves to handle hawks or owls.

Never put any wild bird into a cage. Its feathers may become frayed against the metal bars, compromising its ability to fly.

The best way to help a bird after a window strike is to gently place it right side up on a branch in a dense shrub to see if it can perch properly. If it can, it has a chance of recovering on its own. If it can't, put it in a small cardboard box, propped if necessary in a "donut cushion" fashioned out of tissue. For most backyard birds, a shoebox is perfect. Close the box and place it in a quiet place. Every ten or fifteen minutes, take the box outdoors, open it, and see if the bird flies off. Never open the box indoors. And don't release a songbird after dusk—wait until morning. If the bird is ready to leave, it will usually be able to take off from the box. If not, hold it in your hand as you try to release it, but don't toss it in the air to "launch" it. Just open your hand and be patient—you can gently touch its tail to see if that speeds up the process.

Most birds with minor concussions recover within an hour or two if they're going to recover at all. If blood or black spinal fluid is coming from the mouth, the bird is most likely fatally injured. Otherwise, there is at least a chance that it will recover. If the bird doesn't fly away soon, get it to a wildlife rehabilitation facility as soon as possible, transporting it in a cardboard box or a large paper sack.

8 Build or choose a home with the least impact on the natural world

All of us compete with birds and other wildlife for space and habitat. As our own species spreads out, wild habitats become fragmented or lost altogether. This land-use pattern promotes deer, skunks, cowbirds, predators, and other "edge" species at the expense of those that thrive in forest, grassland, and wetland interiors. The more habitat each person consumes, the greater the total impact on the natural world.

A growing human population places higher demands on natural resources and contributes to the loss of natural habitat. Exacerbating the problem, Americans are living on increasingly larger lots and building increasingly larger homes, individually appropriating more space and resources and leaving less room for wildlife and the regeneration of resources that we all depend on.

Making urban homes and neighborhoods as pleasant as possible is one of the best ways to protect the natural world. Living in an apartment or condo in a city has a far smaller per-person impact on the natural world than living anywhere else. The smaller the area required for each human, the more land can remain natural. So the more habitable our urban areas are, the happier people can be without contributing to continued sprawl.

Most big cities are built on shorelines or in other areas with important natural resources. The vast majority of birds that migrate from the tropics to northern forests pass through cities during their migration. Promoting and enforcing strong regulations with regard to sewage, garbage, industrial waste, and other pollutants and encouraging comfortable, efficient, and affordable mass transit can protect the natural environment and make cities more healthy and livable for humans. When cities retain as much "green space" as possible, they not only help birds and other wildlife directly but also become more pleasant for all of us. According to the Seattle Audubon Society, "A livable city needs a vibrant, healthy urban green infrastructure, an interconnected system of fish-bearing creeks, backyard habitats, community gardens, neighborhood parks, greenbelts, and wetlands—for wildlife and people to enjoy." When cities become unlivable, people tend to migrate

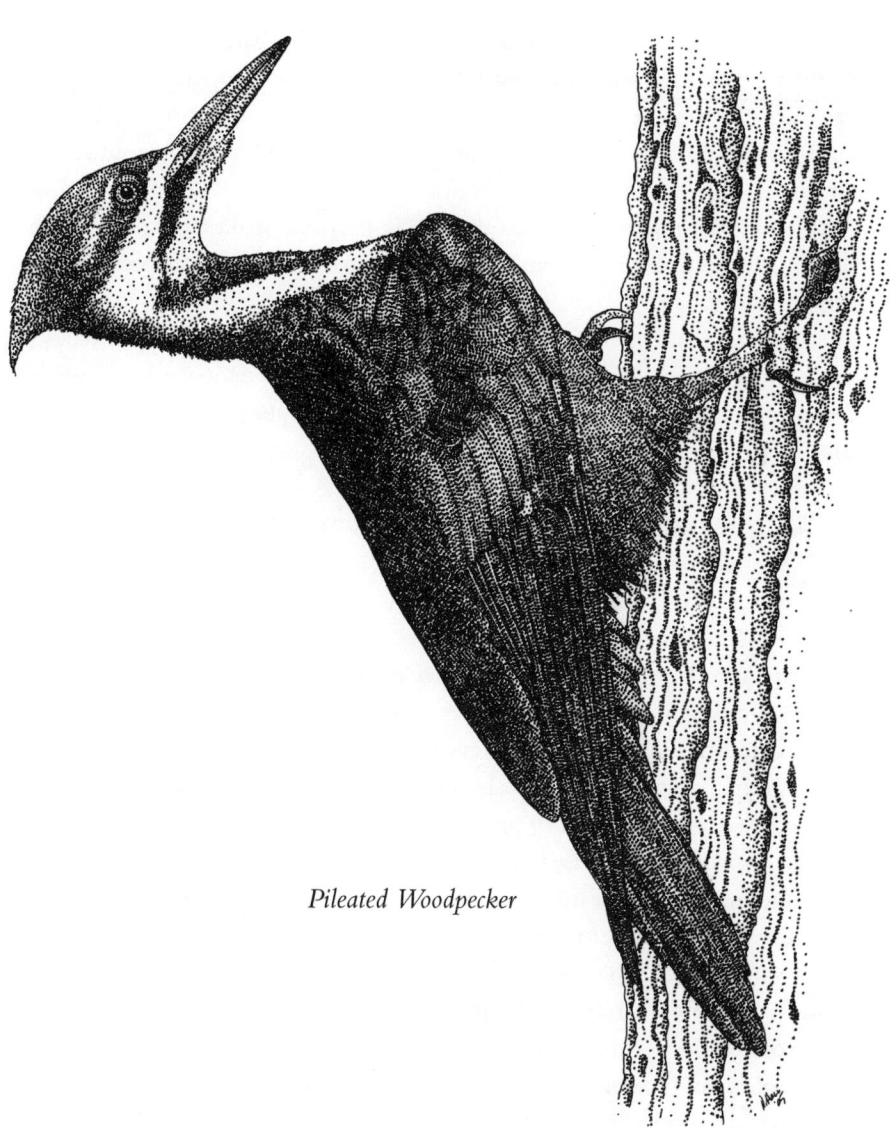

Pileated Woodpecker

to the suburbs, building bigger houses on bigger lots and taking up more natural habitat.

Many people dislike cities and are happiest when they live in natural settings, among natural sights and sounds. People who find satisfaction in a large home on a sprawling lot are going to buy just that, if they can afford it. But by making our homes and lots as bird-friendly as possible, we can at least minimize our personal impact on the natural world and, as a bonus, almost invariably make our home environments healthier and more pleasant for us, too.

Live in the smallest home on the smallest lot that makes you happy. Join neighborhood groups that work actively to make our cities as pleasant for humans and urban wildlife as possible, and support programs that encourage nature study in urban areas, such as the Cornell Laboratory of Ornithology's Urban Bird Studies. Henry David Thoreau wisely understood that "in wildness is the preservation of the world." But on a planet populated with billions of humans, in cities is the preservation of the wildness.

9 Avoid buying or building a home on a floodplain, coast, or shoreline

Like all animals, human beings are drawn to water. Unfortunately, habitat near bodies of water is among the most vulnerable to damage from development. The effects of normal flooding and high-water situations are worsened when houses, pavement, and turf replace the natural vegetation and wetlands associated with shorelines. Houses not only diminish the habitat quality but also contribute to the severity of storm and flood damage, since their very presence reduces the amount of moisture the soil can absorb and increases the amount of debris, sewage, fuel, and other toxic chemicals released from damaged houses and automobiles.

When towns and cities preserve coastal lands as green space, they provide a valuable resource for residents and tourists to enjoy and reduce the pressure on their own infrastructure and emergency responders during and after storms and floods. People with flood damage should use their insurance settlements to relocate rather than to rebuild, especially if floods are likely every twenty years or less.

Of course, people will always be drawn to shorelines despite the danger to nature and to themselves. If you already have a shoreline home or have a deep and specific desire to get one, take special care to landscape your property to preserve as much of the natural environment as possible, design your windows to minimize both bird strikes and breakage in storms, and make sure that all construction meets the most up-to-date standards to minimize storm damage.

10 Buy lumber or furniture with a Sustainable Forestry Initiative or Forest Stewardship Council logo, or buy used

The earth is losing forests at an alarming rate for many reasons, including cattle production, agricultural crop production, commercial logging for lumber and pulp, and development. Deforestation causes enormous and wide-scale environmental problems that hurt us as well as birds and other wildlife. Choosing products that are grown and harvested using sustainable methods helps all of us.

Global problems caused by deforestation include increased carbon dioxide (CO_2) and other gases. When trees are cut and burned to establish cropland and pastures, the carbon that was stored in the tree trunks (wood is about 50 percent carbon) joins with oxygen and is released into the atmosphere as CO_2. According to "Earth Observatory":

> The loss of forests has a profound effect on the global carbon cycle. From 1850 to 1990, deforestation worldwide (including the United States) released 122 billion metric tons of carbon into the atmosphere, with the current rate being approximately 1.6 billion metric tons per year. In comparison, fossil fuel burning (coal, oil, and gas) releases about 6 billion metric tons per year, so it is clear that deforestation makes a significant contribution to the increasing CO_2 in the atmosphere. Releasing CO_2 into the atmosphere enhances the greenhouse effect, and could contribute to an increase in global temperatures.

Deforestation can cause dramatic changes in local climates. In Costa Rica, reduced rainfall and increasing temperature likely contributed to the extinction of the Golden Toad. This beautiful amphibian lived in the highland "cloud forests" near Monteverde, so called because of the frequent formation of clouds and mist as the moisture-laden Caribbean winds rise up the eastern slopes of the mountains. The humidity in those breezes is enhanced by moisture expelled from the leaves of lowland forests. But by the early 1990s, only 18 percent of the Costa Rican lowland forests east of the peaks remained. Pastures don't humidify the winds as forests do, and the atmosphere above pastures is warmer than that over forests. So the winds off these pastures must rise farther up the slopes before clouds condense. Golden Toads depended on high humidity, and their sudden and dramatic disappearance gave intimations of more extinctions to come.

We think of deforestation as a Third World problem, yet in the Pacific Northwest, less than 15 percent of the original old-growth forest ecosystem remains. According to the Seattle Audubon Society, although the Northwest Forest Plan decreased logging by 80 percent, the Forest Service continues to use mature and old-growth forests for 90 percent of their timber volume. During the 1800s, the white pine forest dominating the Great Lakes region was almost entirely logged. Now most of that region's forests are dominated by aspen, a pioneer species that is usually clear-cut for paper and wood products such as plywood and particleboard long before the forest can mature. And chip mills in the southeastern United States contribute to the clear-cutting of more than a million acres of forest every year.

When buying furniture and other wood products, remember that used products save trees. And when buying new, remember that furniture made of saw lumber comes from forests that were allowed to grow to maturity, making it a better choice than particleboard or plywood, which come from forests managed for short rotation and are manufactured with an array of toxic chemicals. As with food, it's far better to buy wood that was grown locally. Besides it minimizing the environmental problems associated with transporting lumber, you'll generally get more accurate information about wood that was harvested nearby than about products from far away.

The Sustainable Forestry Initiative (SFI) and the Forest Stewardship Council (FSC) are organizations devoted to encouraging the responsible management of the world's forests. They set standards to ensure that forestry is practiced in an environmentally responsible, socially beneficial, and economically viable way. Their certification programs are endorsed by hundreds of environmental organizations.

11 Recycle thermometers, button batteries, fluorescent bulbs, and other mercury-containing objects

When we junk an old car or throw out garbage, whether it is incinerated or put in a landfill, any poisons within will eventually work their way into the environment. Mercury, which is dangerous for birds and humans even at extremely low levels, is added to a surprising number of common household items and may be released into the air and water when these items are thrown out. Computers, other electronics, and batteries contain many toxic metals and should be recycled or disposed of at a hazardous waste facility. Even automobiles contain mercury—the fleet of American-made cars for the 2000 model year contain 10,000 pounds of mercury in their light switches. Foreign-made cars had phased out all mercury by 1995.

Neurological damage and reproductive failure from mercury poisoning have been documented in many species. Bald Eagle eggs often fail to hatch when mercury is concentrated at more than 1.0 part per million. Concentrations as high as 19.1 parts per million, levels that cause sterility, have been found in the feathers of eagle chicks. Some adult birds have been killed outright by high concentrations; others have shown impaired flight, aberrant behaviors, and kidney lesions.

Although coal-burning power plants are one of the biggest sources of atmospheric mercury, incinerating municipal garbage is also a huge source. Making sure that our garbage doesn't contain mercury is critical. Unfortunately, mercury is added to products that most of us don't even think about. When we dispose of these items, mercury can seep into groundwater or be released into the atmosphere to come back down to earth in rain. By recycling every household item that has mercury, we limit our contribution to the problem. Of course, selecting products that don't contain mercury at all would be best, but sometimes we have to weigh more complex issues. For example, where electricity is generated from burning coal, high-efficiency fluorescent bulbs might save enough electricity to offset the amount of mercury the bulbs contain, especially if you recycle them. Unfortunately, when lightbulbs burst or break, vaporized mercury escapes into the atmosphere. Before recycling, all burned-out fluorescent bulbs should be tightly sealed in plastic.

The National Wildlife Federation's *Mercury Products Guide* lists the following common items that contain mercury:
- Fever thermometers (choose electronic thermometers)
- Car door and refrigerator light switches
- Some gas-fired stoves and dryers (with mercury flame sensors as a safety device)
- Products with automatic shut-off switches, such as steam irons, curling irons, space heaters, and sump pumps
- Fluorescent bulbs, halogen lights, neon lights, and many automobile headlamps

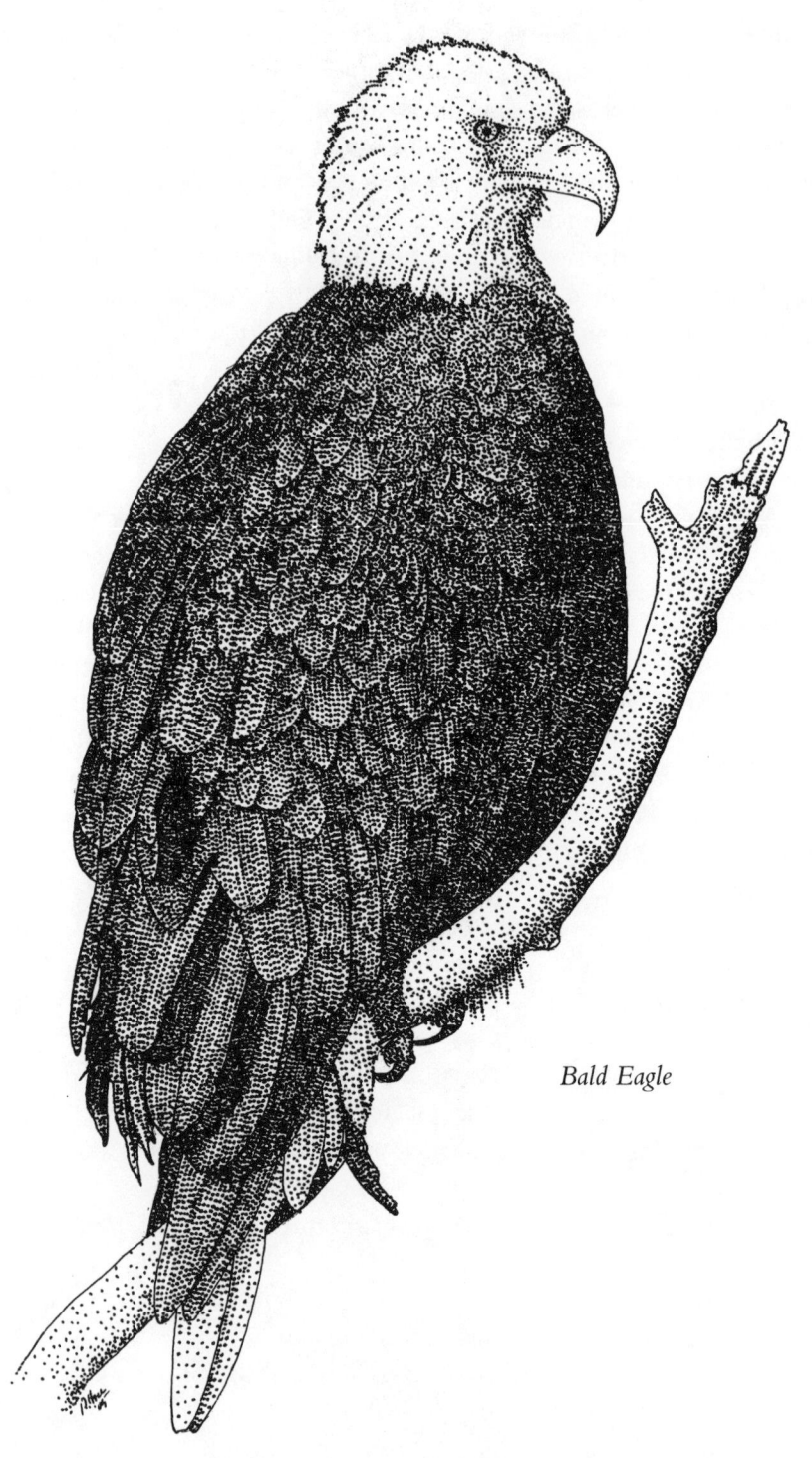

Bald Eagle

- Some computer monitor screens, especially laptops with mercury in the backlighting mechanism
- Portable phones with mute or privacy switches
- Some cosmetics that use mercury as a preservative (of course, you might not want to use these on your skin in the first place)
- Button and camera batteries

If enough people were aware of just how many common household items contain mercury, and if enough of us refused to buy products with mercury, corporations would develop safer alternatives. Meanwhile, it's a good idea to take inventory of what products in our houses might have mercury. When they are no longer used, they should be taken to a hazardous waste disposal site, where the mercury will be recycled.

12 Be a conservation-conscious consumer

Americans constitute less than 5 percent of the world's population, yet we produce almost 25 percent of the world's greenhouse gas emissions and consume nearly 33 percent of the world's electricity, 43 percent of its gasoline, and nearly 30 percent of its paper. Much of this is nothing but waste. Packaging and other components of our everyday purchases and belongings often have serious environmental implications. Eliminating as much waste as possible will minimize our personal impact on birds and protect resources for future generations.

Some consumer products pose serious dangers to the environment and to birds that we don't even suspect. For example, the sudden decimation of three vulture species in India, Pakistan, and Nepal had a shockingly unexpected cause. These vultures were a critical part of the mountain ecosystem, rapidly consuming dead cattle and other livestock and thereby protecting wildlife and people from the dangerous pathogens that can multiply quickly in rotting carcasses. The vultures served a cultural role, too: some members of the Zoroastrian religion have an ancient tradition of disposing of their dead on mountaintops, exposing them to scavengers who carry the spirits of the dead to the sky. In rocky, mountainous regions where burial is difficult or impossible, these vultures provided a sanitary as well as a spiritual function.

Beginning in 1996, people started noticing that the vultures were disappearing. By 2000, the vulture population in India had dropped a shocking 95 percent. Researchers conducted exhaustive testing of tissue samples from freshly dead vultures but found no evidence of conventional viral or bacterial infectious diseases, pesticides, poisons, heavy metals, or nutritional deficiencies. They determined that the vultures had died of renal failure. But why? The cause of this unprecedented and devastating decline left scientists stumped.

Finally, in April 2003, the researchers pinpointed the cause. Vultures were dying after eating carcasses of animals that had been given a new, inexpensive anti-inflammatory medication related to ibuprofen called diclofenac. First used in veterinary medicine in 1993, it instantly became popular in South Asia because of its low cost and effectiveness at reducing lameness and fever in livestock, even though diclofenac doesn't actually cure any conditions but simply reduces symptoms. Scientists discovered a 100 percent correlation between renal failure in dead or dying vultures collected in the field in Pakistan and the presence of diclofenac. Subsequent experiments in Pakistan on unreleasable juvenile vultures demonstrated that very small doses of diclofenac (one-tenth the recommended dose for mammals) caused death from renal failure and that fatal amounts of diclofenac could be ingested by vultures eating dead livestock treated with the recommended veterinary doses.

How could anyone have anticipated that such hardy, adaptable birds could die from a common, properly used medication that alleviates pain and fever in livestock? There are few examples of such dramatic and sudden consequences for birds, but keeping abreast of such issues is important.

Here are a few consumer products that have a serious impact on bird life.

Cleaning agents. When choosing among various brands of cleaning agents and detergents, select those that use the smallest amount of phosphorus, which promotes eutrophication of lakes and streams and "dead zones" in the ocean. Many dishwasher detergents contain very high amounts of phosphorus per cup; others contain significantly less, and some are phosphate-free. Comparing phosphate levels on labels can help guide you toward the best choices.

Clothing. The clothing we wear has huge environmental implications. Cotton has an especially high environmental cost. According to the Organic Trade Association:

- Approximately 10 percent of all pesticides sold for use in U.S. agriculture were applied to cotton in 1997, the most recent year for which such data are publicly available.

Turkey Vulture

- Eighty-four million pounds of pesticides were sprayed on the 14.4 million acres of conventional cotton grown in the United States in 2000 (5.8 pounds per acre), ranking cotton second behind corn in total amount of pesticides sprayed.
- More than 2.03 billion pounds of synthetic fertilizers were applied to conventional cotton in 2000 (142 pounds per acre), making cotton the fourth most heavily fertilized crop behind corn, winter wheat, and soybeans.
- The Environmental Protection Agency considers seven of the top fifteen pesticides used on cotton in the United States (acephate, dichloropropene, diuron, fluometuron, pendimethalin, tribufos, and trifluralin) as "possible," "likely," "probable," or "known" human carcinogens.
- It takes roughly one-third pound of chemicals (pesticides and fertilizers) to grow enough cotton for just one T-shirt.

Choosing clothing made from organic cotton eliminates many of the problems of commercially grown fiber.

Electronics. Computers, printers, televisions, stereos, video games, digital cameras, and other electronics are manufactured using a wide variety of toxic metals and other dangerous chemicals. Some manufacturers are working hard to recycle the materials in their products. Hewlett-Packard, for example, provides a postage-paid envelope with every replacement printer ink cartridge it sells and provides free recycling of its printers and other products as well. Dell provides free recycling for one old computer when you buy a new one. When you shop around for electronic products, make each company's recycling policy a factor in the decision-making process.

CDs and DVDs. CDs cause environmental problems both when manufactured and when disposed of. For music and movies, buy used CDs and DVDs whenever possible. If your computer has a DVD writer, use DVDs instead of CDs for storing data—you can fit much more data on a single DVD than on a CD. And keep abreast of ways to recycle used CDs and DVDs. Virtually all CD recycling facilities charge a fee. Wouldn't it encourage conservation if we were charged a larger fee to throw them in the garbage?

Most consumer products are packaged, some excessively so. The pressure this puts on landfill space is often exaggerated; the real issue of excessive packaging is the waste of natural resources and the pollution associated with paper, cardboard, and plastic production. Encourage retailers and manufacturers to use less packaging.

Some corporations have sounder environmental policies than others, and some use a portion of their profits to make meaningful contributions to environmental organizations, conservation projects, or human health projects (which often directly benefit the environment as well). Being aware of corporate policies helps us make wiser choices as consumers.

It can be dismaying and overwhelming to consider the environmental implications of the products we use every day. But making conscious and informed choices will protect both the birds and us. It's the right thing to do.

3

CONSERVATION OF NATURAL RESOURCES

E VERY TIME WE SWITCH ON A LIGHT, TURN ON A FAUCET, OR PRINT out an e-mail, we have an impact on birds. Reducing our own use of natural resources and fostering what the National Audubon Society calls a "culture of conservation" can have an enormous benefit for a huge variety of birds.

13 Conserve water

Water is a truly renewable resource: evaporating and returning to the air, forming clouds, and then raining down on us, with the cycle repeating over and over. The amount of water on the planet remains constant. What changes is the amount of clean, drinkable fresh water for humans and wildlife.

Humans need only one to two quarts of water per day to stay alive, but we use much more. According to Cornell University's *Science News* (January 20, 1997), each American uses about 100 gallons of water a day for drinking, cooking, washing, disposing of wastes, and other personal purposes—much higher than the world average of about 22 gallons per person per day. Agricultural and industrial water use is even more intensive. Farm policies in the United States subsidize the cost of irrigation, exacerbating the problem. As the population increases, the amount of clean water available in lakes, rivers, and streams, as well as the uncontaminated groundwater supply, is being depleted. Much of the groundwater used for agriculture, industry, and municipalities is being depleted much more rapidly than it's being renewed.

How critical is water conservation for birds? Let's consider just one situation: that of the Aransas National Wildlife Refuge on the Texas Gulf coast. People have known for a long time that the fresh water flowing into the refuge is critical for Whooping Cranes and other species that live in the estuary. Cranes, like the humans living in San Antonio and other Texas cities, depend on water from the Edwards Aquifer, a source of spring water that feeds the Guadalupe and San Antonio Rivers. Rainwater and runoff also provide fresh water for the rivers, but during dry spells, aquifer springs may contribute more than 80 percent of the fresh water entering the bay. When people remove this water from the aquifer for drinking, bathing, irrigation, feeding livestock, manufacturing, and other uses, the fresh water entering the estuary from the rivers declines, salinity goes up, and the ecosystem changes.

In years when insufficient fresh water flows from the rivers into the estuary, marsh salinity increases, and blue crab populations decline. Blue crabs are the primary food source for wintering Whooping Cranes, so when salinity is high and blue crabs are few in number, more Whooping Cranes die over the winter. "We found when salinity in the marshes reaches twenty-three parts per thousand (seawater is thirty-five parts per thousand), the Whooping Cranes have to fly to fresh water to drink at least twice a day. This forces the cranes to use up more energy reserves and increases the risk of predation whenever the birds leave the marsh," Tom Stehn, Whooping Crane coordinator at the Aransas National Wildlife Refuge, told me. The cranes that survive have less to eat and are forced to use up their fat reserves, which they need to survive their 2,400-mile spring migration with enough energy left over to nest successfully. Stehn notes that there is a direct correlation between Whooping Crane breeding success in summer and the population level of blue crabs the previous winter.

It's not only Whooping Cranes that depend on freshwater inflows to the estuary. Other endangered or threatened species that live in the bay include Brown Pelicans, Reddish Egrets, and Piping Plovers. The human population of Texas is expected to double in the next fifty years. How will Texans meet their own needs as well as those of Whooping Cranes and other birds, especially as changing weather patterns exacerbate the degree and duration of droughts?

In Florida, burgeoning development has put Everglades National Park in jeopardy. In Nebraska, the flow of the Platte River, where migrating Sandhill Cranes stop over every spring, is a fraction of its historical level. Much of the arid West is becoming even more arid. In the Southwest, the exploding human population has depleted already limited freshwater sup-plies, with international implications. Millions of acres of junglelike wilder-

Whooping Crane

ness in northern Mexico are now sterile salt flats because of heavy water use in the United States.

In the days before the Hoover Dam was completed in 1936, Aldo Leopold recorded clouds of waterfowl in the Sonoran Desert's largest wetland, the Cienega de Santa Clara. Leopold traveled the Cienega by canoe with his brother in 1922, calling it a "milk and honey wilderness." "The river was nowhere and everywhere, for he could not decide which of a hundred green lagoons offered the most pleasant and least speedy path to the Gulf," Leopold wrote. "So he traveled them all, and so did we." The Cienega is but a shadow of what it once was, and it is threatened by more damage from the Yuma desalting plant, which, if it goes into production, will feed its toxic saline dregs directly into the Cienega.

The ever-increasing voraciousness for fresh water ensures that problems such as this will become more prevalent. We will continue to lose the freshwater reserves that we should be protecting for our children and grandchildren, as well as for birds and other wildlife.

The worst water problems in the nation are in the West, where water conservation is urgent for both humans and birds. Yet flying over major cities, one can't help but notice the many swimming pools sparkling in the sun. Squandering limited water supplies in arid areas increases the likelihood of wildfires and leads to the concentration of toxins that run off into rivers and groundwater supplies. Even in areas of the country where there is much more fresh water, such as the Great Lakes region, groundwater and drinking water supplies are becoming contaminated due to intensive agricultural practices and toxins from industry and people. When sewage plants carry too heavy a burden, managers sometimes hasten the treatment process by releasing a blend of contaminated and cleaned water, which increases the danger of disease for both humans and birds. One dangerous organism, cryptosporidium, got into Milwaukee's drinking water in 1993, causing about 400,000 people to get sick and killing more than 100. In the face of that, little attention was paid to the loss of birds and other wildlife.

Chemicals are so pervasive in the environment that one study found 287 different contaminants in human umbilical cord blood. These contaminants included pesticides, fire retardants, and mercury. A June 2005 *Washington Post* article reported on the alarming amount of pharmaceuticals in our nation's waterways, the result of drugs being tossed down the drain and flushed down the toilet. These chemicals, including hormones found in birth control pills, may have human health risks, since water treatment plants remove only a fraction of pharmaceutically active compounds. Nobody is sure what the effects are, how these substances interact, or their full impact on wildlife. Nonetheless, most government officials don't seem particularly interested in the issue.

When I was in graduate school, one of my friends who became a biologist for Exxon liked to say, "Dilution is the solution to pollution." This may be true to a point, but year after year, as our freshwater supplies stay constant or dwindle and the amount of toxins we release steadily increases, pollution becomes more concentrated, not more diluted. In one of the largest and ostensibly one of the cleanest lakes in the world, a series of storms in September 1990 caused storm sewers to overflow and led to a sewage spill, washing raw sewage and even some medical wastes into Lake Superior. In Duluth, where I live, birders found sick and dead birds all along the shore. One birder brought me three sick Sanderlings; she had found these little shorebirds, weak and emaciated, along a popular beach. Parasites multiply rapidly on birds that are too sick to preen, and these birds were covered with lice and mites. As I examined them and dusted them with a mild insecticide, a louse on the sickest bird bit me, apparently transferring whatever pathogens were in the bird. A couple of days later, I became seriously ill with a high fever, hallucinations, and difficulty breathing. My symptoms were similar to psittacosis (parrot fever), but blood samples proved negative for that and every other disease I was tested for. My doctor laced me with a broad-spectrum antibiotic, and I recovered. The Sanderling died, however, and a Common Nighthawk I was caring for at the same time also succumbed. We Duluthians swim and boat in Lake Superior and draw our drinking water from it, all the while leaking our wastes into the water and trusting that human beings will prove a bit sturdier than little sandpipers.

As public utilities become increasingly burdened by the growing population, and as the anti-tax movement makes it harder to maintain them, we can expect this kind of dangerous situation to happen with increasing frequency, hurting all of us. Even simple sewage backups and overflows can contaminate lakes and rivers. Conserving and using our precious water resources responsibly helps us all.

How can we make a difference? First and foremost, don't waste water. The Web sites of the Environmental Protection Agency and many municipal water providers suggest simple ways that we can save water at home. Also, don't place extra burdens on sewer systems and wastewater treatment plants. Don't wash down drains or flush any of the following items:

- Paper products. These don't dissolve and add to the burden of sludge.
- Lint and hair. These may clog the drain or the sewer system.
- Condoms, underwear, and other nonbiodegradable solids.
- Oil, paint, and other toxins. Take these to your local toxic waste disposal site.
- Cat litter. The sand and gravel can block a sewer line.

14 Conserve electricity

Every time we switch on an electrical appliance, we hurt birds. Every technology that produces electricity or delivers it to our homes kills birds, some more than others. Up to 2 million birds died when they mistakenly landed in oil pits to bathe and drink in 1997 alone. There are no estimates of the number of birds affected by oil and gas spills, oil and gas extraction and transport, toxicity from mercury and other power plant emissions, and the effects of acid rain and global warming. Even the cleanest source of electricity, wind power, can kill birds outright. And no matter how the electricity is produced, transporting it along transmission lines also kills birds. Conserving energy can at least minimize the problems for birds.

Whatever method the local power company uses to produce electricity, it has an impact on the environment and the birds that share it with us.

Coal, gas, and oil. Electricity produced by the burning of fossil fuels, especially coal, has the highest environmental cost. Mining for coal can degrade or destroy huge areas. For example, in Pennsylvania, 3,500 miles of streams and creeks are now sterile as a result of acid runoff from coal mines. The mining of the coal beds in Montana, which were first discovered by Lewis and Clark, has led to terrible degradation. It costs billions of dollars to reclaim land after mining, and toxic water left behind may remain poisonous for generations. Mountaintop mining in Tennessee is destroying critical habitat for the threatened Cerulean Warbler.

Coal-burning power plants are the single largest source of mercury pollution, which comes down to earth in rainwater and poisons lakes, rivers, and streams. According to the U.S. Geological Survey, coal-fired utilities and industrial boilers contribute over 86 percent of the mercury in the atmosphere. A 1999 report by the National Resources Research Council, *Mercury Falling: An Analysis of Mercury Pollution from Coal-Burning Power Plants,* states, "A high percentage of commercial fish, such as tuna and pollock, are now contaminated with traces of mercury. Concern over mercury contamination in 40 states has led government agencies to warn consumers not to eat bass, trout and other sport fish caught in over a thousand lakes and streams." Meanwhile, the blood and tissue mercury levels in loons, Osprey, Bald Eagles, and Belted Kingfishers are increasing.

The amount of fossil fuel required to burn coal is enormous. It takes about 200,000 gallons of oil simply to start a coal burner. Diesel fuel is needed for extracting, transporting, and cleaning the coal, and then the ash must be transported to a landfill and buried. Our tax money provides subsidies to coal companies and to states with coal mines to clean up streams and repair roads, allowing corporations to make their profits without taking into account the real costs of coal production. Nobody has ever figured out the true economics of coal-produced electricity.

Extracting and transporting gas and oil also cause pollution, oil spills, and other dangerous environmental problems. Our dependence on oil has led to wars that have exacted a horrific human toll, to say nothing of the damage done by bombs, land and water mines, bullets, defoliants, and other military technologies to a war zone's environment and its inhabitants.

Burning any fossil fuel, especially oil and coal, spews nitrogen oxides, sulfur dioxide, particulate matter, mercury, and carbon dioxide into the atmosphere. Small amounts of toxic metals such as arsenic, cadmium, chromium, and nickel are also released. Major environmental issues related to these pollutants include smog (particulate matter and ground-level ozone) and acid rain. The latter affects the composition and growth of forests in the eastern United States and Canada, which in turn affects insect populations and thus insectivorous bird species. Acid rain also depletes the soil of calcium, reducing the amount available to the invertebrates that provide food for birds. This loss of calcium in birds' diets apparently causes eggshell thinning and less calcium in the bones of the nestlings of some species, such as the Wood Thrush.

The release of carbon dioxide by power plants burning fossil fuels contributes to global warming, which is already having a serious impact on the migration patterns and ranges of birds, damaging their ecosystems and exacerbating the damage from tropical storms and hurricanes, which are increasing in strength due to rising ocean temperatures. Higher ocean temperatures also contribute to the decrease in plankton and fish populations in northern waters, which has caused a catastrophic loss of seabirds.

Nuclear. In 2001 nuclear power plants provided about 20 percent of the electricity in the United States. Nuclear power plants normally release few contaminants into the air, making them far cleaner than coal or petrochemical plants. But the United States has not reached any kind of consensus about the safest and most prudent ways to deal with nuclear waste products, which remain contaminated for centuries or even millennia. Seepage of nuclear waste can seriously endanger groundwater, crops, and wild plants, as well as humans and animals that get their water and food from them. Also, the possibility of a reactor accident is a clear and present danger, especially in this time of terrorist threats. How likely and how potentially dangerous are such accidents? Home owner and auto insurance policies specifically exclude nuclear plant accidents from their coverage, and Congress strictly limits the liability of utilities and nuclear plant builders and indemnifies Department of Energy private contractors from nuclear incidents, even in cases of gross negligence and willful misconduct, through the Price-Anderson Nuclear Industries Indemnity Act.

Clearly, a nuclear reactor event can cause enormous and lasting damage to the environment and all living things. Conserving energy reduces the amount of nuclear wastes produced and reduces the number of reactors built, thus reducing the likelihood of accidents.

Hydroelectric. Hydroelectric power is clean, insofar as it doesn't release contaminants into the air. But hydroelectric plants affect not only local waters but also streams and lakes far downstream. The transport of suspended solids can be significantly reduced below reservoirs, affecting the oxygen content of lower-lying lakes. Reservoirs also trap nutrients, making them unavailable downstream. The collapse of the population of landlocked salmon in the Pacific Northwest was most likely caused by the construction of several dams that reduced the nutrient content of downstream lakes. Hydroelectric plants also affect the temperature of downstream waters. The more people conserve energy in areas that use hydroelectric power, the fewer dams needed.

Wind. Wind is a renewable, clean energy source, making it the most environmentally friendly source of electricity. The problem is that wind turbines kill birds and are even more dangerous to bats. According to *Avian Monitoring Studies at the Buffalo Ridge, Minnesota Wind Resource Area: Results of a 4-Year Study,* a report prepared for Northern States Power Company, "Results of monitoring studies conducted in Europe and California indicate that raptors (birds of prey), passerines (songbirds), shorebirds and waterfowl are the most susceptible to turbine collisions. Several factors, including avian abundance and composition, geographic area, prey abundance and wind plant characteristics, determine the potential for avian mortality." The Minnesota study found that most of the fatalities were nocturnal migrants and that large numbers of bats were killed by the turbines as well.

Many of the best places to build wind turbines, with the most reliable and optimal wind conditions, are along shorelines and bluffs—precisely the places where bird migration is the heaviest. In California, the huge wind farm at Altamont Pass in Alameda County kills between 881 and 1,300 raptors annually, almost all during the winter migration season. But the effects of wind power on birds aren't entirely understood yet. A 2005 radar study of large bird movements near a wind farm off the coast of Denmark indicated that birds simply flew around the farm or between the turbines; less than 1 percent flew close enough to be in danger of colliding with the giant structures.

Even a small wind turbine can cause mortality. A friend of mine who built one for his own power generation was startled one night by a sudden power outage. He went out to investigate and discovered the mangled carcass of a Snowy Owl that had been killed by the turbine blades.

Wind turbines, especially on wind farms, can also cause habitat fragmentation and disturbance. Seven of twenty-two grassland species that typically nested in an area where some Minnesota wind farms were constructed were found in smaller numbers after turbine construction. Grassland habitat is already diminishing at a rapid rate, and most avian species associated with it are also declining, so wind farms may reduce their potential nesting habitat even further. The best alternative in agricultural areas is to place wind turbines in row crop fields (corn, soy, wheat, or barley), where the habitat doesn't support grassland species anyway.

Avian deaths at wind turbines are gruesome, but clearly, wind power is far better for birds than coal and oil. William Mueller, conservation chair of the Wisconsin Society for Ornithology, wrote:

> I think moving toward alternatives to fossil fuels is so important that I believe some limited avian mortality at wind farms is unfortunate but may be necessarily acceptable. That goes down hard for many folks—it's rather like sawing off your foot when you have gangrene—extremely unpleasant, and it cannot be seen as a "good" outcome, but is inescapable. I only hope we do take extreme care about coastal sites and learn more about the effects on bats, and maybe do mitigation by turning some sets of turbines off during peak migratory periods and the like.

Even though turbine kills are relatively small in magnitude, as wind power becomes an increasingly popular alternative to dirtier forms of power generation, we need to find ways to minimize bird kills. There may be ways to construct turbines to give birds auditory or visual cues to help them avoid collisions. Focused research is necessary, especially before wind farms are located near migration pathways and stopping points. But again, conserving electricity will minimize the number of turbines needed, thus protecting birds.

No matter how electricity is produced, delivering it along transmission lines is dangerous to birds. In July 2005 a year-old Whooping Crane that was part of the reintroduction program in Wisconsin died after colliding with a power line over a cornfield. The U.S. Fish and Wildlife Service estimates that up to 174 million birds are killed by collisions with power lines each year, and more than a thousand hawks and eagles are electrocuted. A U.S. Fish and Wildlife Service technical report published in 1987 showed that 68 percent of birds flying in the vicinity of power lines do not react to them, and some birds that do react to one wire flare up and strike another. Flying birds have difficulty gauging their distance from wires suspended in the airspace in front of them.

At the end of the 2003 Sandhill Crane spring migration season along the Platte River in Nebraska, people from the Audubon Rowe Sanctuary picked up 150 carcasses of cranes that had been killed by power lines. This number did not include birds that had been crippled or killed and then carried off by scavengers or predators or crippled cranes that died after wandering away from the lines. In the spring of 2004, I visited the observation blind at the Rowe Sanctuary on the morning of March 10. As dawn approached, thousands of cranes took off in a thunder of wings. After they disappeared to spend the day feeding, one lone crane remained, its wing horribly skewed. This bird, apparently injured by the power lines the night before, had joined the others to roost and now wandered into the weeds to spend the day alone. Ten minutes after the flock had departed, one crane returned and circled over and over, calling. I suspect that this lone adult was the mate of the crippled bird. Thus, a single power line collision may have resulted in the loss of two birds from the reproductive cycle for at least that year.

The power lines strung across the Platte have long been known to kill cranes. When I visited the sanctuary in the spring of 1996, seventeen dead cranes had been picked up one morning under the power lines. Volunteers and staff of the Rowe Sanctuary worked with the local power company to fit the lines with little plastic spirals called bird flight diverters, which help the cranes see and gauge their distance from the wires. The "Firefly Bird Diverter," a more sophisticated model, consists of a heavy-duty plastic card with a special reflective coating that is highly visible to birds. The $3^{1}/_{2}$ by 6-inch card hangs from a swivel attached by a clamp to the power line or a tower guy wire. The card rotates in winds as light as three to five mile per hour, alerting birds to the obstruction. The coating glows at night for up to ten hours, so it can help prevent nocturnal collisions as well. Sadly, even with the diverters in place, there can be collisions, especially during foggy conditions.

It can be prohibitively expensive to retrofit existing power lines with any kind of flight diverters. And despite the fact that diverters are cheap to make and easy to install when transmission lines are initially erected, most transmission lines in the nation are still built without them.

Far fewer birds are electrocuted by power lines than killed in collisions with them, but electrocution is still a significant cause of avian mortality, especially for raptors and other birds with large wingspans. James Dwyer, a graduate student at the University of Arizona's School of Renewable Natural Resources, discovered that electrocution is responsible for 80 percent of all Harris's Hawk deaths in the Tucson area. In 2004 he was working with the Tucson Electric Power Company to place bird guards on utility poles within 1,000 feet of known Harris's Hawk nests to reduce the number of deaths. As with flight diverters on wires, it's expensive to retrofit utility poles with bird guards, and although the power company deserves credit for cooperating with the project, power companies have known for many decades that their structures are lethal to birds, yet they have constructed millions of power poles without these safeguards. As with so many issues, bird electrocutions are bad for humans as well. One power outage in Saginaw, Minnesota, in the spring of 2001 was started when a Trumpeter Swan, taking off or landing in a small pond, was electrocuted by power lines. Its smoldering body ignited a grass fire. In 2004, a major fire in the foothills of Santa Clarita, twenty-two miles southwest of Los Angeles, charred over 5,000 acres and caused the evacuation of 1,600 homes; that fire was ignited by the burning body of a Red-tailed Hawk electrocuted by a power line.

As the burgeoning population demands more electrical power, the largest power companies build up power grids to allow them to supply energy to larger markets, requiring more transmission lines covering more land and endangering more birds. To make a real difference, the best thing we can do is to limit the amount of electricity we buy from power companies. In most places, it's cost-effective even in the short term to invest in solar cells that heat water for household use. Unfortunately, it's far more expensive to build a system of solar cells to generate electricity, although good systems can provide most or all of a household's electricity and even create a surplus that can be fed into the power grid. Many environmental groups, the Environmental Protection Agency, and most power companies provide free information about ways to conserve electricity in the home.

15 Reduce paper use, choose recycled paper, and recycle the paper you use

The invention of paper was one of the most important advances of humankind. For centuries, it was the only means of communicating scientific, philosophical, spiritual, and artistic ideas over time and space. But paper production has a dark side, requiring the intense harvesting of young trees and highly polluting processes to manufacture it. Now that we can communicate so much more efficiently electronically, using paper for things such as unsolicited mass mailings is wasteful and destructive.

According to the Audubon Society, "Globally, paper use has increased more than sixfold over the past five decades. One-fifth of all the wood harvested in the world ends up being manufactured into paper, a process with environmental costs ranging from deforestation to species loss to pollution. The United States, with less than 5 percent of the planet's population, uses 30 percent of its paper." On average, each American consumes 738 pounds of paper a year. Less than one-third of this paper contains any recycled content.

As our paper use climbs, more forests are cut on short rotation cycles, meaning that forests are clear-cut while they are still covered with aspens and other softwoods, before natural succession leads to mature hardwood growth. Aspens and other early-succession trees provide much of the fiber for paper production in the United States; much of the rest comes from tropical forests.

In the northern forests where I live, aspens are wonderful trees. Their buds provide food in winter and early spring for grouse, and their sap provides food for sapsuckers, whose drill holes in turn provide food for hummingbirds, kinglets, warblers, phoebes, and more. Old aspens are the preferred nest trees for Pileated Woodpeckers and for Boreal and Saw-whet Owls, who nest in old Pileated cavities. But there can be too much of a good thing. Too many aspens means more deer, whose overpopulation has led to overgrazing and habitat destruction, to say nothing of garden damage and traffic accidents. And because so many U.S. and Canadian forests are being managed to provide pulp for paper and wood products (particleboard and plywood) rather than saw lumber, we're reducing the habitat of wildlife that requires more mature forests, such as Scarlet Tanagers and Rose-breasted and Evening Grosbeaks.

Boreal Owl

The paper production process also causes serious environmental damage. Pulp mills are voracious water users. Their freshwater consumption can seriously harm habitat near mills, reducing water levels and raising water temperature, harming many fish in the process. But reducing the water consumption at mills would concentrate the effluents to lethal levels. Paper mills emit into the atmosphere particulate matter, carbon dioxide, sulfur dioxide, hydrogen sulfide, volatile organic compounds, chlorine, chloroform, dioxins, furans, and chlorine dioxide, along with hormone-disrupting and carcinogenic chemicals such as chlorinated phenols and polycyclic aromatic hydrocarbons. Disposal of paper mill sludge pollutes soil, air, and water. In laboratory tests, mill effluent caused reproductive impairment in zooplankton and invertebrates, reducing food for fish. And toxins that collect in zooplankton and invertebrates can bioaccumulate, becoming increasingly concentrated up the food chain.

When it comes to paper use, as with other natural resources, the watchwords are *reduce, reuse,* and *recycle.* Taking steps to reduce junk mail is something that we can all do; go to www.obviously.com/junkmail/ for some ideas. Buying recycled paper for both personal and professional use can also protect significant amounts of forest.

4

PETS AND BIRDS

MANY PEOPLE WHO LOVE WILD BIRDS ARE ALSO PET OWNERS. IT'S easy to enjoy both, and with a few precautions, we can keep our pets safe from predators and keep wild birds and their habitat safe from our pets.

16 **Keep cats indoors**
There are about 78 million pet cats in the United States, and about 48 million of them are allowed to roam outdoors. At least as many stray and feral cats run wild. Most pet cats don't kill many birds, but even small numbers can add up when there are so many cats. And some individual cats kill a lot of birds. On an early October morning during a heavy migration period, I found seventeen dead Yellow-rumped and Palm Warblers on the ground in a two-block area in my neighborhood; as far as I could determine, all had been killed by a single cat. Dr. Stan Temple of the University of Wisconsin estimates that in Wisconsin alone about 7 million birds are killed by cats each year. The American Bird Conservancy estimates that cats kill hundreds of millions of birds in the United States each year and about three times as many mammals, which significantly reduces the prey base for raptors and shrikes.

Some populations of birds are more susceptible to cat predation than others. Bobolinks, meadowlarks, and other grassland species that nest on the ground in agricultural areas are especially vulnerable to farm cats. These species are declining for a number of reasons, but cats are certainly one of the major causes.

Sometimes people "rescue" birds from their cats, but these birds are almost invariably doomed. I was a wildlife rehabilitator for many years and took in a wide variety of birds that had been injured by cats. To the unpracticed eye, many had no apparent injuries because feathers can hide not only puncture wounds but also tears, gashes, and blood. One woman brought me a White-breasted Nuthatch that she had taken from her cat. She thought that it had only lost a few tail feathers, but beneath the belly feathers, I saw in horror that the entire pygostyle (the fused vertebrae of the tail) had been ripped out, along with skin, muscle, and a chunk of intestine. The nuthatch was in shock, and I held it as its life ebbed away. Meanwhile, this woman drove home feeling virtuous for "saving" this little creature and continued to let her cat outdoors.

Another person brought me a female Evening Grosbeak that had been mangled by a cat. One wing was broken, and to anchor it in place as it healed, I put a wrapping around the bird's middle and taped the broken wing to that. I administered antibiotics, and after a day or two, she started eating well and looking perky. I grew attached to her during the ten days I cared for her as she mended. But the day I took off the bandages, she took a deep breath (as if relieved to get the burdensome wrappings off), opened her wings for a practice flight, and keeled over dead. Apparently, the cat had broken several of her ribs. With the bandages in place, the bones remained immobile, but when she opened her wings, the broken bones punctured her lungs and killed her.

Unlike our lungs, bird lungs are flat and situated just below the back ribs. Most of the volume of air that a bird breathes in and out passes through the lungs into huge balloonlike air sacs that fill much of the abdomen, part of the neck, and various spaces in between. When a cat reaches out and claws a bird's back or bites into it while carrying it off, the lungs are invariably damaged. And because cat saliva is rich in bacteria, cat bites are prone to infection. The vast majority of cat-injured birds I cared for ended up dying.

Cats are predators by nature. But unlike foxes, coyotes, hawks, owls, and other wild predators, we subsidize cats, providing them with food and shelter and taking care of them when they're sick or injured. On a single suburban block, three or four cats might thrive, whereas a family of foxes would require far more space and would either move on or die out when they depleted their prey. Even the most well-fed cats have a natural instinct to chase and toy with birds and rodents, and the fitter a cat is, the more effective at killing it becomes. But killing for a living is hard for domesticated animals. Outdoor cats can be hit by cars; be injured in fights with other cats; be killed by dogs, foxes, or other predators; or contract serious diseases such as feline leukemia. In urban areas where rats and mice pose a serious risk for human health, rodents convulsing after consuming poison may entice cats to finish them off, poisoning the cats as well. Roaming cats are also subjected to some of the same natural hazards that wild animals are. I've heard several stories of Great Horned Owls and large hawks killing or wounding cats and small dogs. Cats allowed outdoors live, on average, only three to five years, compared with more than fifteen years for indoor cats. People often romanticize the wild nature of their cats, but I've taken in four cats that I rescued as strays, and all four seemed perfectly content to stay indoors. Animal welfare groups and the American Veterinary Medical Association recommend keeping cats indoors.

Cats that toy with or feed on wild birds and mice are most likely to carry toxoplasmosis, a protozoal infection that is extremely dangerous for unborn babies and newborns. Cats prefer to defecate in loose, sandy soil, so they often use sandboxes or cultivated gardens, exposing small children and gardeners to their droppings, which harbor the infectious organisms.

Some outside cats are so set in their ways that they really do become distressed when confined indoors. If you choose to let your cat outdoors, keep it harnessed or leashed. There are also enclosed kitty pens with complex pathways that allow cats to feel like they're on the prowl outdoors without giving them access to birds. And designers of "invisible fences" are now creating models specifically for cats.

If you witness a neighborhood cat killing birds, find a courteous way to inform the owner and ask that the cat be kept indoors. At least suggest that the cat be kept inside during baby bird season and major migration events or that it be let out only at nighttime. Cats usually hunt visually and kill mostly rodents at night.

17 Don't keep exotic birds or wild birds for pets, and never release exotic birds into the wild

Humans have kept domesticated birds for thousands of years. Pet birds can provide us with companionship, relieve stress, and even give warnings in the event of intruders, fire, or other dangerous situations. But pet ownership entails responsibility. Pets should be truly domesticated, able to lead genuinely satisfying lives in captivity, descended from generations of animals that have lived their lives with humans and can breed readily in captivity.

Yet every year, millions of birds are taken from the wilds of Asia, Africa, and Latin America and sold as pets. This capturing of native birds has been banned for decades in Australia, Great Britain, and the United States, although reduced funding has made enforcement increasingly difficult here. Sadly, it's all too easy to capture and transport birds from poor nations that lack either strong bird protection laws or the means to enforce them. Outrageously, as many as 80 percent of smuggled birds die before reaching their final destination. Some are injured or killed by other animals, including monkeys and larger birds, that are smuggled with them. Often, hundreds of wild birds are crammed into small crates, tubes, pipes, or the nooks and crannies of vehicles and are not given sufficient food, water, or ventilation for the long, hot journey. Their beaks are often taped closed to prevent them from biting their captors or calling out. Tragically, the birds that are most popular as pets tend to be the ones that are most aware of what is happening to them. Members of the parrot family in particular are highly intelligent and social, closely bonded to mate and family. Anyone who has worked closely with parrots, cockatiels, lovebirds, or parakeets understands their capacity for genuine suffering from this kind of brutality.

People who capture birds for the bird trade typically cut down trees or slice open nest cavities with machetes, not only directly impacting bird numbers but also destroying habitat. The trade in wild birds and the resulting habitat destruction now threaten more than 1,000 species with extinction, according to the Defenders of Wildlife. Because of this, in 1992 the United States passed the Wild Bird Conservation Act (WBCA). According to Defenders of Wildlife, "Before the WBCA was enacted, the United States was the world's largest importer of wild birds, importing more than 7.4 million birds between 1980 and 1991, primarily for the pet market." The number of birds imported to the United States dropped significantly after passage of the WBCA, and the American pet bird industry has flourished.

Unfortunately, some common pet birds that readily breed in captivity are still captured from the wild by poachers and sold to distributors and pet shops at cheaper prices than they would have to pay for birds raised by responsible breeders. Birds bred in captivity make better pets, especially when socialized with humans from the time they hatch.

Many people who buy pet birds don't realize how demanding and noisy they can be or how painful their bites are. Sometimes when people grow tired of a bird or simply can't handle it anymore, they release it outside. Escaped pet birds have established feral populations in many cities in the

Scarlet Macaws

United States, especially in Florida, California, and Texas. One species, the Monk Parakeet (often called the "Quaker" by pet owners), is native to temperate areas of South America, but escaped and released Monk Parakeets have established colonies as far north as Illinois, Connecticut, Massachusetts, Rhode Island, and New York and are becoming abundant in southern states. So far, the species doesn't seem to be a serious problem in urban areas, but as with all exotic species, these feral populations of birds compete with native species for food and nesting sites and can introduce diseases to native populations. Released pet birds on Hawaii are the source of many of the diseases that mosquitoes spread to the native species, and farmers and fruit growers are concerned about these exotic birds damaging crops.

If you're thinking about buying a pet bird, first speak to the breeder or seller to ascertain that it was bred in captivity. Make sure that the bird seems comfortable with you and bonds easily with humans. When cleaning pet bird cages, never dispose of used seeds outdoors, where they can spread diseases to wild birds. If you compost used seed or bird droppings, make sure that your compost pile is screened to keep wild birds out.

What if it doesn't work out? If you can no longer keep a pet bird, bring it to a humane organization. If a pet bird dies, bury it or dispose of it safely to prevent any disease organisms from reaching wild birds.

18 Control your dog

When I was a licensed bird rehabilitator, someone accidentally left a door open to the room where an injured nighthawk was healing, and my springer spaniel wandered in and picked the bird up in her mouth. Betsy was well bred for hunting, with a very soft mouth, but the poor bird flailed away in a panic, and by the time I heard the commotion and came running, it was breathing its last. I examined its body closely, and although many feathers had fallen out, there were no open wounds. I think the bird simply died of fright.

The first Blue Jay I ever cared for was a young fledgling that I rescued from the mouth of a golden retriever. I didn't know the dog—I'd come upon the scene while walking in a park—but fortunately for the little jay, the dog had a soft mouth and was obedient enough to hand the bird over to me. And equally fortunately, the little fledgling was still too inexperienced to panic, so it didn't come to the same end as the nighthawk. This bird had a couple of small bleeding wounds, but dog saliva is not as laden with bacteria as cat saliva is. At the time, I didn't have enough experience to recognize signs of infection, but the bird fully recovered.

I've heard many accounts of dogs injuring birds, including baby ducks and geese, songbirds, and even hawks and owls that were presumably picked up while hunting or feeding on the ground. Even dogs that don't chase or kill wild birds can harm them. Running loose in woods or fields, dogs can inadvertently charge over the eggs or chicks of ground-nesting birds. And dogs are especially dangerous on beaches. Least Terns and Piping Plovers nest along sandy beaches and dunes, and their eggs and chicks are easily trampled. Allowing dogs to run on beaches also leads to dog waste runoff, raising the bacterial load for both birds and humans. Many dogs also like to dig, which can cause serious problems along riverbanks and lakeshores and damage rare vegetation.

Keep your dog leashed in natural habitats unless it is well trained and comes immediately when you call. Attending a dog obedience class will both make your dog a more pleasant companion and help protect wildlife. Never allow a dog to run loose on any beach where birds nest or feed. Never allow your dog to dig up streambanks or other sensitive habitat or to destroy natural vegetation in vulnerable habitats. Always carry a supply of plastic bags with you for waste cleanup. This will prevent nutrients and disease organisms from running off into lakes and seeping into groundwater supplies.

Well-trained dogs are actually quite compatible with birds. I've seen a Chipping Sparrow tug at fur from my golden retriever, Bunter. The first two times Bunter was sound asleep, but the third time she was awake, indulgently watching the little bird as if realizing that it just needed some nesting material. When you brush your dog in spring and early summer, put clumps of fur in a clean suet cage or wedged into tree bark for nesting birds, unless you use Frontline or some other topical flea or tick killer, which may make the fur toxic.

PART II

ENHANCING THE
NATURAL HABITAT
OF YOUR BACKYARD

5

LEARN ABOUT
YOUR OWN BACKYARD

THE FIRST STEP IN ENHANCING YOUR BACKYARD HABITAT IS TO understand what plants and animals live in your area.

19 **Identify and keep track of your backyard birds**

I grew up in a blue-collar industrial suburb of Chicago. One morning when I was about seven years old, I looked out my upstairs bedroom window and saw dozens of tiny, colorful birds in the branches of a maple tree. Some were yellow and black and white; one glowed with brilliant, flaming orange; one sported elegant bluish, black, and white plumage; one had bright yellow cheeks and a black bib. Each one was different. They were exquisite—vivid and beautiful, much brighter and more exotic looking than the robins and sparrows I usually saw in my yard. My mother thought that they might be escaped canaries, but they were much more brilliant than my grandpa's pet canaries. I imagined that these must be "angel birds," resurrected from the heroic canaries that had sacrificed their lives to save the coal miners my grandpa had told me about. One by one they vanished. Never again did I see such an extraordinary sight, but the vision stayed in my mind and heart.

About fifteen years later, I received my first field guide for Christmas. When I came to the "Wood Warbler" pages, there they were—those same angel birds, illustrated in full glory. According to the maps, most of them didn't breed in the Chicago area, but dozens of species had to pass through Chicago to get from their tropical wintering grounds to their breeding territories in the northern forests. Perusing the pages of the field guide, I saw a rainbow of birds that apparently ranged through the city, including Baltimore Orioles, Rose-breasted Grosbeaks, and Ruby-throated Hummingbirds. Of course, the maps were pretty general. These birds couldn't live

Rose-breasted Grosbeak

right in the city. Or could they? I soon bought the booklet "Chicagoland Birds: Where and When to Find Them," published by the Field Museum of Natural History, and was amazed at the possibilities.

When my husband and I went back to visit our childhood neighborhood the next spring, there they were. All manner of birds I'd never dreamed of were flying about on my block: catbirds and Brown Thrashers, Wood Thrushes and Scarlet Tanagers, and dozens of warblers in the trees. That little book opened my consciousness to a world I'd never imagined, yet it was the same world that had been there all along. For me, opening my first field guide was like Helen Keller's revelation at the water pump. For the first time in my life, I was able to notice and appreciate the beauty and value of what had always been there.

Learning about your local birds is a critical first step in helping them. Once you know which species could and should nest or winter in your geographic area and which pass through during migration, you can grow appropriate plants, set out appropriate bird feeders, and get involved with local issues that may affect local habitat and the birds that need it. Paying close attention to neighborhood birds also helps you notice when their numbers change, and learning to recognize birds by sight and sound is an important first step in developing the expertise to help with surveys that keep tabs on avian populations.

How do you identify birds and learn about the species in your neighborhood? A field guide and binoculars are the most important tools for a birder. You can get plenty of information about how to choose the right tools, how to use them to identify birds, and how to find organizations and other sources of information about birding in your state at the Cornell Laboratory of Ornithology's Web site at www.birds.cornell.edu/programs/AllAboutBirds/. This site also has lots of information about each species, including their calls and songs, photos, and often video clips. The lab has also developed many citizen science programs that allow you to put your growing skills to good use by helping to monitor bird populations.

As you learn about your backyard birds, keep track of them. Start a "life list" of all the wild birds you identify, everywhere you find them. In addition to a life list, many birders keep separate lists divided by location, from their own backyards and favorite local parks to various counties, states, countries, and continents. Competitive birders follow specific rules developed by the American Birding Association so that they can compare their lists with those of other competitive birders. If you don't care to submit your lists for comparison, you can set your own rules.

The most interesting part of keeping any list is watching it grow. My own backyard list, which I've been working on for twenty-three years, has 162 species. I live on a major migration pathway, so my yard has some built-in advantages, but no matter how long or short your backyard list is, every new bird brings a sense of pleasure and pride. As I always say, no one should go through life listlessly.

20 Learn about the flora and fauna in your neighborhood and region

Most well-educated adults have never had an opportunity to study the basic plants and animals native to their areas, or even their own backyards. Many educated adults can't identify in the field the natural resources that their local economies depend on. When we don't understand basic ecological principles, such as natural forest succession, it's harder to make wise decisions about forestry issues. When we don't understand basic aquatic ecology, we don't recognize the signs of vegetation choking our lakes and streams or the harm caused by eutrophication. Democracy depends on a well-educated citizenry that can make wise decisions about the issues of the day, but as the world grows more complicated, it becomes increasingly difficult for people to be knowledgeable about the many issues that policy makers must deal with. This is a sad shortcoming of our educational system, but fortunately, it's also something that can be corrected—and you can even have fun doing it. Taking inventory of your backyard habitat will prepare you for the next step: enhancing that habitat.

It's an easy matter to visit a library, bookstore, or nature shop and browse through the field guides to trees, flowers, insects, mammals, reptiles, and amphibians. Consider purchasing a few guides dealing with the wildlife that you find particularly interesting. Learn to recognize the most common trees, wildflowers, and creatures native to your region. Then go beyond mere identification and learn more interesting facts about these plants and animals and how they interact with other species.

6

Manage Your Backyard Habitat

As the world grows more urbanized and crowded, our backyards—be they multiacre country estates, tiny balconies jutting out of city apartments, or anything in between—can provide a peaceful and lovely refuge from the hectic world. Our yards can and should provide a refuge for birds, too. Nearly 80 percent of the habitat on which wildlife depends is privately owned, and every year more than 2 million acres of wildlife habitat in the United States are lost to residential use, creating an enormous conservation opportunity, and responsibility, for individual households. What can we do to make our yards as bird-friendly as possible?

21 Grow an assortment of trees, shrubs, and other plants to provide food and cover for a variety of birds

As the human population surges, natural habitat dwindles and backyards become increasingly important refuges for birds and other wildlife. Backyards will never be ideal for species that depend on forest interiors or unbroken prairies, but many birds can thrive in our yards if we provide suitable food, water, cover, and nesting sites.

In the 1970s the National Wildlife Federation (NWF) developed a backyard habitat certification program that provides materials to help you make your backyard the best habitat possible. To be certified by the NWF as a backyard habitat, your yard must have five things:

1. Food. Grow native vegetation that produces acorns, berries, and other seeds or supports insect life to supply food for wildlife. For NWF certification, feeders can supplement natural food sources for birds.

2. Water. Provide a constant, reliable source of water in birdbaths, ponds, pools, or shallow dishes. Dripping or moving water is especially attractive to wild birds. Standing water in birdbaths and in ponds without fish or frogs must be cleaned every two to three days to prevent mosquitoes (which can carry encephalitis and West Nile virus) from hatching. Follow sound water conservation practices in keeping with regional water availability.

3. Cover. Create cover for wildlife with densely branched shrubs, hollow logs, rock piles, brush piles, stone walls, evergreens, meadow grasses, and deep water. This helps protect wildlife against predators and the elements.

4. Places to raise young. Offer wildlife safe places for courtship and for nurturing young. Mature trees provide den sites for squirrels and nesting places for birds. Milkweed provides nesting fibers for goldfinches as well as food for hummingbirds and monarch butterfly larvae. Salamanders, frogs, and toads thrive in ponds or water gardens, where ducks may nest too. Nest boxes provide safe nesting sites for cavity-nesting birds.

5. Sustainable gardening practices. The way you garden or manage your landscape affects wildlife in your yard and your entire neighborhood. Planting natives, reducing chemicals, and building healthy soil are just some of the things you can do to help wildlife and conserve natural resources.

There are many materials available from the library, local and state garden clubs, environmental organizations, state departments of natural resources, and the Internet to help you select plants to improve the bird habitat in your yard, including lists of cultivars that provide food or nest sites for particular species in different regions of the country. Some birds are especially attracted to specific plants—waxwings, robins, and bluebirds to various berries; hummingbirds to various nectar- and insect-rich flowers; Red-headed and Acorn Woodpeckers, Scarlet Tanagers, and jays to oaks; Evening Grosbeaks to box elders and maples; Purple Finches to raspberries; orioles to elms; grouse and sapsuckers to aspens; and redpolls to birches. It's critical to follow guidelines specifically for your geographic area to ensure that the habitat you provide is appropriate for the birds likely to appear in your yard.

Living plants aren't the only ones that provide shelter for birds. Many birds hide and nest in brush piles as well as in dense vegetation. In my own

American Robin

yard, a brush pile that was popular with migrant sparrows, local cardinals, and a host of other birds became an attractive and useful part of the landscape thanks to the Purple Finches that planted (via their droppings) a lovely stand of raspberries in and around the brush they used as a retreat.

A pile of dead branches can be unattractive, but fortunately, the value of a brush pile for birds isn't harmed (and is usually enhanced) by planting shrubs or perennials around it. Brush piles often attract native sparrows. I've had as many as twelve species feeding together on sunflower and white millet seeds spread around my backyard brush pile. Most of the cardinals that appear in my backyard also feed near the brush pile, where they can beat a hasty retreat if the neighborhood Merlin flies over.

Brush piles set near water can also provide a safe haven for salamanders and frogs. Unfortunately, they're sometimes good hiding spots for natural predators too, such as the occasional weasel or skunk. This isn't a problem in my backyard, where my dogs keep most other mammals away, or in rural areas where predators are an important part of the natural environment. But it can be a serious issue in prairie pothole regions, where slash from aspens provides enough cover to allow predators to sneak up on and kill large numbers of nesting waterfowl. If you develop a problem with animals preying on your birds, spreading around handfuls of cat or dog fur brushed from a pet will deter many of them. Unfortunately, brush piles can also hide neighborhood cats.

Dead and dying trees can provide nesting havens for woodpeckers and other cavity-nesting species. But it's important to remove dead trees that are within falling distance of your house, sidewalk, or road.

22 Root out invasive exotic plants

In North America, native animal and plant-life forms have evolved over millions of years and are still evolving. Plants and wildlife that are introduced into this huge ecosystem sometimes cause sudden, dramatic changes that may take native species thousands of years to adapt to on their own. Meanwhile, as native plants lose the competition to aggressive invasives, their decline hurts native wildlife. The annual cycles of native plants are well timed to the comings and goings of native birds, providing vegetal food and insect resources precisely when birds need them.

In some cases, a native plant that normally has a small population suddenly experiences a population explosion, usually because of changes we humans have caused. In the Florida Everglades, for example, because of the nutrient overload from agricultural runoff and human sewage, the cattail population has exploded, crowding out saw grass and the many birds and other animals characteristic of the Everglades that depend on it.

Some exotic plants have become genuine scourges, crowding out natives while providing little if any benefits to native wildlife. Garlic mustard is a rapidly spreading woodland weed that is displacing native wildflowers in much of its range throughout the northeastern and midwestern United States and Canada, south to South Carolina, and west to Kansas, North Dakota, Colorado, and Utah. It dominates the forest floor and can displace most native herbaceous species within ten years of its first appearance. This plant is a major threat to the survival of woodland herbaceous flora and the wildlife that depend on it. Unlike most other plants that invade disturbed habitats, garlic mustard readily spreads into high-quality forests.

Cheatgrass is spreading throughout rangeland in the American West and crowding out sage grass, an essential component in the diet of the Greater Sage Grouse. This splendid bird was clearly created on a day when somebody was in a whimsical mood; the male's annual courtship ritual is a bizarre and exuberant display of testosterone. But because of habitat degradation, especially the loss of native sage grass, the bird suffered a devastating population crash in the twentieth century that didn't stabilize until the mid-1980s and still shows no evidence of recovery.

Sometimes it's hard to appreciate just how damaging an invasive exotic plant can be. Unless you're familiar with the native vegetation, an area can appear verdant and healthy even when it's been completely taken over by exotic weeds. In 1876 kudzu was introduced into the United States; it is now known as the "foot-a-night vine" and the "vine that ate the South." Kudzu vines destroy forests by blocking sunlight from trees and the understory, even as unknowing passersby marvel at the lush vegetation.

Most tourists and many residents of Florida don't realize how badly invasive plants have damaged the ecosystem. The problems are masked when birds and plants are still in evidence. But the invasion into the Everglades by melaleuca and Old World climbing fern has damaged critical foraging and nesting habitats for the Wood Stork and Everglades Snail Kite. Invasion of coastal beach dunes by Australian pine has harmed the nesting of endangered sea turtles. Many biologists believe that, after outright habitat loss, invasive exotic species pose the greatest threat to biodiversity.

A species new to an area can open a Pandora's box long after its original introduction. The melaleuca tree was introduced to Florida in the early 1900s as a potential lumber source and to "dry out" the Everglades. For decades it seemed to be harmless. Then, in the late 1960s, its population suddenly exploded and it began to invade South Florida's natural areas.

Another example of an intentional introduction that got out of control is multiflora rose, which was originally brought to the eastern United States in 1866 as rootstock for ornamental roses. Beginning in the 1930s, the U.S. Soil Conservation Service promoted it for erosion control and as "living fences" to confine livestock. In the 1970s many state departments of natural resources were advocating the planting of multiflora rose as cover and food for wildlife and in highway median strips, to serve as crash barriers and to reduce oncoming automobile headlight glare. But farmers started noticing that on pastures and unplowed land, it disrupted cattle grazing; then ecologists discovered how much it had disrupted natural ecosystems. Multiflora rose now occurs throughout the eastern half of the United States and in parts of Washington and Oregon, tolerating a wide range of soil, moisture, and light conditions and thus invading fields, forests, prairies, some wetlands, and many other habitats. Multiflora rose grows aggressively and produces large numbers of fruits (rose hips) that are eaten and then dispersed by a variety of birds. That sounds good for birds, but the dense thickets of multiflora rose prevent most native shrubs and herbs from thriving, limiting the availability of food to a much narrower time frame. Buckthorn has the same effect.

Even in recent years, some organizations and agencies have introduced new species into areas as "biological controls," sometimes swapping one problem for another or causing new problems without putting a dent in the original one. For example, rats were inadvertently introduced to Hawaii when the ancient Polynesians first arrived, and more came on explorers' ships. They caused tremendous economic and ecological harm, damaging crops and native vegetation and destroying ground-nesting birds' eggs and young. To solve that problem, people introduced mongooses, fierce little predators just the right size to prey on rats. Unfortunately, rats are mainly nocturnal, while mongooses do most of their hunting by day. Suddenly, ground-nesting birds were getting a double whammy—from the nighttime depredations of rats and the daytime attacks by mongooses—with no improvement at all in the rat situation.

Despite warnings by naturalists and scientists, cane toads were introduced in Australia in 1935 specifically to control the cane grub and the scarab beetle, which attack sugarcane plantations. Too late, people discovered that the toads' highly toxic skin poisons pets and wildlife, and the toads carry diseases that can be transmitted to native frogs and fishes. The voracious cane toads eat huge numbers of honeybees, creating problems for beekeepers and farmers. They also prey on other native fauna, including small lizards, frogs, birds, fish, and mice, and they compete for food with native insectivores. Yet they don't eat the insects that they were intended to control.

In recent decades, the multicolored Asian lady beetle has been released several times by the U.S. Department of Agriculture throughout the eastern United States in an attempt to establish it in North America. It took a long time for beetles released in Louisiana and Mississippi in 1979 and 1980 to become established and spread, but by 1994, the species was found in Alabama, Georgia, South Carolina, and Florida. They are now widely found in North America, with frequent reports from the South, Northeast, Midwest, and as far west as Oregon. The beetles eat some insect pests but have become annoying pests themselves.

Just because a plant or animal is native to one part of the United States doesn't mean that it won't cause problems in other areas. Bruce Newhouse, president of the Native Plant Society of Oregon, writes, "The best rule is to not think of 'native' in a grandiose, meaningless sense (such as native to North America), but always to think of *local* native species, propagated from local stock. Plants not from one's local area might not offer the same benefits as locally native species, and may be either invasive, or hybridize, destroying the genetic individuality of local populations."

It takes an enormous amount of labor-intensive work to make even a dent in eradicating an introduced species once it gets established. In South Florida alone, local, state, and federal agencies have spent more than $28 million in an effort to eradicate melaleuca since 1991. And sometimes the cure can be far worse than the disease, especially when land managers resort to powerful herbicides to control invasive exotics. When the timing and method of application are carefully chosen to minimize the impact on animals, native plants, soil, and water, this can sometimes be justified. "Spot spraying" is always safer for the environment. It kills far fewer nontarget plants; limits exposure to wildlife, domestic animals, and humans; and minimizes runoff and groundwater contamination. But spot spraying requires many more man-hours than applying pesticides with airplanes or large machinery. As local, state, and federal budgets continue to be eroded, such decisions will be based on the cheapest route rather than the safest one for humans, birds, and the environment.

Many state departments of natural resources and nature organizations produce pamphlets and posters illustrating exotic weeds. Get into the habit of pulling them whenever you find them. When you hike on public lands, carry a plastic bag in your pocket to dispose of these weeds without allowing their seeds to spread.

23 Recognize and foster beneficial insects and spiders

Many insects and spiders are either beneficial or harmless. Fostering a backyard habitat where these creatures can flourish will provide a natural food source for beautiful birds such as warblers, tanagers, and orioles while also providing natural pest control.

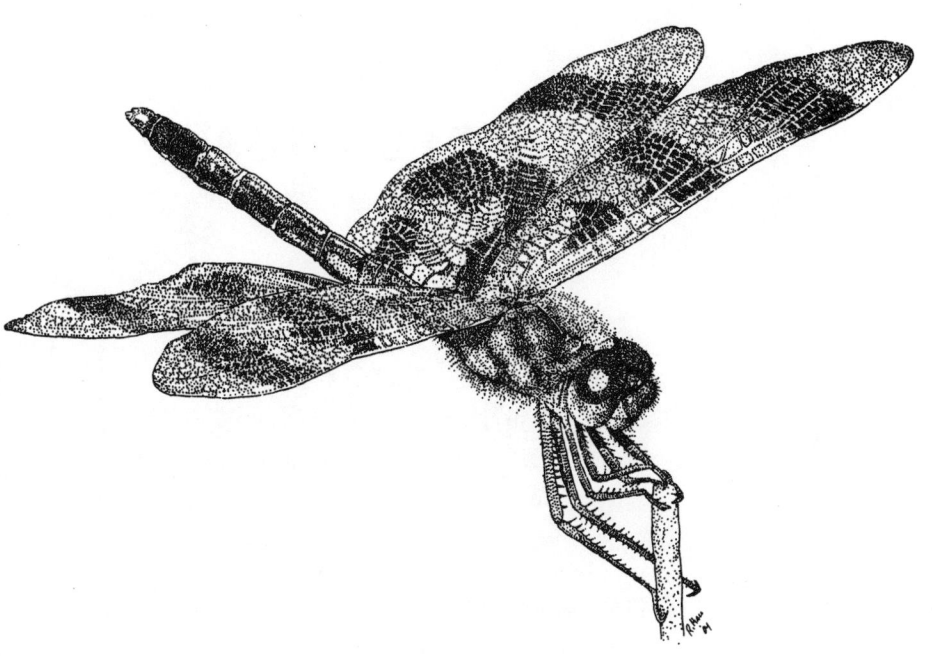

It is far better to attract beneficial insects to your yard by enhancing the natural habitat than by purchasing ones to release. Among other things, you're more likely to keep a healthy balance between predator and prey, so that the predaceous insects won't kill butterflies and other innocuous insects as well as the target prey. Increasing plant diversity in your yard not only helps insects; it also provides better habitat for birds. Grow an assortment of flowering plants so that there will be blooms from early spring through late summer. As a general rule, beneficial insects are attracted to tiny flowers that offer both pollen and nectar. To maintain beneficial insects, shallow pans of drinking water may be valuable, but never allow water to stand for more than a couple of days before replacing it, to keep mosquitoes from breeding. Leaving leaf litter under shrubs may provide beneficial insects with a cool, moist shelter. Never use zapper lights to kill outdoor insects. These lights attract and kill far more beneficial insects than pests. And of course, avoid pesticides, which are generally more lethal to beneficial insects than they are to pests. Most state departments of natural resources and university cooperative extension programs provide information about the best native plants to grow to foster beneficial insects.

7

LIMIT POLLUTION

WHEN WE HEAR THE WORD *POLLUTION,* MOST OF US THINK OF smokestacks belching toxic fumes or chemical plants seeping gunky effluents into lakes or rivers. But a great deal of the pollution that affects our water quality comes right from our own backyards. Lawn and garden fertilizers and pesticides, motor oil and antifreeze, and nutrients and pathogens from pet wastes can all percolate through soil to enter groundwater supplies or run off into storm sewers or directly into lakes and rivers. Finding ways to prevent this will help both birds and humans.

24 Limit outdoor water use

The world is facing a water crisis that is becoming urgent for humans and wildlife. In Australia in 2004, much of the continent's water was being rationed and reservoirs were being emptied. Due to changing weather patterns and a global warming trend; water contamination from pesticides, excessive nutrients, and other harmful chemicals; and heavier demand by a growing population, this problem is mushrooming throughout the world. As with so many other environmental issues, humans and birds are in this situation together, but we're the ones with the intelligence and the moral imperative to do something about it.

Growing lawn turf or shade trees in arid areas squanders water. Native plants that are adapted to dry conditions can be more attractive, provide proper habitats for native wildlife, and require much less maintenance. On average, about 35 percent of household water usage goes to tending lawns and gardens; in hot, arid places such as Arizona, it can be as high as 60 percent. Xeriscaping will improve your backyard habitat for native birds, provide you with an attractive yard, and save water.

In areas with periodic rainfall, one way to significantly reduce the amount of municipal water usage by your household is to put rain barrels at the corners of your home under downspouts. Water from rain barrels can be poured into buckets and used to wash cars, water lawns and garden plants, and fill birdbaths and backyard ponds, lowering your bills and reducing demand on local water treatment services. It's important that rain barrels be properly covered to prevent mosquitoes from breeding in them and that they be emptied within five to seven days of a rainfall to prevent algal growth. Also, you can keep small buckets beside indoor sinks and use them to collect running water that would otherwise go down the drain. This can be a fine source of birdbath water.

Many agencies and conservation organizations provide tips on how to save water. You can find these resources on the Internet and in your local library.

25 Limit nutrient runoff from your yard

I grew up in a suburb of Chicago intersected by Addison Creek. In the 1950s and 1960s, so many nutrients, especially phosphorus from detergents, poured into our sewers that the creek was dangerously polluted. As the water got churned up by a local dam, suds foamed up. On windy days, masses of suds floated through the air, often passing over my yard three blocks from the creek.

Plants require phosphorus and other nutrients to grow, but when nutrients become too concentrated in the soil, they cause "fertilizer burn," which can kill lawn grass. In my Duluth, Minnesota, neighborhood, many lawns treated by commercial lawn-care services appear brown by midsummer because they've been overfertilized. And even when liquid fertilizer is applied at lower levels, much of it runs off or seeps through soil to contaminate open water and groundwater. When nutrients become too concentrated in lakes, rivers, streams, and ponds, aquatic plant growth can become so dense that leaves on the surface keep light from reaching more than a few inches underwater. The oxygen produced by these overgrown plants is limited to the water's surface, while at lower depths, dead leaves and plants decompose, depleting dissolved oxygen in the water. Few aquatic insects and fish can survive in oxygen-depleted water, but mosquitoes flourish because they breathe via an abdominal tube to the surface.

In my own childhood town, the creek was an ugly shade of brown, smelled bad, and supported only a few bullheads and crayfish. My friends and I could find no ducks, geese, or gulls swimming in it. But mosquitoes flourished despite frequent DDT spraying. During that same period, Lake Erie became so eutrophic that it was considered a dead lake.

The level of phosphorus in laundry detergents was significantly reduced in the 1970s, but dishwashing detergents were left unregulated, and excessive fertilizer use continued to grow. In the ocean, when nutrients become too concentrated and change the water chemistry, they affect the timing of the availability of plankton, or even destroy it. Plankton is the very foundation of the ocean's food web. Nutrients originating from heavy use of agricultural and landscaping fertilizers, vehicle and factory emissions, and agricultural, pet, and human wastes work their way into fresh water and ultimately find their way to the sea, where there are now nearly 150 dead zones. These dead zones are increasing, and they pose as great a threat to fish stocks as overfishing, according to the United Nations Environment Program (UNEP) in its *Global Environment Outlook Year Book 2003*. And the effects of nutrient runoff are exacerbated by rising ocean temperatures. In 2004 there was an unprecedented decline in seabird nesting on islands in the North Sea and Bering Sea due to a crash in the sand eel population. Sand eels are small fish that provide food for cod and birds and in turn depend on plankton. In 2004 the sand eel population disappeared from vast areas of the northern seas.

Dead zones have doubled in number over the last decade, with some extending over 27,000 square miles (about the size of Ireland), according to UNEP. Fish-eating ocean birds, from razorbills and puffins to albatrosses and shearwaters, depend on healthy fish populations, as do human beings. As with so many other environmental issues, protecting our fresh and ocean water supplies from excessive nutrients is as important for us as it is for birds.

Spreading compost or a slow-release organic fertilizer can provide lawns and gardens with the same nutrients as liquid commercial fertilizers but at a slower, safer rate. Compost conditions and holds moisture in the soil, decreasing runoff and allowing plants to withdraw greater amounts of nutrients and toxins before seepage reaches groundwater. And plants growing in well-conditioned soil require less watering.

Nutrients from pet waste, piles of leaves, and sump pumps and detergents from washing cars and boats can also run off lawns and driveways

Common Murre

when we aren't conscientious about the problem. It's important to place compost bins or piles where seepage is least likely and to dispose of pet waste in garbage (where it will end up in a landfill) or to bury it where seepage is slowest.

One beautiful way to both help wildlife and protect storm sewers from excessive nutrient runoff is to build a rain garden—a shallow depression in your yard planted with native flowers and grasses selected to quickly soak up rainwater and melted snow from downspouts, driveways, and sloping lawns. Water soaks into the soil and replenishes groundwater rather than adding to runoff. Consult the Internet or gardening books to find the best plants and positioning for rain gardens in your area.

You can also get tips for reducing nutrient runoff from your municipal water provider, sewage treatment facility, university extension service, and environmental organizations.

8

MANAGE LAND WISELY

NEARLY 80 PERCENT OF THE LAND THAT WILDLIFE DEPENDS ON IS IN private hands. Those of us who own farmland, forest, grassland, or other large pieces of natural property can provide huge benefits for birds, usually while enjoying and using the land for our own interests as well.

26 Remove unnecessary fencing

When I was on a birding tour in Arizona in the early 1990s, our group spotted what looked like a dead raptor hanging from a fence by a strip of red cloth. Several of us jumped to the conclusion that a farmer had killed it. When we looked with binoculars, we saw that it was a Barn Owl, and since few of us had ever had a close-up view of this exquisite bird, we walked over to the fence. As we approached, suddenly the bird fluttered its wings. It was alive! That's when we realized that the apparent strip of cloth tying it to the barbed wire fence was actually the bird's bleeding legs. We surmised that while carrying a pack rat back to its nest, one of its dangling legs had been snagged by a protruding barb, slicing a three-inch incision and then catching. As the owl thrashed, its other leg was scraped and punctured. A couple of us managed to extricate the bird while our friends emptied out a Styrofoam cooler and punched large holes in the top. We put the owl inside and got it to a nearby veterinary clinic. The wounds required stitching, and the bird needed steroid ointments and antibiotics, but two days later it was well enough to be released where we found it.

Most birds in this predicament are not found in time to be rescued, and the situation was not a fluke. Collisions with fences are a significant cause of mortality for some species, particularly grassland gallinaceous birds. In one study of radio-tagged Lesser Prairie Chickens, over 25 percent of adult bird mortality was due to collisions with fences. Indeed, this is the primary cause of mortality for female prairie chickens. Prairie chickens and Sharp-tailed Grouse are accustomed to walking through grass, which is soft and pliable. Their first encounter with a fence is usually their last.

Fences can serve valuable functions for people. And birders often like fences because many grassland sparrows use them as perches. But when open habitat is no longer grazed or a fence is no longer necessary for another purpose, it should be removed.

27 Cut hay and alfalfa as late in the breeding season as possible

One June morning I came upon a newly mowed hayfield in northern Wisconsin. Even though the machinery was gone, I could hear that it had been mowed before I saw it—a dozen crows and five ravens were scouring the ground and squabbling over food. What were they picking at in the rows of drying meadow grass and flowers? The mangled bodies of baby birds. This field had held nesting Savannah and Le Conte's Sparrows, Sedge Wrens, Eastern Meadowlarks, Bobolinks, Upland Sandpipers, and Northern Harriers. In much of North America, June is the month when most ground nests hold eggs or helpless nestlings. Unfortunately, it's also the month when young hay has the highest protein content.

Fortunately, beef cows and horses don't require the high amounts of protein that dairy cows do. And many people who own pastureland don't raise livestock at all—they have it cut for aesthetic purposes or simply to prevent it from becoming shrubland. Changing the haying schedule can be an inconvenience for the landowner, but that usually pales in the face of all the lost eggs and nestlings when haying happens in May, June, and even early July. Marge Gibson, founder of Raptor Education Group, Inc., writes, "Many years ago hay was cut only twice per year. The first cutting was about July fourth, but now with the cutting coming in late May or early June there is no way ground nesters can pull off a brood with success." The farmers know they see fewer Meadowlarks, Bobolinks, grassland sparrows and of course Northern Harriers and Short-eared Owls, but often do not realize that they are the cause of the failure with early hay cutting.

How can you tell whether it's safe to cut hay or alfalfa? Meadowlarks often sit on exposed branches or even sing while holding insects in their mouths when they have nestlings. And Gibson notes, "When male Bobolinks are sitting on telephone lines or fence lines the female is still on eggs. The male will begin to make himself scarce once the young are hatched as he is doing most of the hunting for food as the female protects the young from predators. The young go from hatching to fledging in 10 to 14 days. Fledging means for Bobolinks that they leave the nest but still hide in the high grasses in the field until they are flying well which is about 18 to 20 days. So, when the male begins to be 'absent' for most of the day on the fence posts/telephone lines you have about 20 days until you can cut the hay. Give them more if you can."

When a delay in hay cutting represents a significant hardship to a farmer because of time or financial constraints or because the high protein content of early hay is important for livestock, the farmer should cut early. But if farmers are aware of the presence of nesting birds, fewer pastures will be cut while vulnerable eggs and nestlings remain. Farmers with relatively small pastures can scythe their fields, but that's not feasible for most farmers. Before cutting early with heavy machinery, the farmer or a birder should try to scout the field first and flag nests so that they can be given a wide berth.

28 Manage wooded land for birds as well as trees

As paper production increases and as we make more furniture and building materials out of wood products rather than solid lumber, forests are cut at younger ages. When any forest is clear-cut, it grows back, of course. But the first trees to return are pioneer or early-succession species, such as aspen, that grow well with a lot of sunlight. Only after these pioneer species grow and provide shade can other trees, such as maple, beech, and basswood, start to grow.

Different birds have different habitat needs. There's no such thing as a generic forest—there are characteristic species mixes for scores of forest types. A few birds are so specific that they must have one particular tree dominating their habitat. Kirtland's Warblers nest only on the ground beneath the lowest branches of jack pine trees. Other birds depend on something associated with the trees. For example, Northern Parulas build their nests of *Usnea* lichens in northeastern forests and Spanish moss in southeastern forests. Other species are more flexible. Scarlet Tanagers can live in a wide variety of deciduous or mixed deciduous-coniferous forest types, but they prefer mature forest, especially with oaks. White-headed Woodpeckers, of the far western mountains, require montane coniferous forests dominated by pines, with tree species varying geographically.

For most people who own forestland, one of their considerations is the bottom line, which in this case is determined by the value of the lumber, how long it takes to produce, how much it costs to protect it against insects and disease, and how much it costs to cut and transport. But most owners also enjoy the aesthetics of their forests and don't mind spending a little time and money to ensure that their land serves wildlife as well. The expense of protecting forests from insects and diseases goes up dramatically on monoculture tree farms. When there is a mixture of trees, diseases don't spread as readily or become as virulent. Monoculture forests don't support much wildlife either.

Unfortunately, for many decades, "supporting wildlife" was synonymous with "producing white-tailed deer." But it is becoming increasingly obvious that deer cause many problems for humans and birds alike, changing natural vegetation, the composition of forests, and the quality of habitat in the forest understory. Native plants are being overbrowsed to the point where some are becoming endangered and even extirpated from large areas. And studies show that deer eat a surprising number of eggs and nestlings of ground-nesting species. Despite these problems, the all too common occurrence of deer-automobile collisions, and the declining number of deer hunters across most of the nation, many state departments of natural resources are still working to maintain high deer populations. This situation is exacerbated by the increasing amount of forest acreage managed for pulp and paper, since aspen is an important food for deer. Ironically, although aspen is an equally important food for Ruffed Grouse, deer-related damage to the forest understory and perhaps directly to grouse nests is likely a significant factor in this species' current population decline.

Excluding deer from woodlots can be an important way of fostering birds. But that is far easier said than done, and some of the most effective ways of excluding deer, such as by planting buckthorn and other nonnative plants that deer don't eat, can cause other serious problems. Deer overpopulation won't be controlled until there is a widespread acknowledgment of the problem and a willingness on the part of state agencies and the U.S. Forest Service to stop catering to deer hunters and the paper and pulp industries and to start managing more acreage for mature and old growth. Deer hunting can be extremely dangerous for birders and others who visit the woods during hunting season, but when the deer population is excessive, both the legal take and the length of the hunting season should probably be increased. The long-term goal must be to reduce the deer population to healthier and sustainable levels.

Ovenbird

The biodiversity of our woodlots and private forests should be fostered by actively planting and nurturing a variety of native trees, especially later-succession species. When one of my middle-aged friends started planting oaks and other trees that take many decades to reach maturity, some people told him that it was a waste, since he'd never live to see a profit from them. But he's already being rewarded by the assortment of birds that now spend the winter or summer in his woods or pass through during migration. In the long run, fostering diversity in our forests will protect them from diseases that spread like wildfire through a monoculture, and it will promote a more enduring, healthy natural environment.

29 If you live on a lake, river, or stream, preserve the natural quality of the shoreline and surrounding habitat

Something deep in our souls draws us to the water. But the expression "you always hurt the one you love" is especially true of open water and the surrounding habitat. We often build cabins and homes on lakes because we love falling asleep to the haunting cries of loons, awakening to the ethereal songs of thrushes, and spending our days swimming and boating in sparkling waters. Unfortunately, when we bring our more civilized sensibilities to a wild lake, we may alter the natural setting and damage the very qualities that we love.

Fortunately, with care, attention, and a little education, we can maintain and improve the aesthetic value of shoreline property while preserving water quality and enhancing the habitat for birds and other wildlife. Maintaining a buffer of native grasses, broad-leafed plants, shrubs, and trees between the water and the more managed areas of your property, and limiting the amount of turf in the yard, can reduce runoff and help control the local goose population. Reduce or eliminate the use of pesticides and fertilizers near open water. There are many sources of information on the wise management of lakefront properties. Carrol L. Henderson's *Lakescaping for Wildlife,* published by the Minnesota Department of Natural Resources, is a good start.

30 If your property provides space for power lines, communications towers, or wind turbines, make sure they are bird safe

The U.S. Fish and Wildlife Service estimates that up to 174 million birds are killed by collisions with power lines and more than a thousand hawks and eagles are electrocuted at power lines each year. Millions of nocturnal migrants are attracted to the lights on TV and radio transmission towers and killed each spring and fall. Wind farms are a relatively new development on the landscape, but in some areas they are already the cause of significant avian mortality.

We all use electricity and communications technology directly or indirectly. Most book manuscripts are now produced on computers and delivered to publishers via e-mail (saving vast quantities of paper and toxic inks), so even if virulently anti-technology readers don't use telephones, television, radio, or other modern communication methods or even electricity from a power grid, they are still indirectly benefiting from them. And wind turbines produce far cleaner electricity than any alternative except for solar power. Clearly, we're not going to go backward in time to the days before these technologies existed, nor should we want to.

But there are better and worse ways of constructing power lines and power poles, communications towers, and wind turbines. It is unconscionable to erect power lines anywhere near water, bluffs, or other migratory pathways without putting bird flight diverters on the wires. And it's gross negligence to put up power poles that aren't designed to prevent bird electrocutions, since fires and power outages harm humans and destroy property as well as kill birds. It's difficult to get accurate scientific documentation about other issues, but if you have control over power line construction through your property, pressure the utility—loudly and publicly, if necessary—to provide these minimal safeguards. Unfortunately, public regulators often give carte blanche to corporate powers at the expense of the fundamental rights of landowners.

Communications towers are safest when they are freestanding, since birds (and humans) are more likely to collide with guy wires than with the tower itself, especially during daylight. Towers lower than 100 feet are safer than taller ones because they seldom require the lights mandated by the Federal Aviation Administration to prevent airplane collisions. Although lights may be necessary to protect our own well-being, they disorient nocturnal migrants flying in the vicinity, including warblers, thrushes, tanagers, and other beloved songbirds, causing them to collide with the tower, guy wires, and one another. In a twenty-five-year study of bird mortality at the 1,010-foot tower at Tall Timbers Research Station near Tallahassee, Florida, birds were killed nearly every night from mid-August through mid-November. Moderate numbers of migrants were killed under perfectly clear skies, but the toll increased markedly with overcast conditions. According to ornithologist Bill Evans at Towerkill.com, "Theoretically the small kills on clear nights were not from birds drawn to the tower lights but from birds that happened to be flying near the tower and didn't see a guy wire—blind collision." Evans notes, "It is important to clarify that the lights apparently do not attract birds from afar, but rather tend to hold birds that pass within a certain illuminated vicinity. . . . When passing the lighted area, it may be that the increased visibility around the tower becomes the strongest cue the birds have for navigation, and thus they tend to remain in the lighted space by the tower. Mortality occurs when they run into the structure and its guy wires, or even other migrating birds as more and more passing birds cram into the relatively small, lighted space." Even an isolated tower nowhere near a migratory pathway can be deadly. Between 1957 and 1994, a 1,000-foot tower in Eau Claire, Wisconsin, that was monitored daily during migration killed 121,560 birds of 123 species. If you receive a request to rent space for a tower on your property, you have a right to demand that the tower be freestanding and lower than 100 feet. In 2000, the U.S. Fish and Wildlife Service issued "Service Guidance on the Siting, Construction, Operation and Decommissioning of Communications Towers," which is available from the government or online at Towerkill.com.

There is not yet enough research on wind turbines to determine how to minimize bird and bat collisions. Grassland bird numbers do decline when turbines are present, so they are better sited on fields of row crops than in pastures and grasslands. Wind farms kill unacceptable numbers of raptors on some bluffs; similar kills will probably be documented along many waterways where migrants pass through and waterfowl spend time. Research is necessary to learn whether turbines can be designed to give visual or auditory cues to help birds and bats avoid them. Meanwhile, if anyone wants to use your land for a wind farm, require them to conscientiously monitor bird kills using the most advanced, accurate methods. Just picking up carcasses is not sufficient. Foxes, coyotes, raccoons, cats, crows, and other scavengers quickly learn to pick up dead birds, so what remains for a once-a-day monitor may not be an accurate reflection of the kill. The United States has known for many decades that we need to develop alternatives to fossil fuels. It's shocking that so much time was wasted before we finally started to take advantage of wind power, and it's distressing that we're now in such desperate straits that we're constructing huge wind farms in such sensitive places as Horicon Marsh in Wisconsin, one of the most important wetlands in the United States. Landowners have the most power to demand that utilities develop technologies that will at least minimize kills.

9

———

CONTROL PESTS SAFELY

THROUGHOUT HUMAN HISTORY, PEOPLE HAVE BEEN PLAGUED WITH natural pests, including insects, weeds, and wild animals. Just as any self-respecting Blue Jay looks out for itself and its family members first, we humans understandably and justifiably protect ourselves and members of our own species first. But some of the methods we use to control one pest turn out to cause more problems than they solve. Our understanding of how to synthesize and manufacture complex organic chemicals evolved much more rapidly than our understanding of how these chemicals and their metabolites can affect human and animal physiology and complex ecosystems. Many corporations now have a vested interest in using pesticides as a first line of attack against any and all pests. Tragically, the worst disease-carrying mosquitoes are developing resistance to pesticides, and dangerous mosquito-borne illnesses that hurt people and birds are increasing.

There are many other possible defenses against mosquitoes and other pests. Pesticides, like antibiotics and other powerful pharmaceuticals, should be used only when simpler, safer alternatives won't work. This protects both us and the environment, and it ensures that when pesticides must be used to address critical situations, they will be effective.

31 If you must control mosquitoes, do so safely

From earliest times, humans and birds have suffered from mosquito-borne illnesses. We think of malaria, yellow fever, encephalitis, and dengue as human diseases, but mosquito-borne disease organisms take a huge toll on birds too. For example, West Nile virus has killed many more birds than humans. In Hawaii and other oceanic islands where mosquitoes were introduced during historic times, native human and bird populations have been decimated, and some bird species rendered extinct, due to disease transmission by these blood-sucking pests. These diseases are especially problematic in tropical areas, where mosquitoes flourish despite decades of environmental pesticide applications.

Many insecticides are known to have serious environmental effects, but the most famous is DDT. According to an Environmental Protection Agency press release from December 31, 1972:

> A persistent, broad-spectrum compound often termed the "miracle" pesticide, DDT came into wide agricultural and commercial usage in this country in the late 1940s. During the past 30 years, approximately 675,000 tons were applied domestically. The peak year for use in the United States was 1959 when nearly 80 million pounds were applied. From that high point, usage declined steadily to about 13 million pounds in 1971, most of it applied to cotton.

DDT was also used in many areas in a failed attempt to control gypsy moths and the bark beetles that spread Dutch elm disease.

DDT was banned after a long public debate about the role of toxic chemicals in the environment. One side was originally articulated by Rachel Carson in her book *Silent Spring,* written as she was suffering from breast cancer and published just two years before she died. Even today, many continue to insist that DDT and its metabolite, DDE, which was found in human breast milk, do not pose a health risk to humans, despite current research establishing that DDT levels in pregnant women's blood were correlated with preterm births and low birth weight, major contributors to infant mortality.

Carson wrote, "We allow the chemical death rain to fall as though there were no alternative, whereas in fact there are many, and our ingenuity could soon discover many more if given opportunity." Her facts were meticulously documented, her evidence and conclusions supported by a huge number of independent scientists. When the chemical industry couldn't dispute Carson's facts, they resorted to ad hominem attacks on the author herself. Laura Orlando wrote in the March–April 2002 issue of *Dollars & Sense: The Magazine of Economic Justice:*

> Industry's attack on Rachel Carson was swift and vicious. The chemical companies banded together and hired a public relations firm to malign the book and attack Carson's credibility. The pesti-

cide industry trade group, the National Agricultural Chemicals Association, spent over $250,000 (equivalent to $1.4 million today) to denigrate the book and its author. The company that manufactured and sold the pesticides chlordane and heptachlor, the Velsicol Chemical Company of Chicago, threatened to sue Houghton Mifflin.

Milton Greenstein, legal counsel and vice president of *The New Yorker*, was called by at least one chemical company and told that the magazine would be sued if it didn't pull the last installment it planned to run of Carson's book. Greenstein responded, "Everything in those articles has been checked and is true. Go ahead and sue." John Vosburgh, editor of *Audubon Magazine*, which published excerpts from *Silent Spring*, said pretty much the same thing when *Audubon* was threatened. According to Carson biographer Linda Lear, Velsicol's lawyers suggested to Vosburgh that printing "a muckraking article containing unwarranted assertions about Velsicol pesticides" might "jeopardize [the] financial security" of magazine employees and their families. Vosburgh was so incensed that he wrote an editorial that appeared with the book excerpts, criticizing the chemical industry's response.

Even today, corporate interests continue to vilify Rachel Carson as if she had single-handedly (and seven years after her death) banned DDT, and as if the ban was based entirely on DDT's effect on birds rather than on valid concerns, now proved, about its potential to harm human beings. Gilbert L. Ross, M.D., medical director of the American Council on Science and Health, wrote a widely quoted letter to *U.S. News and World Report* (January 31, 2000):

Ms. Carson's writings may have been responsible for the chirping of "untold numbers of birds" who owe their lives to her. But, should we not also remember the millions of malaria victims in the third world whose voices have been prematurely stilled due to the banning of the DDT she demonized? It is Ms. Carson's spiritual cohorts who hope to stifle the potential of food biotechnology to feed the hungry masses, thus following in their mentor's misguided footsteps.

Ross neglects to point out that although Carson wrote a well-documented and influential book, her death took her out of the national dialogue that led the Nixon administration to begin regulating pesticides. Ross also neglects to mention that DDT is still legal in some of the Third World countries where malaria rates are increasing and where other mosquito-killing insecticides are heavily applied as well. Indeed, the heavy application of DDT for agricultural and other purposes is blamed for mosquitoes' built-up resistance to the pesticide, rendering it ineffective against dangerous malaria vectors in West Africa, Iran, Pakistan, India, Sri Lanka, Greece, Egypt, Central America, and Colombia. And Ross doesn't acknowledge that, as a wide-spectrum insecticide, DDT killed enormous numbers of bees and other pollinators, insects essential for producing many of the crops and fruits that "feed the hungry masses."

Rachel Carson's concerns about the effects of DDT were proved correct, but some studies suggest that DDT might play a role in protecting human health without entering natural or agricultural food chains. Since the 1940s, DDT has been applied indoors on upper walls and ceilings where mosquito-borne diseases threaten human lives. This practice has been an effective control against the spread of malaria in the Mississippi Valley of the United States and in Italy, Venezuela, Guyana, India, and several other countries, with little or no effect on humans and pets. But regulation and control of such indoor use of DDT for malaria control should be in the hands of the Environmental Protection Agency (EPA) and the Centers for Disease Control and Prevention, not the Department of Agriculture, with appropriate safeguards to protect people, pets, and the natural environment from contamination.

Nowadays, there is a safer alternative to DDT for outdoor use in combating mosquitoes—the larvicide Bti. This strain of Bt (*Bt israelensis*) kills aquatic insect larvae belonging to the order Diptera, including mosquitoes and blackflies, but it doesn't affect mayflies, dragonflies, caddisflies, or other species belonging to different orders. Bti poses virtually no threat to humans, birds, or beneficial insects. Because it targets larvae, it is sprayed over water, unlike mosquito adulticides, which are sprayed over land.

Using targeted larvicides, making netting and repellents more readily and cheaply available to people in mosquito-infested areas, developing effective repellents and pesticides for indoor use by vulnerable people, and focusing research on specific disease organisms and vaccinations would provide more effective short- and long-term disease control than continued

Three-wattled Bellbird

outdoor spraying of broad-spectrum insecticides. A wiser use of resources for the chemical industry would be to develop specific biochemical agents that can disrupt physiological processes unique to mosquitoes rather than to continue denying or distorting proven research and vilifying a woman who has been dead for forty years and cannot defend herself or respond to new information.

Of course, DDT was not the only insecticide in use in the 1960s. Today, 12,000 pesticides are registered by the EPA for use in the United States. Wayne Sinclair, M.D., and Richard Pressinger, M.Ed., compiled a body of information about the dangers of insecticides. Searching through six medical journals, they found reports of health risks from the mosquito-control pesticide Dibrom (naled) and the pyrethroid pesticide permethrin, including genetic damage, cancer potential, neurotoxicity to unborn children, and harm to marine life. Shockingly and ironically, they noted that pesticide applications appear to be dramatically increasing the incidence of encephalitis, perhaps because of immune system damage to the wildlife that carries encephalitis or to the mosquitoes' own defenses against the disease. Or it may be related to the fact that a higher percentage of dragonflies and other insect predators are killed than mosquitoes, removing a significant cause of natural mosquito mortality.

West Nile virus first appeared in New York in 1999. In the year 2000, more than 80,000 bird carcasses were found throughout the state and brought in for analysis. Funded by the National Audubon Society, Dr. Ward Stone did detailed necropsies on more than 4,000 of those dead birds. Thirty-one percent tested positive for the virus, but 48 percent had died from pesticides and other environmental toxins. Despite massive outdoor spraying, West Nile virus continues to spread. In Minnesota, the prevalence of the disease in a seven-county mosquito-abatement district that relies on pesticide use is about the same as in the remainder of the state.

Unfortunately, many of the mosquitoes implicated in disease transmission in the United States are those that reproduce in small, even tiny, stagnant water sources such as gutters, puddles, children's toys, tires, birdbaths, and other containers and water sources that can't be sprayed with Bti efficiently or effectively. Any effective mosquito-abatement project must include public education, and every community and individual must take responsibility for eliminating as many of these small sources of standing water as possible. Encouraging mosquito-eating bats and swallows to live in your area by installing appropriate nesting and roosting boxes can provide some additional help.

When she was small, my daughter developed a rare, severe reaction to mosquito bites, so it was imperative that we minimize or even eliminate mosquitoes from our house and prevent Katie from getting bitten outdoors. Some of the steps we took to protect her would also work for people with compromised immune systems and others vulnerable to West Nile virus and other mosquito-borne illnesses.

- We kept the window screens in excellent condition, with no tears or holes that might allow a mosquito to pass through.

- At dusk, we closed all the window shades and curtains and turned off the porch lights to keep mosquitoes from being attracted to the house.
- We hung a "bug zapper" light outside Katie's bedroom door and used it as a nightlight, to keep any indoor mosquitoes from entering her room.
- We got into the habit of cleaning birdbaths every two or three days and turning over sandbox toys to keep rainwater from collecting in them. We cleaned out the gutters every spring.
- After we discovered some mosquito larvae in a laundry tub, where water had collected in a shallow indentation near the open drain, we started being more conscientious about wet areas in the basement.
- When Katie played outside, she wore lightweight pants, a long-sleeved tight-weave shirt, and a hat, all of which had been heavily sprayed with insect repellent. (Katie's mosquito sensitivity was worst when she was a baby and toddler, too young to safely use insect repellent on her skin.)

32 Use weed killers and fungicides only as a last resort

According to the U.S. Fish and Wildlife Service and the National Audubon Society, about 7 million birds are killed each year by household lawn pesticides. Herbicide use is growing at a particularly rapid rate, with home owners using over 50 percent more than they did twenty years ago. According to 1999 figures released by the EPA, 74 percent of U.S. households use some type of pesticide; 40 million use herbicides. There are many safer alternatives.

When I was a bird rehabilitator, a woman brought me two nestling robins that were suffering from neurological damage. One was on its side, unable to balance itself. Neither could lift its head to beg for food. Both of them trembled with violent spasms every few minutes. She told me that she'd found one adult dead on the ground beneath the nest tree and another adult and two nestlings dead inside the nest. I asked her if any lawns in the vicinity had been treated within the past two days, and she answered, "Why, yes! We sprayed our yard just yesterday. But it can't be that—those chemicals were approved by the EPA." The spray was a "weed and feed" formulation with a herbicide (weed killer) and a fertilizer. Apparently, the adult robins had run on the lawn while the grass was still wet, and when they returned to the nest to feed their nestlings, their belly feathers smeared the toxins directly on the nestlings' bare skin. Perhaps when the adults preened or pulled earthworms out of the freshly sprayed lawn, they ingested the toxins themselves.

Both baby robins were dead within a few hours. I called a few agencies and rehab facilities, trying to get their bodies necropsied to determine for certain what had killed them. But necropsies are expensive, and every veterinarian and scientist I talked to said that there wouldn't be enough tissue to analyze in such tiny birds. Also, many pesticides break down into different, often less toxic chemicals within days after application. This is good for animals exposed to them after that time, but the neurological damage caused when the chemicals are active doesn't miraculously reverse.

Marge Gibson, past president of the International Wildlife Rehabilitation Council and founder and director of Raptor Education Group, Inc., in Antigo, Wisconsin, is one of a growing number of people who believe that pesticide manufacturers should be required to use some sort of chemical markers to make it easier to trace chemical killers. Chemical manufacturers decry environmentalists for their blanket indictments of pesticides, but they refuse to make it easier to pinpoint which of the 12,000-plus pesticide products currently registered for use in and around our homes cause the greatest damage; they prefer to protect their formulations as trade secrets.

Most Americans believe that pesticides are tested by the government to ensure their safety for humans and wildlife. But this is simply not true. Chemical companies do their own testing and submit the results to the EPA for review, setting up the potential for "selective" reporting. And pesticides are not "approved" by the EPA. The agency may register pesticides if there is no documented and significant evidence that they cause harm or if the manufacturer can make a case that the benefits outweigh the harms, but there is virtually no enforcement to ensure that pesticides are limited to their prescribed uses, and there are no regulations requiring that pesticides be tested for their effects on songbirds. Since the late 1980s, field testing to determine whether a chemical might cause unexpected environmental consequences is no longer required for registration. And almost no research has been conducted on the effects of multiple pesticides used together, even though pesticides are often applied in complex mixtures and may cause far worse problems in combination than alone.

Despite the lack of research, it's clear that pesticides, including herbicides, kill birds, as I observed firsthand and as Dr. Stone's necropsies on

New York birds established. Atrazine, one of the most widely used herbicides in agriculture, which is also registered as a weed controller on lawns and golf courses, has been found to be a hormone disruptor, causing frogs to develop both male and female sex organs even at extremely low concentrations. At higher levels, it's connected with a variety of problems, including stopping photosynthesis in aquatic systems, thus depleting oxygen. According to *National Geographic Today* (April 16, 2004), "Atrazine, a top selling weed killer in the United States and the world, has been found to dramatically affect the sexual development of male frogs, turning them into hermaphrodites—creatures with both male and female organs—at concentrations 30 times lower than those deemed safe by the U.S. Environmental Protection Agency. 'What struck us as unbelievable was that atrazine could cause such dramatic effects at such low levels,' says Tyrone Hayes, an associate professor of integrative biology at the University of California, Berkeley, who led the frog study." Yet in October 2003, the same month that the European Union banned atrazine, the EPA decided to permit its ongoing use in the United States, with no new restrictions.

According to the American Bird Conservancy, one of the most common herbicides for home use, glyphosate (the active ingredient in Roundup), "can be acutely toxic to non-target plants, including aquatic plants and algae. The effects of this toxicity on natural plant succession alters the ecology of treated areas. In most cases, the plant species diversity will decrease, and along with it, the numbers of insects, mammals and birds utilizing these areas as habitat." (www.abcbirds.org/pesticides/Profiles/glyphosate.htm)

Roundup also weakens crops, leading to a vicious spiral of increasing farmer dependency on chemicals to solve many of the problems caused by other chemicals. In a study conducted by T. B. Moorman and colleagues at the U.S. Department of Agriculture's Southern Weed Science Laboratory in Stoneville, Mississippi, glyphosate reduced the ability of soybeans and clover to fix nitrogen. A study conducted by G. S. Johal and J. E. Rahe of the Center for Pest Management at Simon Frase University in Burnaby, British Columbia, found that glyphosate made bean plants more susceptible to disease. At Dalhousie University in Halifax, Nova Scotia, D. Estok and others found that glyphosate reduces the growth of beneficial mycorrhizal fungi, which are important for soil quality.

Even worse, the effects of this heavily used weed killer aren't limited to plants. Utah State University Extension reported in "Utah Pesticide and

Toxic News" (July 2005), " 'The herbicide Roundup is lethal to some tadpole species,' says a University of Pittsburgh researcher who tested the compound in experimental tanks. The surfactant used in the formulation appears to be the culprit. Roundup, manufactured by Monsanto, is the second most commonly applied herbicide in the U.S. and has been considered relatively nontoxic to animals. Rick A. Relyea, an assistant professor of biology . . . concludes from previous research conducted in Australia that the lethal chemical is probably not glyphosate, the active ingredient in Roundup, but polyethoxylated tallowamine (POEA), the surfactant in the product that allows glyphosate to penetrate leaves. About 10 years ago, scientists found that pure glyphosate is not very toxic to some Australian tadpole species, Relyea says. But they discovered that both Roundup and pure POEA are quite toxic to these same species." (http://extension.usu.edu/files/newsletters/July%2005.pdf)

The American Bird Conservancy profile of glyphosate, which cites supporting studies, says that products that contain glyphosate are dangerous to mammals: "Most toxicity tests cited by industry and the EPA [Environmental Protection Agency] investigate toxicity through oral exposure routes. The toxicity of glyphosate and the common surfactant POEA is much greater through inhalation routes of exposure. . . . Experimentally induced inhalation of Roundup by rats produced 100 percent mortality in 24 hours. Humans ingesting as little as 100 ml of Roundup have died (suicide attempts using Roundup have a 10 to 20 percent success rate)." The same report cites studies indicating that glyphosate, especially in combination with the surfactant used in Roundup, is toxic to fish and invertebrates.

M. I. Youset and other researchers at the University of Alexandria in Egypt and the University of Tromso in Norway found that sperm production in rabbits was diminished by 50 percent when they were exposed to glyphosate. And a study published in 1998 in *Environmental and Molecular Mutagenesis* found that an unidentified chemical in Roundup caused genetic damage in the livers and kidneys of mice exposed to the herbicide. Unfortunately, Monsanto doesn't have to reveal what ingredients are in Roundup because the formula is a trade secret protected by patent regulations. In California, where pesticide-related illnesses must be reported, glyphosate was the third most commonly reported cause of pesticide illness among agricultural workers, and the most common cause in landscape workers. Symptoms experienced after Roundup exposure include eye and skin irritation, headache, nausea, and heart palpitations. There is no testing on human beings to learn of the short- or long-term effects of these toxins; the only indication that a chemical may be harmful to human beings is by guesswork based on its effects on animals. We react swiftly when a canary keels over in a coal mine, but we ignore the warning of wild bird deaths and even severe human illnesses.

Although Monsanto claims that Roundup breaks up into harmless substances, it has found to be extremely persistent, with residue absorbed by subsequent crops more than a year after application. According to the American Bird Conservancy, "Glyphosate's toxicity is compounded by its persistence in the environment. Recent research suggests that even when glyphosate binds soil particles, it will cyclically 'desorb' or lose its attraction to soil and become active as a herbicide." As well, the World Health Organization (UNEP, 1994 Glyphosate. Environmental Health Criterion #159, Geneva, Switzerland) found that glyphosate's half-life in forest pond sediments was 400 days.

American households spend nearly $2 billion on an estimated 80 million pounds of pesticides every year, and eventually some of the toxins work their way into groundwater and run off into lakes, rivers, and streams. According to a 1999 U.S. Geological Survey (USGS) report on the quality of our nation's waters, "At least one pesticide was found in almost every water and fish sample collected from streams and in more than one-half of shallow wells sampled in agricultural and urban areas." Conservationist Rob Fergus notes, "A couple of western studies I have seen (an Idaho report on the Boise area and a USGS survey of Willamette River tributaries in Oregon) suggest that watersheds with a suburban component are the ones most likely to have pesticide concentrations in excess of acute toxicity levels for aquatic life. The pesticides most commonly exceeding acute concentrations are precisely the ones commonly used in gardening and lawn care. This makes sense when you consider that individual suburban users of pesticides, applying them to very small acreages, are less limited by costs than farmers, and likely to overapply the chemicals. So there is a lot to be gained by encouraging suburban residents to moderate and, better yet, eliminate their use of common yard chemicals."

When applied to an entire lawn, the herbicides in "weed and feed" applications are applied even to sections of lawn that are weed free. When consumers apply lawn pesticides themselves, they can at least spot-spray individual dandelions rather than applying toxins to every square inch of lawn. Most lawn care services don't limit herbicide applications to weeds alone; they develop formulas for each region of the country based on climatic averages, regardless of any given year's actual rainfall and temperature conditions, and all treated lawns in the region receive identical doses year after year, whether they are covered with thousands of dandelions or have only one or two. This increases the exposure for wildlife, pets, and human beings, and it hastens the rate at which weeds become resistant to herbicides. As weeds grow more resistant, farmers and home owners use increasing amounts of herbicides in a vicious and unending circle, providing spiraling profits for chemical manufacturers and increasing the incidence of asthma, allergies, and cancer for the rest of us.

There are many alternatives to lawn and garden pesticides. Plants native to an area are already adapted to the natural rainfall, humidity, temperature, and soil conditions. They can more easily withstand weed, insect, fungus, and other pest damage than can introduced plants that are stressed by the unfamiliar weather and soil conditions. Native plants also provide more habitat for native wildlife. Minimizing the area of manicured lawn will not only reduce your need for lawn pesticides but also provide many other benefits. Select grass varieties that were developed for your region. Never use a lawn care service that applies pesticides to the entire lawn; insist on spot-spraying weeds only.

There are many other tricks for reducing or eliminating our reliance on herbicides. Corn gluten meal applied in early spring and fall may prevent the germination of dandelions, crabcrass, and other common lawn weeds. Overseeding bare spots in the lawn, core aerating the lawn, and adding organic mulch or compost will improve soil quality and help prevent weed growth. You can learn about the many safe alternatives to lawn and garden pesticides from gardening books and in pamphlets available from your local cooperative extension office. "Audubon at Home," a program developed by the National Audubon Society, encourages individuals to take action to improve the environmental health and habitat quality of their yards and neighborhoods. Many alternatives to pesticide use are listed on its Web site (www.audubon.org/bird/at_home/).

33 Eliminate or minimize the use of lawn and garden insecticides

Even though DDT and other pesticides failed to curtail the bark beetles that carry Dutch elm disease or stop the spread of the gypsy moth, many people continue to turn to insecticides to deal with insect pests in their yards. According to the EPA's 1999 figures, 58 million households use insecticides. In the 1999 USGS report, over 10 percent of the urban streams sampled contained a mixture of the insecticides diazinon and chloropyrifos. In a recent study of pesticide exposure among children living in a major U.S. metropolitan area, traces of lawn and garden chemicals were found in 99 percent of the 110 children tested. Concentrations were significantly higher in children whose parents reported that they used pesticides in their yards.

Even after an insecticide is proved to be harmful, it still takes time and effort to end its use. The U.S. Fish and Wildlife Service issued a draft biological opinion in 1993 indicating that parathion might adversely affect over 170 species. Parathion was also implicated as a human carcinogen and as a cardiovascular, developmental, endocrine, neurological, reproductive, respiratory, and skin toxicant. Nevertheless, it took a decade and a massive campaign by the American Bird Conservancy and others to halt the use, sale, and distribution of the product in the United States. Even today, parathion is still being used in Latin America, where farmworkers, tropical birds, and migratory birds from North America continue to be hurt by it.

In many cases, home owners use unnecessary insecticides, which are included in many basic lawn formulations applied by commercial lawn care services. These are invariably bad for birds and of little or no value to home owners, who are usually most interested in controlling dandelions. But, in addition to fertilizers and dandelion-killing herbicides, lawn care services often apply insecticides on the off chance that a particular lawn is infested with cutworms. Most of these companies refuse to supply home owners with a list of the ingredients they use, claiming that it's a trade secret. So it's impossible to know for sure how dangerous these applications are.

It's wise for home owners to avoid using Bt too, even though it's safer than most insecticides. The variety used on lawns and gardens, Btk, kills all caterpillars, including monarch butterfly and luna moth larvae. Caterpillars are essential in the diets of warblers and other birds, so Btk reduces their food supplies. And there is evidence that many insect pests are growing resistant to Bt, as they have to so many other insecticides. Because of the importance of pest control for agriculture, many farmers will continue to apply at least some insecticides, but home owners should find alternatives whenever possible to at least slow the pace at which resistance develops. There are many options for noninsecticide pest control that are easy to use for lawns and small-scale gardening, including fostering native insect-eating frogs, toads, beneficial insects and spiders, bats, and insect-eating birds. You can learn about all kinds of pesticide alternatives from extension services, conservation organizations, Audubon at Home, the National Wildlife Federation, and organic gardening associations.

34 Control rodents safely

Rats and mice pose serious hazards to wildlife and humans. On Hawaii and other islands where rats have been introduced, they've brought populations and even whole species to the verge of extinction. On Gough Island, in the Atlantic between the southern tips of Africa and South America, introduced mice have learned how to attack and kill Tristan Albatross chicks that are 200 times their size. Researchers discovered in 2005 that a shocking 80 percent of the chicks were being lost, primarily due to these mouse attacks. Also, fleas carried by rodents may harbor diseases. Rats and mice, like the humans they have evolved with, are intelligent and adaptable, but except when they are kept for research purposes or as pets, they pose a threat to humans and native wildlife.

We need to control problem rodents, but we must take precautions so that our methods don't hurt birds, other wildlife, or human beings, causing even greater problems. Pesticides registered for rats and other mammals are extraordinarily toxic to humans, birds, and all other wildlife. Many rat poisons are anticlotting agents that remain toxic in the tissues of dead and dying rats. Poisoned rodents can be picked up by pets or taken by predators and scavengers, which in turn ingest the toxins. At sublethal levels, this secondary poisoning may not immediately kill a hawk or an eagle, but since these birds often receive minor cuts and scrapes during their hunting activities, they can still "bleed out" with even low levels of anticoagulant rat poisons in their systems. And because rats breed quickly, causing major infestations, the large number of poisoned animals at a site increases the likelihood that hawks will eat several affected rats, ingesting enough poison to kill the raptors.

At times, rat or mouse infestations may become so dangerous that professional exterminators must be called in. But the extraordinarily dangerous pesticides they use should be considered the last resort when rodents are causing demonstrable, significant, genuinely dangerous health or ecological problems. Every effort must be made to set the bait where it will not be discovered or taken by other animals and to quickly remove dead and dying rats before predators or scavengers can find them. Rat poisons are cruel—death is slow and painful—so for humane reasons, too, they should not be used except in extraordinary situations when human health or the survival of an ecosystem is at risk.

How can we keep the number of rodents down without using such drastic measures? In most situations, sealing off food and nesting sites and maintaining healthy populations of natural predators are the safest and wisest long-term defenses. Where grain is stored, rat poisons are a temporary and dangerous solution; it is better to focus on denying them access to the food in the first place. Never use Tanglefoot or other sticky pest control formulas outdoors. If you must use them indoors, be prepared for a traumatic experience for yourself as well as your target pest. Rats and mice make surprisingly loud distress calls when desperate; they may gnaw off feet that are stuck in these products, and if their bellies get stuck, they may struggle so hard that they are disemboweled. Many of us have trouble directly killing a mouse or rat, for reasons ranging from squeamishness to moral repugnance. Snap traps are no more cruel than other methods and, when set indoors, are far less likely than poisons to hurt children, wildlife, and pets. It's best to affix snap traps to something heavy so that a trapped rat or mouse doesn't drag itself to an inaccessible place, lengthening its suffering and presenting you with another unpleasant problem.

People who maintain bird feeding stations must not subsidize rats and mice. Minimize the amount of spilled seed that sits overnight at feeding stations, and never offer bread to birds—it has minimal nutritional value for native birds and is an open invitation to rats and mice. Store birdseed in the basement, shed, porch, or garage in well-sealed bins. Metal bins are best, because rodents can't chew their way in. And if you do notice a rat at your bird feeding station, close down shop for at least a week.

10

Know How to Deal with Wildlife Problems

Ｗhen we enhance our backyard habitat, we attract not only songbirds but also other wildlife—sometimes species that we don't particularly want. And even our favorite birds can cause problems, such as woodpeckers damaging siding or cardinals flying repeatedly into windows, battling their reflections. Knowing what to do when you have a problem with wildlife will make your backyard habitat more enjoyable.

35 **Learn what to do when you find injured or sick birds**
We people have made the world so inhospitable for birds that every year over a billion are killed and millions, perhaps billions, more are injured by striking cars, windows, power lines, and communications towers; poisoned by pesticides and other toxins; oil soaked after spills; and attacked by cats and dogs. It seems fitting that when we are the direct cause of injuries to wild birds, we should do our best to help them recover.

Many people believe that injured birds are less fit genetically and that it's better to eliminate them from the gene pool, but most human-caused problems and even many natural causes of bird injuries are random, taking out fit and unfit individuals indiscriminately. Individual birds have value and deserve our respect and help for no other reason than simple humaneness. Working with even the most abundant species provides rehabbers with experience and knowledge that will come in handy when working with endangered and threatened birds. And most rehab centers provide valuable educational services using common birds, making the general public more aware of the problems wild birds face and how to better protect them.

Sometimes, it's more compassionate to leave a badly injured bird to die, when capture and confinement would distress it without relieving pain, improving its chance of survival, or removing a disease vector from the wild. But sometimes a bird's life can be saved by taking it to a rehabber. Unfortunately, untrained individuals often don't know how to capture an injured bird, safely transport it, or find a rehabber in the first place.

If you find a bird on its side or one that seems dazed and unable to fly, far from any window, road, wires, or towers, it may be sick rather than injured. It's difficult for inexperienced people to diagnose an illness or to successfully nurse a diseased bird back to health, and it's illegal to hold a wild bird for any purpose without a license. Some serious communicable illnesses are possible, too. Although bird diseases are seldom transmitted directly to humans, there are exceptions. I became extremely sick after being bitten by a louse on a sick bird, and the disease organism was never isolated. Other rehabbers with many years of experience have never heard of another case like mine, so this is apparently a rare occurrence. Nevertheless, when you encounter a sick bird, you should take precautions to avoid getting sick yourself.

If you find a bird that may have died from West Nile virus or another human health risk, contact your state health department or department of natural resources to find out if they are testing birds to verify the status of the disease in your area. If you find a sick bird that may be infected, call a professional rehabber to find out what to do. In some cases, rehabbers can't take birds that may be infected, because this could put other birds in the facility at risk.

The greater likelihood when you encounter a sick bird is that it has been poisoned with pesticides or lead. Of 4,000 dead birds necropsied in New York State, almost half had died from pesticides and other toxins. Birds can get sick from many commonly used lawn chemicals or from ingesting lead shot or sinkers. Although ducks and geese can be legally hunted only with nonlead shot, upland birds such as grouse, pheasants, and doves still can be legally shot with toxic lead in most places, even though we've known for decades that they too, along with ground-feeding songbirds such as bobolinks and meadowlarks, may ingest lead shot and be poisoned.

Wear gloves to pick up any sick bird. To capture a hurt or sick bird that is trying to flee, toss a lightweight towel over it. Place it in a sturdy box. If you happen to have a piece of Astroturf or some wood chips or cedar shavings handy, cover the bottom with that. Otherwise, paper towels work better than newspapers because they aren't as slippery. If the bird is unable to sit upright, prop it with a tissue "donut cushion" or wedged between rolls of paper towels. Never house or transport an injured wild bird in a cage, even temporarily; the bars will fray its feathers.

To immobilize a badly drooping wing in a safe position to prevent further injury while transporting a bird, the best thing to use is Vet Wrap, a product that sticks only to itself, but unless you're a doctor or a veterinarian, you're not likely to have that handy. Hairdresser tape (the kind used to hold bangs in place) works well too, but that can be hard to find. Duct tape is much too sticky, and cellophane tape is too stiff. Masking tape can be used, but it's best to stick and unstick it on a table a few times to weaken the adhesive so that removal won't pull out many feathers.

Get any sick or injured bird to a licensed rehabber as quickly as possible. If you're transporting a wild bird in your car, keep the radio off or at least set at a low volume.

Fledglings have very short tails for a week or more after leaving the nest, and this is perfectly natural. If a bird's tail feathers are pulled out, they will grow back in, typically within a few weeks. Many adult birds adapt quite well to flying without most of their tail feathers. I've watched two different adult chickadees lead normal lives after a predator had pulled their tail feathers out. In both cases, it was easy to recognize the birds from day to day as the feathers grew in, so I was certain that they both recovered completely. If tail feathers are merely broken or frayed, however, they won't be replaced until the bird molts. Licensed rehabbers often attach replacement feathers when necessary (called "imping") but this is painstaking and requires expertise. It also requires feathers, which are illegal for nonlicensed people to possess.

Cat bites cause puncture wounds, and cat saliva is heavily laden with dangerous bacteria. If you find a bird that was attacked by a cat, get it to a rehabber immediately. Without antibiotics, it will certainly die within a few days, even if it seems fine initially after the attack.

Make sure that you keep the number of the nearest rehab facility near your phone, with your other emergency numbers. Rehab facilities almost never receive government funding, so please support these centers generously.

36 Learn what to do when you find a baby bird

Every summer I get at least a hundred calls from people who have found baby birds and want to know what to do. Many people are afraid to pick up baby birds for fear that the mother will detect the scent of human hands and no longer take care of them. Although recent research indicates that many birds have a better sense of smell than ornithologists once believed, birds identify their babies pretty much the way we humans do—by sight and sound, not odor. So if you pick up a fallen nestling, you can restore it to its nest without fear that the parents will reject it.

Many of us have a powerful instinct to bond with small, helpless creatures, and sometimes a person who has every intention of bringing a baby bird to a rehabber ends up trying to raise it. But possessing any wild bird violates state and federal laws. In the case of baby birds raised by well-meaning but inexperienced people, these birds have a much poorer chance of survival and a poorer quality of life if they do survive.

Most baby birds fall into two categories, *precocial* and *altricial*. Precocial birds, such as ducklings, shorebirds, and barnyard chicks, hatch covered with soft down, open their eyes within minutes or hours, and quickly leave the nest, following their mother to food. Parent birds may hold food up to the mouths of precocial chicks, or they may tap at food to show the babies what is edible, but the babies don't open their mouths wide to beg, as robins and jays do.

Precocial chicks must learn very quickly upon hatching how to survive, so these species *imprint,* usually on the first moving, vocalizing thing they see, which is virtually always their mother. If an imprinted baby bird is separated from its family, it will have trouble adapting to feeding without its mother and siblings nearby. Fortunately, an imprinted chick can often be released in the vicinity of another mother and same-size chicks of its species and successfully join that family. If you find a wild duckling, killdeer, or other fuzzy chick, get it to a rehabber or release it near its own or a potential foster mother as quickly as possible. On rare occasions, one precocial chick hatches after the others have already left the nest. In this case, since the wild chick hasn't seen its mother, it may imprint on a person picking it up. Chicks imprinted on humans, especially shorebirds, may starve to death because they feed, by instinct, on food items presented by their mother, using subtle clues that we simply can't match. Imprinted chicks are adorable, and it is heartbreaking to watch them die, but that nearly always happens if an untrained person tries to raise them.

Altricial chicks undergo two stages of development—*nestling* and *fledgling*. If a nestling falls from a nest, it can be put back without risk. Fledglings can be placed back in the nest, but like human toddlers, they'll hop right back out. You can recognize altricial nestlings because they have a lot of bare skin and cannot hop at all. They sometimes fall out of nests in high winds or storms or are plucked from a nest by a crow or jay and dropped when mobbed by the parents or other birds. Rarely, a nestling may restlessly wiggle out of the nest when it's infested with lice or mites. If you can return a nestling to its own nest, do so. The parents will not reject a baby that has been touched by human hands. If you cannot return it to the nest or if the nest has been destroyed and can't be repaired, get the bird to a rehabber as soon as possible.

Altricial fledglings can hop or walk. Cavity-nesting fledglings such as woodpeckers and swallows can fly fairly well from the time they emerge from the nest, but many fledglings cannot fly for several days or more. These are the birds that people most often mistake as abandoned. Sadly, the vast majority of fledglings "rescued" by people were actually being properly cared for by their parents when the well-meaning person intervened. When a nestful of babies fledges, each little bird hops or flits about, exploring the world and periodically making sounds that attract its parents to feed it. The parents can't be with all the fledglings at the same time—keeping a whole brood of fledglings together would be like trying to keep four or five toddlers together in a toy store. So please don't assume that a baby bird hopping around alone is an orphan or has been abandoned. Within a couple of days of leaving the nest, most fledglings in a family band together and retreat to more secluded areas.

If you're worried about children, cat attacks, or other dangers facing a fledgling in the open, pick it up and carry it to a nearby tree or shrub. The parents will certainly be able to find it. Taking a fledgling from its parents is cruel to both the bereft parents and the baby, whose best chance of survival is to be raised and educated by its parents.

Never feed any baby bird crackers, bread, or milk. The most nutritious diet to feed an altricial chick until you can get it to a rehabber is a commercial hand-feeding mixture for baby birds that you can purchase at a pet shop. Kaytee Exact Handfeeding Diet, a powdered mix, provides a reasonably good diet for the short term. This is not a complete diet for most wild birds, however, and should be supplemented with other food items appropriate for the species. For example, most songbirds require mealworms or other insects, and robins and waxwings are also fed some fruits. Feed nestlings every fifteen to thirty minutes, as much as they can comfortably eat, during daylight hours. If you must take a break for up to a couple of hours once or twice a day, that's okay, but to parent birds, raising their babies is a full-time job, and if you are assuming that responsibility, you should do it properly.

Most nestlings defecate as soon as they swallow. In the wild, this ensures that the parent will still be at the nest to clean up. Most nestlings eliminate these wastes via a fecal sac—the feces and urine are encased in a strong membrane that can be carried off by the parents and disposed of elsewhere. If a nestling's droppings are slimy or messy, this is evidence that it is sick or that the diet lacks important elements.

Confining a fledgling to a box or cage, or even a whole house, is like keeping a human toddler in a crib. This is a critical stage in a young bird's development, when it learns proper coordination and many of the skills that will keep it alive. If you don't know how to teach a baby bird to survive in the wild, you do it a terrible injury by keeping it. In some cases, such as with swallows, a fledgling remains with its parents through its first migration. Parents teach their offspring feeding and survival strategies and the migration route. Without its own or foster parents, such a fledgling has little chance of surviving. Baby robins remain with their father for weeks after fledging, and baby jays normally remain with their parents for months. Without parents to teach them basic survival strategies, they have a much poorer chance of making it on their own. So do your best to get any baby bird to a licensed rehabber with the necessary expertise and facilities. Many rehabbers use "foster parent" birds to teach their fledglings the necessary survival skills.

Remember, it is illegal to keep any native American bird, and many nonnative species, as a pet. You won't be arrested or fined if you rescue a bird and do what's necessary to keep it alive until you find a licensed rehabilitator. If you feel genuine compassion for a wild creature, you have a moral as well as a legal responsibility to give it a chance at a long, healthy life in the wild.

37 Know what to do if a bird gets into your house or garage

If you discover a bird in your house, take a deep breath. There's no need for both of you to panic. First, close any doors to other rooms to keep the bird in a confined space. Close the shades and curtains and turn off any lights to make the room as dark as possible. If the room has a door to the outside, open it and slowly move behind the bird to guide it outside. If there is no exit, open a window from behind the still-closed curtain; then open the curtain, but keep any glass surfaces covered to keep the bird from hitting the glass. Slowly move behind the bird and guide it toward the open window.

If no windows can be opened, keep the room darkened and try to toss a towel over the bird. Then you can pick it up and release it outdoors. If the bird perches in a high place and stays put, it's often best to wait until dark. Then use a flashlight to find your way to the bird. In this case, if you still have the patience, it's usually best to keep the bird in a cardboard box overnight and release it in the morning. If the bird is injured, bring it to a rehabilitator.

Sometimes birds get trapped in garages. The most common situation is for a hummingbird to be attracted to the red emergency pull on an open garage door and then get confused. When birds are lost or disoriented, they tend to move to higher perches, where they are in less danger from predators and have a wider view. The best way to lure a hummingbird down is to set your most conspicuous hummingbird feeder as close to the open garage door as possible. If you don't feed hummingbirds, put a red handkerchief or something else bright red near the door. When the hummingbird comes down to investigate or feed, it will find its own way out.

38 Put a cap or screen on your metal chimney

Several years ago, a Snowy Owl with a radio transmitter dropped down the chimney of an abandoned hotel in Superior, Wisconsin. The bird was located by a raptor researcher only because he managed to zero in on the bird's transmitter signal. When he reached the emaciated but still living bird, he discovered the mummified bodies of two other snowies and several pigeons that weren't lucky enough to be wearing transmitters when they needed help. When the story was recounted at a Duluth Audubon meeting, two other people told of the same thing happening elsewhere in town.

Snowy Owl

Fewer birds fall down chimneys than crash into windows, but when a bird suddenly appears in the fireplace, it's traumatic for us, to say nothing of the poor bird. Pigeons, European Starlings, and House Sparrows are the most likely birds to end up in this predicament, but over the years, I've heard of owls, nuthatches, creepers, and woodpeckers dropping down chimneys. Tumbling down a length of chimney can cause serious injury to a bird. One White-breasted Nuthatch brought to me had been slashed by a sharp edge as he fell down a chimney. He had a badly swollen foot and a gash in his abdomen and died the same night.

This is one of the easiest bird problems to prevent. All you need to do is put a cap on your metal chimney. Home improvement stores offer many choices of chimney screens and caps. This simple solution not only protects birds but also prevents a potentially distressing and messy predicament for you.

39 Solve bird problems carefully, responsibly, and proactively

No matter how devoted to birds you are, in some situations, birds can cause problems. Finding safe and humane ways of dealing with these issues is important for our own peace of mind as well as for the birds. Bird problems are as varied as birds themselves.

Fish-eating birds. Herons, pelicans, eagles, osprey, cormorants, and kingfishers compete with humans for fish, which can make them unpopular. Fish declines attributable to birds are only a tiny fraction of those due to habitat degradation, pesticides, manure and other nutrient runoff, mercury and other toxins, power plants, shoreline erosion, commercial and even sport fishing, and dams, but birds make an easy scapegoat. Every year the U.S. Department of Agriculture's Animal and Plant Health Inspection Service issues permits allowing farmers and fish farmers to kill millions of migratory birds. In Washington state, where salmon are endangered due to devastating habitat degradation from dams, unsustainable forestry practices, and erosion, permits are issued to kill thousands of migratory birds each year, including herons, ducks, gulls, grebes, and cormorants. Yet little is done to address the root causes of salmon declines, and there is no research-based evidence that birds have any effect whatsoever on the return of adult salmon. According to an *Arkansas Times* article by Leslie Newell Peacock (August 5, 2004), a single Arkansas fish farm owner was given permits to kill 400 Great Blue Herons, 400 Great Egrets, 100 American Coots, 100 American White Pelicans, and 5 Snowy Egrets in 2004 alone.

Research by the U.S. Department of Agriculture (USDA) found that cormorants have little or no effect on sport fish, choosing gizzard shad and yellow bass over largemouth bass and crappie. Although they have a more serious effect on catfish, another USDA study found that a nonlethal method to reduce cormorant fishing on catfish ponds was "cost-efficient and easy to set up." Cormorants are killed not only when they are actually causing problems; adults and babies are killed in their nesting trees, often many miles

*Double-crested
Cormorant*

from any fish farms. In the 1970s, the Double-crested Cormorant was listed as a threatened species in many places. But since then, both pelican and cormorant populations have surged, partly because they've recovered from the effects of DDT, and partly because of the subsidies humans provide at poorly designed fish hatcheries and fish farms. Bird populations, like sunlight and rainfall, are natural situations that fish farmers need to accept and adapt to as part of their cost of doing business. There are effective, nonlethal methods of reducing bird predation on fish farms, and managers should use them.

Fish farmers aren't the only ones who don't want to share fish with birds. In Duluth one spring, I received many phone calls about a Great Blue Heron that was fishing on the banks of a local river, side by side with human fishermen. Sometimes the heron would approach someone who'd just caught a fish, and sometimes the bird actually took fish from the fishermen's buckets. Most of the anglers were charmed rather than annoyed. Then, after a few weeks, one fisherman clubbed the bird to death, an offense that isn't just cruel and wrong but also illegal. Unfortunately, he got away with it because none of the witnesses could or would identify him. Sportfishermen don't always appreciate avian competition, but birds are an important natural resource too. People who are concerned about declining fish populations need to look at the root causes rather than blaming birds.

That said, some conflicts between cormorants and people are based on real problems. Large cormorant populations are associated with habitat alteration at nest colonies, which can lower property values and affect other colonial waterbirds. In addition, it can lead to vast accumulations of guano on ships, buildings, breakwaters, and other waterway structures; nutrient overload that lowers water quality; and possible transmission of fish diseases or parasites. Although cormorants eat a lot of "rough fish," their take of other species can be significant. Studies indicate that although cormorants usually have only small impacts on fish populations, local impacts may be significant. For example, smallmouth bass constitute less than 2 percent of a cormorant's total diet, but this amounts to about 21 to 35 percent of the bass available in the Eastern Basin of Lake Ontario. When departments of natural resources try to balance the needs of all their constituencies, they sometimes make the decision to harass or even kill cormorants. Once this decision is made, the best approach for bird lovers is to encourage them to choose the safest and most humane methods to at least minimize potential environmental harms and undue suffering.

People who raise koi and other exotic fish in small backyard ponds understandably get annoyed when Great Blue Herons or other birds fly in and eat their fish. Since the whole purpose of these ponds is aesthetic, it doesn't make sense to cover them with nets. The most effective way to protect them is to design the pond to deter birds. Herons fish from a standing position, so they need fairly shallow water. Deep water and steep banks will protect fish from them. If the pond surface area is small, you don't need to worry about attracting cormorants and loons, which need running space to take off. The possibility of these exotic fish introducing exotic diseases into a natural system is a problem that most backyard fish owners don't fully appreciate.

Canada Geese. Unlike most birds, Canada Geese can digest grass, making their droppings particularly unpleasant. Since geese learn how to negotiate life from their parents rather than doing most things by instinct, some geese have adapted to living near people, cars, and buildings. These birds have increased and multiplied, and their many offspring know no other life. Large flocks often gather on lawns near lakes, rivers, and streams—an unnatural habitat that increases the likelihood that their droppings will run off into the water.

Less serious environmentally, but still a nuisance, are geese gatherings on golf courses, church lawns, and residential lawns. The obvious long-term solution is to replace unnatural turf with natural vegetation, but that won't work on golf courses. Some people lay down green plastic mesh where they have a goose problem. The geese seem to dislike the feel of this and go elsewhere; again, this isn't practical for golf courses. Probably the most effective way of discouraging geese from invading areas such as golf courses and airports is to use trained dogs. Obviously, you can't have dogs running around a golf course all day long while people are trying to play, but if a handler runs the dogs every morning and evening for an hour at first and last light when the geese are building their nests, this may encourage them to nest elsewhere. But the problem with exploding populations, whether they are deer, geese, or humans, is that eventually, all the elsewheres become filled too. Not until we get over our obsession with monoculture lawns will we even begin to solve the goose overpopulation problem.

Bird-on-bird predation. Once in a while, home owners get upset or frustrated by hawks, owls, or shrikes visiting a feeding station to pick up an easy meal. Some people enjoy watching these birds and simply make sure that there are enough hiding places near feeders to protect alert songbirds. One year, a Merlin nested on my block and appeared in my yard just about every day, but at different times. It would cruise down the street just above the sidewalk, dropping to within a foot or less of the ground as it passed my house. Then it would wheel around a spruce tree in the corner of my front lawn at high speed, completely hidden from the view of birds at the feeders in the side yard, until it was within striking distance. The songbirds would scatter, but at least half the time the Merlin would be successful and grab one. As hard as this was on the individual birds the Merlin took, and as sad as it made me at times, the Merlin pair raised two chicks and then moved on, and they haven't nested on my block since. Like all creatures, Merlins are just trying to make their way in the world.

If a raptor's daily visits are upsetting, you might want to close down the feeder for a week or so to break the habit. Otherwise, it's just as well to assume a Zenlike attitude toward birds of prey, which are fully protected by state and federal laws. If their killing ways disturb you, remember that even bluebirds are considered vicious serial killers by insects.

Gull overpopulation. Like other birds undergoing population explosions, gulls, especially Ring-billed Gulls, are exploiting the many new sources of food provided in the urban and suburban environment—easily available garbage, various invertebrates living in our expansive lawns, and handouts from people. Until we stop subsidizing them and maintaining huge areas of turf, the gull problem will remain serious. The overpopulation of gulls, like that of crows, causes ecological problems because gulls take so many eggs and chicks of terns, plovers, and other shorebirds. On foggy mornings during migration, I've watched Ring-billed Gulls in Duluth snapping up warblers in midair as the exhausted little migrants dropped down after the night's flight. Leaving dog food where birds can find it and feeding bread at feeders exacerbates the gull problem. Beautiful as they are, gulls simply do not need subsidies from us.

Birds at airports. Gulls and a wide variety of other birds can pose a serious hazard at airports. Damage to U.S. civil and military planes costs more than $600 million annually. Bird-plane collisions also put the lives of aircraft crew members and passengers at risk. More than 195 people have been killed worldwide as a result of aircraft strikes since 1988. Since 1975, five large jet airliners have had major accidents in which bird strikes played a significant role. In one case, about three dozen people were killed. The horror of human beings dying eclipses the environmental destruction, but that too is an element of bird-plane collisions. As a result of a bird strike that disabled an engine on a B-747 departing Los Angeles International Airport in August 2000, the pilot had to dump eighty-three tons of fuel over the Pacific Ocean before returning to land safely.

There are a number of effective techniques that can reduce the number of birds in the vicinity of airports. In general, the techniques fall into three categories:

1. Make the environment unattractive for birds, which may involve draining a swamp, getting rid of a prairie dog colony that provides food for predator birds, or simply cutting the grass.
2. Scare the birds away. This can sometimes be accomplished with pyrotechnics and fireworks or remote-controlled aircraft. Airfield managers must continue to use these techniques, however, or the birds will quickly return. Birds often learn to cope with loud noisemakers, figure out that owl decoys are fakes, and ignore scarecrows.
3. Reduce the bird population. As a last resort, sometimes airports must shoot birds that won't leave. They have to get permits to kill most species and can't harm endangered animals.

One extremely effective way of keeping birds away from airports (and golf courses) and minimizing environmental damage is to employ border collies to chase them away. These intelligent working dogs are tireless and responsible and so effective that one Florida airport was bird free within two months of hiring a dog and handler.

Pigeons. Rock Pigeons were one of the first species introduced to North America by European settlers, who brought the birds here for food and to raise as pets, racers, and messengers. Although pigeons weren't intentionally introduced to the wild, feral populations quickly became established. Unlike most introduced species, pigeons have invaded very few natural habitats, don't compete with native birds for natural food or nesting sites, and provide a lot of entertainment and pleasure in urban habitats. Pigeons have saved thousands of human lives by carrying important messages in wartime and blood samples from hospitals to laboratories in peacetime. And they serve as a reliable food source for reintroduced Peregrine Falcons, especially in urban areas. Rock Pigeons are similar in size to the now-extinct Passenger Pigeons, which once formed a significant prey base for peregrines.

Unfortunately, pigeons can sometimes be a nuisance and occasionally pose a health hazard where they are exceptionally numerous or are nesting in enclosed quarters where their droppings collect. When they gather at grain elevators and railroads, they feed on spilled seeds, seldom posing a serious economic problem, although that spilled grain also attracts rats and mice, which can be harmful.

There is no situation in which a pigeon infestation requires poison with anticoagulants. Pigeons virtually never pose ecological problems, and although old, moldy roost sites can definitely cause health problems, cleaning and sealing them off does not require killing the birds, especially with dangerous toxins. The avicide Rid-A-Bird and other pesticides with fenthion are no longer legal, for good reason. Under no circumstances should fenthion ever be used, since it is utterly indiscriminate in the birds it kills, and the toxin in just a single bird killed by fenthion can be enough to kill a bird of prey or scavenger feeding on the carcass.

Tanglefoot and other nontoxic sticky coatings used to keep pigeons off eaves and other structures may temporarily deter them, but at a huge cost. Animals aren't scared away by it—they're coated with it, and it causes undue suffering to any bird or mammal that happens to come in contact with it. If an animal gets stuck, it may bite off its legs in order to escape. If it does escape intact with Tanglefoot on its body, it's unlikely to survive. Tanglefoot is not water soluble, and it destroys the waterproofing of fur or feathers. To repair just one Red-tailed Hawk coated with the substance, Scott Diehl, manager of the Wisconsin Humane Society Wildlife Rehabilitation Center in Milwaukee, had to anesthetize the bird three times for special cleanings.

To keep unwanted pigeons from roosting and nesting in attics and on eaves and other structures, close off entryways. To dissuade them from roosting in areas that don't lend themselves to being sealed off, helium balloons can be effective. Birds are often frightened by the balloons' unexpected movements, since nothing they encounter in the natural world "falls up." Brightly colored Mylar balloons are scary enough so that by the time the helium has leaked out, the pigeons have usually found other roosting places. Plastic owls and snakes may work temporarily, but birds are smarter than people give them credit for and quickly figure out that these are fakes. Gluing loose feathers on an owl decoy or getting one with a movable neck joint may succeed a bit longer, but local birds will eventually learn that they can safely ignore it.

In some communities, pigeons are controlled by providing attractive pigeon nest boxes. Then, when the eggs have been laid, people switch them with wooden decoy eggs to limit reproduction. This method requires vigilance and man-hours, but it is actually much easier and cheaper than conscientiously searching out dead and dying pigeons after using poisons.

Woodpeckers. Woodpeckers can be annoying when they bang on your downspout at five in the morning, or they can cause more significant damage by digging holes in your cedar siding. To deal with them, you need to figure out what they're doing.

Woodpeckers "drum" to advertise their territory, and they choose the noisiest, most resonant percussion instrument they can find, because the farther the sound carries, the wider their territorial boundaries. According to the Cornell Laboratory of Ornithology, woodpeckers drum on aluminum siding; the trim boards and fascia boards of wood, brick, and stucco houses; and metal downspouts, gutters, chimneys, and vents. Birders often get a kick out of listening to woodpeckers, but if the noise is too bothersome, you can temporarily cover the area they're hammering on with insulation or a towel to send them elsewhere.

Woodpeckers hoping to roost or nest in your house can cut fairly large holes into the wood. They are most likely to attempt to dig out large holes when your house is in a wooded area and is sided with natural or dark-stained wood. Most attractive for them, according to the Cornell Lab, is clapboard siding, board-and-batten siding, tongue-and-groove siding, and, less often, resawn shakes and shingles. Woodpeckers are most drawn to redwood and cedar. When beginning to drill nesting or roosting holes, woodpeckers often make several attempts, starting a hole in one spot and then starting a new one. This is how a single house can end up with so many large holes. Woodpeckers are most quiet when probing for insects within the siding. In these situations, they can leave dozens or even hundreds of tinier holes.

In the West, Acorn Woodpeckers sometimes gouge a huge number of holes in a building, into which they stuff acorns for storage. Some people in sturdy houses laugh this off or enjoy the rustic look, but many people are not amused.

So what can you do about woodpecker damage? Removing woodpeckers by trapping or even shooting virtually never works, because whatever attracted the first bird will quickly attract another one. Tanglefoot and other sticky coatings stain the wood and cause serious problems for wildlife without preventing future problems—a cruel and shortsighted answer that is unwarranted in this situation.

Here are some recommendations:

- Repair every woodpecker hole as soon as possible. Aluminum flashing can be used to cover existing holes or to line the corner or fascia boards of the house. You can paint it to match the color of your siding.
- Hang aluminum foil strips, brightly colored reflective tape, or windsocks down from above or helium balloons up from below. Bright pinwheels near the damage may help, too. Woodpeckers may also be dissuaded by owl decoys with moving parts or recordings of hawks.
- Lightweight nylon or plastic netting can be attached from overhanging eaves to the siding of the damaged building. One type of netting is called BirdNet, manufactured by Bird-X. To keep the birds from reaching through the net, leave at least three inches between the net and the siding.
- Provide plenty of suet feeders. These may entice woodpeckers away from your house if they are hunting for insects. Unfortunately, suet may attract more woodpeckers to your property, some of which might then discover your house.
- As long as a nest is not already established, roost or nest holes should be plugged with wood putty during the daytime. If the birds already have eggs or young, the holes can be sealed after the nestlings have fledged, usually by midsummer. If you act as soon as you notice woodpecker damage, they will be dissuaded before the cavity is constructed.
- If woodpeckers are poking into the holes of carpenter bees, get rid of the bees. These insects prefer either natural or stained wood; wood that is painted (oil base or polyurethane) is less likely to be infested, because the hard finish deters bees. If you prefer natural or stained wood, the Cornell Lab recommends spraying the area with a preventive insect control such as Cypermethrin; if the bees are already established, consider using an insecticide specifically designed to control wasps and bees. It should be sprayed into the entrance holes in late evening or at night when the bees are inside the tunnels. After twenty-four hours, plug the tunnel entrances with cork, a wooden dowel, or wood putty to keep bees from recolonizing.
- If your house is sided with grooved plywood, the Cornell Lab recommends painting it to seal core gaps and prevent insects

from tunneling into the wood. Alternatively, caulking along the sides of the vertical grooves will cover entrances to gaps in the core. Once the gaps are caulked, repair the damage so the old holes don't attract foraging woodpeckers.

- For houses sided with wooden shakes, shingles, or board and batten, the Cornell Lab recommends hiring an exterminator to spray the outside of the house with insecticide and then replacing the damaged shakes or boards. Once the insects are gone, the woodpeckers won't be attracted.
- In the case of Acorn Woodpecker damage, sealing every hole and then covering the area with hardware cloth or plastic netting should solve the problem.

Sapsuckers probing for sap are the only woodpeckers that regularly dig into healthy tree tissue. Sap running from their drill holes provides one of the chief natural foods for the first hummingbirds that arrive before flowers bloom in the spring. The sap also feeds a wide variety of warblers, flycatchers, kinglets, and other songbirds and seldom does permanent damage to the tree. But in the event that a sapsucker is tapping a prized ornamental tree, wrapping aluminum sheeting or burlap around the area is nearly always effective.

House nesters. Phoebes and swallows nesting on houses annoy some people who don't like the messy mud nests, don't appreciate the droppings below the nests, and don't like being attacked by protective parent birds. These birds eat flying insects, including mosquitoes, almost exclusively, giving tolerant people a practical bonus, and their graceful flight is wonderfully entertaining. If you can't tolerate their nests, you need to be proactive, washing down the mud the moment it appears—before the nest is built and the first eggs laid—and then putting up helium balloons or covering the area with plastic to prevent future building. Building a nest shelf in a more acceptable area of the house or garage can solve the problem for you while accommodating the needs of the birds.

Jays. Blue Jays and Steller's Jays often raid the nests of other birds, especially robins. I've watched Blue Jays do this on many occasions, and in every case, the jay was an adult that carried the "plunder" off to feed its mate or nestlings. Jays typically raise five babies a year in a single clutch, and it takes only fourteen to eighteen days for baby jays to fledge at close to their full adult weight, so parent jays need to find a lot of protein-rich food during this brief nestling period. Once the babies are full grown, their diet becomes typical of adult Blue Jays; the vast majority consists of vegetal matter (especially acorns and other mast, along with berries and seeds), with most of the animal matter in the form of insects and, at feeders, suet. But at all times, jays are opportunistic omnivores.

When jays fly into a feeding station, often all the other birds fly off. After observing this pattern for many years, I've concluded that it's because jays have a silhouette similar to that of a Sharp-shinned Hawk, with rounded wings and a long, narrow tail. Birds who wait to verify an identification before flying off aren't likely to survive very long. But once skittish birds see that it's just a jay, they quickly return.

Jays are noisy, and although we may find that annoying, other birds appreciate it because the jays are so effective at warning the whole avian neighborhood about predators and other danger. If you don't want jays visiting your feeders, however, try using hanging feeders.

Blue Jays are found in just about every habitat as long as there are some shade trees, and their population isn't increasing. As a matter of fact, Breeding Bird Survey data show a slight but significant decline in Blue Jay numbers across the United States, with most of the decline in the East. Steller's Jays are merely holding their own. As with hawks, if you can't learn to appreciate jays, adopting a Zenlike attitude toward them will at least save you some irritation.

Crows. The American Crow belongs to the same family as jays, but unlike its diminutive relatives, its population has exploded. Crows have learned to exploit Dumpsters and garbage bags, dog kennels, gardens, roadsides, and birds smacking into windows and communication towers for food. In cities, where shooting is prohibited, crows don't have to worry about their two biggest population-limiting factors—hunting and winter food availability. When provided with a high-quality diet year-round, along with large spruce trees for nesting in established neighborhoods, how could crows help but thrive? Unfortunately, crows can annoy us with their raucous caws, and they take a large number of songbird eggs and nestlings—far more than jays, because crow babies are much larger and require much more protein to reach full size. In my neighborhood in Duluth, I haven't seen a single robin pair fledge young from any tree nest in ten years. Because crows are so abundant and observant, virtually all the successful robins in my area now nest on window ledges, basement window wells, or porch lights. Several people have told me that in the Twin Cities, crows are even learning to raid robin nests on houses.

In other areas, crow populations have been decimated or even extirpated by West Nile virus. Although that disease has killed birds belonging to hundreds of species, crows are uniquely vulnerable. In laboratory studies, 98 to 100 percent of crows exposed to any amount of the virus die. Because of their large size and conspicuousness, dead and dying crows serve as an important warning of where West Nile virus is spreading. It's possible that the disease will reduce crow numbers throughout the continent, but eventually, resistant populations will reestablish.

The crow problem arose because our current urban and suburban lifestyle subsidizes them. Crows, like humans, are intelligent, opportunistic omnivores with fascinating, complex social structures. Henry Ward Beecher wrote that if men could fly and bore black feathers, few would be clever enough to be crows. Problems with crow overpopulation will continue in many areas until we learn to keep our garbage sealed from them, feed our dogs in less accessible dishes, drive more carefully to reduce their roadkill meals, and remove and destroy road-killed animals rather than leaving them for scavengers to eat. If we develop the collective will to stop providing easy food sources, when the crow populations in virus-affected areas recover, they should remain at more appropriate levels rather than exploding all over again.

Window collisions. Every year I get calls and letters about birds, usually American Robins and Northern Cardinals, repeatedly flying into windows, patio doors, and car mirrors. Some people are irritated by the noise or the mess, but most are more concerned about the birds. What are these birds doing? And what can we do to stop this behavior?

When songbirds grow territorial each year, they do their best to keep other adults of the same species and sex outside of their territorial boundaries. When a territorial male robin or cardinal discovers another male on his territory, he becomes agitated, raises the feathers on his head, and assumes a dominant posture. Normally, that is enough to make the intruder leave. If not, the territorial resident flies to a singing perch and bursts into song; if that doesn't work, he chases the intruder off. When a male bird notices his own reflection in a window or mirror, he gets agitated, raises the feathers on his head, and assumes a dominant posture. But shockingly, from the bird's point of view, instead of flying away, the "intruder" gets equally agitated, raises its head feathers, and assumes an equally dominant posture. The first time this happens, the real bird usually goes to his favorite song perch to sing. When he doesn't hear a responding song, he's more certain than ever that this is his territory. But when he checks, the reflected bird is still there. Each time this happens, he gets more agitated, but his agitation is always matched by the reflection. When the hapless bird finally flies in to chase the other bird away, the reflection flies at him in exactly the same way, and they collide. The real bird seems shocked that no matter how aggressive he gets, and no matter how hard he fights, the reflection matches his level of aggression. The real bird becomes more and more determined to drive the upstart away.

Robins and cardinals are not stupid. But during the nesting season, their territorial urge is even more powerful than their urge to eat or sleep. Defending their territory is how they ensure that there will be enough food for their babies. Ironically, the whole time a bird is fighting its reflection, it is not doing the things that will ensure its babies' survival. It needs to eat, sing (if it's a male), build a nest and incubate eggs (if it's a female), and chase real competitors away.

The only way to stop this destructive behavior is to break the reflection. Fortunately, you don't have to break the window to accomplish this. The simplest way, if it's a small window or mirror, is to tape some paper or cardboard over it, on the outside, and keep it in place for three or four days until the bird gets busy enough with other things to forget about the "intruder." It's harder to cover a picture window or a patio door. One technique that sometimes works is to paper over the area where the bird has been hitting and then hang shiny helium balloons nearby. Permanently covering the outside of the window with CollidEscape will both eliminate the reflection and allow you to see out. Fortunately, this behavior usually stops as soon as the clutch hatches, so no matter how you deal with it, within a week the problem is usually over.

Starlings. European Starlings were introduced to the United States on March 16, 1890, in Central Park in New York City. At the time, many "naturalization societies" throughout the world were intentionally introducing various animals from one continent to another. Most of these species died out, but the introduction of starlings was a rousing success. The particular club that introduced starlings was working toward the goal of establishing in Central Park every species ever mentioned in a play by William Shakespeare, and unfortunately, Shakespeare was a better playwright than an ornithologist. In *Henry IV, Part I* Hotspur says, "I'll have a starling shall be taught to speak nothing but Mortimer." In Shakespeare's time, starlings were popular cage birds, thought of as "poor man's mynahs" because anyone could catch one for a pet, unlike their relative from India.

Starlings can imitate a wide variety of sounds, but Shakespeare didn't realize that it would be impossible to teach a starling to speak "nothing but Mortimer." Even if a starling could be kept in a chamber that was absolutely silent except for someone droning "Mortimer" over and over, most starlings would experiment with rearranging the syllables of the word. Shakespeare made many apt observations about birds, but if he had been more knowledgeable about starlings, we wouldn't be plagued with them today.

Starlings are fascinating creatures. My family had a pet starling named Mortimer for many years. He never learned to speak, but his song was a string of imitations of sounds in our home—the tea kettle, the telephone, birds heard through the window, distant lawn mowers, and even the smoke alarm. Listening to starlings outdoors, it's often easy to figure out where individual birds have spent time by the different recognizable sounds in their repertoire. And the way flocks wheel about in unison in high-speed flight is breathtaking and amazing.

But like Rock Pigeons, starlings can be serious nuisances. Their droppings occasionally build to unhealthy levels, and their noise is a constant irritation. Unlike pigeons, starlings can also cause huge ecological problems. They are cavity nesters, appropriating nest holes from flickers, Red-headed Woodpeckers, and other larger species. Starlings are more aggressive than these other birds and have a special weapon in their beak musculature. On most songbirds, the muscles exert pressure when the birds close their beaks, allowing them to crack seed and nut shells or to break off chunks of food. Starling facial muscles are arranged to exert force as the starling pulls its beak open, allowing it to stick its beak into the soil and then open it to expose grubs and other food items beneath the surface. A starling can use the beak in a deadlier way, too. If a woodpecker lights outside a hole appropriated by a starling, the starling can stab the woodpecker and then open the beak, exacerbating the injury. Because of this aggressive nest appropriation, starlings have had a serious impact on some species, including Red-headed Woodpeckers and bluebirds.

To control starlings, it's most important not to subsidize them. Make sure that any songbird nest boxes have holes too small for starlings to squeeze through—check with the North American Bluebird Society and the Purple Martin Conservation Association for suggestions about nest box design. If starlings are nesting on your own house, dissuade them by closing off nooks and crannies or temporarily setting up helium balloons that will float near their access points. If starlings are visiting your feeding station, it's helpful to switch to hanging feeders, because most starlings prefer steadier footing. During midsummer days when starling babies are fledging, close down your suet feeders.

Starlings are not native, so they are not protected by the laws that protect native birds. If a starling has invaded a martin house or bluebird box, it is perfectly legal to toss out the eggs and nesting materials. In some urban and agricultural situations in which starlings are causing economic or health problems, they are doused with detergent water, usually in their roosts at night. This destroys the waterproofing and insulating value of their feathers, and they die of hypothermia. This is a horrible way for the birds to die, but at least it doesn't hurt nontarget species or cause lasting environmental damage. Poisons are never an appropriate way to deal with starlings.

Blackbirds. In some places, grackles, redwings, and other blackbirds have become fairly serious pests, subsidized by agriculture. Winter wheat and other crops provide food during winter, when these birds historically had their highest mortality. According to current estimates, Red-winged Blackbirds are the most abundant land bird in North America. As beautiful as they are, they can cause problems for farmers. Millions of redwings and other blackbirds are intentionally killed every year by pesticides, trapping, shooting, and roost spraying with detergent water, especially by sunflower growers. Despite this, in North and South Dakota alone, the redwing population increased about 33 percent between 1996 and 1999. Blackbirds are not the worst problems facing these farmers. Every year, sunflower growers throughout the United States lose an average of 6 percent of their crop to disease, 7 percent to insects, 5 percent to weeds, and 3 percent to waste when harvesting with combines; farmers in North and South Dakota, where the redwing problem is worst, lose only about 1 to 2 percent of their crop to birds. This sounds negligible, but a few farmers bear the brunt of the damage—every year about 500 growers lose more than 25 percent of their crops to blackbirds. Interestingly, a USDA Animal and Plant Health Inspection Service (APHIS) study estimates that despite the huge increase in the redwing population, their damage to sunflower crops has not increased at all.

One novel plan was a 2001 proposal by APHIS to kill 6 million Red-winged Blackbirds in the Dakotas over three years by setting out poisoned rice during spring migration. Migrating birds would be lured down by the rice during the season that they feed on waste grain rather than crops and so aren't causing any damage at all. The intention was to reduce their numbers before the birds reproduced. But the proposal would have indiscriminately killed all birds attracted to the rice, including bobolinks, meadowlarks, and native sparrows, as well as any scavengers and predators that fed on the poisoned birds. Also, there was absolutely no research ascertaining that the redwings migrating through the area in the spring were the same populations that caused problems in fall. As of this writing, the program hasn't been approved. It would be much more environmentally sound and probably just as cost-effective to provide crop insurance for sunflower growers and compensate those few farmers who lose a significant portion of their crops to blackbirds.

In the backyard, blackbirds aren't nearly as troublesome as they are on farms, and birders take a lot of pleasure in visiting marshes in the spring to see redwings perched atop cattails advertising their territories. But blackbirds certainly don't need subsidies from humans, and some species, particularly grackles, are aggressive toward smaller birds, occasionally killing them. Blackbirds prefer to feed on the ground, so when they're abundant, don't allow spilled seed to collect near your feeders. Switching to hanging feeders during heavy blackbird visits can reduce the problem too. When grackles or starlings collect in my backyard, I simply let the dogs out, and the birds fly away.

Cowbirds. Cowbirds are in the blackbird family, but they are unique among North American birds in being brood parasites. This means that rather than constructing their own nests, cowbirds lay their eggs in the nests of other birds, allowing them to incubate the cowbird eggs and raise the babies. Cowbirds hang around with their foster parents for several days after fledging but do not imprint on them. When they can find enough food on their own, they instinctively leave and start associating with other cowbirds.

Brown-headed Cowbirds were once closely associated with bison, eating insects and seeds from the prairie soil trampled by the beasts. Because bison were nomadic, cowbirds were unlikely to parasitize the same hosts year after year, and prairie birds evolved to deal with them. Before settlement, the most significant limiting factor for cowbird populations was their dependence on the bison population. But even as humans extirpated the bison, they introduced livestock that cowbirds instinctively gravitated toward, and humans also began providing cowbirds with plenty of disturbed soil and abundant food. As a result, their population exploded, and their range expanded to areas where songbirds had never been exposed to nest parasitism before.

Some reports indicate that a single cowbird can lay forty or even sixty eggs in a season, although the average is probably much fewer. But clearly, a large population of cowbirds invading an area where few or no songbirds had developed strategies to deal with nest parasitism could cause grave problems. Fortunately, despite the large and sudden range expansion in the past two centuries, the cowbird population in North America is currently stabilizing or even decreasing, according to Breeding Bird Survey data.

Before laying an egg, a female cowbird tosses out one of the host's eggs, so right off the bat, a cowbird egg represents a 20 to 25 percent loss in potential reproductive success for the host birds. Baby cowbirds are not aggressive toward their foster siblings (it is European cuckoos that push other eggs and nestlings out of the nest soon after they hatch), but because female cowbirds tend to select smaller host species, baby cowbirds have an advantage. When songbird parents attend the babies, they don't seem to recognize them individually or to remember which one has been fed most recently, so they simply stuff food into the largest, most conspicuous mouth—invariably, the cowbird's. In years when food is abundant, most of the babies get plenty to eat, but when food is harder to come by, the cowbird's survival comes at the expense of one, two, or even three brood mates. Margaret Morse Nice found that in addition to the lost egg, on average, one Song Sparrow nestling died for each cowbird successfully raised.

Nest parasitism may be a problem for individual broods raised with a cowbird, but overall, it has little effect on many species, including Song Sparrows and Chipping Sparrows. These fairly short-distance migrants arrive early in spring and often nest two or even three times in a season. But cowbirds can cause serious losses among neotropical migrants, which arrive later and depart sooner, generally nesting only once a season. The problem is exacerbated for endangered migrants. A full 90 percent of Black-capped Vireo nests are parasitized in open canyon woodlands in Fort Hood, Texas; 80 to 90 percent of Bell's Vireo and Yellow-breasted Chat nests are parasitized in desert riparian habitat in the lower Colorado River valley; and 50 percent of Lazuli Bunting nests are parasitized in shrubland prairie habitat in western Montana.

When ornithologists first made a connection between the range expansion of Brown-headed Cowbirds and the decline of endangered species such as Black-capped Vireos and Kirtland's Warblers, they began protecting the vulnerable populations by trapping and killing cowbirds, with varying success. Now research is focused on determining just how serious the cowbird threat really is. According to Vincent Muehter in a National Audubon Society report,

> Conservationists and the public tend to overestimate the significance of parasitism as a major cause of declining songbird populations. A recent study failed to show population-level effects of cowbird parasitism on host species and refuted key predictions about impact of parasitism. This research was based on the reasonable premises that (1) host populations should decrease in areas where cowbirds are increasing, and increase in areas where cowbirds are decreasing (Breeding Bird Survey data); and (2) heavily parasitized hosts should decrease while less commonly used hosts should increase or maintain stable populations (Ontario Nest Record data).
>
> Cowbird control programs on Endangered Species have had some success in meeting their ultimate goal: increasing local host populations. In the Least Bell's Vireo, populations increased following cowbird control and efforts to improve breeding habitat. In the Kirtland's Warbler, cowbird control and habitat restoration combined to bring populations in Michigan back from 200 breeding pairs in 1972 to about 400 breeding pairs in 1998. . . . However, four years of cowbird control have not helped restore Willow Flycatcher populations in California, suggesting that habitat, not cowbirds, is the key limiting factor.
>
> Scientists suggest that cowbird control is a short-term solution that ignores the real problem of habitat degradation as a result of agriculture, grazing and development. They cite studies showing limited geographical reach of control and those showing no long-term benefit without indefinite support. Scientists caution against diverting limited human and financial resources to cowbirds and neglecting the root causes of why species are at-risk. Scientists, however, support limited control to help restore local populations of Threatened or Endangered species.
>
> Scientists advocate protection and restoration of host breeding habitat, and improvements in grazing and agricultural practices.
>
> Cowbird control initiatives should answer three practical questions: (1) Does control fix the root causes driving high rates of

parasitism? (2) Do the benefits outweigh the inevitable long-term financial costs? (3) Is control an effective "stop-gap" measure to keep an endangered species viable until root problems can be corrected?

Cowbirds feed in open areas and invade forests only along edges to search for nests. Forest fragmentation increases edges and thus increases the potential for cowbird parasitism, which is one more reason why defending natural areas from urban sprawl and protecting intact portions of state and national forests are so important.

House Sparrows. House Sparrows were introduced to the United States many times during the 1800s by homesick European immigrants who missed the familiar cheeping, by religious settlers who wanted to bring to America birds mentioned in the Bible, by foolish optimists who hoped that the sparrows would feed on insect pests or the bugs and seeds in horse manure, and by many other groups. The first documented introduction that I could find was by Nicolas Pike, who released eight pairs in Greenwood Cemetery in Brooklyn in the spring of 1850, but other releases were happening at the same time. Some towns and cities even set up friendly competitions to see which could get House Sparrows established first. The sparrow population exploded, then stabilized and even fell. Now it's fairly stable, although sparrows have declined in some areas where House Finches have appeared. In Europe, however, House Sparrow numbers have declined dangerously.

Like European Starlings, House Sparrows nest on buildings and in cavities and nest boxes. And like starlings, House Sparrows are extremely aggressive in appropriating and defending nest boxes. However, House Sparrows are small enough to fit through the entrance holes to bluebird and martin boxes and small natural cavities, which causes grave problems for these birds. House Sparrows can destroy eggs and kill nestlings and even adults of these species. So in rural and suburban areas, they pose serious threats to native bluebirds and martins. As nonnative birds, House Sparrows are not protected in the United States; eggs or nestlings can be removed from nest boxes, and adults can legally be killed.

In urban areas, House Sparrows aren't nearly so bad. They fill a niche that wouldn't be filled by any native birds, feeding on crumbs and weed seeds and nesting in nooks and crannies of buildings. When I was a child, House Sparrows used to cheep in the shrubs beneath my bedroom window, and I'd listen to them every night as I went to sleep, imagining the adventures they were recounting to one another. Today, I love watching how they adapt to and exploit new sources of food and warmth. At expressway rest stops, they frequently hop up to newly parked cars to snatch crushed insects from the grilles. During extreme cold snaps in northern Minnesota, I often watch them fly up to cars the moment a neighbor pulls in the driveway and turns off the engine. Before the driver even gets out of the car, several sparrows have flown under it, where they bask in the engine's heat for many comfortable moments until it cools down. For me, these urban sparrows are as endearing as Charles Dickens's Artful Dodger.

But even in urban areas, House Sparrows compete with native birds for food, especially when weary migrants are passing through. Cities are often built on rivers and lakeshores, precisely the routes that many migratory birds use. Providing at least some feeder fare that House Sparrows don't like can help these hungry strangers passing through town.

40 Find safe ways to solve problems with squirrels, raccoons, and other mammalian wildlife

When we improve our backyard habitats for birds, other wildlife moves in as well. Deer, raccoons, skunks, foxes, bears, coyotes, rabbits, and other wild animals are often attracted to human habitation, especially where they can find appropriate food, shelter, and water. And as we humans voraciously gobble up more natural habitat for our own homes, we give native wildlife fewer options. It's better for the natural environment when we build our homes in already settled areas and don't contribute to sprawl. But out of necessity, more wildlife is finding its way into major urban areas. When these wild animals are hit by cars, their carcasses provide huge amounts of calories that maintain unnaturally high populations of crows and other scavengers and also allow dangerous pathogens to flourish.

Where such wildlife is uncommon, home owners may welcome the sight of such interesting and beautiful creatures, but when their populations get out of hand, trouble follows. Deer and rabbits can seriously damage gardens and wild plants, as well as natural habitat. Deer also eat a surprising number of eggs and chicks of ground-nesting species and are a vector for Lyme disease. Raccoons, skunks, foxes, and coyotes can harm pets and may harbor rabies. Raccoons not only eat eggs and nestlings but sometimes kill and eat sleeping adult birds as well, including fairly large ones. ("Tex," the famous Whooping Crane imprinted on George Archibald of the Interna-

tional Crane Foundation, was killed by raccoons.) Bears can damage bird feeders and pose a danger to pets and humans. Squirrels and chipmunks occasionally damage homes, foundations, sidewalks, and gardens. Even where outright squirrel damage is negligible, many people don't like them eating at bird feeders.

When mammal populations are at normal levels, they can enrich our lives and are an essential part of a healthy ecosystem. But how do we keep their numbers manageable? First and foremost, never subsidize unwanted mammals in your yard. Never leave dog food out where coyotes, foxes, or other animals (including crows) may find it. If mammals are attracted to your brush pile, set out clumps of dog or cat fur to dissuade them. If you maintain a feeding station and scatter seeds on the ground for migrating birds, provide only as much as the birds can consume in a day, and rake up spilled seed regularly. Take corn off the menu if it attracts unwanted mammals. If you have problems at suet feeders, stop offering it or bring it in at night. To keep raccoons (and sometimes squirrels) off your feeders, smear a light coating of petroleum jelly on a short length of the pole. Raccoons are fastidious and don't like to get their fur messy. Don't use Tanglefoot or anything sticky. Various peppers are used to discourage squirrels from eating birdseed, but I am concerned that even though birds don't necessarily taste the pepper, it may injure their mouth or esophagus.

PART III

SUPPLEMENTING

BACKYARD HABITAT

11

BIRD FEEDING BASICS

FOR NEARLY TWO CENTURIES, PEOPLE IN THE UNITED STATES HAVE taken pleasure and satisfaction in feeding birds. Henry David Thoreau enjoyed the birds at Walden Pond and enticed them closer by setting out bread crumbs. Emily Dickinson wrote about her beloved songbirds and apparently fed them crumbs too. Bird feeding has benefits beyond being a time-honored American tradition. Attracting birds to our yards with feeders affords us an excellent look at a wide assortment of birds, making us more skilled at identifying them and more aware of seasonal changes and migratory patterns. It gives us the opportunity to keep track of bird distribution and population changes. And bird feeding also gives us a feeling that we're benefiting birds by giving them sustenance.

But are we helping or hurting birds by feeding them? Are we fostering the spread of disease among them? Are we making songbirds more vulnerable to attacks by cats and hawks? Are we changing migration patterns or distribution? Are we subsidizing deer, raccoons, bears, and other potential nuisance animals? Are we drawing birds close to our houses where they might be killed by our own windows? Understanding the issues involved with bird feeding and taking steps to avoid potential dangers will help ensure that bird feeding is as beneficial to birds as it is to us.

41 Understand the pros and cons of bird feeding

Feeders provide humans with the opportunity to see and enjoy backyard birds and learn about their habits. Most people who become involved in conservation first recognized the importance of birds and other natural resources because of intimate encounters with individual wild animals, including birds at feeders. And feeders have provided ornithologists and resource managers with data to track the spread of diseases, such as conjunctivitis in House Finches, and an easy way to monitor the distribution and abundance of many species. A lot of valuable data are obtained from "citizen science" projects that involve observation at feeders, such as Audubon's Christmas Bird Count and the Cornell Lab's Great Backyard Bird Count and Project Feeder Watch. Clearly, bird feeding adds to our understanding and knowledge of birds, aiding in conservation.

Bird feeding also helps individual birds directly, providing them with easy food resources during extreme weather and food shortages and keeping some birds alive that would otherwise die. During the cold, wet month of May 2004, a huge variety of birds took refuge in my backyard, including several species seldom found at feeders. As many as five Scarlet Tanagers, seven Baltimore Orioles, thirty Cape May Warblers, and even a Bobolink spent days or weeks in the yard. So few insects were available at the time that people hiking through northern forests in Minnesota were finding dead insectivorous birds that had apparently succumbed to starvation. Feeders also provide temporary safe harbors for migrants that have wandered out of their normal range. When a *Selasphorus* hummingbird (either a Rufous or an Allen's Hummingbird) appeared in my yard, far out of her range one cold November day, she was clearly hungry, in no condition to fly the 2,000 miles to reach her species' normal winter range without replenishing her body's reserves. She remained for sixteen days and then disappeared at mid-morning on December 3, when the temperature reached the twenties and was warmer in the southeast, the direction she was presumably headed. I'm afraid that if she didn't encounter anymore feeders, she probably didn't survive long enough to get to her proper wintering range. Desperate birds like this one may take refuge at feeders and may even borrow time at them, but the feeders didn't entice them out of their normal range or cause their ultimate demise. And in some cases, such as the warblers visiting my yard that cold spring, feeders probably keep some healthy but cold and starving birds alive until springlike weather finally comes. A young Ruby-throated Hummingbird stopped at my feeder for a long feeding bout one October day, long after others of its species had left northern Minnesota. That bird had probably hatched late and was behind schedule preparing for migration, but once its body was primed for travel, it stayed focused on the journey, stopping only for a meal before zipping off again. Very few hobbies provide so many benefits and pleasure to both people and wildlife while causing so little harm to either.

Because feeders often become gathering places for large numbers of birds, and because they provide food resources that can give local birds longer life spans and greater reproductive success, bird feeding may be a tool for wildlife managers. For these same reasons, feeders may subsidize invasive nonnative birds and native species whose populations are too high and, in rare situations, foster the spread of disease organisms. Those of us who feed birds must recognize these potential problems and work actively to prevent them. In some serious local or regional situations, bird feeding may need to be regulated.

One of the most important concerns about bird feeding is subsidizing problem species, especially exotics such as European Starlings and House Sparrows and overabundant native species such as Ring-billed Gulls, Canada Geese, and some blackbirds. Hand-feeding pigeons, ducks, gulls, and geese at urban and suburban parks provides great pleasure for some people and benefits both people and wildlife by fostering sympathy and affection for the latter. But doing so can also contribute to their overpopulation, creating a nuisance for other people and hurting other species and natural habitat. Concentrations of ducks and geese in urban parks can add significantly to the nutrient and bacteria loads of local beaches. And feeding in early winter can entice some urban ducks to remain in an area longer than is safe. In the winter of 2003, dozens of ducks died overnight when ice formed rapidly in a little inlet of Lake Superior near a city park where many people fed them. Perhaps these birds would have moved on earlier if they hadn't been so dependent on people for food, but since most urban duck populations include Mallards from domestic duck stock (as did this particular flock), it's uncertain whether these birds would have migrated, regardless of feeding. Because individual towns and cities have specific bird population issues and different local attitudes, regulations or prohibitions about feeding in public parks need to be addressed on a case-by-case basis.

Backyard feeding is unlikely to cause the vast majority of wild birds to remain in a location longer than usual, although feeders do provide food for individuals whose migratory timing or route varies from the norm and injured birds that aren't capable of migration. Stray orioles, thrashers, and some others may remain at feeding stations well north of their species' typical range for an entire winter. Many of the rarities found on Christmas Bird Counts are birds that remained farther north than their normal range and are regularly visiting feeders. But orioles, thrashers, hummingbirds, and most others time their migration for the weeks when natural food is most

abundant rather than when food is starting to disappear. So food availability is not the deciding factor that keeps individual wild birds past their normal departure time, especially long-distance migrants. Some hummingbirds that find themselves north of where they "belong" in early winter may take refuge at a feeding station, but without that feeding station, they'd simply die unnoticed. Some birds that linger may be injured, but most birds overwintering north of their "typical" range simply represent a normal variation within their species. Many short-distance migrants such as blackbirds, juncos, and native sparrows are wintering north of their historical winter ranges because of changes in agriculture, habitat, and climate. A few nonmigratory species such as cardinals, titmice, and Red-bellied Woodpeckers have been steadily extending their year-round ranges northward in recent decades. Bird feeding contributes to the survival of individuals, so it has certainly played a role in their gradual range extension, but it hasn't been the only or even the primary factor. For example, cardinals have been expanding northward since the 1800s, possibly because railroad track right-of-ways were kept cleared of snow, where grain occasionally spilled. And ornamental trees and shrubs planted in cities and towns have played an important role in changing bird distribution.

42 Take precautions to keep your feeder birds safe from toxins and diseases

When I was rehabilitating wild birds, I sometimes got phone calls from anxious people who had sick or dying birds in their yards. In one case, the caller later learned that her birdseed was contaminated, and many other people who had purchased seed from the same supplier had also lost birds. Another caller's feeding station apparently became infected with botulism during a very wet spring. In both cases, the people felt devastated about hurting the birds that they were trying to help.

To maximize the advantages and minimize the potential harm of bird feeding for individual birds and local populations, it's important to take some basic precautions. Here are a few guidelines to prevent bird diseases at feeding stations:

- Rake up shells and wasted seeds frequently and dispose of them in compost bins that are screened or covered to keep birds out.
- Make sure feeders provide drainage so seeds dry quickly after a rain. If seeds are sprouting in a platform feeder, clean it out and add drain holes. Many platform feeders are floored with screening to promote good drainage.
- Regularly clean feeders with a solution of 10 percent bleach and 90 percent water and allow them to dry completely before refilling.
- Store seeds in a dry place to prevent fungus and other disease organisms from contaminating the supply.

There are a few dangerous organisms that can hurt backyard birds. None of the diseases they cause, except House Finch conjunctivitis, is commonly seen at feeders, but knowing what to look for and how to prevent outbreaks or transmission will help you avoid sad situations.

Aflatoxins. Birdseed, especially corn and peanuts sold specifically for bird feeding, can be contaminated with aflatoxins. These poisons are produced by two fungi that are common and widespread in nature, *Aspergillus parasiticus* and *Aspergillus flavus,* which grow most rapidly in warm and humid environments. Aflatoxins are highly dangerous for humans and livestock, so seed sold for human consumption and animal feed is screened by the U.S. Department of Agriculture. Seed sold for bird feeding isn't legally required to be screened, and some seed sold for this purpose may not be. Research conducted by Dr. Scott Henke of Texas A&M University found that 17 percent of birdseed samples tested in Texas contained relatively large amounts of the toxin and that feeding birds contaminated seed can be very harmful. Consumers should demand that seed purchased for bird feeding be screened for this dangerous toxin.

Aflatoxins develop most easily in seeds packaged in plastic bags, because condensing moisture fosters fungal growth. To avoid this, don't buy corn in non-breathable plastic bags. Make sure it's fresh; store it in a clean, dry place; and keep your feeders and the ground beneath them meticulously clean. Choose peanuts sold for human consumption.

Aspergillosis. Aspergillosis is another fungal disease that is usually caused by *Aspergillus fumigatus,* which is commonly found in decaying vegetable matter, including moldy birdseed. A bird becomes infected by eating or inhaling mold spores from contaminated foods. The fungus produces lesions in the lungs and air sacs, causing difficulty breathing, emaciation, and excessive thirst. Birds often appear to have difficulty walking. When their eyes are infected, there may be a white opacity accompanied by a discharge. Healthy birds normally resist the disease, but birds with depressed immune systems are especially vulnerable. Occasionally, outbreaks of the disease cause significant mortality in certain species. Aspergillosis outbreaks at feeders are preventable by keeping feeders clean, the ground beneath them well raked, and spoiled seeds and shells well covered where you dispose of them (preferably, in a screened compost bin).

Avian pox. Birds don't get chickenpox, but they do get two forms of avian pox. (Oddly, chickenpox most likely got its name because it isn't particularly dangerous, so it was considered more "chicken" than the similar but deadly smallpox.) In the more common form of avian pox, wartlike growths appear on the featherless areas of the body around the eye, at the base of the beak, and on the legs and feet. When limited to the eye areas, the disease may be mistaken for conjunctivitis. In the rarer form, plaques develop on the mucous membrane of the mouth, throat, trachea, and lungs. These make breathing and feeding difficult and increase susceptibility to secondary infections, which kill the bird.

Avian pox can be caused by several strains of poxviruses and has been reported in at least sixty species of birds from twenty families, including turkeys, hawks, owls, and sparrows. The virus can be spread by direct contact with infected birds or contact with contaminated surfaces or through contaminated food or water. If you see a bird that may be infected with avian pox, it's a good idea to close down the feeding station for a week or two and make sure that the ground is raked and feeders are cleaned before resuming feeding.

Bird flu. Bird flu occurs on overcrowded, unsanitary poultry farms. According to the Centers for Disease Control and Prevention:

> Type A influenza viruses can infect several animal species, including birds, pigs, horses, seals and whales. Influenza viruses that infect birds are called "avian influenza viruses." Birds are an especially important species because all known subtypes of influenza A viruses circulate among wild birds, which are considered the natural hosts for influenza A viruses. Avian influenza viruses do not usually directly infect humans or circulate among humans.
>
> Influenza A viruses can be divided into subtypes on the basis of their surface proteins—hemagglutinin (HA) and neuraminidase (NA). There are 15 known H subtypes. While all subtypes can be found in birds, only 3 subtypes of HA (H1, H2 and H3) and two subtypes of NA (N1 and N2) are known to have circulated widely in humans.
>
> Avian influenza usually does not make wild birds sick, but can make domesticated birds very sick and kill them. Avian influenza A viruses do not usually infect humans; however, several instances of human infections and outbreaks have been reported since 1997. When such infections occur, public health authorities monitor the situation closely because of concerns about the potential for more widespread infection in the human population.

Since 1997, only one wild bird in the United States has tested positive for avian flu, a Peregrine Falcon. People have contracted the disease from contact with infected poultry and from other humans. Intensive production practices foster conditions in which bird flu and other diseases flourish. Overcrowded birds are more stressed, and cruel practices such as debeaking add to their stress level, making them far more vulnerable to illness. The excessive use of antibiotics also contributes to their stress level and, dangerously, to the virulence of bacterial diseases, making the birds more susceptible to viral infections due to their weakened immunity. In the final analysis, the probability of contracting bird flu from other people or from mass-produced grocery store poultry is greater than the chance of contracting it from wild birds. There is no known connection between bird flu and bird feeding. At this time, the best thing we can do to protect ourselves from bird flu is to buy organic, free-range poultry from a trusted local grower.

Conjunctivitis. Mycoplasmal conjunctivitis is an eye disease limited mostly to House Finches and, to a lesser extent, American Goldfinches, predominantly in the eastern half of the country. The eastern population of House Finches was introduced from a handful of individuals released in New York in the 1940s, so these birds are fairly closely related to one another. Apparently, most of the eastern birds are genetically susceptible to this disease. Infected birds may have red, swollen, runny, or crusty eyes. In the worst cases, the eyes become swollen shut or crusted over, leading to blindness. Infected birds may sit quietly, their feathers puffed out a bit, scratching one eye with a foot or against a tree. Although some infected birds recover, most probably die from starvation, exposure, or predation.

Many people associate this disease with bird feeding because so many of the sick birds are detected at feeding stations, but House Finches are flocking birds whether at feeders or away from them. According to the Cornell Lab, the worst period of disease transmission is late summer and fall, when Houses Finches visit feeders only sporadically. Disease prevalence is lowest during midwinter, when finches visit feeders much more regularly. And the epidemic did not affect any native eastern bird species common at bird feeders during the period that it reduced the eastern House Finch population by 60 percent. The disease took several years to reach the western population and (as of this writing) has infected comparatively few western House Finches. In the West, where the species is native and abundant, including at feeders, the House Finch population is more genetically diverse and at least somewhat resistant to the disease.

If you detect an infected bird using a tube feeder with a design that requires it to turn the side of its face toward the feeder, take the feeder down, clean it thoroughly, and don't put it back out while infected birds are visiting. As with other bird diseases, if you notice any sick or dying birds in your yard, it's a good idea to close down your feeding station entirely for at least a week. Make sure you report any infected birds to the Cornell Lab's

House Finch and American Goldfinch Disease Survey, either on its Web site (http://birds.cornell.edu/hofi/index.html) or by phone (800-843-2473).

Salmonella. Salmonellosis, or salmonella poisoning, is caused by bacteria belonging to the genus *Salmonella* and is a common cause of mortality in birds. Although it is found more often in natural settings than in backyards, feeder birds can be infected, and unfortunately, the symptoms are not always obvious. As with most sick birds, those suffering from salmonellosis may appear fluffed up and depressed. They may also have swollen eyelids, and the feathers near the vent may be stained and pasty. They are often lethargic and easy to approach. Unfortunately, some infected birds not yet showing outward signs of illness can spread the infection to other birds via their droppings.

Salmonellosis is transmitted primarily from bird to bird by fecal contamination of food and water, although it can also be transmitted by ingestion of contaminated feed or from physical contact. The disease can cause significant mortality. If you notice a bird that may be suffering from salmonellosis, it's important to close down your feeding station and birdbath for a couple of weeks. Rake all areas where birds have been gathering, and clean all feeders thoroughly. The original infection probably arose elsewhere, but it's important to prevent it from spreading to other birds. Ground-feeding birds are particularly susceptible to salmonellosis, so make sure that you rake frequently.

Trichomoniasis. Trichomoniasis is a disease caused by the protozoan *Trichomonas gallinae*. It most commonly affects pigeons and doves and the predators that feed on them, but it can also be spread to feeder birds when infected doves are present. This disease is characterized by raised lesions in the mouth, esophagus, and crop, so an infected bird may have trouble closing its mouth. The disease may be present in the mouth secretions of birds that appear to be healthy but are carriers, especially pigeons. The oral secretions of infected birds can contaminate feeders, the ground beneath feeders, and birdbaths, which can in turn expose many other birds to the disease. Mortality from this disease varies but can be quite high. Changing birdbath water frequently and raking beneath feeders will protect your birds from this disease. Discouraging pigeons from gathering at your feeding station can be an important preventive measure.

West Nile virus. This disease, spread by mosquitoes, biting flies, and possibly other blood-sucking parasites, is highly lethal to horses and many species of birds, especially jays and crows. Less than 1 percent of humans bitten by mosquitoes harboring West Nile virus get seriously ill, but for this 1 percent, the disease can be extremely serious. It affects the brain similar to encephalitis and can cause permanent neurological damage; it's fatal in 3 to 15 percent of serious cases (that is, in 0.03 to 0.15 percent of people exposed to the virus). The disease is most dangerous for the elderly and those with compromised immune systems, who must be protected from mosquito bites. Fortunately, the vast majority of people bitten by infected mosquitoes do not get sick or have only mild symptoms. In contrast, 99 to 100 percent of crows exposed to the virus in laboratory tests died. And West Nile virus seems to kill infected birds very quickly.

To prevent the disease in the first place, it's important to refresh your birdbath every few days, keep gutters cleaned, and eliminate any other sources of stagnant water to deter mosquito breeding. West Nile virus is most frequently transmitted by mosquitoes belonging to the genus *Culex*— the mosquitoes most closely associated with human habitation.

If you find a bird that may have died from West Nile virus, wear gloves when you pick it up and double-bag it in plastic. Then call the county health department to find out whether it is testing birds to verify the presence of the disease in your area. Testing is expensive, so if the authorities are already aware of the presence of the disease in your area, they may not want the carcass. In that case, keep it double bagged and dispose of it in the trash to prevent further disease transmission.

What should you do if you notice a diseased bird at your feeding station? According to the Cornell Lab:

> Only veterinarians or federally licensed wildlife rehabilitators can legally treat wild birds. Therefore, if you find a diseased bird, it's best to report it to your state or local wildlife agency. If you are advised to take the bird in for an examination, try to catch the bird by throwing a light towel over it and placing it in a box with air-holes. If you find a dead bird, place it in a double plastic bag and into the garbage (wear gloves).
>
> If a sick bird comes to your feeder, minimize the risk of infecting other birds by cleaning your feeder area thoroughly. If you see several diseased birds, take down all your feeders for at least a week to give the birds a chance to disperse. Keep the feeders down until you no longer see diseased individuals. And remember that prevention is the key to avoiding the spread of disease. Regularly clean

your feeders even when there are no signs of disease and prevent overcrowding by adding more feeders or setting up different types of feeders that allow only a few birds to visit at one time. And store your seed where it will remain as cool and dry as possible.

Pesticide poisoning. Pesticide poisoning often affects backyard birds, especially within two or three days of pesticide applications. An affected bird may be disoriented or have trouble balancing. It may be lying on its side, unable to sit at all. Although many lawn chemicals break down into less toxic substances within a few days, the damage they do to birds during their most toxic period is usually permanent and often fatal. I once cared for a newly fledged Blue Jay that a woman had seen hopping in her neighbor's freshly sprayed lawn. Hours later when she looked out, the little jay was lying helplessly on his side, unable to move. When she brought him to me, I examined him closely and found no injuries whatsoever, although his belly feathers were sticky and bore a faint odor. His eyes were bright, and he opened his mouth to beg, so I fed him several times that day. His digestive processes were fine, but he had very little muscular control and could not balance himself. I continued to feed him and fashioned a little sling from some handkerchiefs so that I could carry him with me during my daily activities to ensure that he stayed upright and was getting enough mental stimulation; at night I put him in a plastic bucket lined with paper towels to prop him up. I'd never done physical therapy on a bird and didn't know anyone who had, but each day I'd open and close his wings and move his legs to keep the muscles working at least a little. The little bird seemed comfortable and curious, was interested in his surroundings, made appropriate vocalizations, and even gained weight, but for many weeks he showed no improvement in his ability to balance. Finally, after almost three months, I set him on a table and he remained upright for several seconds before toppling. Over the following days, he was able to balance for longer periods, and one day he tried to hop. Now that he finally had a little muscular control, he became restless in the sling and seemed frustrated when I put him inside the padded bucket, where he was unable to see what was going on around him. So I lined a ten-gallon aquarium with cloth diapers and paper towels and brought him into our busy family room, since jays and their relatives are very intelligent and don't thrive without mental stimulation. He seemed so delighted to be in the aquarium that I let him sleep there that night. In the morning, I was devastated to find him dead. He'd apparently wedged himself between the glass and the diaper I'd lined it with. One shoulder, on the side where he'd fallen so many times, was poorly feathered, and the bare patches of skin against the cool glass had caused him to die of hypothermia in his sleep.

The prognosis for birds who've been poisoned by lawn pesticides is bleak, and it's also extremely difficult and often prohibitively expensive to test them to verify the cause of their illness. Many pesticide applications include a combination of different herbicides and insecticides (and sometimes fungicides), and most lawn care companies won't divulge the ingredients in their applications (trade secrets), so it's almost impossible to determine which pesticides killed a backyard bird or even whether pesticides were involved. There isn't enough tissue in a small bird to get a good sample, especially if the bird didn't actually ingest the toxin but just got some on its feathers and skin or breathed fumes. It is unconscionable to set out birdseed in yards that are treated with these dangerous chemicals.

When you purchase corn, make sure that it is intended for feeding, not planting, and never buy corn or other seed that is coated with a pink or red dye. That colored coating is capstan, a fungicide used on seeds meant for planting. It can kill mammals as large as horses and is very toxic to birds.

43 To deter hawks, close down your feeding station for a few weeks

Merlins, Cooper's Hawks, American Kestrels, and even Redtailed Hawks and Peregrine Falcons have become adapted to cities and suburbs. Some of these hawks have become adept at taking birds from feeding stations. Hawks are a natural hazard that songbirds have to deal with everywhere and usually aren't a significant problem, even though some of us feel outraged when a hawk takes one of our chickadees.

If your yard is visited by resident or migrating hawks, make sure that your feeders are very close or affixed to your windows to ensure that birds don't crash into the glass in a panic when a hawk flies in. It's sad enough when a hawk takes a few birds, but deaths from window collisions are a complete waste. Also, make sure that you have a good mix of plants to provide adequate cover. If you're concerned about a resident hawk taking too many birds, close down your feeder for a few days—the hawk will quickly develop a different hunting route. Never set out poison or try to trap a hawk. They are protected by federal and state laws.

Peregrine Falcon

Some people ask me why I'm more concerned about cats than hawks in my neighborhood. Hawks are natural predators native to America. If the prey base in an area becomes depleted, hawks move on, allowing the prey to replenish itself. We humans subsidize our pet cats, so they don't depend on birds or mice for food. Cats can thus be maintained at far higher densities than any natural predator population could be, destroying prey populations but not moving on to allow them to recover.

44 Patronize feed stores that support conservation

Back in the 1930s, hunters started paying for conservation with every dollar they spent on guns and ammunition. The Federal Aid in Wildlife Restoration Act, popularly know as the Pittman-Robertson Act, was approved by Congress on September 2, 1937, and took effect July 1, 1938. The purpose of this act is to provide funding for the selection, restoration, rehabilitation, and improvement of wildlife habitat; wildlife management research; and the distribution of information. Funds are derived from an 11 percent federal excise tax on sporting arms, ammunition, and archery equipment and a 10 percent tax on handguns.

At this point, there is no similar program to support birds and their habitat by taxing birdseed, binoculars, spotting scopes, or field guides, so birders aren't supporting the conservation of birds at nearly the same level that hunters have supported the conservation of game animals. But by choosing to buy our bird feeding supplies from stores that support conservation, we can indirectly support important research and species protection.

Some national bird store chains support research into bird food preferences and the nutritional needs of various species and also make contributions to local, national, and international conservation projects and nonprofit organizations. National chains of bird food sellers, because they buy seed in huge quantities, have the power to influence the policies of their suppliers. Conservation-minded consumers should pressure retailers to buy seeds from farmers who do not use bird-killing pesticides, to refuse to buy seeds imported from Burma or other countries with devastating human rights and environmental policies, and to make sure that the seeds they buy have been screened for aflatoxins and other hazardous chemicals and organisms.

45 Participate in citizen science feeder projects

Since the first Christmas Bird Count in 1900, Americans have been participating in organized "citizen science" projects that collect data about bird populations. The Christmas Bird Count, sponsored by the National Audubon Society, has become a model for such projects, amassing fairly standardized data from across the continent for a specific time each year (early winter) and allowing researchers to discern trends in various species' numbers. As valuable as Christmas Bird Count data are, the count period is too early in the season to provide much detailed information about winter finch movements, so the Cornell Lab and the National Audubon Society initiated the Great Backyard Bird Count, which provides a continentwide survey of bird numbers in February. Data from both projects can be mapped, providing an excellent picture of where populations for many species are concentrated.

The Cornell Lab has several other citizen science projects, including Project Feeder Watch, which provides a picture of where many species are year-round, and Project Pigeon Watch and Urban Bird Studies, which provide fascinating information about birds living in urban settings. Cornell also amasses data from nonprofessionals for its House Finch disease study and other important and interesting projects, such as its chickadee winter survival study. Cornell and Audubon also collaborated to initiate a new program called eBird, which allows birders and feeder watchers throughout North America to enter every bird they see afield and in their own backyards into a database. Advanced birders in each state help verify details to confirm rarer species and unusual numbers. As more people become aware of eBird and start contributing their sightings, this project has the potential to become one of the most valuable sources of information about year-round bird numbers ever developed.

12

BIRD FOOD RECOMMENDATIONS

WHEN WE THINK OF BIRD FEEDING, WE USUALLY THINK OF SEED. But there are many different kinds of birdseed and numerous other foods that are just as important in a well-managed feeding station.

46 Offer safe and appropriate birdseed

Many North American birds eat seeds. Some finches belonging to the family Fringillidae feed on virtually nothing else, but most birds eat other foods as well. Birds that eat seeds either break the shells open to eat the heart or swallow the seeds whole, letting their gizzards grind down the shells. Birds are as varied as the plants that produce seeds. Some species, such as crossbills, have beaks specifically structured to open certain kinds of seeds; others, such as most blackbirds, can open a wide variety of different seeds. Some of the birdseeds most often provided at feeders are discussed here, in approximate order from most to least useful.

Sunflower seeds. A huge variety of birds, from chickadees to grosbeaks, feed on sunflower seeds, so if you provide only one kind of bird food, this is the best choice. There are two main varieties: black oil and striped. Striped sunflower seeds are larger and have thicker shells than black oil sunflower seeds, so the striped ones are more difficult for smaller birds and birds with weaker beaks to open. If you're inundated with House Sparrows, it's wise to switch to striped sunflower seeds until they've moved on.

Black oil sunflower seeds have a higher fat content than striped. Fat is a high-energy food that birds metabolize efficiently, so the extra calories and fat make black oil seeds more valuable during the cold days of winter when birds maintain their body temperature by shivering, requiring extra calories. I use black oil seeds almost exclusively at my feeders. Some of the birds that feed on sunflower seeds are ground feeders, especially doves, sparrows, towhees, and cardinals. Don't spread on the ground more seed than the birds will eat in one day, especially in wet weather.

Sunflower seed shells contain a plant growth inhibitor, so some people recommend not placing raked-up hulls on compost piles that will be used on gardens. However, this compost may help keep weeds at bay when placed between garden rows. To keep birds from feeding near decaying seeds and other compost, which may harbor fungi, keep your compost bin closed or screened.

A moth that lays its eggs within sunflower seeds can become an annoying problem when the seed is stored in the house. The caterpillars feed on the sunflower seeds, increasing the likelihood of fungal and bacterial growth, so these moths make the seed somewhat dangerous for birds, too. The U.S. Fish and Wildlife Service recommends that seed distributors store seeds in air-conditioned spaces to help control these pests.

Sunflower seed is grown primarily for human food, especially vegetable oil, and because of its obvious popularity with birds, U.S. farmers lose about 2 percent of their entire crop each year to birds. Bird clubs and those of us who feed birds should encourage birdseed retailers to investigate how their suppliers control blackbirds and to boycott those that resort to poisons. A national agricultural insurance system, paid in part by a tax on birdseed, could protect farmers from serious losses while protecting birds, humans, and the environment we share from dangerous pesticides.

Sunflower hearts and chips. If you live in an apartment or just don't want to deal with sunflower seed shells, you can offer hulled sunflower hearts or sunflower chips. These are also very good for birds with soft beaks, such as tanagers, so they appeal to an even larger set of birds than are attracted to whole sunflower seeds. Sunflower hearts spoil quickly, especially in wet weather, so provide them in small covered or tube feeders or in well-drained open platforms, and freshen the chips frequently. Store them in a cool, dry room in tightly sealed packaging to prevent sunflower moth damage.

Niger seed, or thistle. Goldfinches, siskins, and redpolls eat many small weed seeds, and among their favorites is thistle, a noxious weed that can't be sold in the United States. Niger (sometimes spelled Nyjer) thistle, grown in India, Ethiopia, Burma, and Nepal, is just as attractive to birds and is sterilized, so it won't germinate here.

Burma has a terrible record of human rights abuses and habitat destruction, so finding niger seed distributors that purchase exclusively from other countries is best. According to EarthRights International:

In recent years, Burma has emerged as one of the three top exporters of niger seed to the United States. In 2000, India was the number one source of niger seed, followed by Ethiopia, Burma, and Nepal. In a two month period (April and May 2001), U.S. companies imported over 3,000 tons of niger seed from Burma, which they valued at $1.6 million. This projects to an annual rate of 18,000 tons and almost $10 million. At the retail level, this translates into more than $50 million in sales.

Some of the U.S.'s biggest birdseed distributors . . . sell mixes that contain niger seed from Burma.

But Burma is hardly a "reputable" supplier. Government watchdogs like the International Labor Organization and the U.S. Department of Labor have concluded that the use of forced labor in Burma is "widespread and systematic." Based on these findings, U.S. government agencies are prohibited from purchasing goods made in Burma. . . .

We urge consumers not to purchase any birdseed mixes that contain niger seed from Burma. We also ask that you contact birdseed distributors' headquarters and local retailers and urge them to halt this practice that directly supports the repressive regime that rules Burma.

The U.S. government has had a ban on niger seed from Burma now for the last three years. Overall, birdseed accounts for only about 2 percent of Burma's exports. (Two far more significant Burmese exports are apparel, which involves the use of forced labor, and teak, which contributes to deforestation.) Continue to alert bird food retailers to your concerns about niger seed from Burma and ask them to boycott companies that sell Burmese niger thistle. Concerted international pressure on Burma may eventually force it to improve its environmental and human rights practices.

To feed niger seed, use little mesh bag feeders called thistle stockings, which finches cling to while feeding, or tube feeders with small openings. Finches are sociable, flocking birds that can feed almost shoulder to shoulder, so feeders with many ports work well for them. Use large feeders that can accommodate many finches only when you actually have many finches—otherwise, the seeds will sit uneaten for days or weeks and spoil.

Niger seed is expensive, so if you're inundated with finches and want to keep them happy within a more reasonable budget, mix thistle with sunflower chips. If your thistle tube feeder doesn't block seed from falling below the lowest hole (most feeders have an open tube all the way to the lowest perch, a couple of inches below the lowest feeding hole), the seed on the bottom will become rancid and moldy. To prevent this, fill the bottom with clean sand or marbles to just below the lowest feeding hole. When you don't have many finches and the seed isn't used up quickly, set out only a small amount and freshen it regularly.

White proso millet. White millet is popular with ground-feeding birds, including quails, doves, native American sparrows, juncos, towhees, and cardinals. Unfortunately, it also attracts cowbirds, House Sparrows, and blackbirds, which are already subsidized by human activities and kept at unnaturally high population levels by agricultural practices and habitat changes. When these species are present, skip the millet; virtually all of the more desirable species that feed on white millet also like black sunflower, which doesn't attract as many cowbirds or House Sparrows. In my own yard, I scatter white millet on the ground only during migration periods, when native sparrows are abundant. My neighborhood has very few House Sparrows.

Safflower seeds. Safflower is a favorite of cardinals, and grosbeaks, chickadees, doves, and native sparrows feed on it as well. According to many books, House Sparrows, starlings, and squirrels don't like it, but in some areas, certain individuals seem to be developing a taste for it. Because safflower is offered primarily for cardinals and grosbeaks, open platform feeders or large hopper feeders are the best choices.

Milo or sorghum. Milo is eaten by many birds, especially ground feeders in the Southwest. The Cornell Lab conducted seed preference tests and found that Steller's Jays, Curve-billed Thrashers, and Gambel's Quails prefer milo over sunflower seeds. According to Carrol Henderson, House Sparrows don't like it very much, although cowbirds do. If you buy mixed seed, look at the label to make sure that the little red seeds are milo or sorghum, not red millet.

Shelled and cracked corn. Corn is eaten by grouse, pheasants, turkeys, quails, cardinals, grosbeaks, crows, ravens, jays, doves, ducks, cranes, and many other species. Unfortunately, it's also very attractive to House Sparrows, cowbirds, starlings, geese, deer, and bears, none of which should be subsidized. Don't offer corn if these species are a problem. Even worse, corn

Mourning Doves

is the bird food that is most likely to be contaminated with aflatoxins, which are highly poisonous to birds. Never buy corn sold in non-breathable plastic bags, because condensation fosters fungal growth. Many of the birds that like cracked corn are ground feeders, but spreading corn on the ground may increase the likelihood of contamination with fungus. Spread only a small amount at a time, and be very conscientious about keeping the feeding area raked.

Never offer corn that is coated with a red dye. This means that it has been treated with fungicides and is intended for planting. It is highly toxic to humans, other mammals, and all birds.

Rapeseed. Rapeseed is eaten by only a few species, such as quails, doves, finches, and juncos. Unless you have these species at your feeder, any rapeseed in the mixture is going to spoil and foster fungal growth and potential disease.

Golden millet, red millet, flax, and buckwheat. These seeds are not nearly as popular with most birds as white millet, so they are more likely to be left over to spoil. Most inexpensive grocery store seed mixtures contain at least one or two of these, adding bulk but reducing the quality and potentially increasing the likelihood of disease transmission. Also, grocery store mixes are usually packaged in plastic bags, where condensing moisture can promote the growth of fungus and other disease organisms.

Canary seed. This is very popular with House Sparrows and cowbirds, so it should not be offered. Other birds that feed on canary seed, such as doves and native sparrows, are just as happy with sunflower seed, and canary seed isn't particularly nutritious compared with other seeds.

Wheat and oats. Many species eat wheat and oats, especially gallinaceous birds, but they are also popular with starlings, House Sparrows, and cowbirds and should not be used. Sometimes these are added as fillers to bird mixes, but they can quickly spoil.

Popped corn. Popped popcorn is sometimes eaten by thrashers, but since it's likely to spoil after being soaked in rain or even heavy dew, it isn't a good choice. Never offer microwave popcorn or buttered popcorn.

47 Offer peanut butter and nuts

Peanut butter is nutritious and has a high energy content, so it is often a component of bluebird mixes. The easiest way to offer it is smeared into the crevices of tree bark or stuffed into the holes of hanging log feeders. It's fun to hang old pinecones stuffed with peanut butter on tree branches—this is a favorite feeder type for chickadees and a delightful project for small children.

In his book *A Complete Guide to Bird Feeding,* John V. Dennis reports cases of birds choking on peanut butter. Because of its sticky texture, it can gum up their mouths, so mix peanut butter with a generous amount of cornmeal to make it grittier. In summer, peanut butter may get too goopy to use even with cornmeal, but during northern Minnesota winters, I offer unadulterated peanut butter—when frozen, birds have no problem with it. Birds don't seem to have a preference between chunky and creamy. Because peanut butter is produced for human consumption, it is screened for aflatoxins and other contaminants and is safe for birds.

Peanuts in the shell are popular with jays and even much smaller birds. In my own yard, chickadees frequently carry off small peanuts in the shell to eat on a branch. Once I watched a chickadee pick up a huge peanut—

one with three kernels, which probably weighed a full third of the chickadee's weight. The tiny bird took off, steadily losing altitude and barely making it into a nearby lilac bush. There it spent the next hour chipping away and eating while its flock came and went several times.

Peanut kernels, hearts, and chips are also popular with jays and a huge variety of other birds. Unfortunately, like corn, peanuts sold for animal consumption may be contaminated with aflatoxins, especially when sold in plastic bags or improperly stored. Until all peanut producers are required to screen peanuts sold for bird feeding for aflatoxins, we consumers should refuse to buy peanuts that might kill the birds we are trying to feed. Peanuts sold in grocery stores for human consumption have been screened and are safe for birds.

Peanut hearts and kernels are often offered in mesh cages. Make sure the mesh is wide enough to allow the birds easy access to the seeds, and avoid painted ones—paint chips can be ingested. I provide peanut hearts in a small acrylic feeder affixed with suction cups to a second-story window, which squirrels can't reach. Unless your birds go through peanuts very quickly, small feeders that are freshened frequently are better than large ones. Bring peanuts in during rainy spells. Peanut chips are often mixed with niger thistle for finches. Make sure these mixtures stay fresh.

Mixed nuts (cracked so that birds can get at the meat) and acorns are popular with a variety of birds. Make sure the nuts don't get wet. Since squirrels and chipmunks love nuts as much as birds do, buy feeders designed or placed to exclude them. Otherwise, plan on spending an inordinate amount of time and effort trying to keep squirrels at bay, or learn to enjoy them.

48 Offer suet

Most birds that winter in northern climates are adherents of the Atkin's diet—that is, they thrive on low-carbohydrate diets that are heavy in fats and proteins. Those of us concerned about clogged arteries may find it hard to believe, but unadulterated animal fat is actually a healthy food for many birds.

The term *suet* technically refers to the hard, fatty tissue around the kidneys of cattle and sheep, used in cooking and for making tallow. However, many people use the word to refer to any fat trimmings from beef. Either way, it's very popular with many backyard birds, especially woodpeckers, chickadees, nuthatches, jays, catbirds, orioles, and starlings. Over the years,

I've had four species of warblers at my suet feeders. Tanagers also occasion-ally visit suet feeders, especially during spring migration.

Suet can be fed to birds raw (as it comes from the grocery store) or ren-dered—melted down, usually in a double boiler, and then strained. Ren-dered suet can be poured into cupcake papers, aluminum foil cake pans, or similar molds and then chilled. Rendered suet stays fresh and solid much longer than raw suet; in warm weather, raw suet quickly becomes rancid.

There are many recipes for making more complicated suet cakes, avail-able in bird feeding books. Several varieties of commercial suet cakes are available; some even contain dried insects or fruits in addition to rendered suet. Commercial suet cakes are especially good to use in summer because they stay fresh for a long time.

Suet, either raw chunks or prepared cakes, is usually offered to birds in suet cages. These can be bought from bird feeding stores or made from plastic-coated wide-weave metal mesh or hardware cloth. Suet can also be smeared directly onto tree bark or stuck into the crevices of pinecones that are then hung from tree branches. A teacher in my area once had a Red-breasted Nuthatch die after becoming entangled in an onion bag holding suet, so I no longer recommend using mesh bags. Some people are con-cerned that metal suet cages might pose a danger in extreme cold. I've never heard firsthand of any birds injured by getting stuck to cold metal, but to be safe, I always buy plastic-coated suet cages.

Hunters often tie venison rib cages to the trunk of a tree, where birds can pick at the fat and peck into the bone for weeks. It may be important to consider your neighbor's view when figuring out where to place such a treat, but it provides high-quality food for birds. Make sure that no buck-shot or bullets remain.

People used to set out congealed bacon fat and other drippings for birds. Although birds seem to relish the flavor, and although the fat is good for them, it's risky to offer bacon or other processed meats to birds. Sodium nitrites are harmful to humans, so they are almost certainly harmful to birds.

Should you feed suet to birds in summer? They don't need it when insects are available, but adult chickadees and woodpeckers often take quick meals at feeders to sustain their energy levels as they bring the majority of the insects they catch to their nestlings. And when baby woodpeckers and orioles fledge, the parents frequently bring them to feeders, providing us with a lovely sight and a firsthand view of how successful nesting has been that season. But soft suet can make a bird's belly or facial feathers sticky, reducing their insulating and waterproofing ability. There are even reports of woodpeckers losing all the feathers on their faces after feeding at goopy suet. Rancid suet can also harbor dangerous bacteria. Make sure to set out only rendered or commercially prepared suet cakes in warm weather. As fun as it is to see them, I don't like the idea of offering suet to attract fledglings, because growing birds need more protein than fat in their diets.

49 Offer fruits and jellies

Although most songbirds require diets that are high in protein and fat, some need a higher-energy diet, which they get mainly from fruits and nectar. Some species that never visit feeders for birdseed will come for fruits. You can offer grapes, currants, apples, bananas, raisins, oranges, and other fruits. Never offer more than your birds are taking within a day or two, and make sure to compost the leftovers as soon as there is any sign of mold. In the tropics, birds are accustomed to picking up fruits at feeders. Here in the United States and Canada, fruit-eating birds expect their fruit to grow on trees or shrubs and are often oblivious to fruits in feeders. But after one or two birds discover this source of food, others will soon follow their lead.

Orioles and catbirds are very fond of grape jelly, as are robins, some woodpeckers, and occasionally even tanagers. Some orioles visit feeders for orange marmalade or grape jelly all summer, long after they've stopped feeding on real oranges. This is fine for adult birds, which often need a quick supply of calories when they're incubating eggs, brooding young, or hunting insects for nestlings. But jellies are not appropriate for fledglings, which need much more protein than carbohydrates. If adult birds are bringing their young to your feeders, it's time to take in the jelly. If you enjoy seeing these young birds, set out mealworms for them instead. The sugars in jelly are much more concentrated than they are in natural foods, so if you offer jelly, make sure you provide clean drinking water in a birdbath.

Jellies should be spooned into jar tops or similar small containers. Never set out more than a spoonful or two—birds may get mired in it, especially after the surface becomes sticky. One cold spring, I had dozens of migrating birds visiting my jelly. I had to be away from home for several hours, but because the temperature was below freezing and I felt that my orioles and tanagers were depending on me, I set out a large bowl of jelly for them. I came home to find a Red-breasted Nuthatch hopelessly stuck. I fished him out and gave him three baths with warm water, drying him with paper

Baltimore Oriole

towels and allowing him to preen between baths. It took almost four hours for him to be clean and dry enough to be released. Luckily, jelly washes out with plain water, so I didn't need soaps or detergents, which can compromise natural oils. This situation could have ended much worse—the little bird could have succumbed to hypothermia before I discovered him. And thanks to my experience as a licensed bird rehabber and the fact that this particular nuthatch was accustomed to taking mealworms from my hand, he wasn't very stressed. In fact, he ate lots of mealworms during his recovery period. After his release, he didn't return to my feeders all day, but the next morning, there he was, good as new.

As potentially dangerous as this was, I didn't consider ending my jelly feeding. That spring was very cold, and natural food was so scarce that a huge variety of birds took advantage of my feeding station. But to prevent such an accident from happening again, I put out more feeders with much smaller amounts of jelly in each.

50 Provide water for drinking and bathing

Birds are physiologically able to conserve water more efficiently than mammals can, but they still require drinking water to survive. Because they can fly to ponds, lakes, and other natural water sources, in most areas they get by quite well without birdbaths. In winter, their bodies are extremely good at conserving water, and they can eat snow or drops from melting icicles. But providing water in backyard habitats can support a larger number of birds, and easily available, safe drinking water makes their lives easier. Birds are attracted to the sound of water running or dripping, so recirculating fountains and slow drips attract many more birds than simple birdbaths do.

Plastic and ceramic birdbaths may have slippery slopes. If yours does, add sand or rough stones to the bottom to provide birds with better footing. In summer, the best location for a birdbath is in the shade, to minimize evaporation and algal growth. The activity at birdbaths often attracts neighborhood cats and other predators, and birds with wet feathers are often clumsy fliers, so it's best to situate birdbaths near trees or shrubs where the birds can retreat if a predator is spotted.

Cleanliness is important. Some birds, most notably grackles, dispose of their nestlings' fecal sacs over water. In natural settings, they choose lakes or streams, but in urban and suburban settings, they may use swimming pools, shiny automobiles (on sunny days, the shimmering surface has a watery appearance to a grackle's eyes), or birdbaths. And when birds bathe, dirt, germs, parasites, and droppings remain behind. Also, the mosquito species most likely to carry encephalitis and West Nile virus often lay their eggs in birdbaths. Be sure to change the water every two or three days to keep it clean and to destroy mosquito eggs before they hatch. A quick weekly scouring with a wire-bristle brush and a hose is usually adequate maintenance.

Birds are also attracted to lawn sprinklers set to provide a fine spray. It's best to run these in the early morning or evening, when cooler temperatures minimize evaporation. If water shortages are an issue, recirculating ponds and sprinklers may be inappropriate. In this case, you can suspend a water-filled container with a slow leak—a tin can with a small puncture in the bottom or a water bottle with the drinking spout barely open—from an overhanging branch. Set a small birdbath underneath to catch the dripping water. Once or twice a day, refill the drip source from the tap or even from the birdbath itself.

Constructing a backyard pond will provide water for your regular birds and attract passing migrants as well. If you want to stock your backyard pond with aquatic plants, fish, frogs, or other creatures, make sure to use only species that are native to your area. (Beautiful as they are, exotic fish such as Koi are not a good idea; they will attract predators and may expose native wildlife to exotic diseases.) These ponds are best constructed so that they are filled by natural rainfall rather than municipal water supplies, which is especially important if water shortages are an issue.

Should you provide water in winter? Even though birds seem to espe-cially enjoy birdbaths when their natural sources are frozen solid, heated birdbaths use electricity; wasting energy is ultimately a much more serious

problem for bird populations than winter water shortages are. Fresh water set out in the morning may remain unfrozen for several hours, but during extreme cold, water vapor can be dangerous if it condenses on feathers. During freezing weather, birds simply should not bathe. I've read of several instances of birds, usually starlings or Mourning Doves, bathing in heated birdbaths in winter and then, after flying off, suddenly dropping like stones when their wet wings or tail feathers froze. If you do provide water in winter, cover the birdbath with a nonmetallic mesh grille (perhaps constructed of wooden dowels) that allows birds to insert their beaks for drinking but prevents them from immersing their bodies.

51 Supply birds with calcium and other minerals

Because they lay eggs, birds have very high calcium requirements. Calcium can be at a premium under many circumstances, but the situation is becoming dire in some areas where acid rain has leached calcium from the soil, making it less available in invertebrates as well as in grit. In these areas, ground-feeding birds such as Wood Thrushes are becoming calcium depleted and laying eggs with thinner shells. Also, seed-eating birds require grit in their gizzards to help them grind down their food. Providing grit and crushed oyster shells purchased from pet shops and eggshells from the kitchen can help birds enormously.

Because the risk of salmonella is high in raw eggs, all eggshells except those that have been hard-boiled should be baked for twenty minutes at 250 degrees Fahrenheit. Allow the eggshells to cool, and then crush them into pieces smaller than a dime. The Cornell Lab recommends offering them on the ground, in a dish, or on a low platform feeder, separate from seed feeders. The lab has conducted tests to determine where various species prefer to pick up eggshells: chickadees and nuthatches prefer feeders, quails and swallows prefer the ground, and many birds show no strong preference either way. A huge variety of birds has been recorded picking up eggshells, including orioles, tanagers, warblers, and thrushes. Crows, jays, blackbirds, and swallows seem to take the most.

13

FEEDING SPECIAL BIRDS

AMONG THE MOST POPULAR OF ALL BACKYARD BIRDS ARE HUM-mingbirds. They're easy to feed but require special feeders. And some birds that people don't usually think of as feeder birds, such as bluebirds, can be enticed to feeders for special treats.

52 Attract and feed hummingbirds safely

Hummingbirds are lovely and enormously entertaining. Because of their extraordinary metabolic rate (hummingbird hearts have been recorded beating more than 1,200 times per minute), they need a lot of fuel relative to their size to sustain life. Ruby-throated and Rufous Hummingbird eggs are as tiny as peas. The embryos may die if the eggs become chilled, so female hummingbirds must be able to feed and return to their nests very quickly during cold or rainy weather, especially if the temperature is below freezing. Abundant food resources can mean the difference between nesting success and failure.

Sugar water is the standard hummingbird feeder fare. Under normal circumstances, you can use one-quarter to one-third cup of sugar per cup of water. Natural nectars vary in their sugar content, and these concentrations are within normal ranges. During cold, rainy periods, it's not a bad idea to keep it on the strong side to provide needed energy; during drought conditions, use less sugar to prevent birds from becoming dehydrated. When you mix just enough solution to use right away, there's no need to boil the water.

Never substitute honey for sugar—the water becomes cloudy, and fungus and bacteria grow far more readily in honey than in processed sugar. Food coloring is unnecessary and may be harmful. The color and design of hummingbird feeders are what attract hummers. I never use commercial hummingbird mixtures, which are simply sugar and artificial coloring. Plain sugar is cheaper and probably healthier.

I know of one report of a hummingbird collapsing with hypothermia while feeding from a perch early on a cold morning. The person who reported this believed that as the bird filled up with almost freezing sugar water, its body temperature dropped to critical levels. He suggested using feeders without perches during cold periods, since muscle activity from hovering helps maintain body temperature. Although I don't know of any studies that have replicated these observations, it's a good idea to set out fresh hummingbird nectar first thing in the morning, so the water will be warmest when the birds are coldest.

If you use feeders with large enough perches, orioles also drink sugar water. You can offer sugar water in bowls, but you're more likely to attract ants than hummingbirds. Some woodpeckers feed on sugar water, especially Downy and Acorn Woodpeckers, and other species occasionally develop a "sweet beak." One cold spring, a Cape May Warbler learned to hover for a few seconds at a time at my window hummingbird feeder, coming many times a day for over a week.

The greatest danger to birds from sugar water is spoilage. Fungus and bacteria flourish in it, especially in warm weather. In addition, sugar water ferments, forming alcohol and other organic compounds. This process also happens more rapidly in warm weather. Hummingbirds feeding on sugar water that has been left out only three or four days can develop enlarged livers, so it's important during warm weather to change the solution frequently. It's also a good idea to keep hummingbird feeders in the coolest, shadiest places available. Hummingbirds are extremely territorial and tend to chase one another away from feeders, so to accommodate the most hummingbirds and to keep the water freshest, it's better to set out five or six small feeders with one or two ports each than to set out one or two large feeders with five or six ports each.

Wasps harass hummingbirds and can sting and even kill them. To protect your hummingbirds, use bee guards on your feeders. If they still cause problems, Carrol Henderson recommends discouraging bees and wasps by rubbing Avon Skin-So-Soft, Off Skintastic, or other insect repellents around the feeder ports. Be careful not to get these substances near the nectar, however. One summer when I had a serious problem with yellow jackets, I started vacuuming them out of the hummingbird feeders. Within an hour of the first time I did this, a couple of my hummingbirds figured out that the noisy vacuum was vanquishing the wasps and started hovering at the windows, making chittering sounds. One female would repeatedly tap on the glass and stare at me to alert me that wasps were present. I'd crank the window open and start the vacuum while the hummers perched or hovered just two or three feet away. They'd zip over to the feeder the moment I turned off the vacuum, before the window was even closed.

Ants are also attracted to hummingbird feeders. Smearing a dab of petroleum jelly or insect repellent on the wire holding a suspended feeder can keep ants at bay. Some hanging hummingbird feeders have an ant guard, a middle section of the feeder that can be filled with water. This works like a moat at the castle door to keep ants from crawling into the feeder. No matter how bad an ant or wasp problem is, never use pesticides near hummingbird feeders.

Sugar water is not sufficient to sustain hummingbirds for any length of time. Hummingbird gardens are the best source of both nectar and insects. There are many resources available to help you select appropriate hummingbird plants for your area. Flowers that attract many small insects are just as important as flowers that produce lots of nectar. One interesting way of providing insects, suggested by Carrol Henderson, is to set out chunks of melon or banana in a mesh bag. Hummingbirds and other fly-catching species can dart at the bag and catch the fruit flies that appear. In fruit-growing agricultural areas, this may not be a wise idea.

Encouraging spiders and fostering lichens will help local hummingbirds, which use lichens and spider silk in nest construction. Some hummingbirds prefer to build their nests near trees where sapsuckers are maintaining fresh drill holes, which guarantees a nearby source of food and minimizes the amount of time they're off the nest during incubation. So fostering sapsuckers will also encourage hummingbirds.

Many people believe that keeping feeders out into autumn will entice hummingbirds to remain in the north longer than they should, but that simply isn't true. Immature hummingbirds may remain at feeders for weeks after the adults migrate, but especially in the case of Ruby-throated Hummingbirds, the young birds have such a powerful migratory instinct that they will leave as soon as their muscle mass and fat levels can support the rigors of the flight. Anna's, Rufous, and Calliope Hummingbirds and Green Violet-ears occasionally find themselves farther north in late fall and winter than a hummingbird would normally be. This represents normal variation and may be augmented by lower survival rates in the tropics, where com-

Ruby-throated
Hummingbird

petition for dwindling habitat is getting worse. More Rufous Hummingbirds appear to be wintering in the United States, but this is only tangentially related to and supported by bird feeding. Although feeders clearly help these individuals and may ultimately contribute to the success of birds with a genetic tendency to remain farther north, the feeders do not entice them to stay; they simply provide some assistance to the birds that choose to do so. In years when nesting is late, young birds that would otherwise starve may be kept alive longer, or even be able to get their weight up to attempt migration, if they encounter late feeders. An immature Ruby-throated Hummingbird once stopped at my feeder in October, long after I thought I'd seen the last one of the year. It took a long, filling drink and then moved on. The feeder may have given it a needed boost during its travels, but it did not entice the bird to remain.

In the event that a hummingbird remains in your area after normal fall migration, when flowers and insects are no longer available, adding protein to a sugar water mixture can help it survive and remain healthy. Special commercial hummingbird mixtures such as Nektar Plus are ideal. These spoil extremely quickly, however, and should be used only in exceptional circumstances. When a Rufous Hummingbird appeared at my feeder one November, I mixed mealworms in a blender with a sugar water solution to provide her with protein. This sustained her during several freezing days when no wild insects were available. I had six hummingbird feeders out, but only one with the mealworms added. When temperatures were below 20 degrees Fahrenheit, that was the feeder she visited at least 90 percent of the time.

When hummingbirds turn up in northern areas in winter, they're likely to be unusual species wandering outside their normal range. If you happen to observe an out-of-season hummingbird, notify the local bird club or state ornithological society, and expect birders to start arriving to study the bird. Some species are hard to distinguish in the field, so birders take a lot of photographs for documentation. There are about fifty banders in North America specifically licensed to handle hummingbirds. These people have a lot of experience and know how to capture and measure these birds safely. Only a few of these individuals have a special endorsement that allows them to remove a tail feather to verify identification. Although a feather can be extremely useful for identifying a rare species, removing one in the case of a wintering hummingbird doesn't seem warranted. Whenever a feather is removed, the bird's body instantly starts diverting energy and nutrients into feather production. This isn't a problem when resources are abundant, but in times of scarcity or when a bird is already stressed by low temperatures, it seems less justifiable. Usually, photographing the tail feathers of a bird in the hand provides all the documentation necessary for accurate identification. Trapping the bird in a cage trap is much safer than using a mist net, where the bird is more likely to lose feathers and be hurt or stressed during removal.

The U.S. Fish and Wildlife Service no longer issues permits allowing people to trap out-of-range hummingbirds to move them to "more appropriate" areas, partly because the vast majority of birds died during capture or transport. Hummingbirds are surprisingly hardy. The Rufous Hummingbird that visited my yard survived both a blizzard and a night when the temperature dropped to 6 degrees Fahrenheit. But sadly, some wintering hummingbirds do die. Because information about the bird's species and body condition at the time of death is valuable and may ultimately help other hummingbirds, it's a good idea to retrieve the carcass of any winter hummingbirds that succumb. By paying attention to where a wintering hummingbird roosts during the day and at night, observers have a better chance of finding a body if the bird suddenly stops appearing. If the bird appears throughout one day and then doesn't appear the next morning, chances are it died overnight. If it stops coming at midmorning, chances are good that it moved on.

53 Attract bluebirds and other insectivorous birds

Bluebirds have long been treasured by Americans. Their pleasing songs, lovely plumage, and gentle ways make them one of the most popular songbirds. Clearings for native and colonial settlements and especially farms and orchards provided ideal bluebird habitat for both feeding and nesting. Bluebirds hunt in open fields by perching in dead trees or on stumps (fence posts are perfect), dropping to the ground for insects. Also, woodpecker holes in fence posts and natural cavities in apple trees make ideal nesting sites. But beginning in the 1940s and 1950s, several changes in agricultural practices made farms less hospitable for bluebirds. Farmers started treating damaged tree limbs before diseased branches rotted away to provide natural cavities. At the same time, more farmers built fences with metal posts. And even worse, farmers began using pesticides. Meanwhile, the exploding populations of introduced House Sparrows and European Starlings produced greater competition for the dwindling number of potential nest cavities. Although one of the worst pesticides for birds, DDT, was banned in 1971, other insecticides still in use can hurt bluebirds and decimate their food resources.

Providing nest boxes and limiting pesticide use have improved bluebird population levels greatly. But monitoring bluebird boxes and cleaning them out at the end of the breeding season furnish sad proof of the hardships caused by extremes in weather: the desiccated bodies of bluebirds and their eggs or nestlings. Starvation and hypothermia during unusually cold springs are the normal causes of mortality in bluebirds. Although bluebird populations can flourish despite seasonal losses, dead bluebirds seem a heartbreaking waste, especially when there are ways to help them. Birds survive cold temperatures much more easily when they have plenty of food and stores of body fat, which provide the energy needed to shiver, thus heating their bodies and preventing hypothermia. Providing food for local bluebirds greatly increases the chance of them making it through bad weather.

The best food to offer bluebirds is mealworms, the larvae of small, black, flightless beetles belonging to the genus *Tenebrio*. They're agricultural pests that infest flour and other grain products. They're available in pet shops, bird feeding stores, and sometimes bait shops but are cheaper to buy in quantity from mail-order companies such as Grubco or Rainbow Mealworms.

It's important to keep in mind that mealworms are part of a food chain. If there are toxins in their tissues, those toxins will be transferred to the birds that eat them. Mealworms ordered through the mail usually arrive packaged in wadded newspaper. Transfer them to new quarters as soon as possible to minimize the amount of toxic newsprint ink they consume. House mealworms in plastic buckets with an inch of oatmeal, cornflakes, cream of wheat, wheat bran, or other dry grain product on the bottom. For moisture and vitamins, occasionally add pieces of raw potato, carrot, or apple. Particularly during spring and summer, boost your mealworms' vitamin content by adding a baby-bird hand-feeding powder (such as Kaytee Exact, available at pet shops) to the mealworm bucket.

If you don't want the mealworms to breed, when they are close to maximum size, refrigerate them with some food to keep them alive but growing very slowly. Don't freeze them—they get mushy when thawed and spoil quickly. During severe cold spells, frozen mealworms stay fresh and are popular with birds, but when the temperature rises to the upper twenties and thirties, they quickly go bad. When the temperature hovers near freezing, you can set mealworms in a heated birdbath filled with sphagnum moss; adding fruit to the mixture makes this irresistible.

Providing enough mealworms to satisfy even a single family of bluebirds can become prohibitively expensive, so most people supplement the mealworm diet with other nutritious items. Bluebird conservation organizations provide recipes for suitable foods such as peanut butter, suet, sunflower hearts, grapes, berries, cherries, raisins, currants, and other fruits. Bluebirds in many areas also appreciate calcium supplements, which are easily provided by setting out crushed eggshells (when not from hard-boiled eggs, bake for twenty minutes at 250 degrees).

Bluebirds are not traditionally feeder birds, so it takes a certain amount of effort to get them to figure out what bird feeders are all about. Simply setting out wiggling mealworms on a low platform in view of a bluebird hunting perch will entice birds right away, but they'll have lots of competition for those expensive delicacies. As soon as your bluebirds learn to associate the feeding tray with food, start using a feeder designed to exclude most other species. As cavity nesters, bluebirds naturally enter holes that other birds simply don't, so most bluebird feeders capitalize on this by offering the food within some sort of small enclosure. Simple plans for bluebird feeders are available in Carrol Henderson's bird feeding book and from bluebird organizations.

Bluebirds aren't the only birds that come to feeders for mealworms. I've had chickadees and Red-breasted Nuthatches that quickly learned to take them from my hands. During the few springs that Scarlet Tanagers have appeared in my yard during migration, they've eagerly come to window feeders for mealworms. I've also enjoyed watching woodpeckers, jays, thrushes, catbirds, Chipping and Lincoln's Sparrows, vireos, and warblers eat mealworms.

Do mealworms entice birds to stay at feeders longer than they normally would? This is highly unlikely. Many species time their migration to coincide with the period of richest food supplies, regardless of whether feeding stations are around. Although I keep mealworms available throughout the spring and fall migration, I've never had migratory species from summer stay longer than they normally would, and I've never observed spring or fall migrants in my yard later than normal. In winter, mealworms may well sustain some out-of-range individuals that would otherwise die, but there is no evidence that this contributes to the passing on of genetic weaknesses. Of course, we should never feed birds that show any signs of sickness (rather than injury) at a feeding station, where illness can quickly spread. Sick birds should be taken to a rehabber.

54 Help out uncommon backyard birds that need it

Several years ago, a man living in the woods of northern Wisconsin, near Lake Superior, was delighted to report that a Bald Eagle came down to his large platform bird feeder every day for breakfast. Each morning, the man put out a peeled hard-boiled egg, and the moment he went back inside, the eagle flew down from its perch in a large pine tree for an easy meal. Perhaps the eagle had been raised near a campground or a lakeshore where fishermen cleaned their catch, and the eagle had learned to associate people with food, or maybe the eagle somehow figured out that this man was a friendly source of food. Birds, especially omnivores and scavengers, are surprisingly adaptable and open to learning, particularly when hungry. Of course, encouraging powerful raptors to spend time near people is generally not a good idea for the birds; eventually, they're going to get too close to someone who isn't so comfortable with their presence.

In northern Minnesota where I live, we periodically experience winter invasions of northern owls. Many of them are emaciated, although their dense feathers make them look perfectly fine until they keel over dead. People want to help these owls, so when they find fresh mice in their garage or basement traps, they set them out on their bird feeders or a deck railing for the visiting backyard owls. A surprising number of birds learn to take the mice and even recognize the people providing them. It's very important to make sure that these mice are fresh, that they were killed in traps rather than by poison, and that they were healthy before they died. Some people even purchase live mice, gerbils, or hamsters from pet shops for hungry owls, but this is not a good idea. Pet shop animals can harbor many diseases that wild birds have no defenses against.

In regions where Sandhill Cranes wander about in residential areas, some people set out buckets of corn just for them. It's important to make sure that any cracked corn you offer is safe from aflatoxins. In hot, muggy areas such as central Florida, where a lot of people feed cranes, it's especially important to take corn and other seeds inside or cover them well when it's raining.

Some people try to entice Great Blue Herons and other wading birds to buckets of minnows or other baitfish. Based on stories I've heard from fishermen, herons are already far too willing to take bait that was not intended to be shared.

Gardeners frequently develop an acquaintance with backyard robins and toss them earthworms. My backyard robins come to a window platform feeder and eat from a plastic bowl filled with mealworms. I'm not sure how they first discovered the mealworms, which I originally set out for chickadees, but they've become regular feeder birds.

The strangest effort I've heard of to attract a particular bird was when a birding columnist for a northern Wisconsin community newsletter tried to lure a Turkey Vulture to his backyard by setting out a road-killed raccoon. I sent his column to humor writer Dave Barry, who sent me back a postcard with the simple words, "Vulture chow."

14

HELPING NESTING BIRDS

ONE OF THE HABITAT CHANGES CAUSED BY PEOPLE DURING THE past two centuries is the reduction of available nest cavities for native American birds. Indiscriminate clear-cutting and managing forests for paper and wood fiber production rather than saw lumber have contributed to this situation, since larger species of woodpeckers require larger, older trees. Older forests with decaying trees are valuable food sources for woodpeckers as well, but nest sites can be the limiting factor for woodpeckers and especially for other cavity nesters that can't excavate their own holes, such as Wood Ducks, goldeneyes, bluebirds, Great Crested Flycatchers, wrens, and Lucy's and Prothonotary Warblers. Flourishing populations of House Sparrows and European Starlings have exacerbated the cavity shortage for native birds. When a local habitat provides adequate food and cover but insufficient nesting sites, artificial nest boxes and platforms can make an enormous difference to local populations. In some cases, nest boxes have helped whole species make a comeback.

55 Provide nest boxes and platforms, and monitor them responsibly

For hundreds, perhaps thousands, of years, Americans have been providing housing for wild birds. The earliest Americans provided hollowed-out gourds for Purple Martins. The Purple Martin Conservation Association notes that "documents from the 18th and 19th centuries suggest that these early Americans attracted martins to their villages because they functioned like scarecrows, chasing crows away from their corn patches, and vultures away from their meats and hides hung out to dry. The mutually-beneficial relationship established then, still exists today."

Unfortunately, improperly designed or situated birdhouses can cause eggs or nestlings to die from excessive heat or cold or to drown. When they are not monitored and maintained properly, debilitating and even lethal parasites can flourish. And birdhouses designed by well-meaning but uninformed people can be open invitations to House Sparrows and European Starlings, both of which are threats to native American birds and do not need housing subsidies. With just a few precautions, however, providing nest boxes or platforms for birds can be a wonderful hobby.

The first step is to decide what species you want to attract and then learn about its nesting requirements. The Cornell Lab's Birdhouse Network can give you a lot of helpful hints. Organizations such as the North American Bluebird Society, Project Loon Watch, or Purple Martin Conservation Society focus on particular species and can provide state-of-the-art information on monitoring techniques and precautions, hole size and shape, house design, and potential predators.

Wood Duck

Keep in mind a few basic precautions:

- Wood provides far more insulation than metal and is preferable in any birdhouse construction.
- Never use wood that was treated with mercury or other toxins or painted with lead-based paint.
- Don't set houses too close together (except when setting out bluebird houses in pairs to reduce competition from Tree Swallows). In particular, don't set two loon nest platforms on the same lake, don't set Wood Duck nest boxes in view of each other, and don't set owl nest boxes anywhere near each other.
- Don't place wren houses near any other birdhouses. Wrens occasionally puncture the eggs of other birds nesting near their territories.
- Purple Martins have better nesting success in gourds than in wooden "apartment" houses. If you use the latter, houses with dividers between apartments are better than those without.
- Perches at a birdhouse entrance hole encourage House Sparrows without helping native birds at all. If you purchase ready-made houses with perches, remove them.
- Wood Duck houses should have little wooden slats, hardware cloth, or some other rough surface between the bottom and the entrance hole to help the ducklings climb out after they've hatched.

56 Make flat roofs nighthawk-friendly

As soon as Americans constructed their first permanent buildings, nighthawks and swifts moved in. On flat rooftops, nighthawks feel safe from most predators, and rock-ballasted flat roofs are quite similar in look and feel to the bare ground on their natural nesting sites. The Common Nighthawk is declining over much of its range, apparently suffering from predation by a burgeoning population of crows and gulls, a reduction in the urban population of mayflies and other fairly large emergent aquatic insects (an important food source during migration and the nesting season), and changes in flat roof construction. I've heard of bird banders handling nighthawks with blistered feet, probably caused by landing on roofs with these newer designs. The solid roof color makes these

Common Nighthawk

normally camouflaged birds more conspicuous, and the smooth surface may permit eggs to roll. Mark Alt, president of the Minnesota Ornithologists' Union, has devoted some time to studying different roof types and their suitability for nighthawks. He describes four basic types of flat roofs:

1. A built-up roof is made by pouring a blend of hot asphalt and rubber over a roof and letting it set. This kind of roof can get extremely hot, so it is unsuitable and even dangerous for wildlife.
2. A rock-ballasted roof consists of tar paper or a rubber membrane held in place by the weight of rocks, usually smaller than baseballs. Alt notes that the surface resembles a dry riverbed or rocky lakeshore. In addition to Common Nighthawks, Killdeer and Forster's Terns can safely nest on this kind of roof.
3. PVC membrane roofs are constructed of plastic sheeting glued into place. This plastic is usually white, and its smooth surface and high reflectivity make it overly warm and subject to wind.
4. Sheet metal reflective roofing, with its mirrorlike finish, produces dangerous glare and heat.

Fortunately, cities are increasingly looking at rooftops as potential green spaces. Vegetation on rooftops can help reduce urban temperatures, produce oxygen, and absorb pollutants. If you live or work in a building with a flat roof, consider getting involved in the process of converting the roof to green space. Also take the needs of nighthawks into account. If making the rooftop a green one isn't possible, advocate for rock-ballasted roofing. On either green roofs or non-rock-ballasted roofs, placing gravel pads in the corners may create suitable nesting areas for nighthawks.

57 Make masonry chimneys swift-friendly

Chimney and Vaux's Swifts nest in hollow trees and masonry chimneys. In many areas, these species are declining due to the loss of natural nesting sites. Maintaining nonmetal chimneys provides critical nesting sites for these birds.

The Driftwood Wildlife Association of Austin, Texas, provides guidelines for making masonry chimneys safe for both home owners and swifts:

> Since Chimney Swifts are in North America only during the warmest part of the year, there is seldom a conflict over time-sharing rights of a chimney.

For a chimney to be suitable for swifts, the inside must be made of stone, firebrick or masonry flue tiles with mortared joints. These materials provide enough texture for the birds to cling to the walls. Metal chimneys are unsuitable and should always be capped. Any animal which enters a metal flue will fall to the bottom and be unable to climb the slippery walls.

Proper maintenance is crucial for any chimney whether it is to be used by Chimney Swifts or for winter fires. Wood fires produce flammable creosote residue which coats the inside of a chimney. If left unattended, this material will build up and the entire layer may ignite. A resulting chimney fire will spew burning cinders onto the roof and surrounding structures. In extreme cases, intense chimney fires can cause an explosion. In most cases, an annual cleaning by a professional will keep the chimney walls clean and safe.

Chimney Swifts build their nests by attaching small twigs to the chimney wall with their glue-like saliva. When completed, the shallow half-cup nest protrudes two to three inches from the wall. By keeping the chimney free of creosote buildup, home owners help assure successful nest building, decreasing the chances of the nest falling before the birds have fledged. The best time to clean a chimney is in mid-March when the wood fire season is over and just before the Chimney Swifts return from their Amazon Basin wintering grounds.

When cleaning the chimney, the damper should be inspected and should remain closed during the nesting season. This will prevent birds from flying into the house and becoming trapped or injured. A closed damper will also prevent a nest which does break loose from falling into the fireplace. It also lessens the transfer of sound and will make the chimney quieter for the birds and home owner. In older homes some fireplaces may not have dampers, or they may be inoperative. In these cases, a large piece of foam rubber (do not use fiberglass insulation) can be wedged up from the fireplace to serve this purpose, while the swifts are in residence.

There may be occasional conflicts between humans and swifts, but these can often be resolved to everyone's satisfaction. Evelyn L. Bull writes in *Birds of Oregon: A General Reference:*

Public support for swifts can be illustrated by the case of the chimney at Chapman School in Portland. For several years, the school's heating plant remained closed until the [Vaux's] swifts left in the fall, forcing the children to dress accordingly. Finally, Dave Eshbaugh, Executive Director of the Audubon Society of Portland, spearheaded a program to raise funds to rebuild the heating system and allow the chimney to remain unused for heating purposes. Funds came from citizens, metro, Portland Public Schools, and several foundations. The University of Oregon decided not to demolish the unused chimney on Agate Hall largely because of public support for the swifts.

58 Provide nesting materials

Setting out good nesting materials in clean suet cages or wedged into bark on trees or shrubs is a great help to backyard birds. It's best not to use white or bright colors (except for white feathers used by Tree Swallows), and natural fibers are better than synthetics.

Never set out dryer lint for nesting birds. Although the soft, fluffy lint feels suitable both to us and to birds, after it gets wet and then dries, it becomes brittle and crumbly and could cause a nest to fall apart. Any type of string or twine should be no longer than about six inches to prevent possible strangling.

Suitable nest materials to offer birds include the following:

- Cotton quilt batting
- Frayed binder twine or yarn, cut into six-inch lengths (choose dull colors)
- Thin strips of rags from natural fiber cloth, about one inch by six inches
- Dog and cat fur (easily available after brushing)
- Horse hair and sheep wool; make sure to cut long hair from manes and tails shorter than six inches
- Milkweed down (planting milkweed is even more helpful to birds)
- Small white feathers retrieved from old pillows or a poultry farm
- Discarded snakeskins, perhaps from someone who raises snakes (Great Crested Flycatchers in particular are drawn to snakeskins)

- Alfalfa stems and other high-quality natural fibers, cut into four-
  to five-inch lengths
- Small twigs, dead leaves, dry grass, bark strips, pine needles

Providing a small muddy puddle away from roads can also be very helpful for birds that use mud in nest construction, especially robins and swallows. Fostering spiders in your yard is useful because many birds utilize
spider silk in their nests. And encouraging lichens on dead wood, moist
rocks, or tree bark can provide important nesting materials for hummingbirds and small songbirds.

PART IV

Helping Birds Away From Home

15

ON THE ROAD

WHENEVER WE START OUR CARS, WE POLLUTE THE AIR AND USE finite natural resources. And once we pull out onto the road, we risk colliding with birds. Automobiles kill as many as 60 million birds a year in the United States alone. Although people are not going to stop driving anytime soon, and birders in particular will continue to travel long distances just to see birds, there are things we can do. Modifying our driving habits, properly maintaining our cars, and choosing cars with high fuel efficiency can save birds, conserve valuable resources, and limit our contribution to the habitat degradation and pollution associated with extracting, transporting, and using oil products.

59 When buying a car, make gas mileage and low emissions important criteria

In the 1970s, when the Organization of Petroleum Exporting Countries (OPEC) raised oil prices to unprecedented levels and the United States was faced with shortages, the country responded with several gas-conserving measures, including requiring auto manufacturers to improve the fuel efficiency of their fleets. At first, this requirement had a dramatic effect on the average gas mileage of passenger vehicles (the average fuel efficiency in 1974 had been only 12.9 miles per gallon), but when minivans and sport-utility vehicles (SUVs) were classified as light trucks rather than passenger vehicles and exempted from the requirement, the average fuel economy of vehicles on the road actually declined. By 1991, it was at the worst level in two decades, according to *Forbes*. With SUVs and minivans so popular, automakers and oil companies continue to profit from Americans' taste for gas-guzzlers.

Black-capped Chickadee

Meanwhile, as our highways become more congested, daily rush hours in metropolitan areas become increasingly worse, causing each commuter's drive time and thus car emissions to increase. In 2004 the Texas Transportation Institute's annual Mobility Report noted that in 2002, snarled traffic cost travelers in the eighty-five largest U.S. cities 3.5 billion hours a year, compared with 700 million hours in 1982. In 1982, 30 percent of urban highways were congested, meaning that traffic wasn't free-flowing, whereas in 2002, 67 percent of urban highways were congested. This is clearly a waste of time, but it's also a waste of precious natural resources. For gasoline-

powered nonhybrid vehicles, idling and moving through congestion produce the worst gas mileage of all. So all the problems associated with poor
fuel efficiency are exacerbated by our increasingly congested highways.

Barring stronger government regulations (which worked in the past),
the only way automakers will get serious about improving fuel efficiency is
if consumers demand it. The statistics for gas mileage and greenhouse gas
emissions, air pollution ratings, and safety information on new and used cars
and trucks are available from the Environmental Protection Agency (EPA).
Interestingly and ironically, the worst gas-guzzlers of all—large vehicles with
a gross vehicle weight over 8,500 pounds, such as larger pickup trucks and
the biggest SUVs—are currently exempt from furnishing such data to the
EPA; fuel-efficiency rules apply only to automobiles and "light trucks." Yet
small businesses qualify for a special tax break when purchasing SUVs,
including the most egregiously polluting and fuel-wasting models; this tax
break is unavailable for vehicles of other classes.

As with so many things, buying a fuel-efficient car helps people as well
as birds. It protects the air we breathe and limits contributions to climate
change. And fuel economy saves money. According to the EPA, the owner
of a vehicle that gets 40 miles per gallon (mpg) will spend $562 less each
year on gasoline than the owner of a 20 mpg vehicle, so if you own your
car for four years, the 40 mpg vehicle will save about $2,250, assuming
15,000 miles of driving and a fuel cost of $1.50 per gallon. As of this writ-
ing, gas in my city cost $2.29 per gallon. You do the math.

When you're in the market for a car, make fuel efficiency and reduced
emissions high priorities in your selection, and any time you fill out a consumer questionnaire about your car, mention how important fuel efficiency
and low emissions are to you.

60 Drive at the slowest speed that is safe, courteous, and convenient

During the winter of 2004–2005, the largest irruption of northern owls ever recorded brought thousands of Great Gray, Northern Hawk,
and Boreal Owls into northern Minnesota, Wisconsin, and North Dakota.
Birds that had spent their entire lives in the northern wilderness suddenly
found themselves on country roads and even major thoroughfares and interstate highways. As many as ten owls could be found on the twenty-mile
drive along the highway between Duluth and Two Harbors, Minnesota,
some sitting right on signs and telephone poles at the edge of the road. And

over the season, many of these inexperienced birds were killed by cars. Virtually every day in December and January I received phone calls—some days as many as five or six—from distraught people who had collided with an owl or come across one dead on the road. These collisions were a topic of conversation throughout the area, in grocery stores and doctors' offices. I asked many people whether they thought it would be better for these owls if we all slowed down a bit. Almost without exception, people said yes. But then they added that it would probably be too dangerous to slow down unless everyone else did. No one wanted to start the trend.

Great Gray Owls are huge and conspicuous and therefore fairly easy to avoid. But just a few months before their winter invasion, there was a fall migration fallout of Yellow-rumped Warblers in Duluth. Cool air and warmer land temperatures grounded the little birds all over the city, especially on sun-warmed areas such as roads. So many were being run over that several crows and jays had actually learned to sit atop traffic lights and wait, swooping down on the dead and dying birds during red lights. There were so many dead warblers that the jays and crows weren't even eating the ones they retrieved; they were stashing them in conifers and under leaves, as they do when caching seeds. I found that driving 25 miles per hour was the fastest I could go and still avoid hitting any of the tiny birds. It's easy to drive that speed when you have the road to yourself, but trickier in traffic. Again, the "I'd drive slower if everyone else did" mind-set was at work. Interestingly, when I did slow down to a bird-safe speed during this time, no other drivers showed impatience. Perhaps during migration phenomena of this magnitude, radio and television news commentators could remind their listeners to slow down a bit. Such events are rare and usually last only a few days. Couldn't we humans accommodate birds during such brief periods?

Of course, birds gather on roadsides throughout the year. The United States is crisscrossed by over 8 million lane miles of roads, and 6.3 million of them—over 75 percent—are in rural areas. Early in the morning, many sparrows and thrushes gather on roadsides to pick up grit or insects and worms illuminated by streetlights. So many are killed by cars that many crows, ravens, and jays have learned to take early-morning excursions above highways to capitalize on the carnage; some even migrate above highways, where they can spot these flattened fast-food opportunities as they go. There is evidence that Red-headed Woodpecker numbers have been adversely affected by highways because of their habit of swooping across clearings at lower heights than other woodpeckers do.

Collisions with automobiles kill 60 million to 80 million birds a year, and thousands to millions more die each year from oil spills and other causes directly related to fueling our cars. According to EPA figures, the optimal highway speed for fuel efficiency in the average car is 55 mph, and fuel efficiency drops dramatically above 60 mph. That's why the Nixon administration lowered the speed limit to 55 on interstate highways in the 1970s during the gas shortages. My hybrid car's optimal speed for the best gas mileage is about 40 mph; I consistently average over 60 mpg at that speed. As a finite natural resource, the gas we burn today simply won't be available for our children and grandchildren, and the more gas we use, the more we contribute to the many problems associated with oil production. When we're in a hurry for a good reason, driving the speed limit is certainly justifiable. But otherwise, driving more slowly—at a speed that's convenient for us and safe and courteous for other drivers—protects the air and water and saves gas, money, lives, and wildlife.

Of course, driving slowly can't prevent all collisions with birds and other wildlife, but speed is definitely a major factor. When we slow down, not only are we better able to detect and react to animals in the road ahead; we can also notice and enjoy wildlife along the way. On a country road, slowing down from 60 to 45 mph makes the drive time 33 percent longer, but it can increase both the enjoyment and the safety of the trip.

Minimizing roadkills helps in other ways as well. Many people who complain about excessive crow populations never even think about how crows and other scavengers profit from road-killed animals. With the extremely tight city, county, and state budgets in many areas, highway crews aren't concentrating on roadkill removal, and even crow populations aren't sufficient to quickly clear away all the decaying animals. Pathogens can build up quickly in carcasses and can be carried to our homes and yards on the feet or bodies of scavengers, including house flies. Preventing roadkills in the first place is in everyone's best interest.

Good driving habits will help avoid collisions with deer, birds, and other wildlife. Any time a car is following closely behind you, allow it to pass as soon as possible. You don't want someone right on your tail if you have to brake for an animal in the road. If a car approaches rapidly from behind, it's safest and most courteous to speed up until you reach a safe place for the car to pass you, or find a place where you can pull over. Always wear your seat belt. According to several insurance Web sites, most people injured in animal-related crashes were not wearing their seat belts.

Be extra vigilant in the early morning and evening—the most active time for wildlife. In low-light conditions and at night when there is no oncoming traffic, use your high-beam headlights to pick up eye shine at a distance. As soon as you detect a deer or other animal, slow down and turn on your low-beams so the animal doesn't "freeze" in the headlights.

If you spot a bird, deer, or other animal in the road ahead of you, what's the best response? First of all, be completely aware of the traffic around you. If you're on a quiet country road with no one behind you, brake and stop as far from the animal as possible and beep your horn. If there is a distant car behind you, pump your brake a few times to alert the driver to slow down. If you see an oncoming vehicle, flash your lights to alert the other driver that the animal is there and might cross into his or her lane. Never swerve—you may confuse the animal or lose control of your vehicle. Look for other animals after one has crossed the road. Deer and many ground-feeding or gallinaceous birds are found in pairs or groups.

61 Remove dead animals from roadways (if it's safe to do so) and help turtles across the road

Road-killed animals attract scavengers, including crows, ravens, vultures, and even Bald Eagles, putting these birds at risk too. Roadkills also attract rats, mice, and flies, and dangerous pathogens can multiply quickly in decomposing road-killed animals which are transported all over via scavengers' feet and droppings. So removing carcasses from roadsides is a public health issue as well as a wildlife issue. The reduction in government services as a result of tax reductions has ended roadkill removal in many jurisdictions.

One summer afternoon when I was driving along Highway 13, a two-lane road in northern Wisconsin, I saw a Turkey Vulture in the road ahead eating from a skunk carcass. I slowed down as the vulture galumphed to the shoulder and awkwardly flapped up into a nearby tree. I could see in my rearview mirror a car about a mile behind me. By the time the vulture got back to its meal, it would need to leave again or be struck. So I did what anyone with an overdeveloped maternal instinct would do under the circumstances: I pulled over, got out of my car, picked the dead skunk up by the tail, and hurled it beyond the roadside ditch. All the while, the vulture kept its eyes fixed on my face. After I tossed the carcass, I'm certain the bird gave me a surprised and grateful "gee thanks, lady!" look. It immediately dropped down to resume its feast as I stood watching less than ten feet away.

Of course, whenever I recount this story to others, the typical response is, "Ewwwwww!"

Picking up dead skunks can be rather distasteful, and germs are an issue. I keep baby wipes in my car for just such an emergency. Many—perhaps most—people simply do not want to deal with roadkill. But dead animals attract scavengers, making roads more dangerous for them and us. I've seen two dead adult Bald Eagles killed at raccoon carcasses, both during nesting season. What a waste!

Roadkill is one thing, but it's a relatively easy matter to help turtles across the road. Your assistance will be worthless, however, if you put the turtle back on the side it was coming from. During egg-laying time, they head for the spot where they hatched, lay their eggs, and then head back to where they now live; they simply will not be deterred. But if you carry the turtle across the road to where it was headed, you improve its chances of surviving the egg-laying ordeal and reduce the chance of yet another road-kill subsidizing crows and luring eagles and other scavengers to their deaths.

62 Know what to do if you encounter an injured bird on the highway

Most birds struck by cars die very quickly, but some survive for a while. Injured, struggling birds along a highway can distract drivers, leading to accidents. In many cases, the bird's injuries are too severe to be repaired by even the finest rehab facility, but other birds, if given prompt treatment, can make a complete recovery. When dead and dying birds are left along roadsides, they attract predators and scavengers, which in turn can be hit by cars.

What is the best thing to do when you see an injured bird on the road? Before you can even consider stopping, you must have the proper equipment to perform a rescue. A paper bag big enough to comfortably hold the bird with little room for maneuvering is the simplest way to transport an injured bird. Lining the bottom of the bag with paper towels gives the bird's feet something to grip; even better is a piece of Astroturf. Keep assorted paper bags, a few paper clips, and a roll of paper towels in your trunk at all times, along with a pair of heavy leather gloves, latex gloves, and both a kitchen towel and a large bath towel. Organize them in a medium-size cardboard box, which can be used if you encounter a bird too large or strong for a paper bag. A roll of 3M Vet Wrap (for humans, the same product is called 3M Coban) can come in handy to hold up a badly injured wing so it doesn't dangle, leading to more damage during transport. Keep the telephone numbers of the nearest wildlife rehabilitation facility, the department of natural resources, and the state highway patrol stored in your cell phone, but also write them conspicuously on the box, just in case. You may never need this rescue kit, but you'll be glad you have it if you do encounter an injured bird. Having a large bath towel in my car was a godsend when I came upon a grounded Peregrine Falcon fledgling in downtown Duluth. She needed just a little assistance to get back to the roof where her nest box was. A week later, she was flying over the city in perfect form.

When you discover a hurt bird along the road, the first thing you must do is to make a virtually instantaneous assessment of the traffic situation. If you're on a quiet country road, there probably won't be a problem pulling over. If you're on a busy interstate highway going through a city during rush hour, you shouldn't even think of pulling over. Most other situations require you to assess the risk and make a decision. When the situation is too dangerous to stop your car, ask one of your passengers to use a cell phone to call a rehabber and get help there as soon as possible. Most rehab facilities have developed protocols for working with the highway patrol to safely remove struggling animals from roadsides. However, many highway patrol officers and police, and even some conservation officers, don't know how to deal with injured animals. In northern Minnesota, some birders noticed a hurt Great Gray Owl along a narrow, winding country road; they drove a quarter mile to a driveway where they could safely turn around to go back and rescue it, but they were just seconds too late; as they approached, a sheriff pulled over and shot the bird. The first priority for law enforcement is to prevent humans from being injured, and that's where their training is focused. So when you find injured wildlife, it's best to notify wildlife rehabbers first. They'll know which authorities to call.

If you can find a safe place to stop, pull over and turn on your emergency flashers. The next issue is getting the bird from the roadside into the bag or box. If possible, it's best to have two people approach the bird from the road from different directions; that way, if the bird tries to flee, it will be running away from traffic rather than toward it. Your goal is to toss a towel over the bird and then, wearing gloves if the bird may have strong claws, talons, or beak, scoop the bird up, place it in the bag, roll it closed, and secure it with paper clips. You do *not* want a bird fluttering around your car while you're driving! With a sparrow or warbler in a paper sandwich bag, just folding the top down may be enough, but a paper clip provides more insurance. If a wing is dangling and the bird isn't struggling too hard, you can try to gently set the wing against the body, as well matched to the other wing as possible, and roll Vet Wrap or a towel around the bird to hold the wing in place. Be careful not to wrap too tightly—birds breathe using air sacs that fill many spaces in their bodies, and wrapping too tightly can cause suffocation. If you're uncertain about doing this, it's better to leave the wing and just get the bird into the bag.

If possible, drive directly to a rehab facility. The people there will need to know your name, the date and place where you found the bird, and what caused the bird's injuries, if you know. Rehab facilities aren't allowed to charge a fee for taking birds, and they get no government funding except, in rare cases, for specific research or conservation projects. They depend on contributions from donors like you.

Northern Cardinal

16

WHILE BIRDING

THOSE OF US WHO ENJOY BIRDING HAVE A VESTED INTEREST IN THE long-term survival of birds, just as hunters do in game animals. Although birding isn't a consumptive sport, we do put stress on birds through the simple act of watching them. By being mindful of the pressures we put on birds and honoring the American Birding Association's code of ethics, birders can enjoy the pastime now and far into the future.

63 Be mindful of automobile use when birding

Birding is an automobile-intensive hobby. One of the greatest joys in birding is adding a new species to one's life list. When a rare bird is found, birders share the word on Internet listserves, telephone hotlines, and cell phone text messages, and within minutes or hours of a discovery, other birders descend on the site. When a rare hummingbird turned up in my own backyard in November 2004, dozens of birders arrived within a few days to add it to their city, county, state, and even life lists. Many of them came from the Twin Cities, over 150 miles away, and some came from even farther. And during the owl invasion of 2004–2005, well over a thousand birders from all over the continent and many from abroad descended on northern Minnesota.

Chasing these rarities uses valuable natural resources and contributes to declining air and water quality, increased traffic, and highway deaths of birds, but chasing is part of the essence of birding for many of us. Rather than casting blame on those who jump in their cars at the first news of a rarity or feeling guilty about our own chasing, it's more productive to be mindful of the resources we use and the associated harms and to thoughtfully reduce our negative impacts whenever possible.

Because some of the best birding locations in the country happen to be along rutted, rocky dirt roads, some birders prefer to drive heavy-duty SUVs rather than smaller vehicles that get better gas mileage. My car's hybrid engine not only saves a lot of gas but also shuts off the gas engine when I stop, making it wonderfully quiet when listening for birds. The car's low clearance does make it a poor choice in a few circumstances, but considering how much money I save on fuel and how much I saved on car costs in the first place, I don't mind renting when I need something bigger. In most cases, it's more economical to buy a small car for day-to-day use and rent an SUV for those occasions when its size and ruggedness are genuinely useful.

For day-to-day birding, choosing a nearby place and exploring its nooks and crannies on foot can be even more satisfying than combing country roads and birding from the car. I "adopted" a park within walking distance of our apartment when we lived in Madison, Wisconsin, and went birding there every morning before work during spring migration and at least weekly throughout the rest of the year. By exploring just this one place, I discovered a few rarities to share with my fellow birders, learned many subtle things about the behavior and habitat needs of various birds, and could even recognize individual birds by song and appearance. When we moved from Madison, my "Picnic Point" list included 200 species.

While we lived in Madison, I rode the bus to work in winter and during bad weather. One bus stop was near a part of Lake Monona where the local power company's warm water discharge kept the lake open all winter. I liked to catch an early bus, get a transfer, and hop off at that spot to check out the ducks (and sometimes a Snowy Owl) in the area, then take the next bus the rest of the way to work. Of course, many of the best birding areas aren't serviced by public transportation, but when one is, why not take advantage of it?

On fine days in the warmer seasons, I rode my bicycle to work. Madison has a wonderful bike path system, and by giving myself enough time, I could enjoy lots of birds on the way to and from work.

On weekends, I loved going birding farther afield. Some birders treasure being alone to enjoy their field time. But if you don't mind birding with others, you improve your birding miles-per-gallon factor by carpooling. And having at least one extra set of eyes significantly raises the number of species you see, especially on the road between stops. When a rare bird is found some distance from where you live, carpooling will both save gas and make the excursion more enjoyable.

Here are some other tips for reducing your fuel consumption while birding:

- Keep your car in tune, the oil and air filters clean, and the tires properly inflated. If your car has a faulty oxygen sensor, your gas mileage may improve as much as 40 percent when you get it repaired, according to EPA figures. Using oil other than the auto manufacturer's recommended grade can lower fuel efficiency.
- Never carry unneeded items, especially heavy ones, in the trunk or backseat. According to EPA figures, an extra 100 pounds of cargo in the trunk reduces a typical car's fuel economy by 1 to 2 percent.
- Use cruise control and overdrive when appropriate.
- Aggressive driving (speeding, rapid acceleration and braking) can lower your gas mileage by 33 percent at highway speeds and 5 percent around town, according to EPA figures. After stopping for a good bird on the roadside, take off gently unless you need to merge into traffic.
- According to the EPA, a roof rack or carrier provides additional cargo space and may allow you to meet your needs with a smaller car. However, a loaded roof rack can decrease fuel economy by 5 percent or more. Reduce aerodynamic drag and improve fuel economy by placing items inside the trunk whenever possible.

By conscientiously doing what you can to minimize your driving and maximize your fuel economy, you can enjoy chasing rarities without squandering more natural resources than necessary.

64 Honor the American Birding Association's ethical code for birders

We birders have an obligation to protect the birds we enjoy even while we're looking at them. Birders who disturb vegetation to get better views of nests risk flushing an incubating parent; when birds fly off their nests in a panic, they occasionally dislodge or hurt eggs or babies. Disturbances at nest sites can also attract snakes, crows, raccoons, eagles, gulls, and other nest predators. Those who walk off trails to chase a rarity risk step-

ping on nests. Observers stomping through a Long-eared Owl roost can easily disturb and flush these shy birds, which must then search in daytime for alternative roost sites, often while being harassed by crows. Birders descending on a marsh at night may play recordings or clunk two stones together to entice a Yellow Rail to call back, and then surround the bird until it flushes for everyone to have a view. This technique can damage habitat, destroy nests and eggs, or even injure an adult by causing it to collide with a tree or a birder in the dark. At an American Birding Association convention in Duluth in 1988, birders descended on a nearby marsh and flushed a Yellow Rail, which was caught in midair by one birder. An article published in the June 1988 issue of *Birding* described the sound of the rail hitting the birder's hand as a loud "thwack." The writer added, "Ooh, I'll bet that one stung his hand," without even speculating about how that impact would have felt to a two-ounce bird.

Birding activities can also become a nuisance for other people, both birders and nonbirders. When huge numbers of Great Gray Owls descended on northern Minnesota during the winter of 2004–2005, over a thousand birders from all over flocked to see them. One morning while driving down a county highway, I came upon a birder cussing angrily. He had just seen his first Great Gray Owls—two sitting right next to each other. After allowing several people to view them through his spotting scope, he had set up his camera to digiscope them. Suddenly, another car pulled up and two people jumped out. They slammed the car doors and ran right between the camera and the owls, causing the birds to flush before the birder got his picture. He was understandably furious.

These same throngs of birders upset many local people in the area. The closest town, Meadowlands, has a population of only 766, and people living out in the woods don't expect to have to deal with so many strangers driving the back roads, often training their long lenses directly toward window feeders. The problems were exacerbated because the owl invasion came during a time when the government was issuing terrorist alerts. In one instance, someone spiked the roadside to flatten the tires of unwelcome cars, and someone else painted threats on his garage against any birders found in the vicinity. When a community is angry about birders, that antipathy may extend to the birds themselves, which can harm conservation efforts and put the birds in danger. Although spiking roadsides and issuing threats are extreme, not to mention illegal, it's also unacceptable for birders to disrupt the lives of others.

The American Birding Association has developed an ethical code for birding. It reads as follows:

1. Promote the welfare of birds and their environment.

    1(a) Support the protection of important bird habitat.

    1(b) To avoid stressing birds or exposing them to danger, exercise restraint and caution during observation, photography, sound recording, or filming.

Limit the use of recordings and other methods of attracting birds, and never use such methods in heavily birded areas, or for attracting any species that is Threatened, Endangered, or of Special Concern, or is rare in your local area;

Keep well back from nests and nesting colonies, roosts, display areas, and important feeding sites. In such sensitive areas, if there is a need for extended observation, photography, filming, or recording, try to use a blind or hide, and take advantage of natural cover;

Use artificial light sparingly for filming or photography, especially for close-ups.

1(c) Before advertising the presence of a rare bird, evaluate the potential for disturbance to the bird, its surroundings, and other people in the area, and proceed only if access can be controlled, disturbance minimized, and permission has been obtained from private land-owners. The sites of rare nesting birds should be divulged only to the proper conservation authorities.

1(d) Stay on roads, trails, and paths where they exist; otherwise keep habitat disturbance to a minimum.

2. Respect the law, and the rights of others.

2(a) Do not enter private property without the owner's explicit permission.

2(b) Follow all laws, rules, and regulations governing use of roads and public areas, both at home and abroad.

2(c) Practise common courtesy in contacts with other people. Your exemplary behavior will generate goodwill with birders and non-birders alike.

3. Ensure that feeders, nest structures, and other artificial bird environments are safe.

3(a) Keep dispensers, water, and food clean, and free of decay or disease. It is important to feed birds continually during harsh weather.

3(b) Maintain and clean nest structures regularly.

3(c) If you are attracting birds to an area, ensure the birds are not exposed to predation from cats and other domestic animals, or dangers posed by artificial hazards.

4. Group birding, whether organized or impromptu, requires special care. Each individual in the group, in addition to the obligations spelled out in Items #1 and #2, has responsibilities as a Group Member.

4(a) Respect the interests, rights, and skills of fellow birders, as well as people participating in other legitimate outdoor activities. Freely share your knowledge and experience, except where code 1(c) applies. Be especially helpful to beginning birders.

4(b) If you witness unethical birding behavior, assess the situation, and intervene if you think it prudent. When interceding, inform the person(s) of the inappropriate action, and attempt, within reason, to have it stopped. If the behavior continues, document it, and notify appropriate individuals or organizations. Group Leader Responsibilities [amateur and professional trips and tours].

4(c) Be an exemplary ethical role model for the group. Teach through word and example.

4(d) Keep groups to a size that limits impact on the environment, and does not interfere with others using the same area.

4(e) Ensure everyone in the group knows of and practises this code.

4(f) Learn and inform the group of any special circumstances applicable to the areas being visited (e.g. no tape recorders allowed).

4(g) Acknowledge that professional tour companies bear a special responsibility to place the welfare of birds and the benefits of public knowledge ahead of the company's commercial interests. Ideally, leaders should keep track of tour sightings, document unusual occurrences, and submit records to appropriate organizations.

Please follow this code and distribute and teach it to others. The American Birding Association's code of birding ethics can be freely reproduced for distribution or dissemination.

65 Report bird sightings to the local birder hotline, state ornithological society, and eBird

Much of what is known about American bird distribution and population levels has been contributed by people who enjoy birds as an avocation rather than a job. Many of the bird specimens that led to the original scientific descriptions of North American birds were collected by army officers and surgeons in the 1700s and 1800s. Abert's Towhee, Bendire's Thrasher, Clark's Nutcracker, Coues' Flycatcher, Hammond's Flycatcher, McCown's Longspur, McKay's Bunting, Scott's Oriole, and Williamson's Sapsucker were all named for American military officers who contributed to ornithology out of a deep personal interest. Arthur Cleveland Bent, who spent many decades compiling the most comprehensive life history accounts of North American birds available until the 1990s, was a businessman. Most of what we know about population increases and decreases in North American songbirds since 1966 comes from volunteer birders through the Breeding Bird Survey, and volunteer birders have provided most of the information available in state bird atlas programs. Only through solid information can any conservation efforts be effective at helping birds.

Some birders are "listers," diligently keeping a life list or separate lists of birds seen in various locations or during specific periods. Other people keep no lists at all. But maintaining field notebooks in which we record the birds seen, the dates and places they were seen, the numbers of individuals seen, and the weather and other conditions provides extremely valuable information for our personal use and for ornithologists and conservationists.

These records can be kept by hand or on computer. Some software allows you to check off species and record the number of birds seen, along with the date and place, in a PDA, which then synchronizes with your computer. The best software programs allow you to generate reports for specific places or time periods, allowing you to easily report seasonal sightings to state ornithological records committees and to quickly pull up notes about any species.

Keeping records digitally makes them easy to access. I have over a dozen field notebooks from my first years of birding, but it's very hard to find the specific day in the late 1970s when I found a Bell's Vireo at my favorite park in Madison or the date that one of my students found a Prothonotary Warbler there. Since the early 1990s I've been keeping most of my records on a software program called AviSys. I can now easily look up all the times I've seen a Golden-winged Warbler anywhere (as long as I've entered the data in AviSys). It takes time to transfer all my old sightings from my field notebooks into this software program, but it allows me to reminisce as I work. The payoff comes when someone needs information about the presence or absence of a particular species at a particular place during a particular time.

In the event that you spot a rare or hard-to-identify species, recording a careful description in your field notes can be valuable; it can help you decide what you've seen and convince an ornithological records committee that you really did see it. Practice drawing birds of various shapes, and pay attention to the various body parts as shown in the front of most field guides. Drawing birds is helpful not only in documenting various species but also in helping you become more observant about shape, color patterns, and other features. Perfecting field skills is something that all good birders, from beginners to advanced, should strive for.

It's important to share your records. Many localities and most states and provinces have birder hotlines to let interested birders know about rare birds via telephone, e-mail, or cell phone text messages. So when you spot a rarity, share it with others. Sometimes, beginners or even experienced birders make errors. Make sure that you've seen all the salient field marks of a rare bird before reporting it. In general, though, it's better to report a possible rarity, giving others the chance to see it and verify your identification, than to stay quiet for fear of being ridiculed.

Most states and provinces have ornithological societies that welcome documented sightings of birds. Find out what organization collects these records in your area. Some take reports over the Internet, and some use written report forms. Unlike local and state birding hotlines, these organizations must verify all unusual sightings to maintain an accurate official checklist of a state's avifauna, so they have much higher standards of documentation. Don't be offended if a particular sighting isn't accepted. It doesn't affect your own personal lists, unless you're in a competition. The sport of birding sometimes collides with the science of ornithology, but overall, both benefit from honoring the aims and contributions of the other.

One of the best ways to keep track of your sightings and to benefit other birders, ornithologists, and conservationists in your area and around the world is to report them to eBird. According to its Web site:

eBird, a project developed by the Cornell Lab of Ornithology and the National Audubon Society, provides a simple way for you to keep track of the birds you see anywhere in North America. You can retrieve information on your bird observations, from your backyard to your neighborhood to your favorite bird-watching locations, at any time for your personal use. You can also access the entire historical database to find out what other eBirders are reporting from across North America. In addition, the cumulative eBird database is used by birdwatchers, scientists, and conservationists who want to know more about the distributions and movement patterns of birds across the continent.

The eBird database that you are helping to create can be used by

- *you,* to track your personal observations and maintain lists of all of the birds you've ever seen, those recorded at specific locations, or recorded over specific periods of time; or to create lists of birds recorded from various locations and dates based on the records of other eBirders.

- *other birders and amateur naturalists,* allowing them to learn about the birds in your region.

- *scientists,* to uncover patterns in bird movements and ranges across North America, including migratory pathways, wintering and breeding ranges, arrival and departure dates, range expansions and contractions, and a host of other important environmental relationships.

- *conservationists,* to identify important areas for birds based on current range distributions, and to track population trends that can be used to create management plans for endangered, threatened, and at-risk species.

- *educators,* who may use the cumulative database to teach students about birds and the scientific process, including collecting, analyzing, and interpreting results.

- *anyone,* to discover where species can be found throughout the year; which birds are regularly found at specific locations across North America; when certain species arrive or depart from their breeding and wintering grounds; and many other possibilities.

66 Donate your old binoculars and field guides to a local school, nature center, or organization such as Birders' Exchange

When I started birding in 1975, there weren't many kinds of binoculars to choose from. Now there are hundreds of models of standard binoculars, as well as some with image stabilizing, built-in digital cameras, and night vision. There are also many more spotting scope models. Birders now push their optics to the limits, even taking photographs through a technique called digiscoping. More space in birding magazines is devoted to comparisons of sophisticated optical equipment. Many birders still use the same pair of binoculars they've had for twenty years or more, but a growing number buy new optics every few years, allowing their old binoculars to languish on a shelf. Meanwhile, birding and conservation organizations in Old World and New World tropical countries are in desperate need of optical equipment. That's why the American Birding Association started its Birders' Exchange program. According to the American Birding Association:

> Birders' Exchange takes new and used birding equipment and educational materials and matches it with local scientists, conservationists, and educators working to conserve Neotropical migratory birds and their habitats in Latin America and the Caribbean. Such items are also critical for community outreach and education.
>
> Equipment donated through Birders' Exchange is necessary to support a range of conservation activities to protect Neotropical migrant birds—from educating school children to conducting scientific research. The combination of these and other activities is promoting long-term results toward the conservation of birds and their habitats.
>
> Please consider donating some of the following items:
> - Binoculars—we especially are in need of rubber armored and/or waterproof binoculars
> - Digital cameras
> - GPS units
> - Spotting scopes
> - Tripods
> - Field guides to Neotropical birds
> - Field guides to North American birds

- Ornithology texts
- Laptop computers
- Backpacks

The equipment must be in good working order. For example, the binoculars must be in proper alignment, the focus wheel in operation, and the glass without flaws.

Occasionally we ask for other materials as the special requirements of projects demand. Contact us ahead of time if you have other gear to contribute to see if we have a proper match. Birders' Exchange also needs contributions to continue its work. All contributions are tax-deductible to the extent permissible by law. Birders' Exchange will acknowledge all contributions by letter.

Your old optics can also help birds and people closer to home when you donate them to a local school or nature center. Before donating, make sure that the equipment is wanted and will actually be used. Another option is to "adopt" a budding birder and pass on your old optics to him or her.

67 Be careful when using recordings and laser pointers in the field

One of the simplest ways to lure songbirds in for a close look is to play recordings of their songs. As equipment becomes smaller, it becomes easier to use this playback technique when birding. The problem is that birds respond to recordings because they're stressed. When a male bird hears the song of another bird of his species (and sometimes other species), his heart rate rises and he gets agitated. He often stops what he's doing and starts singing himself or even approaches the source of the sound to chase away what he perceives to be an intruder on his territory. Since it is natural for birds to check out one another's territory and respond in exactly this way, this is usually not a major issue. However, playback is best used to lure an already singing bird closer rather than to grab the attention of a bird going about some other business. Sometimes a birder or a guide will play a song of a nonsinging bird to lure it out for a quick look. This isn't harmful in isolated incidents, but it shouldn't happen more than a handful of times to any single bird.

In some situations, however, playback can be genuinely harmful. In the case of very rare species, especially "hotline birds" that attract a lot of birders, or in very popular birding destinations, birds can spend too much of their time responding to recordings rather than doing the things they need to be doing. While a bird is responding to a recording, and usually for many minutes after, it's focused on finding the intruder rather than checking out other possible dangers on its territory, feeding or caring for its young, or finding food for itself. There are some popular birding destinations where playing recordings is prohibited because the birds are already under intense birding pressure. Violating these prohibitions is highly unethical.

Birding guides are now using more high-tech methods to point out birds. For a while, people were using small hand mirrors to shine the reflected light around the bird they wanted people to see. But mirrors are unreliable when it isn't sunny and are hard to control precisely. When I saw a Red-faced Warbler in Arizona and pointed it out to one of the other people on the tour, he tried to show it to the rest of our group with a mirror but flashed the light directly on the bird, scaring it away. Some guides are now using laser pointers, but I don't think that this is a good idea. For one thing, there is always the risk of accidentally shining the light into the bird's eyes or the bird flitting into the light beam. My son has a blind area on one retina caused by a child playing with a laser pointer when they were in fifth grade; the beam only shone in my son's eye for a second or two. Some people are steady-handed and can do an excellent job of keeping the pointer away from the bird, but when we're focused on a bird, we're not noticing what's beyond it, especially through branches and foliage. We don't know what insects, amphibians, or other animals, including birds, the beam might be reaching. If you must use a laser pointer, keep it on for the shortest time possible, and take great pains to keep the beam away from every person and animal.

17

DURING
OUTDOOR RECREATION

MANY OF THE ACTIVITIES THAT HUMANS ENJOY OUTDOORS HAVE an impact on birds. When we are mindful of this fact, we can make more conscientious choices about what we do and how we have fun.

68 Be responsible when visiting public parks and gardens

Many people visit urban and suburban parks to enjoy the outdoors, including birds. Feeding ducks, geese, gulls, or pigeons in parks can be pleasurable for people and birds alike; it often sparks a lifelong interest in wildlife and conservation and seldom causes problems. In some areas, however, some of these species have dangerously high population densities, leading to water contamination, competition with other birds, and a greater likelihood of disease outbreaks. Be mindful of local issues regarding bird feeding.

Many people toss pennies into pools and fountains. Unfortunately, American pennies minted after 1982 contain 96 percent zinc and are toxic when ingested by children, birds, dogs, and other living things. Save your pennies or donate them to a wildlife rehabber.

Balloon releases can be dangerous for birds. The worst offenders are Mylar balloons. Extreme caution should be taken to prevent these balloons from escaping into the atmosphere, where they can float for miles before dropping down. If a balloon ends up in an ocean, lake, or stream, it can be swallowed by a bird or aquatic animal, killing it. Latex balloons pose the same dangers, although they degrade more quickly than Mylar. Also, if a balloon catches on a tree, the string or ribbon can strangle birds. Many people like to mark special occasions with balloon releases, but it can be equally satisfying and symbolic to send up soap bubbles, which are harmless. If you buy a balloon for a child, tie the string around the child's wrist or through a buttonhole to minimize the possibility of it floating away.

69 Fish responsibly

My father-in-law was an avid trout fisherman, and I liked to tag along when he went fishing in Port Wing, Wisconsin. I could see and hear myriad songbirds, ducks, shorebirds, hummingbirds, hawks, and other wonderful birds while he focused on fishing, often just downstream of a Great Blue Heron who shared his piscivorous passion. Many of my birding friends are also anglers. It's easy to observe birds while enjoying this quiet, low-impact sport that is best pursued in exactly the kinds of habitat where birds abound.

There are two ways that fishing can harm birds. The first involves tackle. Lead tackle, much of which is designed to look like aquatic bugs or small fish, may lure birds. Hooks can kill birds outright, whether they are swallowed or catch on eyes or mouth parts; lures can slice into the throat or esophagus or poison even the largest herons once they reach the stomach and release lead into the bloodstream; lead sinkers can poison bottom-feeding birds that are dabbling for food and grit. Many state departments of natural resources will trade toxic lead sinkers for nontoxic ones. This will avoid many problems, but even nontoxic hooks and lures can pierce birds internally or externally. Remember that when you release a fish by cutting the line, the hook or lure left in the fish is like a time bomb. If an eagle or heron catches the fish, it may be injured by the hook, and no matter how the fish eventually dies, the hook or lure will be out there for some unsuspecting bird or other creature to ingest. Be mindful of how dangerous tackle can be, and always do your best to bring home exactly what you brought out.

The second danger that fishing poses for birds involves monofilament line. When I was rehabbing birds, I treated several birds that were barely clinging to life after becoming entangled in fishing lines. In the case of one loon with line wrapped around its head, neck, and beak, by the time it could be captured, its mouth was a mass of necrotic tissue. The poor bird had suffered for weeks and ended up dying horribly. I've also seen swallows and other songbirds hanging dead from monofilament line caught on utility lines and tree branches near popular fishing spots.

The Florida Fish and Wildlife Conservation Commission writes:

Most monofilament is non-biodegradable—it lasts about 600 years. Because it is thin and often clear, it is very difficult for birds and animals to see and they can easily brush up against it and become entangled in it. Once entangled, they may become injured, may drown, may become strangled, or may starve to death. Many animals also ingest fishing line. One recovered sea turtle was found to have consumed 590 feet of heavy-duty fishing line.

Monofilament is considered the primary cause of all bird entanglements. Florida Fish and Wildlife Conservation Commission biologists have identified monofilament fishing line as the number-one killer of adult Brown Pelicans. The Tampa Bay Watch estimates that hundreds, perhaps thousands, of birds die in Florida every year as a result of monofilament.

To prevent your fishing line from hurting birds, make sure that you're aware of branches and wires when casting and take precautions to avoid getting your line caught. If it does get tangled, do your level best to remove it rather than just cutting it off. When disposing of old monofilament line, bring it to a monofilament recycling center. Some states provide recycling boxes near fishing spots; building these makes a good Eagle Scout project. If you can't recycle it (monofilament can't be recycled with normal plastics), cut it into very short lengths (less than six inches) before throwing it out.

As more lakes, rivers, and streams become degraded from development, acid rain, mercury, nutrient runoff, pesticide contamination, invasive exotic species, and other problems, fish populations are becoming depleted. This is distressing to commercial and sports fishermen, but by working with conservationists to improve the health of fresh- and saltwater resources, anglers can help ensure the future of their sport and benefit the water systems that we all depend on for recreation, a healthy environment, and our very survival.

70 Encourage bird-friendly golf course maintenance

In 1998 some of my birding acquaintances noticed that television coverage of golf tournaments included, in the background soundtrack, songs of birds that didn't live anywhere near the places those golf courses were located. Apparently, someone at CBS wanted to make the ambience more "natural," without even understanding what constitutes nat-

Canada Geese

ural. I don't know if this was an intentional effort to mislead viewers into thinking that golf courses are more hospitable to birds than they are, but to many birders, it smacked of subtle propaganda.

Lots of birds can and do live on golf courses. According to Ohio State University Extension:

> In the United States, there are approximately 15,000 golf courses, accounting for an estimated 4 million acres. Seventy percent of that area is considered *rough* or *out-of-play*, and has the potential for creating significant wildlife benefits. . . . More golf courses are created each year, with a typical golf course comprising 54 hectares of land. . . . Recently, golf courses have played an important role in the conservation efforts for the Eastern bluebird, tree swallow, purple martin, red-cockaded woodpecker, and even osprey. . . . Golf courses may also provide suitable nesting sites for the declining red-headed woodpecker.

Unfortunately, golf courses have a dark side. The large areas of turf on the burgeoning number of golf courses contribute to the population explosion of Canada Geese and Ring-billed Gulls. Turf also exacerbates runoff problems and requires a great deal of water to be maintained. As water shortages become critical throughout the nation and the world, watering golf courses from increasingly limited groundwater and surface supplies really can't be justified. The vast majority of golf courses also apply fairly large amounts of fertilizers and pesticides to the turf, which can seep into groundwater or run off into open water, sometimes after harming birds or even golfers.

Golfers who want to remain healthy and enjoy their sport should demand that the golf courses they visit follow the best possible practices to minimize environmental harm. It was public pressure after large bird die-offs on golf courses and sod farms that led the Environmental Protection Agency to ban the use of the deadly pesticide diazinon in these areas in 1988. Continued careful study of environmental dangers and pressure to make golf courses as "green" as they look will benefit birds, golfers, and everyone else.

71 Be a responsible boater

I've never met a boater who didn't like seeing Bald Eagles and other cool birds—that's part of what draws people to the water in the first place. But boating can take a heavy toll on birds, especially in terms of air and water pollution, noise, and disturbance at nesting areas. Motorboats should go slowly anywhere near shorelines where birds nest. Waves from the wake can douse nests, especially those of Common Loons, which are normally constructed right at the water's edge.

Most motorboaters are reasonably careful, but many of their boats are polluters, as even the owners can attest after breathing the fumes. The National Wildlife Federation notes:

> The U.S. government allows motorboat engines to be made with no pollution controls. Smog is formed when exhaust gases rise into the air and are "cooked" in the sunlight. The chemicals in smog can kill plants and burn people's and animals' eyes, noses, and throats. Motorboat engines also pollute the water with their exhaust and by spilling oil and gasoline. Every year in the U.S., the total amount of water pollution from motorboats may equal 10 to 15 *Exxon Valdez* oil spill disasters! The chemicals in this pollution can kill fish eggs and other forms of water life. The U.S. Environmental Protection Agency is looking for the best ways to cut down on air and water pollution from boats.

Although government mandates have been extremely successful in lowering automobile emissions and would certainly work just as well with motorboats, consumers can play an important role too. When buying a motorboat, let dealers know how important this issue is to you, and make air and water emissions an important criterion for selecting a boat.

If standard motorboats are polluting, far worse are personal watercrafts (PWCs). The National Parks Conservation Association writes:

> PWCs differ greatly from conventional boats in design, use and effects on the water resource and surrounding areas. As thrill craft, PWCs have disproportionate horsepower to length and weight ratios. While a traditional boat may have a horsepower to length

ratio of 4:1 (a 16-foot craft with a 65-horsepower engine), it is not uncommon for PWCs to have a ratio of 12:1. . . .

PWCs are particularly disruptive to wildlife because of their high speeds, unpredictable movements and excessive noise. Because of their size and maneuverability, PWCs are able to enter remote regions and areas of shallow water, which are often used by fish and wildlife as nesting and reproduction habitat. One study of disturbance flights of common terns in New Jersey found that even at slower speeds, PWCs were a significantly stronger source of disturbance than were motor boats. And data from the Florida Game and Freshwater Fish Commission show clearly that PWCs cause wildlife to flush at greater distances, with more complex behavioral responses than observed in disturbances caused by automobiles, all-terrain vehicles, pedestrians, or motorboats.

Pollution is another major concern associated with PWCs. The overwhelming majority of PWCs are powered by two-stroke engines that are infamous for their propensity to pollute both air and water. A study by the Environmental Protection Agency (EPA) concluded that for most personal watercraft up to 30 percent of their fuel and oil can be emitted directly into the water and air. The polycyclic aromatic hydrocarbons that result from the discharged fuel are toxic to various forms of zooplankton, an important link in the aquatic food chain.

Three times, I've witnessed PWC drivers steer straight into collections of ducks or shorebirds at high speeds. In two cases, all the birds managed to take off in time. In the third, the boater intentionally drove headlong into a family of Wood Ducks. At least two ducklings were killed outright, and the mother's wing was mangled; I couldn't tell how serious her injuries were, but the water was red with her blood. In all three cases, the craft sped away too fast for me to take their numbers to report them. In my opinion, PWC should, as their name implies, be limited to personal waterways—preferably the owners' swimming pools and bathtubs. They have no place in natural waters. As long as they are allowed there, they should be required to have conspicuous numbers that can be easily read from shore.

72 Hunt and shoot responsibly, and support bird-friendly game management policies

Although it's counterintuitive for many people, hunting and bird protection go hand in hand. Much of the natural habitat in North America, and particularly that in the national wildlife refuge system, has been bought, protected, and enhanced thanks to support by hunters through the Pittman-Robertson Act, hunting licenses, and other fees. Throughout most of U.S. history, hunters such as John James Audubon, Theodore Roosevelt, and Aldo Leopold have taken the lead in major conservation movements, and they should take pride in their contributions to preserving the natural environment. I hear from many deer hunters who sit in their stands for hours and have charming encounters with birds, from chickadees to owls. And kindhearted hunters often set out venison ribs or antlers for their backyard birds.

But hunters sometimes give themselves too much credit for bird conservation. Even today, they continue to shoot Greater Prairie Chickens, Sharp-tailed Grouse, Sage Grouse, Northern Bobwhites, and American Woodcocks, yet these species are at historic lows in many parts of their ranges and are abundant nowhere. In Michigan, hunters started demanding the opening of a Mourning Dove season less than two decades after the state's Greater Prairie Chicken population had completely died out. That tragedy was largely due to habitat loss, but hunting certainly contributed to the decline, and as the population dwindled, Michigan hunters could have focused more attention on managing habitat for native prairie chickens rather than for white-tailed deer and exotic pheasants.

After resisting for many decades, hunters finally gave in to demands that they stop shooting waterfowl with toxic lead shot in 1991. In many places, however, they continue to use lead when hunting upland birds, even though there are plenty of studies establishing that doves, gallinaceous birds, and other ground feeders ingest and are harmed by lead shot. In Ohio, Michigan, Wisconsin, and Minnesota—states where Mourning Dove seasons had been prohibited for many decades, until recently—there was no consideration of limiting the new hunt to nontoxic shot. And just about every year, I read of at least one case of a hunter mistaking a Whooping Crane for a Snow Goose. To maintain their credibility as a true force for conservation, hunters need to take their responsibilities toward the birds they harvest more seriously. Currently, major hunting spokespersons seem focused entirely on gun rights rather than conservation, although the two issues are hardly mutually exclusive. There's also a dangerous resurge of interest in shooting large numbers of birds in "canned shoots" on private property, reminiscent of the late 1800s, when the Passenger Pigeon was shot to extinction. This culture of overkill is exacerbated when the vice president of the United States shoots seventy pheasants and a large but undisclosed number of Mallards in a single day.

Nevertheless, virtually all hunters do want what's best for gamebirds and other wildlife. There are a few steps that they can take to protect birds and their habitat. First, waterfowl and upland bird hunters should always hunt with dogs, which significantly increases their chance of retrieving shot birds. Second, hunters who truly care about gamebirds and other wildlife should use only nontoxic shot and bullets outdoors, whether they're shooting birds, deer, or targets; the primary cause of mortality in reintroduced California Condors in Arizona and California is lead poisoning from bullets and shot in the carcasses they eat. Third, it's a no-brainer that hunters should be able to positively identify their quarry before shooting it, but in the excitement of the moment, mistakes can be made. The more time hunters spend looking at birds outside of hunting season, the more quickly and easily they'll be able to recognize both appropriate and inappropriate targets while hunting.

In the case of badly declining species, hunters should voluntarily reduce or even eliminate their take in areas where a species is disappearing. And they should use their political clout to demand that more attention be given to these species. Hunters should also recognize that the population of deer is too high virtually everywhere and work to improve habitat for species other than deer. Even though they should be taken to task for problems associated with hunting, hunters should not be criticized for taking part in their sport, any more than Bald Eagles and Peregrine Falcons should be.

73 Photograph birds responsibly

Wildlife photographers shoot birds without hurting them—usually, at least. The relatively new technique of digiscoping—photographing birds though a spotting scope—allows photographers to get great photos of natural behaviors at much longer distances than they could with most affordable lenses. But no matter what technique is used for photographing birds, care should be taken so that the birds aren't harmed.

Disturbing vegetation around a nest is not only unethical but usually illegal. Searching out nests can sometimes attract opportunistic nest predators, especially crows and Blue Jays. And luring birds of prey with pet-shop rodents can be extremely dangerous near roadsides; it also risks spreading diseases from captive animals to wild populations.

Nowadays, far more people are exposed to wild birds via photographs and video than by spending time in the natural world. When wildlife photographers conscientiously follow safe practices, they provide educational opportunities of inestimable value for conservation.

74 Demand more public land so that snowmobile and all-terrain-vehicle riders can coexist peaceably with birders

Snowmobiles and all-terrain vehicles (ATVs) cause three main problems: excessive noise, air pollution, and erosion. If their operators were mindful of these problems and worked as a force to get manufacturers to reduce both noise and emissions, and if they would police their own numbers to keep everyone on prescribed trails and in legal off-trail areas, they would have fewer clashes with conservationists and environmentalists.

The pollution from two-stroke engines is simply unacceptable in this day and age; the technology is certainly available to devise something that produces fewer emissions. The noise may contribute to the thrill for some operators, but I've seen many snowmobilers wearing high-tech noise-reducing ear protectors, so I suspect that the noise isn't appealing to most of them either.

As more land is taken up for private development, more pressure is placed on public land. In winter, birders and other hikers must often share trails with cross-country skiers and snowmobilers. Since snowmobilers and some skiers pay fees for the privilege of using these trails, many are becoming limited-use trails, with fewer available for birding and hiking. There is clearly a need for more high-quality public land, rather than simply divvying up existing public land among more and more users. But this will happen only when birders, conservationists, snowmobilers, skiers, ATV riders, and everyone else who uses public land join together to demand that more public land be set aside.

75 Practice low-impact hiking

Hiking is probably the lowest-impact use of public land. Hiking on trails is rarely harmful (staying on trails is very important, especially during the breeding season), and hikers can actively help birds in several ways. Always carry plastic bags in your backpack or pocket. If you're hiking with a dog (which should never be allowed to run loose through woodland or grassland habitat during nesting season), clean up after it. Bags are also useful when you pull up purple loosestrife, garlic mustard, and other invasive exotic weeds. Tightly bagging them prevents seeds from being released. Picking up trash, especially items that are likely to hurt wildlife, is something that conscientious hikers do without even thinking. Monofilament line, fishing tackle, balloons, used condoms, six-pack rings, cans, and pop-top rings are probably the most dangerous trash items commonly found. Thin plastic bags are perfect for picking up even the most distasteful items—just put your hand inside the bag, pick up the item, and hold it as you turn the bag inside out.

PART V

HELPING BIRDS ON A LARGER SCALE

18

MAKE FINANCIAL CONTRIBUTIONS

ANYTHING THAT FLITS ABOUT THE PLANET AS FREE AS A BIRD HAS no use for money. But even if birds themselves don't need it, conserving their habitat and cleaning the environment cost a lot of money. Hunters have been footing the bills for land conservation in the United States for many decades, and some people consider that the game they take justifies that state of affairs. But anyone who watches birds—whether on intensive "big days," during a leisurely stroll through a public park, or from the kitchen table—is making use of resources that require protection. There are many ways that we can spend our conservation dollars. Whether we have a lot of money or just a little to donate to conservation causes, we want to be sure that it will be well used.

76 Buy and display a federal Duck Stamp

One of the most exciting recent projects to restore an endangered species is Operation Migration, the program that teaches captive-bred Whooping Crane chicks to migrate from Wisconsin to Florida following an ultralight aircraft. Once they learn their route on the first migration, they return to Wisconsin and then repeat the migrations each year on their own. The birds summer at the Necedah National Wildlife Refuge in Wisconsin and winter at the Chassahowitzka National Wildlife Refuge in Florida. Meanwhile, the natural flock of Whooping Cranes that breeds in Wood Buffalo National Park, on the border between the Northwest Territories and Alberta, spends the winter in the Aransas National Wildlife Refuge.

According to the National Wildlife Refuge Association:

Today, there are 282 million people living in the United States, more than double the number 100 years ago. Experts predict that the population again will double in the next 100 years. More people means more land is developed, more water is used, more minerals are extracted, more roads, etc. Nearly four million acres of land are lost to development each year. When once-pristine land is developed, the conversion fragments the ecosystem and leaves it in small, disjointed patches. As these patches become smaller and more isolated, their ability to maintain healthy populations of a variety of plant and animal species is reduced. Individual species are lost from each fragment, the entire community changes, and the ecosystem becomes degraded. This is happening to varying degrees all over the country.

In the midst of this degradation, our national wildlife refuges hold the line. Refuges, which used to be managed primarily for waterfowl, now are focused on conserving and protecting all species and their habitats. They contain rare and common ecosystems alike—everything from southwest desert to arctic tundra, from tropical forests to coral reefs. Indeed, the entire spectrum of North American ecosystems is found within the 100-million-acre Refuge System. And many rare, native, and endemic ecosystems will survive the explosive growth and development occurring in the United States solely because the Refuge System safeguards them.

- Since 1600, more than a third of our country's forest land has been converted to agricultural and other uses. Of the 740 million forest acres remaining in the U.S., about 50 million (6 percent) are reserved from commercial timber harvest in the form of parks, wilderness, and other land classifications. Because these reserved lands represent such a small piece of the pie, their health is all the more important to conserving the species that depend on them. And since forests found on refuges—about 17 million acres—generally are unavailable for intensive or consumptive uses, they are the most critical for wildlife.

- Some 150 refuges contain various types of marine and estuarine areas that provide habitat for species like the West

Indian manatee, monk seal, sea turtles, and countless shorebirds. The System contains almost 3 million acres of coral
reefs and adjacent ocean habitat, a larger area than is protected by any other public lands or marine system.

- The Refuge System includes about 17 million acres of tundra, eight million acres of brush habitat, six million acres of
  desert, and four million acres of grasslands.
- In addition, 75 designated National Wilderness areas totaling
  about 21 million acres, or one-fifth of the entire National
  Wilderness Preservation System, are found on 65 refuges in
  25 states.

How is this critical program funded? Partly by congressional appropri-
ations, partly by entrance fees, and partly by Federal Migratory Bird Hunting and Conservation Stamps, commonly known as "Ducks Stamps." These
pictorial stamps are produced by the U.S. Postal Service for the U.S. Fish
and Wildlife Service. They are not valid for postage. Duck Stamps were
originally created in 1934 to serve as the federal licenses required for hunting migratory waterfowl. Each waterfowl hunter in every state is required
to have a federal Duck Stamp. The stamps also serve as annual passes for
refuges that charge an entry fee.

Duck Stamps cost fifteen dollars and are sold in many post offices across
the country. You can also buy them on the Internet (www.duckstamp.com)
or at many sporting goods and outdoor stores. Ninety-eight cents out of
every dollar generated by the sale of Duck Stamps goes directly to purchase
or lease wetland habitat for protection in the National Wildlife Refuge System. The federal Duck Stamp program is a highly effective way of funding
the conservation of natural resources.

As the United States becomes more urbanized, fewer people are becoming hunters. To keep the National Wildlife Refuge System strong, birders
need to step in and take up the slack by buying Duck Stamps. Most birders
don't hunt, and many don't visit national wildlife refuges. Why should they
spend fifteen dollars every year for a Duck Stamp that they'll never use? Even
if birders don't personally visit refuges, many migratory birds do. These areas
are rich in habitat that supports not only wintering and breeding birds but
also millions or even billions of migrating birds as they rest and feed along
the way. Although refuges have historically been managed for waterfowl and
other gamebirds, other birds certainly benefit. For example, the amazing

Ivory-billed Woodpecker sightings made in 2004 and 2005 happened at the Cache River National Wildlife Refuge in Arkansas.

Unfortunately, most nonhunters don't realize how important the Duck Stamp program is for acquiring critical refuge habitat for nongame species. And because the hunting population is dwindling even as the total population is rising, putting aside land for habitat is becoming more difficult. When we display a Duck Stamp on a spotting scope or jacket or dangling from binoculars, we open up opportunities for people to notice it and ask about it. Grassroots education can go a long way toward raising public awareness about this essential program.

77 Support your favorite birding spots

When I was a little girl, I used to play on property that belonged to Automatic Electric, a huge industrial complex with a tree-lined creek on its extensive grounds. My family had frequent picnics in Chicago forest preserves, where I would take little hikes by myself while everyone else socialized. It never occurred to me that any of my favorite haunts would remain wild only as long as their private owners or (in the case of the forest preserves) their public managing agencies and the Chicago taxpayers who funded them chose to let them remain that way. Even when I played in my backyard, I could see that none of the birds I enjoyed—not the robins or cardinals or colorful little songbirds passing through—lived entirely in my backyard. As far as enjoying the out-of-doors, we're all dependent on the kindness and funding of strangers. All wild habitat "belongs" to someone or something, either public or private. And whether land is under the control of an individual, a corporation, a conservation organization, or a public agency, decisions regarding its management can be made very quickly, flattening even the most pristine, critical habitat into a discount department store parking lot in short order. We can exert public pressure on governmental agencies to protect public lands or to enforce environmental regulations on private lands, but those agencies are pressured by other interests as well. How can we ensure that there will continue to be wild spaces for our children and future generations, much less for birds and wildlife?

We can make the greatest impact by taking a personal interest in, and responsibility for, the places we know and love best. Belonging to or even starting a "Friends of" organization to support nearby national wildlife refuges, parks, and other public lands is one way. Letting managers and landowners know how much we value a spot and appreciate its quality habitat is also important. Paying entrance and parking fees to parks and private birding spots should go without saying, but some people, even prominent, well-to-do birders, sometimes try to dodge this fundamental duty.

When we're conscious of who or what entity is in charge of managing the land at our favorite birding destinations and show our support with both membership and entrance fees and additional contributions, we can make a huge difference in ensuring that wild habitat stays that way.

78 Support state, national, and international Important Bird Areas

Although all natural habitat supports birds, some areas have greater significance than others in providing breeding or wintering habitat or serving as essential migratory stopovers for bird populations as a whole. To help prioritize habitat protection, the National Audubon Society and BirdLife International are working together to identify a network of the most critical sites. This effort is known as the Important Bird Areas (IBA) program.

The IBA program in the United States and Canada works through partnerships with local, state, provincial, and national organizations, especially the North American Bird Conservation Initiative, to identify those places that are most critical to birds. The international IBA program is a global effort to identify areas worldwide that are most important for maintaining bird populations, where conservation efforts should be focused. In the United States, the IBA program has become a key component of bird conservation programs such as Partners in Flight, the North American Waterbird Conservation Plan, and the U.S. Shorebird Conservation Plan.

You can help identify, monitor, and conserve Important Bird Areas though volunteer action and contributions. Audubon suggests ways that you can get involved, including nominating sites that might fit IBA criteria; volunteering on projects to monitor populations, restore habitat, or eradicate invasive species at an IBA; advocating for changes in laws and policies that would benefit birds of concern at IBAs; developing birding field trips to IBAs in your area; and making financial contributions to your state's IBA program.

One of the most novel ways of financially supporting the IBA program was devised by Wisconsin birder Noel Cutright, who in 2004 conducted

Wood Thrush

thirty-three consecutive Breeding Bird Surveys in Ohio, Michigan, Wisconsin, and Minnesota as a "birdathon" endeavor, raising pledges in a well-publicized effort called his "Quad 30 Campaign." As of this writing, Cutright has raised a total of $49,460.04, earmarked to support the IBA program.

79 Support your state's nongame wildlife program

Because most state departments of natural resources or conservation were instituted to protect fish and game populations, they have historically been funded largely or even entirely by hunting and fishing licenses and fees. In the past three decades, more states have recognized the importance of protecting nongame wildlife as well, but many of these programs are funded entirely by voluntary contributions, often via checkoffs on tax returns.

Many people are understandably concerned about how their tax dollars are spent. Nongame wildlife programs have an excellent record of funding research and managing essential habitat. For example, in the past ten years, the Alabama Nongame Wildlife Program released ninety-one Bald Eagles and sixty-six Ospreys to restore nesting populations and then monitored their nesting activity; built more than 10,000 bluebird nest boxes and coordinated more than 1,000 volunteers to "Bring Back the Bluebird"; managed and protected Gaillard Island in Mobile Bay to produce more than 10,000 Brown Pelicans in eight years (more pelicans than were produced in Alabama in the last century); conducted annual shorebird surveys to help monitor the condition of valuable wetland habitat; assisted in studies of turtles, nongame fish, mussels, rare frogs, bats, and salamanders; and initiated a monitoring program to conserve Alabama's songbirds.

To provide the maximum benefit from limited dollars, most nongame wildlife programs depend on trained volunteers for many projects that involve monitoring populations, restoring habitat, removing invasive exotics, and building and erecting nest boxes and platforms. Being generous with your time, expertise, and dollars can go a long way toward restoring and maintaining nongame populations in your state.

80 Support your favorite local, state, national, and international conservation organizations

There may be a host of problems facing birds, but there are also many nonprofit organizations working to solve them. No one wants to support an organization that uses donations to support its own infrastructure rather than to advance its proclaimed mission, but this isn't always easy to evaluate. There are some tools that can help you figure out which are the most worthy conservation organizations.

The Charity Navigator (www.charitynavigator.org) rates all kinds of nonprofit organizations based on their fiscal policies, as does the American

Institute of Philanthropy (www.charitywatch.org). These rankings may help you decide when choosing between organizations. Many bird conservation organizations are not rated, however, and few local or regional nonprofits provide data to these watchdogs. In addition, some organizations that get a low rating may actually be doing better work than their ranking implies. Every nonprofit organization should provide an annual report so you can decide for yourself.

One of the easiest ways to judge the quality of an organization's educational programs is to take part in them. If you find yourself turning to a particular Internet resource a lot, find out which organization produces it. If an organization provides public programs that are useful and fun and that promote the love, understanding, and protection of birds, their educational programs are worth supporting. If the organization maintains a nature center or some other educational facility, you can judge it by how interesting and useful the displays are and how well it manages the property.

Some organizations that trap and band birds display them publicly before release. Wild birds can be a wonderful resource in public education programs, but the birds' welfare must be considered first. Showing groups struggling, desperate birds not only teaches some very bad lessons but also puts the birds under so much stress that some of them die. Banded birds should be handled for display for only brief periods and should never be held after they start to show signs of stress. Allowing inexperienced people to hold a bird and release it can be such a magical experience that it's worth some risk, as long as an experienced professional is at hand to guide the process. It's often wise to assign two people to show and release banded birds: one to hold and pay attention to the bird, and the other to speak to the crowd.

Some organizations have "adopt-a-bird" programs wherein people make donations to hold and release a particular banded bird. They often get a photo of the bird and a certificate with the bird's band number and information about the species, and if the bird is ever recovered or retrapped, they'll receive a postcard with the information. This kind of program can be an excellent way for nonprofits to solicit donations while conducting their regular research and educational programs. But adopt-a-bird programs often have a dark side. I've seen overly enthusiastic volunteers and employees hold a bird for as long as forty-five minutes while working a crowd, jeopardizing the bird's welfare to solicit funds. This is not only unethical and cruel; it's also against the state and federal rules that regulate banders and those licensed to display birds for educational purposes. Organizations should enforce clear standards about how long birds can be displayed, and it should never appear that a bird is being held hostage for money. If you witness this kind of activity, let the organization know that you find it inappropriate.

Sometimes, banding activities that really aren't unduly stressful or harmful to birds can seem cruel. It is standard operating procedure to keep birds taken from nets in cloth bags or, in the case of hawks, restrained in metal or plastic tubes until the bander can band, measure, and release the bird. Like horses wearing blinders, diurnal birds in dark places are usually subdued and fairly calm. Experienced handlers recognize signs of stress and know how to work quickly, efficiently, and gently when they handle the bird. Inexperienced banders are obviously more clumsy, but they are expected to work under a master bander until they've become proficient.

Some local birding organizations support a banding station or seasonal bird count as their primary research program. Research is useful only when it is published so that other scientists and the general public can take advantage of the information. By law, all bird banding data must be sent to the Patuxent Wildlife Research Center's Bird Banding Laboratory, where it contributes to the huge body of data that establishes longevity patterns, migratory paths and timing, breeding success, and many other essential components of our knowledge base about birds.

Bird banding data can be useful in many other ways, too. By keeping abreast of current ornithological literature, banders can recognize and fill gaps in our knowledge of birds. Bird banders funded by contributions to nonprofit organizations should belong to several ornithological societies, including the Association of Field Ornithologists and at least one of the major national ornithological societies, such as the American Ornithologists' Union, the Wilson Ornithological Society, or the Cooper Ornithological Society. There are also specialty societies, such as Hawk Watch International, the North American Bluebird Society, and the Hummingbird Society.

Banding data can be extremely valuable in fostering public education on a local basis. For example, Sharp-shinned Hawks banded at Hawk Ridge Nature Reserve in Duluth, Minnesota, have been recovered from many locations in Central America and even South America. People in Duluth find this fascinating, so providing this information promotes interest in raptors and migrants in general and instills pride in local natural resources.

How do you judge the quality of research coming out of various organizations? This can be tricky, but an organization's annual report should include a list of recent papers published in the scientific literature by members of its research team, as well as a summary of the past year's banding returns and other research findings. The publishing of papers in major scientific journals is competitive and is often not warranted for local research projects, but the publication of one or two major papers and a few smaller ones in regional and state ornithological journals and other smaller publications every decade, or the publishing of authoritative pamphlets and booklets of regional or local value, is a reasonable expectation to justify donations.

It would be impossible to publish a complete list of worthy organizations that promote bird conservation. But some of my favorite national organizations that work for bird conservation or environmental quality include the following.

The American Bird Conservancy. This organization, given the maximum four stars by the Charity Navigator, uses research to prepare position papers and expert testimony that have had a major impact on several critical issues. Its current high-priority issues are the seabird bycatch from longlines, bird kills at communication towers, horseshoe crabs, the persecution of fish-eating birds, and birds and wind energy. The ABC has also been an extremely effective voice with regard to pesticide issues. It orchestrated a landmark international accord to protect Swainson's Hawks from the deadly insecticide monocrotophos in Argentina and then hired full-time staff to address the problem of pesticide hazards to birds. Its mission is to reduce the exposure of wild birds to hazardous pesticides and to better define when, how, and to what degree specific pesticides pose risks to birds. The ABC Web site is a treasure trove of solid information about this and other important issues.

Cornell Laboratory of Ornithology. The Cornell Lab focuses on research, education, and citizen science programs to promote bird conservation. Its research programs include bird population studies, a state-of-the-art bioacoustics research program, and a library of natural sounds. Citizen science projects include eBird and the Great Backyard Bird Count (both in conjunction with Audubon), Project Feeder Watch, the House Finch Disease Survey, the Birdhouse Network, and Urban Bird Studies. Educational programs include the Web sites All About Birds and Birds of North America, Classroom Feeder Watch, Project Pigeon Watch, a home study course in bird biology, and an annual sound recording workshop.

Fatal Light Awareness Program. FLAP is a Toronto-based nonprofit formed in April 1993 to find a solution to the problem of birds flying into lighted buildings, especially during nocturnal migration flights. During migration seasons, FLAP volunteers patrol Toronto's downtown core in the early-morning hours to rescue live birds and collect dead ones. Also, FLAP publicizes the problem and convinces building staffs, cleaning crews, security, and management to turn off the lights. As awareness of the problem grows, FLAP has been working with concerned groups in other cities to form similar organizations.

National Audubon Society. Audubon spearheaded the Important Bird Areas program in the United States and has taken a leading role in other vital issues, campaigns, and programs, including the Christmas Bird Count, eBird (in conjunction with the Cornell Lab), and Audubon at Home, which gives people the tools to protect birds in daily life. On international issues, Audubon works in partnership with BirdLife International.

National Wildlife Federation. The National Wildlife Federation focuses on land stewardship, water resources, and wildlife conservation issues on regional, national, and global levels. It provides a wealth of educational resources, from magazines to the popular and useful eNature.com.

The Nature Conservancy. The Nature Conservancy's mission is to preserve the plants, animals, and natural communities that represent the diversity of life on earth by protecting the lands and waters they need to survive. It identifies the highest-priority places that will ensure biodiversity over the long term.

Pesticide Action Network of North America. Although not specifically a bird conservation organization, the Pesticide Action Network of North American (PANNA) maintains meticulous records on research and works to protect all of us from pesticides' harmful effects. According to its Web site (www.panna.org), PANNA "works to replace pesticide use with ecologically sound and socially just alternatives. As one of five PAN Regional Centers worldwide, we link local and international consumer, labor, health, environment and agriculture groups into an international citizens' action network. This network challenges the global proliferation of pesticides, defends basic rights to health and environmental quality, and works to insure the transition to a just and viable society." PANNA's newsletter, sent via e-mail, is filled with accurate and up-to-date information about pesticide-related issues.

The Rainforest Alliance. The Rainforest Alliance works to protect ecosystems and the people and wildlife that depend on them by transforming land-use practices, business practices, and consumer behavior. Compa-

Elegant Trogon

nies, cooperatives, and landowners that participate in its programs must meet rigorous standards that conserve biodiversity and provide sustainable livelihoods. Based in New York City, with offices throughout the United States and worldwide, the Rainforest Alliance works in more than fifty countries with farmers, foresters, lodge owners, and tour operators—people whose livelihoods depend on natural resources. Groups ranging from large multinational corporations to small, community-based indigenous groups work to transform the way food is cultivated, wood is harvested, and travel is practiced. The Rainforest Alliance certifies farms as well as forestry and tourism operations that meet its standards for balancing environmental, social, and economic considerations.

Union of Concerned Scientists. The UCS is an independent nonprofit alliance of more than 100,000 concerned citizens and scientists who combine rigorous scientific analysis with innovative thinking and committed citizen advocacy to work for a cleaner, healthier environment and a safer world. It produces many useful resources for learning about conservation and environmental issues that affect humans and birds.

Bird-specific groups. A wide range of organizations focuses on particular birds, such as the International Crane Foundation and Operation Migration, the Hummingbird Society, the Purple Martin Conservation Association, and the North American Bluebird Society. Most states and provinces have ornithological organizations, and there are many local and regional nature centers, bird observatories and sanctuaries, wildlife refuge support organizations, birding clubs, and other worthy groups. Support the ones that campaign for the issues you care about.

81 Support local and regional bird rehabilitation facilities

The goal of wildlife rehabilitation is to provide professional care to sick, injured, and orphaned wild animals so that they can ultimately be returned to their natural habitats. Animals whose injuries or illnesses will prevent them from living successfully in the wild are either humanely euthanized or, in limited cases, placed in an educational facility if the animal is healthy enough and adaptable enough to serve as an educational tool.

Wildlife rehabilitation involves veterinary medicine, basic first aid, and physical therapy. Because groups of birds are so different from one another and from domestic birds, avian rehabilitators also need extensive knowledge about each species they care for, including its natural history, nutritional requirements, feeding techniques, behavioral issues, and caging considerations, as well as any dangers the birds may present to rehabilitators. Rehabbers have to be able to respond to emergencies, sometimes picking up animals in difficult circumstances without putting themselves or other people at risk. Once bird rehabilitators receive their permits, they normally continue to attend conferences, seminars, and workshops; keep up with the published literature; and network with others in the field.

In addition, wildlife rehabilitators spend a lot of time responding to people's questions. I've fielded questions from people in a panic because a bird, usually a Ruffed Grouse, has crashed through a window and is running all over the house bleeding, with broken glass everywhere. Some people call wondering whether they should ask the letter carrier to deliver their mail next door until the phoebes or robins nesting on the front porch fledge their babies. Others are at their wits' end because a cardinal or robin keeps bashing itself against a window, fighting its reflection. Anguished people often call after hitting a bird. Others call after keeping a small nestling for a week or so, feeding it nothing but crackers and milk (both inappropriate for birds), by which time it's too late to save it. Occasionally, people call after finding a sick or dying bird on their lawn the day after it was treated with pesticides; some are distraught and feel guilty, while others refuse to believe that pesticides are the culprit. One man demanded that I come to his house and take some baby Chipping Sparrows out of the nest in his yard before they fledged, so that his cat wouldn't kill them. When I suggested that he keep the cat indoors for a few days, he called me an ugly word, said he hoped that the cat ate all the baby birds, and slammed down the phone.

Wildlife rehabilitation takes care of individual birds, not entire populations, so many people feel that their contributions would be better spent elsewhere. But rehabbing birds does more than restore thousands of birds to the wild each year that were harmed by windows, cats, pesticides, automobiles, oil spills, and other human-caused mishaps. It also gives us important insights into avian physiology and behavior and opportunities to develop techniques that can then be used to help endangered species. And rehabbers provide invaluable one-on-one educational services, even if some people refuse to be educated.

Maintaining and staffing well-run professional facilities can be expensive. By supporting the wildlife rehab clinic that serves your area, you can make a genuine difference in the lives of individual birds, help larger populations, and support conservation education.

82 Support the development of birding trails

In recent years, birding groups have been combining forces with chambers of commerce and local businesses to produce maps to the best birding destinations in the area. Many are located right off major highways, state routes, or small country roads; some are farther off the beaten path. Some birding trail systems are organized around a single natural feature, such as the Great Salt Lake Birding Trails or the Great River Birding Trail, which follows the Mississippi River from its start near Bemidji, Minnesota, all the way down to the Gulf of Mexico. Others cover entire states, such as the Great Washington Birding Trail and the Great Florida Birding Trail.

Many birders are already familiar with birders' guides, books that give detailed descriptions of and directions to the best birding areas in a state or region. Birders' guides provide fairly detailed coverage of avian seasonal distributions, focusing on rare and difficult-to-find species. Birding trail maps don't include such comprehensive information and usually emphasize conspicuous birds rather than possible rarities. They're generally produced in color with beautiful photos, providing information in an accessible and welcoming way, especially for new birders and visitors.

Because of birding trails, a wide range of people have become more aware of the green spaces in their areas. Trail users have the opportunity to discover natural treasures firsthand, making them more interested in protecting beautiful and sensitive areas. People visiting birding trail destinations invariably stop at restaurants, gas stations, and motels, giving those businesses a financial stake in the well-being of the bird populations around them. In these and other ways, birding trails help ensure that these great birding spots will be kept natural long into the future.

19

VOLUNTEER

THE MOVEMENT FOR BIRD AND HABITAT PROTECTION IN THE UNITED States is led in large part by nonprofit organizations and governmental agencies with relatively small budgets. Some of the most successful programs for monitoring birds, removing invasive exotic weeds from public lands, and other important projects are possible only because birders and other people volunteer their time, expertise, and labor.

83 Volunteer at conservation organizations and governmental agencies

Inventories and surveys of wildlife such as birds, frogs, and plants are essential for assessing the habitat quality of an area and setting priorities for habitat restoration and other conservation projects. Some, like the Breeding Bird Survey, take place annually, providing a database that indicates changes in populations over time. Others may take place several times a year to get a baseline assessment of the species composition of an area or to augment past records when developing an area bird checklist. Some surveys, such as various loon and crane watches and frog counts, focus on a single species or group. Others, such as the Breeding Bird Atlas, require an intensive search for evidence of every possible breeding species; these surveys may be conducted from late winter through late summer for two or three years. Breeding Bird Atlases are normally produced on a statewide basis and require the cooperation of many people to produce meaningful results. Virtually all these surveys are conducted by experienced volunteers. In most cases, these surveys require participants to have a fairly high level of expertise, with skill in bird identification by both sight and sound.

Ornithologist Bill Evans of Ithaca, New York, has developed a technique of accurately surveying nocturnal migrants by setting up inexpensive microphones on fairly quiet rooftops and recording the sounds on eight-hour videotapes or directly onto computer hard drives. He has also developed the software needed to analyze such recordings, which is available for free on his Web site (www.oldbird.org). This Web site provides all the information you need to construct an accurate and inexpensive directional microphone in a waterproof housing, conduct the surveys, and analyze and share the data. It also enables volunteers to take part in networks to use their flight call data for environmental education and to promote the understanding of nocturnal songbird migration. Even novices can participate, because the software not only teaches you how to identify flight calls but also analyzes the recordings itself.

Birders of all levels of expertise can volunteer to participate in Christmas Bird Counts, the Great Backyard Bird Count, and other citizen science programs. And anyone can report bird sightings to eBird and to state and local ornithological societies. Some local migration watches also make use of volunteers. Many wildlife rehabilitation centers depend on trained volunteers to help feed and care for injured and orphaned wildlife, clean cages, and pick up injured animals.

Some habitat improvement projects, such as native seed collection, removal of exotic vegetation, and other restoration work, welcome volunteers. Projects such as blazing and maintaining trails; erecting viewing blinds, platforms, and information signs; and basic cleanups don't require any expertise but do require time and labor. Some local bird clubs and state ornithological societies keep track of volunteer opportunities for birders, as does the American Birding Association.

84 Volunteer to help youth organizations develop bird study programs

When my boys were Scouts, I had the great pleasure of helping their troops earn their Bird Study Merit Badges. Boy Scouts earn this badge by reading an informative and surprisingly comprehensive booklet (written by noted field ornithologist and author Scott Weidensaul) and then demonstrating that they know how to use binoculars, recognize the parts of a bird, use a field guide, keep a field notebook, and identify at least twenty species of wild birds by appearance and at least five species by song or call. Other requirements include taking a field trip with experienced birders or demonstrating some understanding of local bird populations, building a feeder or birdbath, or planting a backyard sanctuary. Although the skills required to earn the badge are fairly straightforward, many Scout leaders and parents don't feel knowledgeable enough about birds to help the boys earn this merit badge. It's an easy matter to purchase the inexpensive bird study booklet from the local Boy Scout Council, familiarize yourself with the material and activities the boys must master to earn the badge, and then volunteer to serve as badge counselor.

Girl Scouts have no specific bird study badge, but individual troops can devise special badges. When I was the leader of my daughter's Girl Scout troop, we dissected a Great Horned Owl, built bird feeders, learned to recognize and imitate a wide variety of birds by appearance and sound, and went birding in local and state parks. Although few leaders or parents would have the necessary permits to legally dissect an owl, local birders can certainly volunteer to help girls master basic birding skills that will help them fulfill the requirements of some of their outdoor badges.

Common Loons

Some schools welcome community volunteers to help teachers with various activities. If you're interested, alert local principals of your availability and what you can offer students. Schools are naturally leery of strangers, and teachers are often too busy with the basic curriculum to cover nature study in the classroom, but local birders and classroom teachers occasionally get together to provide excellent bird study units. Some schools also support after-school nature clubs or programs. Even when you can't go into schools personally, local checklists, old field guides and binoculars, and other educational materials may be welcome.

Sometimes a member of a local birding club organizes a junior birding club, offering meetings and field trips for children that run at the same time as the adult ones. These can be very successful, providing fun birding opportunities for children and making it easier for their parents to attend meetings. But the purposes of the club need to be presented clearly to parents, who should not expect to drop off uninterested children and get free babysitting services.

85 Volunteer to present educational programs at local nursing homes, service clubs, gardening clubs, and other groups

One of the simplest ways to educate the general nonbirding public is through public speaking at local clubs. You not only provide information but also raise awareness of the issues faced by local birds and the benefits of making the world more hospitable for birds. I've been doing this for over two decades and find it fun and easy. When I first started, I was terrified— I felt awkward, was scared that I'd make mistakes, and figured that there were many people with more experience and expertise that my audience would rather be hearing. Fortunately, the Wisconsin Society for Ornithology sold a set of slides of birds of the state for a minimal price, and slides from the Cornell Lab filled in any gaps. I soon discovered that I was comfortable speaking as long as the lights were out and everyone was enjoying these wonderful images. It finally occurred to me that even though there were certainly plenty of people with more experience and expertise, I was the one who was able and willing to be there.

Computer software now makes it very easy to put together a great visual presentation. On my own Web site (www.birderblog.com) and many others, you can download still photos, videos, and sound recordings of a wide range of species for free for educational purposes. Many professional and amateur photographers justifiably do not want their work used without permission, so be sure to honor copyright laws and basic ethics. Unfortunately, the projectors that hook up to computers for these presentations are very expensive. Sometimes birding clubs pool their resources with those of other local organizations to share a single projector, and you may be able to borrow it.

Speaking at Rotary, Kiwanis, and other service organizations often opens the minds and hearts of influential citizens who otherwise wouldn't pay much attention to birds. Garden club programs give you an opportunity to discuss how lawn and garden pesticides affect some of the most beautiful backyard birds. Talking at nursing homes and assisted-living centers gives residents a welcome change in their routine and often stirs lovely memories of bird encounters from long ago. If you listen patiently, you'll be surprised how much you can learn.

20

TAKE POLITICAL ACTION

FROM THE DAYS OF THEODORE ROOSEVELT, SETTING ASIDE PUBLIC lands for recreation and habitat protection has been a fundamental way of ensuring that our children would share America's abundance. Programs enabled by the Endangered Species Act have helped restore populations of Whooping Cranes, Kirtland's Warblers, and Peregrine Falcons, all of which are at their highest historical levels thanks to the act signed into law by Richard Nixon. The Clean Air and Clean Water Acts had powerful and immediate effects. Unfortunately, we've allowed the government to weaken them, and water and air quality is sliding back, but at least there's some wiggle room before things get as dire as they were in the 1960s. Anyone who claims that politics has nothing to do with birds just isn't paying attention.

86 Work to make strong environmental protections part of your party's agenda

During the Nixon administration, from 1969 through 1974, there was a bipartisan consensus in the federal government that people needed clean air and water and deserved to enjoy the abundant natural riches bequeathed by our forebears. During that brief era, the United States made enormous strides forward, enacting the Clean Air Act, Clean Water Act, and Endangered Species Act; forming the Environmental Protection Agency; lowering the speed limit to 55 miles per hour; and banning DDT. Almost immediately, we saw huge improvements in environmental quality. The Cuyahoga River, once afire, now supports nesting Bald Eagles. Peregrine Falcons, once wiped out east of the Rockies, now nest in many major cities as well as along cliffs in more remote areas. The total population of singing male Kirtland's Warblers, an easy species to census accurately, was down to a mere 167 in 1974; in 2005 the numbers reached an all-time high of 1,415. And soapsuds no longer billow up from churning water in rivers and streams.

Whenever we do a thorough housecleaning, it feels good to sit down and rest, even though we realize that we're never really done—it takes vigilance and ongoing efforts to keep anything clean, be it a home or a nation. Even the best legislation must be enforced in order to accomplish anything, and laws can always be revised, rescinded, or ignored by subsequent administrations and Congresses. Despite the passage of all these laws, the amount of mercury in the fish we eat continues to rise. A 2005 study by the Centers for Disease Control and Prevention found that more than 90 percent of U.S. residents carry pesticides in their bodies; many of these chemicals are linked to health effects such as cancer, birth defects, and neurological problems. Children, who are particularly vulnerable to the effects of pesticide exposure, had higher levels of some pesticides in their bodies than adults did. Laws created to reduce gasoline consumption were subverted by excluding minivans and SUVs from mileage requirements by defining them as light trucks; as a result, average gas consumption is higher now than it was before the original legislation was enacted. And since the Endangered Species Act was passed, many species have continued to decline. For example, since the early 1980s, the last Greater Prairie Chickens have disappeared from Michigan, Dusky Seaside Sparrows became extinct, and the Greater Sage Grouse population crashed to its lowest historical level, where it remains today.

I was an idealistic high school and college student during the Nixon administration. I never imagined that these laws wouldn't be honorably and completely enforced, or that the country wouldn't continue moving forward and standing as a beacon of progressive conservation. And I certainly never dreamed that knowledgeable people of integrity following in the tradition of Theodore Roosevelt, Gaylord Nelson, Rachel Carson, Morris and Stewart Udall, and Lady Bird Johnson—people currently fighting for the continued enforcement of acts signed into law by Richard Nixon—would be ridiculed and lambasted as "environmental wackos" by popular public figures without any sustained public outcry or demand for professional restraint.

Taking individual action to protect birds and support environmental safeguards is critical. But it is naive to believe that this is enough. Unless we take an active role in setting the political agenda; unless we press our elected leaders to put the needs of human beings above the profit margins of major corporations; unless we make our voices heard at public hearings about important local, state, and national issues; unless we make conservation a high-priority issue and vote accordingly, our nation will continue along its current path, inching closer toward a government of the corporations, by the corporations, and for the corporations.

According to current polls, the vast majority of Americans support a clean and healthy environment and the protection of endangered species. But at election time, these issues usually take a backseat. People may support a candidate solely because of his or her stand for or against legalized abortion, but protecting the unborn should include limiting the amount of mercury and pesticides they're exposed to, and protecting women's reproductive rights should extend to guaranteeing their right to drink hormone-free water. Many hunters vote based on gun issues without taking into account a candidate's record of protecting wildlife populations and habitat, even as waterfowl and upland gamebirds decline. In my area, hunters express a longing for the days when Sharp-tailed Grouse, American Woodcocks, Canvasbacks, and Redheads were easier to find; in many other places, woodcock and grouse hunters have given up completely. The sport of hunting has already been diminished far more by these losses than it could be by any gun law. People who are focused on national security need to consider which candidate is most likely to reduce our dependence on foreign oil by supporting conservation and the development of alternative energy sources. Ironically, much of the money that patriotic Americans are spending at the gas pumps is ending up in the pockets of Saudi Arabians who are funding terrorists to kill our citizens.

This is not meant to discount the importance of a wide spectrum of political issues or the possibility that different approaches supported by different political philosophies can sometimes achieve the same goals. But air and water quality has been demonstrably improved by the Clean Air and Clean Water Acts, and no alternative has ever been so effective. Our society expects individuals to clean up after themselves—if we're caught littering, pouring waste oil down storm sewers, dumping garbage on public land, or burning trash in open containers, we're justifiably prosecuted. Most laws protecting air and water quality simply apply these fair and obvious rules about cleaning up after ourselves to large corporations as well. Of course, the devil is in the details, but clean air and water are so fundamental that it's shocking and distressing that protecting them is barely a blip on the electorate's radar screen, even as cities issue smog alerts and water shortages become more prevalent. Things will improve only when politicians and the people who elect them make environmental quality a top priority once again.

87 Get involved in land-use issues and work for strong protection of natural habitat

One of the reasons that so few people take an active role in political action is that it's so hard to tease out which regulating agencies are involved and to understand the bureaucratic underpinnings of each one. It's even harder to figure out the wisest course of action to make oneself heard at any level of government. Joining local and state chapters of conservation organizations such as the Izaak Walton League and the Audubon Society, or just subscribing to their electronic newsletters, can help you get a handle on pressing issues and specific ways you can help.

When developers propose housing or business projects on public land or on adjacent private land, the issues are sometimes covered in the newspaper. But often, such developments are proposed and approved more quietly. Get to know the people on your local and county zoning and planning boards, and find out how you can stay abreast of proposed developments.

Sometimes private land is left undeveloped and unfenced for so long that there is a public perception that it's public land; when houses or businesses suddenly spring up, especially along lakeshores and other sensitive places, people can be extremely distressed, but usually, very little can be done. Some development projects, however, can and should be stopped. It's important for you to keep a level head, assess your options, and try to achieve the best realistic resolution possible. Some developers are willing to work with conservationists to devise building and landscaping plans that are less harmful to birds or actually benefit them, but this virtually never happens after angry confrontations and harsh rhetoric. Developers are usually represented by lawyers or other paid agents with no emotional stake in the outcome, they put in a day's work and then go home. Conservationists usually have a deep emotional connection to the land they're trying to save; they put together their case, attend meetings, and consult experts, in addition to working forty hours a week at their real jobs. It's not surprising that the handful of committed conservationists working in an area can get burned out, while the developments keep coming. By working with a local organization, people can help one another maintain morale, make sure that no one gets overburdened, and help everyone keep things in perspective. Brainstorming with other conservationists also makes it easier to strategize and to devise creative alternatives to minimize harm when a development project is going forward.

Some of the most important development issues include the construction of lighted communication towers, wind farms, and power lines, especially where migratory birds collect or sensitive species may gather, and the
construction of buildings with large windows, especially tall ones along
migratory pathways. In the case of communication towers, ornithologist
Bill Evans has compiled a wealth of information about the problem, including guidelines that the U.S. Fish and Wildlife Service has developed to help
regulators and communications companies plan towers that will minimize
bird deaths. These resources are available at www.towerkill.com.

When fighting a development project, collect specific data to support
the genuine importance of the area for birds and the number that would be
vulnerable if the project went through. The more thoroughly you understand the risks and ways the developer can modify the project to minimize
the damage, the stronger your case will be and the more likely it is that the
issue will be resolved in a way that is least harmful for birds.

88 Provide the local media with accurate information about local bird issues

Most people who have been the subject of stories in newspapers,
in magazines, or on television know how easy it is for reporters to get the
details wrong. Environmental issues tend to be complex, not well suited for
sound bytes, and beyond the expertise of reporters, making it more likely
that the information will be garbled. Sometimes it's distressing to learn just
how uninformed about birds and nature some supposedly well-educated
reporters are. Before a television interview I was about to give on the Ring-
billed Gull population explosion in Duluth, the news anchor asked me in
all sincerity whether gulls were birds.

Those of us who have studied biology may be shocked that people can
get through twelve years of public- or private-school education and even
earn college and graduate degrees without ever learning what makes birds
different from other animals. I was valedictorian of my high school class and
graduated from college with high honors, yet at the age of twenty-three, I
still needed two field guides and a recording to be certain about the identification of the first bird on my life list—a chickadee. Most of us with a passion for and understanding of birds have researched the subject on our own,
taken an elective course in college, or even majored in biology or ornithology; most people with degrees in journalism have taken few science

courses. And even most people with degrees in the sciences, including the life sciences, manage to finish their educations without gaining any in-depth knowledge about birds.

Despite the nagging suspicion that a television anchorman really should know that gulls are birds, it doesn't pay to act appalled by such a question, especially if I may have to deal with that reporter again. I've always figured that it's better to answer every question in a straightforward, matter-of-fact way, as I'd hope an accountant, lawyer, doctor, plumber, auto mechanic, or electrician would answer my "dumb" questions.

When bird stories or issues are being covered in the news, it would be ideal for a local bird club to put simple, accurate "FAQs" (frequently asked questions) on its Web site that could be quoted directly. If you ever give a telephone interview, don't worry about hesitating before you speak—it's better to put something together in your head so that it's clear and accurate. If you're invited to speak on a radio talk show or the television news, especially a live broadcast, you need to be quick, clear, and concise in order to make your point and maintain your credibility with the audience. Sometimes a good technique is to think of your audience and the reporter as intelligent and inquisitive fifth-graders who want to understand the whole picture but have no background in the subject. If you prefer to think of them as the educated adults they are, at least remember that they deal with a huge array of issues and have limited time to focus on a subject that's of little personal interest to them. The more interesting and engaging your responses are, the more positive the audience response and the long-term outcome will be.

Anyone with a strong viewpoint about any topic tends to grow impatient with those who hold an opposing viewpoint or even those who are trying to look objectively at both sides. As our society grows increasingly polarized with regard to more issues, levels of incivility are rising. When advocating for a healthy environment, which all of us need, it's better to shed light rather than heat on the subject.

89 Attend and testify at public hearings, or find other ways to provide accurate information about important issues

During the height of a controversy in my city, when the Ring-billed Gull population had exploded and people were growing alarmed and upset by them, I got a call from a city councilor asking me to attend an upcoming meeting. He wanted me to present factual information about the issue, especially because another councilor had suggested that the city introduce wild pigs to the harbor area to control the gulls by eating their eggs. This would have been like curing an earache by cutting off your head. The city councilor who had suggested the pig plan may have been uninformed about both birds and wild pigs, but he was an honest and friendly politician who had been reelected many times because the people in his district trusted him. It didn't take much on my part to convince the council, including him, to search for better alternatives.

When birds are at the center of any controversy, be they gulls, geese, or cormorants, the first task is to determine, clearly and honestly, what issues lie at the heart of the conflict. For instance, when golfers are upset about geese, it's usually related to the real inconveniences of slipping on goose poop, being attacked by aggressive geese when playing near a nest, and trying to play with geese standing between the ball and the hole. In dealing with this kind of conflict, our task is to help find safe and practical ways to discourage geese from the golf course, not to pooh-pooh the problems or to go on ad nauseum about what magnificent creatures Canada Geese are.

The U.S. Fish and Wildlife Service estimates that at least 5 million and possibly as many as 50 million birds are killed annually in collisions with communications towers in the United States. There are more than 85,000 towers, over 60,000 of them lighted, dotting the American landscape, and that number is expected to rise dramatically during the next decade as more high-definition television towers and wider cell phone and messaging coverage exacerbate the problem. Little research has been conducted to discover ways of preventing birds from striking towers, including such simple measures as noisemakers, predator calls, streamers, sleeves, balls, paint, extra lights, changing the duration of the strobes or the flash patterns, or changing the colors of the aircraft warning lights.

Public apathy about the issue is understandable—few people even realize how deadly these towers are to birds. In 1988, when I worked to stop the construction of a guyed, lighted tower that was going to be built along an internationally famous hawk migration flyway, virtually none of the public I talked to, including local birders, had ever heard about bird kills at towers. A handful of places, most notably in Florida, Kansas, and Wisconsin, had been monitoring one or more towers for many years. I became involved in the issue because I knew about the enormous bird kills documented at an Eau Claire, Wisconsin, TV tower, beginning when more than 20,000 birds were killed on a single foggy night—September 20, 1957. But it was impossible to get a sense of the national magnitude of the problem or the potential hazard at this specific site near the hawk flyway. We did, however, have decades of precise data about the Duluth area's hawk migration and several years of data about the exceptional magnitude of nocturnal and early-morning nonraptor flights along the shore, not far from the proposed tower. I pulled that data together to explain the potential for harm. I also collected statements from several prominent ornithologists and knowledgeable birders throughout the state attesting to the unique importance of the area for migrating birds and the danger of siting a tower on the migration path. Based largely on the strength of this evidence, the zoning board and the board of adjustment both voted unanimously to deny permits for construction. When the town's three-member board voted the other way, I ended up filing a request in district court for an environmental assessment before construction could proceed. I waged a public-relations campaign, as did the company proposing the tower. It made the mistake of misrepresenting the tower as being essential for 911 emergency service in the township. One call to the county administrator of 911 services revealed the truth: the township's 911 antennas were already in place elsewhere, and the proposed tower had no bearing on emergency services. Even as I exposed the deception, I firmly and consistently kept my primary focus on the specific elements of towers that posed a danger to birds—guy wires and lights—and the unique magnitude of the migration in this specific area. I explained dozens of times, to hundreds of people, how nocturnal migrants can be attracted to the lighted space, become disoriented as they flutter about, and strike the tower, the guy wires, or one another. By neither exaggerating nor minimizing the dangers, staying within my area of expertise, and finding other experts to back up my claims, I garnered so much public support that the company backed down and built a 100-foot wooden pole cemented into the ground to hold its antenna. It was short enough to not require lights and was built without potentially lethal guy wires.

We've constructed tens of thousands of lighted towers since that time, and even more information has come to light proving that communications towers are lethal to birds. But still, little attention is paid to the problem. We can't and shouldn't try to stop the construction of every proposed tower. We should, however, demand that bird kills at all towers be monitored and documented and then use the data to pressure the industry to develop technologies—auditory or visual—to reduce the kill. Every bird killed by one of these towers represents a clear violation of the Migratory Bird Treaty Act of 1918, one of the oldest conservation statutes in existence, which states that no migratory bird may be killed by anyone unless specifically exempted under a permit. This is a strict liability statute, making the "take" of migratory birds without a permit illegal, even when unintentional, incidental, or inadvertent. The research necessary to develop strategies to reduce the kill should be paid for by bird take permit fees, based on the number of birds killed by each tower the previous year.

These unsightly and deadly towers will remain standing until we figure out a better way to send communications signals, perhaps by satellite. Meanwhile, they provide us with useful and even lifesaving benefits. But the number of birds they kill is unacceptably high, and we need to demand that the corporations profiting from them reduce the slaughter. When a tower is proposed in your neck of the woods, request that permitting agencies follow U.S. Fish and Wildlife Service guidelines for construction and siting, and urge daily monitoring of bird kills during spring and fall migration.

When anglers or fish farm managers propose to kill or harass cormorants, their concern is usually competition for fish. This is hardly a new issue—people have been killing cormorants throughout history for the same reason. But beginning in the 1950s, DDT, PCBs and other contaminants drove cormorant numbers down dramatically, especially in the Great Lakes; by the 1970s, breeding cormorants had been completely extirpated from Lakes Michigan and Superior. Since most adults alive today don't have a clear memory of cormorants before this period, the increasing cormorant numbers on these lakes seem like an insidious new development rather than the natural outcome of a species recovering from an environmental scourge. But it's easy for conservationists to go too far in defending cormorants. Presenting statistics about the kinds of fish they typically eat can be misleading, since their local impacts can be significantly greater than statistics indicate. Again, whenever competing interests are at loggerheads, politicians and managers must try to find a solution somewhere between the two extremes. In this case, making an honest effort to find the most environmentally sound and humane ways of reducing cormorant pressure on local fisheries will help. But when the efforts of one group to understand and accommodate the needs of the other group aren't reciprocated, decision makers often end up giving more to the unyielding side, not striking a fair balance at all.

Although it can be helpful to suggest alternatives to a very bad proposal, it's not our duty or obligation as conservationists to have an answer to every problem we point out. Sometimes, stopping a misguided project or the use of a dangerous toxin is the only solution, pure and simple.

90 Support programs that fund habitat acquisition and other important conservation projects

Hunters as a group have political clout, influence, and credibility because they have long "put their money where their mouth is." The money they spend on licenses, fees, and taxes on firearms and ammunition goes a long way in influencing departments of natural resources and

Pied-billed Grebe

national agencies to make management and habitat acquisition for game animals a high priority.

In order for nongame species to receive that level of protection, these departments and agencies must be better funded by nongame interests too. Many people already contribute directly to nongame wildlife programs at the state level through tax checkoffs, but additional funding is required to even come close to the level allocated to game species and habitat. One promising idea was the Conservation and Restoration Act (CARA), proposed in the 1990s, which would have provided as much as $3.1 billion annually to states for conservation purposes. The bill would have authorized the funding of state and federal programs for wildlife restoration, parks and outdoor recreation, coastal conservation, and historic preservation. Funds were to come from a portion of the income from federal offshore oil and natural gas leases. Despite its failure to pass in previous years, by the summer of 2001, CARA was gaining support in Congress and appeared to be headed toward passage that fall. But following the tragic events of September 11, 2001, Congress turned its attention and funding elsewhere, and CARA died. Now, Congress is enacting tax cuts even while waging an expensive war in Iraq, and we face a federal debt that may overwhelm our budget for generations. It's doubtful that CARA or similar legislation will be resurrected again in our lifetimes, even though pressure on public lands continues to grow.

How can we provide adequate funding for habitat acquisition and protection of nongame wildlife? One suggestion is to enact a special tax on birding equipment such as binoculars, spotting scopes, and bird feeding supplies. Some people mistrust any kind of tax, even if they support its ultimate goals, because they don't believe that the government will use the money wisely. But the enormous success of our national and state park systems and national wildlife refuges and the success of past environmental legislation show the value of appropriating funds to acquire and maintain public lands and preserve and protect wildlife. Some people who use binoculars to watch sports or for hunting claim that it's unfair to be taxed for something they have no interest in. But everyone in America who legally buys a gun or ammunition for any purpose at all is taxed for game habitat. It's ironic that a mugger who buys a Saturday night special contributes more to wildlife habitat than many birders do.

21

FOSTER A CULTURE OF CONSERVATION

IN ORDER TO FOSTER A TRUE AND LASTING CULTURE OF CONSERvation, we need to educate the public about the beauty and value of the natural world and about the many connections between conservation, environmental quality, and our own well-being. We as individuals can make a huge difference in raising this awareness.

91 Work to make conservation ethics a mainstream focus again

In the 1960s and 1970s, environmentalism became a national fad in response to filthy air, dead lakes, burning rivers, and the rapid disappearance of treasured wildlife. But as we entered the 1980s, long lines at the gas pumps became short again, oil prices dropped so that people could afford to turn up the thermostat, and smog alerts became less numerous. A perception grew that we'd done everything we needed to do, and it was now okay to ease up on the regulations.

In 2001, the vice president of the United States sniffed that conservation was "a personal virtue" and that there would be no sweaters and lowered thermostats in his office. Talk radio hosts and "ditto-heads" lambasted everyone promoting conservation and clean air and water as "environmental wackos." Thousands of people bought Hummers, vehicles that are too heavy to be classified as light trucks, so via a legal loophole, they don't have to meet any gas mileage requirements at all. The pendulum has swung to the opposite side in a bizarre national orgy of waste, a fad far more destructive than anything ever suggested or done by law-abiding environmentalists.

Whether environmentalism or antienvironmentalism happens to be in vogue at the time, our eternal need for clean air and water and green space is best served by developing what Audubon calls a "culture of conserva-

California Condor

tion." Everything we do to raise awareness of the natural riches and hazards in our world, and everything we do to help people enjoy and value our natural heritage, will contribute to this culture. As people realize how their actions directly affect the air they breathe and the water they drink, we may see those simple but time-honored principles such as "waste not, want not" and "clean up after yourself" being applied not only at home, at school, and in the workplace but also in the world at large.

92 Be aware of weather events that affect local birds

Weather is such an integral part of our day-to-day lives that the weather report is often the most popular part of the evening news, and it's the one thing people insist on hearing every half hour on the radio. Birds that live outdoors, "naked as jaybirds," no matter what the weather have an even more intimate acquaintance with it. Some meteorological conditions are literally uplifting for them; others are disastrous. When we become more in tune with the rhythms of nature, we can sometimes avert avian tragedies.

Duluth, where I live, is situated on the western tip of Lake Superior. Every spring, hawks migrate north and end up somewhere along this largest of the Great Lakes. Thousands then make a left turn and follow the Wisconsin shoreline until they clear the tip of the lake right in Duluth. In the fall, as birds head south, they once again hit the shoreline and this time turn right. Either way, to clear the lake, they have to fly over Duluth. Every fall, about 93,000 hawks are counted at Hawk Ridge Nature Reserve in the city; on a single exceptional day, September 15, 2003, a record 102,329 were tallied. Fall hawk migration events are correlated with weather patterns; by far, the biggest flights happen on September days with west or northwest winds and high pressure. When one bird feels a rising column of air, it spreads its wings and circles, allowing the thermal to carry it upward in a spiral ascent. When another hawk spies the first one rising, it takes advantage of the thermal too. Soon there may be dozens, hundreds, or thousands of hawks swirling skyward. From a distance, a small group may look like delicate smoke tendrils or steam rising from a kettle, which is what one of these collections of spiraling hawks is called. Sometimes it looks like a tornado. Sometimes the top of the kettle is too high to observe with the naked eye, but as the hawks reach the point where the air column stops rising, they pull their wings back, arrowlike, and shoot forward, covering as much ground as they can, losing altitude, until they locate another thermal. Thus the birds pour over my city each September, drawing Duluthians' eyes to the sky.

Not all cities have such regularly occurring and spectacular avian events, but weather affects birds everywhere. In spring, robins work their way northward in a band across the continent that pretty much matches the 37-degree isotherm. In the eastern United States, April showers bring the first warblers, and May flowers sustain the first hummingbirds. When we look closely at NEXRAD radar maps on TV or the Internet, sometimes we can see the tattered forms that early radar technicians called "angels," which indicate large bird or insect movements in the nighttime sky. At first it's tricky to interpret these maps, but John Idzikowski of the Wisconsin Society for Ornithology put together a simple online tutorial (http://my.execpc.com/CE/5F/idzikoj/nexrad/nexweb/nexrad.htm) that shows how to read these migrations. On evenings when radar shows a heavy flight, let your radio and television weather forecasters know about it. They may not be receptive at first, but once a weather report starts mentioning wildlife regularly, the positive response from viewers will likely ensure that it becomes an ongoing feature, especially if you and members of your local bird club can give producers a steady and reliable source of interesting information. Bringing birds into local and even national weather conversations keeps them on the public radar screen, even when all we can see on NEXRAD is a storm system.

In large cities, NEXRAD data can tell us which nights represent a clear and present danger to birds. Cities are often built along major waterways where migrating birds concentrate in huge numbers, so even on clear nights, migrating birds may find themselves in the lighted space of a high-rise and collide with windows. In early morning, as migrants descend from the sky to street level, they may find themselves in a concrete maze. When a lost bird spots a lush ornamental tree, it will naturally fly straight for it, even though that tree may be in a hotel lobby with glass blocking the way. In Chicago in the past twenty-five years, about 30,000 birds have been killed by crashing into the glass at McCormick Place alone. It's a huge problem that occurs in every city, yet most of these deaths are completely and easily preventable if people working or living in the buildings would simply turn off the lights or close the drapes on migration nights. But people need to be reminded when to close the curtains.

That is why the Fatal Light Awareness Program (FLAP) of Toronto came into existence. FLAP works with building owners and managers to encourage them to turn building lights off or pull drapes during migration nights, and it retrieves and aids injured birds come morning. FLAP also works with other cities that want to start similar programs, such as Lights Out Chicago, and it provides information for architects to help them develop less lethal building designs. Volunteers for FLAP and similar programs are pioneers in a world where people integrate nature awareness into daily urban life, which is probably the most fundamental task we face in creating a culture of conservation.

93 Help city parks and local schools provide good bird habitat and observation opportunities for the public

I'm fortunate enough to live in Duluth, a city that still has a lot of public land. And I grew up near Chicago, with its extensive forest preserves and lakefront. But with many cities struggling to stretch dwindling budgets to provide basic services, there is less money for maintaining parks and other public land and virtually no money for acquiring more.

To protect birds and improve our own lives, it's essential that cities maintain quality habitat. We as individuals can do a lot to improve the habitat in existing parks. Pulling invasive exotic weeds, picking up trash, and pressing for the enactment of pet leash ordinances and "pooper scooper" regulations can go a long way toward improving habitat at little cost to the budget. Individuals working with bird clubs and park managers can do even more. We can raise funds to buy and plant native trees and shrubs on city green space. We can help design and plan bike paths that will take pressure off crowded roads and highways and help the public enjoy natural habitat. We can erect and maintain bird feeding stations in appropriate areas for the public to enjoy. And we can offer to lead field trips, such as spring warbler walks and summer songbird strolls, that provide opportunities for the public to learn about and enjoy birds. As a new birder, I was delighted to suddenly notice all the birds that had been in my town all along. Helping others to make this joyful discovery will contribute to the building of a true culture of conservation.

94 Foster a culture of conservation in urban neighborhoods

Most major cities are built along the shores of rivers, lakes, and oceans, where transportation has historically been simplest. Many birds follow these same waterways on their migrations, and a surprising number make rest stops even in the heart of large cities. Fortunately, many large cities maintain parks and other green space, and in enlightened areas, they provide opportunities for people to enjoy birds and other natural treasures. The first Snowy Owl I ever saw flew directly overhead as I walked on the sidewalk along Lake Shore Drive not far from the Chicago Loop. I saw my first Barn and Saw-whet Owls in Lincoln Park. And as of this writing, the last Red-headed Woodpecker I've seen anywhere was spotted in Millennium Park.

When I'm walking along the waterfront in downtown Chicago, I see fewer birders than joggers, bikers, and dog walkers, but our numbers are increasing. Volunteers in Chicago, as in many other cities, now comb downtown streets in early morning during migration to pick up birds injured by windows the night before; they maintain Peregrine Falcon nest platforms on buildings and find other ways to enhance the urban world while helping millions of people coexist with wild birds. In New York City, people like Deborah Allen and Robert "Birding Bob" DeCandido lead birding excursions by day and monitor bird migration at the Empire State Building by night.

Because of their dense populations, cities often initiate basic conservation measures long before suburbs or rural communities do, in an effort to deal with pollution, water shortages, and power outages. Congestion and auto emissions lead cities to adopt efficient public transportation options and to encourage carpooling long before suburbs do, and cities usually develop and encourage people to use bike paths too. Many cities now encourage building owners to develop "green roofs." Buildings in urban centers cover a huge percentage of total acreage, and when their rooftops (especially asphalt) are left bare, they can heat up the landscape to unbearable levels. Green roofs are much cooler and absorb many pollutants while producing oxygen. They're also much more attractive, often providing outdoorsy retreats for high-rise residents in the middle of what appears from the street to be a concrete jungle.

As cities adopt more conservation initiatives, even if they do so for practical and aesthetic reasons rather than to promote bird conservation, more people are discovering the benefits of conservation for their pocketbooks, their personal welfare, and their communities. As an added bonus, the birds we share our world with benefit too. When we encourage the conservation of resources, guard against pollution, and work for habitat improvements, we make cities more livable for everyone. And if a growing culture of conservation in our cities slows migration to the suburbs and beyond, it has a direct impact on wild areas at the edges of sprawl. Quality cities are key to the preservation of wildness.

95 Support efforts to help Third World countries raise their standard of living with minimal environmental impact

As the world population continues to grow, the gap between rich and poor grows even faster, and extraordinary pressures are placed on habitats that are critical for the health of the entire planet. But how can anyone in North America fault poor people in the tropics for slashing and burning rain forests while we are clear-cutting millions of acres of boreal forest each year, much of it for toilet paper and junk mail that could easily be produced using recycled paper?

The United Nations Environment Program (UNEP) was formed "to provide leadership and encourage partnership in caring for the environment by inspiring, informing, and enabling nations and peoples to improve their quality of life without compromising that of future generations." UNEP focuses on a huge array of important environmental issues facing the world and searches for realistic solutions. It produces authoritative and useful resources for understanding the global nature of environmental issues, such as the extraordinary atlas *One Planet, Many People,* which compares and contrasts satellite images of the past few decades with contemporary ones. These images clearly show the huge growth of greenhouses in southern Spain; the rapid rise of shrimp farming in Asia and Latin America; the emergence of a giant, shadow puppet–shaped peninsula at the mouth of the Yellow River; deforestation in Paraguay and Brazil; rapid oil and gas development in Wyoming; forest fires across sub-Saharan Africa; and the retreat of glaciers and ice in polar and mountain areas.

Global environmental issues are so huge and complex that it's impossible to imagine an individual making any significant contribution to their resolution. But learning more about these issues, promoting understanding of them in our communities, and supporting organizations like UNEP that are working hard to find realistic solutions are all things that we can do. Start by visiting UNEP's Web site at www.unep.org.

22

Serve as an
Ambassador for Birds

Virtually all conservation initiatives benefit humans as well as birds. We often justify helping birds out of self-interest, citing the huge amounts of insects and rodents they consume; the plants they pollinate; the meat, eggs, and feathers they produce; and the economic value they provide for people who hunt and photograph them or sell services and equipment to birders. It's much harder to articulate why we should protect birds simply for their own sakes.

But the more we learn about birds, the more obvious it becomes that these creatures have minds of their own. They aren't feathered robots giving programmed responses to stimuli; they are individuals capable of complex learning and communicating with one another and sometimes with us. After a study was released showing individual differences within a species of European titmice, the *New York Times* published an editorial on March 3, 2005, that read in part:

> We take the range of personalities among individuals in our species for granted, yet it seems surprising to think of similar diversity in other species. Many people find the implications of that genuinely shocking. If bird personalities have a strong genetic and evolutionary basis, there is good reason to suspect that human personalities do, too.
>
> Humans do not like to think of themselves as animals. Nor do they like to think that their behavior may have genetic or evolutionary roots. But the richer perspective—morally and intellectually—lies in examining and coming to terms with the kinship of all life. There's a certain tragic isolation in believing that humans stand

apart in every way from the creatures that surround them, that the rest of creation was shaped exclusively for our use. The real fruit of that perspective is, in fact, tragic isolation on an earth that has been eroded by our moral assumptions. Science has something much wiser to tell us about who we are. So do the birds around us.

Even if it's difficult to convince skeptics of the intrinsic value of birds beyond human practicality and aesthetics, that fundamental worth is there. After all, God himself notes the fall of a sparrow.

Anhinga

96 Be a mentor to new birders

When I was new to birding in November 1975, my mother-in-law and I came upon two birders at the Morton Arboretum outside of Chicago. They approached us and volunteered that they had seen Red Crossbills in a pine stand not far from us and a late Nashville Warbler in another area. I felt honored to be welcomed into the birding brotherhood and offered that we'd seen a pretty good assortment of ducks in a nearby lake, including a lot of wigeons. I didn't mention that my first American Coots were among them. I had been charmed by the "cute coots with their white snoots," ruby eyes, and determined way of pumping their necks when swimming. One had even stood on the bank, giving me a great look at its bizarre greenish, lobed toes. These coots were number 110 on my life list, and I had been thrilled to see them, but I had a feeling that these were major-league birders, interested only in rarities. Since the field guide clearly stated that coots were quite common, I didn't mention them. My mother-in-law, not realizing the careful little dance that birders do to size up one another, blurted out, "There were coots there too! That was new for both of us!" The two men looked at us disdainfully and walked away.

I was fortunate to know some advanced birders who were extremely welcoming. One of the main forces in the Capital Area Audubon Society in Lansing, a wonderful birder named Joan Brigham, had taken me under her wing and expressed great interest in all my discoveries. Dave Catlin, an advanced birder and one of my fellow graduate students in the Environmental Education program at Michigan State, shared my excitement when he heard about my first glimpse of warblers. But I'd already learned that the birding community has something of a pecking order. When two birders encounter each other, they engage in a peculiar verbal dance to size up the other, based on not only the size of their lists but also more subtle criteria. Knowing what constitutes a "good bird" is critical, and making any error in identification could mark one as mediocre for life. My fearfulness of making a mistake caused me to be exceptionally wary. One spring I spotted a Summer Tanager—a very rare bird in Michigan—along the Red Cedar River on campus, but I didn't tell anyone for fear of being questioned and perhaps ridiculed. I'd started birding because birds were so beautiful and fascinating, but somehow my joyful enterprise had morphed into a competitive sport.

Fortunately, by the time I left Michigan for Madison, Wisconsin, in 1976, I'd gotten that silly game out of my system. I'd seen some top birders make errors, and I'd discovered that I would rather bird with people who called out every bird they saw—even if they occasionally had to reassess a sighting and say "Oops"—than with those so intent on being 100 percent accurate that they didn't call out birds until it was too late for others to see them.

A few birders still play the pecking order game and try to make the birding community exclusive and exclusionary, but most birders realize that the more birders there are, the more likely we are to hear about rarities and the more people there are to work for bird protection. The focus on rarities has become more intense as telephone and Internet rare bird alerts have made it easier to chase down unusual birds. The mission of the American Birding Association has always been to help with the sport of listing—providing birding guides, checklists, and other tools to help birders amass large lists; creating guidelines to make list comparisons meaningful; and publishing a yearly directory of the birders with the largest lists for each state, country, and continent. State ornithological societies also publish such directories, which require one to see a certain number of species. Thus, for some people, the point of the hobby becomes searching out rare birds to bulk up their lists, rather than enjoying all birds.

Even though seeing rarities is exciting and carefully documenting them is important, birding is more than that. Although it's easy to fall into thinking "oh, that's just another grackle," one of the easiest ways to keep our own enjoyment of common birds fresh is to go birding with beginners. Those grackles that are so abundant (and even annoying after you see one kill a Pine Siskin at your feeder or have to deal with their nestlings' fecal sacs on your car) have brilliant gold eyes, a shiny purple head, glossy plumage, a long pointed tail, and a certain macho exuberance. Experiencing this with a beginner can call to mind the excitement of the day long ago when you saw your own first grackle.

Birding with beginners can be fun, but it's also important for birding itself and for the birds we love. Welcoming newcomers into the fold, patiently listening to their discoveries in the way that Joan Brigham and Dave Catlin listened to mine, giving them useful tips, and showing by example what a joyful enterprise birding is will ensure that birding as a hobby, sport, science, and pastime continues to grow. And in a society that allocates funds based on the size of the interested constituency, the bigger the birding community is, the more likely it is that we'll be able to keep habitat acquisition and protection on the radar screen of the politicians who make land-use decisions and vote on laws that protect our air, water, and wildlife heritage.

97 Don't leave home without binoculars

Most birders take up the hobby after a particular bird somehow sparks their interest. But many people who are thrilled to see an unusually lovely or comical or interesting bird don't know how to identify it or how to find another one like it. As I did on the day I saw dozens of warblers in my maple tree as a little girl, they tuck the memory away and go on with their lives.

Many times when I'm watching a flock of warblers on a popular dog-walking path in a local park or a Snowy Owl on the ice near the Lake Superior shore through the window of a restaurant, people ask me what I'm looking at, and they often stop to look too. Once when I was walking in downtown Los Angeles, I heard some swifts chittering overhead and I wheeled to a stop and pulled out my binoculars. A man curled under some newspapers on a bus stop bench sat up and asked me what I was looking at. I said, "White-throated Swifts!" I then handed him my binoculars, and he looked up with a confused expression. But the moment the swifts came into view, his face lit up. It reminded me of my own first memory of birds: As a little girl, I lived in an apartment in a tired old neighborhood in Chicago. I loved to kneel on the sofa, watch out the window, and wait for a drawbridge over the Chicago River to go up. Each time, pigeons flew up, higher and higher, drawing my eyes away from the grimy city and up to the big, beautiful sky. That memory came flooding back as I watched this homeless man looking up at a sky filled with White-throated Swifts.

When I'm checking out the Peregrine Falcon family nesting in a wooden box on a hotel in downtown Duluth, passersby often stop to ask me what I'm looking at. After I tell them, they almost always step up to my spotting scope to take a look. Peregrines are the fastest bird in the world and so are inherently interesting. The ones in Duluth have been nesting downtown for several years, but most people aren't aware of them. Their delight when they see these birds is joyful to behold.

Once the conversation about the falcons begins, people often recount tales of birds they've seen in their yards, wondering what they might have been. I usually keep a field guide in my vest pocket, and when I pull it out and show them the possibilities, they are often surprised at how easy it is to identify a bird they'd wondered about for months. Many of them walk away saying that they're going to buy binoculars and a field guide.

I started bringing my binoculars into restaurants as a security measure, scared that someone might steal them from my car. But I quickly discovered that having them with me is useful, since I always request a window seat. I've seen a Prothonotary Warbler out the window of a fast-food restaurant in Chicago; loons, mergansers, and migrating hawks out the window of a restaurant in Duluth; and a Snail Kite out the window of the Miccosukee Indian restaurant on the edge of Everglades National Park. As an added bonus, I've had the pleasure of sharing many of these birds with employees and other diners. When a major owl invasion brought birders from all over the world to Duluth, I found myself eating out with birding acquaintances who were in town for the fun. Wait staff were fascinated by this influx of birders, and because the owls were so conspicuous, they almost always had their own owl tales to share. This provided visiting birders with valuable information about good spots to check out, helped restaurant owners to see the value of birding to their own bottom line, and inspired at least a few restaurant employees to join the birding family.

Some birders are reluctant, from shyness or embarrassment, to walk around nonbirdy places with binoculars. But the practical benefits of sharing our hobby with nonbirders can be extraordinary. While living in Madison, Wisconsin, I used to go birding at a campus natural area every morning before heading to work. Picnic Point was technically closed until seven o'clock, but in spring I'd arrive well before six each day. One morning as I was scoping out some Hooded Mergansers in Lake Mendota, a policeman approached, almost certainly to kick me out, although I didn't think about that until later. I was so excited watching the ducks with their comical headdress that I couldn't help but exclaim, "Look! Hooded Mergansers! They're displaying!" I stepped aside so that he could look through my spotting scope, and he was as delighted as I was. He said that he'd seen these birds during hunting season, but hadn't realized that they were so beautiful in spring or had such an interesting breeding display. He didn't kick me out, and after that, whenever he drove past, he would wave and ask what I'd been seeing.

Beyond the practical benefits to us, sharing our hobby with nonbirders helps business owners realize that birding is a hobby worth supporting, and it draws other people in. And the more people there are who support birding, the larger and stronger the culture of conservation and the support for bird preservation will be.

98 Organize an army of birders who are willing to serve as birding ambassadors

Although each individual serving as an ambassador for birds can do a great deal of good, a whole army of ambassadors can do much more. No one can be available around the clock, year after year, to answer questions, help novices, and inspire nonbirders to take up the hobby. Sometimes it's discouraging to deal with the questions people ask, such as whether they should feed their hummingbirds artificial sweeteners rather than sugar so they don't get fat (no, hummingbirds need the calories and carbohydrates in sugar), or whether it's okay to pour a quarter cup of bleach into their birdbath to keep the water clean (no, bleach is toxic; it's okay to use a bleach solution to clean the birdbath, but allow it to dry and then add clean, fresh water). Anyone dealing with the same questions over and over can suffer burnout.

But working with other birders, informally or as part of a birding club, to provide information to the general public in the form of community education classes or local field trips can be a service of inestimable value. When a local bird club has an office and a phone, it can provide valuable assistance to people with basic questions. Bird clubs and individuals can also provide answers to questions via e-mail. Putting together a list of frequently asked questions for a pamphlet or Web site is also a good idea; for example, what to do about noisy woodpeckers, how to keep cardinals or robins from bashing into windows, or what to do when children find baby birds. Being able to refer people to wildlife rehabbers, government officials, and other professionals in the case of serious problems is also useful.

Many times, people ask me what kind of bird makes a particular sound. Over the years, I've figured out which birds people in my area are most likely to be asking about and can guess correctly at least 80 or 90 percent of the time. But now I've got better tools. Over the phone, if I'm close to my computer or CD player, I can play recordings of the likely possibilities, holding the phone up to the speaker. It's so satisfying to hear a caller say, "Yes! That's it!" When I'm away from home, I just pull my Palm Pilot out of my pocket. I've put bird sound recordings on it and can tap a few strokes and play each possibility until we find the right one. These are tools that a bird club or a small army of birding ambassadors can easily take advantage of.

Sharing our knowledge can be tiring, especially for introverts. When we find others who are willing to work together to provide information to the public, the task is easier for all of us.

99 Participate in birding festivals and celebrations of Earth Day, International Migratory Bird Day, and other significant occasions

I was a freshman in college during the first Earth Day in 1970. Twenty million demonstrators from thousands of schools and communities throughout the country participated in this grassroots national teach-in. It was a heady experience, and I was certain that this one event would lead everyone in the nation to an understanding of how important the environment is for all of us.

It may not have been as universally or as permanently inspiring as I'd imagined, but that first Earth Day did motivate millions of people, and it was an exceptional opportunity to draw together bands of conservationists to work toward important changes. That momentum was enough to pressure Congress and the administration to pass the Clean Air Act, Clean Water Act, Endangered Species Act, and a multitude of other measures in what was easily the most important five-year period for environmental progress in the nation's history.

That level of widespread passion can be aroused only during dire times, with rivers afire and the national emblem edging toward extinction. The first Earth Day garnered enormous attention in the media, but now that it's an annual event, most newspapers don't even mention it. But even today, marking Earth Day with fun and educational activities draws many people into the conservation fold and helps keep air and water quality and conservation of natural resources in the minds of many others.

International Migratory Bird Day (IMBD) was created in 1993 by visionaries at the Smithsonian Migratory Bird Center and the Cornell Lab. Now under the direction of the National Fish and Wildlife Foundation and the U.S. Fish and Wildlife Service, IMBD continues to focus attention on one of the most important and spectacular events in the life of a migratory bird—the journey between its summer and winter homes. Today, it is celebrated in Canada, the United States, Mexico, and Central America through bird festivals and bird walks, educational programs, and "Bird Day!" Each annual IMBD has a different theme, such as shade coffee, habitat, or

Horned Puffins

collisions; educational materials, including a striking poster, are created for each year's theme. You can get information and educational materials through the Web site www.birdday.org.

Helping your community celebrate Earth Day and International Migratory Bird Day is a fun and easy way to foster a culture of conservation and serve as an ambassador for birds.

100 Pay attention to birds in popular culture

Every year, people ask me whether it's true that hummingbirds migrate by riding on the backs of geese. The answer is no. Researchers band and weigh hummingbirds in Texas, Louisiana, and other spots along the Gulf of Mexico in the United States and in the Yucatán peninsula, where many of them winter. In spring and fall, the weights of arriving hummingbirds are always less than the weights of departing ones, and physiological studies have found that the difference in weight is fully accounted for by the work involved in flapping the entire 640 miles or so over the Gulf, nonstop, without food or rest.

But if it's so easily proved that hummingbirds don't hitch free rides, how did this well-known myth originate, and why does it persist? I had an insight into this when I was at my mother-in-law's place in Port Wing, Wisconsin, one summer day, watching a male Ruby-throated Hummingbird perched on a telephone wire. Suddenly he started twittering in an agitated way, looking up. I followed his gaze to a Bald Eagle flying high overhead. When the eagle crossed into what was apparently the hummingbird's column of defended airspace, the little guy took off and started dive-bombing the eagle, up and down, up and down like a tiny yo-yo, striking the eagle's nape over and over. A ten- or twelve-pound Bald Eagle is fully 1,600 times the weight of a Ruby-throated Hummingbird. I doubt that the massive raptor even noticed the little twerp, but it kept flying and eventually crossed out of the column of defended airspace. The hummingbird returned to the telephone wire still chittering—dare I say, triumphantly. I suspect that someone saw a hummingbird attacking a larger bird, perhaps a goose; witnessed the hummer either rise or descend from the larger bird's upper back; and leaped to a conclusion without watching the entire encounter. I found one documented case of a hunter bagging a goose with a dead hummingbird entangled in sticky weeds on its upper back, but that can just as easily be explained by the hummingbird's attacking the goose as by hitching a ride.

Traditions about swallows returning to Capistrano and vultures appearing at Hinckley, Ohio, on specific days are a bit of a stretch. In both cases, migrants appear days or even weeks before the appointed celebration, and most people just avert their eyes and play along.

People have many myths, sayings, and traditions about birds, from swallows carrying spring on their wings to Maya Angelou's "I know why the caged bird sings." Sports teams are often named for birds—sometimes appropriately, if they want to exude an aura of strength, agility, and cunning, and sometimes less appropriately. Teams called the "Nighthawks" might not realize that real nighthawks have soft feet that are unable to grasp a branch, much less prey; a calm and gentle disposition; and absolutely no way of defending themselves, except hiding or fleeing.

Many books feature birds, such as the owls in the Harry Potter stories, White Fang's first meal of ptarmigan chicks, and the seabird (a dovekie or murrelet) found by Laura Ingalls Wilder's family in *The Long Winter*. Even Scarlett O'Hara noticed swallows flying about Tara. I hear many birdsongs in the soundtracks of television shows and movies—some appropriate, some impossible in the real world. Noticing bird references in books, movies, and television shows gives you an interesting connection to nonbirders that may pique their interest and draw a few of them to nature study.

101 Think about the many ways that birds have enriched your life, and share them with others

From the time I was a little girl, birds have filled my eyes and ears with loveliness, my mind with fascination and wonder, and my heart with joy and laughter. Sometimes it's hard for me to realize that they don't hold that much meaning for most people. But of all the animals on this planet, birds are the ones that make us most aware of their presence throughout the year, wherever we go. Even people with no emotional connections to birds notice them, if only to wish that they'd fly away and squawk someplace else. Fortunately, most of the time when birds attract our attention, it's not unpleasant at all. Theodore Roosevelt wrote:

> Perhaps the sweetest bird music I have ever listened to was uttered by a hermit thrush. It was while hunting deer on a small lake, in the heart of the wilderness; the night was dark, for the moon had not yet risen, but there were clouds, and as we moved over the surface of the water with the perfect silence so strange and almost oppressive to the novice in this sport, I could distinguish dimly the outlines of the gloomy and impenetrable pine forests by which we were surrounded. We had been out for two or three hours but had seen nothing; once we heard a tree fall with a dull, heavy crash, and two or three times the harsh hooting of an owl had been answered by the unholy laughter of a loon from the bosom of the lake, but otherwise nothing had occurred to break

the death-like stillness of the night; not even a breath of air stirred among the tops of the tall pine trees. Wearied by our unsuccess we at last turned homeward when suddenly the quiet was broken by the song of a hermit thrush; louder and clearer it sang from the depths of the grim and rugged woods, until the sweet, sad music seemed to fill the very air and to conquer for the moment the gloom of the night; then it died away and ceased as suddenly as it had begun. Perhaps the song would have seemed less sweet in the daytime, but uttered as it was, with such surroundings, sounding so strange and so beautiful amid these grand but desolate wilds, I shall never forget it.

Recounting beautiful encounters like this inspires others and encourages them to remember their own lovely experiences with birds.

Many people dealing with cancer have told me about the sense of hope and good cheer they get from the birds at their feeders. Anne Frank was comforted watching birds from her hiding place in the Annex. Alexander Skutch, in *The Life of the Hummingbird,* tells a charming and apparently true story of a man who was befriended by a Rufous Hummingbird. The bird accompanied the man on walks as he convalesced from a serious illness and one day actually saved his life. The little hummer began chittering and flying up to his face as if to stop him, and when the man looked down, there was a venomous snake on the path in front of him. Although wild birds are seldom actual lifesavers, they are often metaphorical ones. Collecting and recounting these important stories about our deep-rooted connections with birds can fill us with joy and wonder and provide others with a deeper understanding of the intrinsic value of birds.

In Closing

WHEN I STARTED WRITING THIS BOOK IN 2003, I KNEW THAT I faced a daunting task. I'd been working on conservation issues for many years and knew how many perils birds face in the world today. But as I researched, I learned more about the sheer magnitude of problems that I was already aware of—50 million birds a year at TV towers? A billion birds a year at windows? And I discovered perils that I'd never even imagined, large and small, from the dangers of fences for prairie chickens to the toxicity of pennies in ponds. How could I not feel discouraged? Like the children in Dr. Seuss's *The Cat in the Hat,* birds face a mess that is "so big and so deep and so tall" that there seems no realistic way to solve it. No way at all.

Before we were even a nation, we worked together in a concerted effort to defeat the most powerful empire on earth and win our independence. Remembering that the only thing we had to fear was fear itself, we made enormous personal and collective sacrifices and survived the Depression, destroyed Nazism, and defeated the nation that had attacked Pearl Harbor. When we set our collective minds and hearts to it, we traveled to the moon, walked on it, and even hit a couple of golf balls up there. Now, if we continue to take steps backward, rather than toward, clean air and water and energy, if we slide away from protecting the resources that belong to every single one of us, and if we abandon the natural habitat that sustains us and that is our rightful heritage, it will not be because we can't make things better; it will be because we choose not to.

In the real world, there is no magical Cat who will ride in and clean up our messes for us. I have a few friends who deeply and truly believe that God will step in and save the day, but I grew up hearing that "the Lord helps those who help themselves." And I can't forget that God charged Noah with saving every species. This mess is our responsibility, individually and collectively. What is the solution? You and I are.

BIBLIOGRAPHY

EVEN AS THIS BOOK WAS BEING EDITED, NEW INFORMATION WAS coming to light regarding bird flu and the environmental impact of the 2005 hurricane season. I've tried to make this bibliography as complete as possible. I have divided it into three sections—Online resources, Books, and Articles in newspapers, magazines, and journals. I'm sure by the time of publication I will have learned of even more useful sources. To provide the most current and complete list of references possible, I will maintain an updated bibliography on my Web site, http://www.lauraerickson.com./

Online Resources

American Bird Conservancy
    http://www.abcbirds.org/
    "A Birder's Guide to Global Warming"
    http://www.abcbirds.org/climatechange/birdwatchersguide.pdf
    "Cats Indoors Campaign"
    http://www.abcbirds.org/cats/
    "Pesticides"
    http://www.abcbirds.org/pesticides/faws.htm
    "Pesticides and Birds Campaign"
    http://www.abcbirds.org/pesticides/
    "Seabird Report"
    http://www.abcbirds.org/policy/seabird_report.pdf
    "Tower Kill Policy"
    http://www.abcbirds.org/policy/towerkill.htm

American Birding Association
  http://www.americanbirding.org
  "Birders' Exchange"
  http://www.americanbirding.org/bex/
American Racing Pigeon Union
  http://www.pigeon.org/lostbirdinfo.htm
Arizona Native Plant Society
  http://www.AZNPS.org/html/state_np_links.html
Beyond Pesticides
  http://www.beyondpesticides.org
  "Diazinon"
  http://beyondpesticides.org/infoservices/pesticidefactsheets/toxic/
  diazinon.htm
BirdPAC
  http://www.birdpac.org/
Bird Strike Committe USA (birds colliding with aircraft)
  http://www.birdstrike.org/birds.htm
Boreal Songbird Initiative
  http://www.borealbirds.org/
British Trust for Ornithology. "The Effect of Climate Change on Birds"
  http://www.bto.org/research/advice/ecc/
Center for a New American Dream
  http://www.newdream.org/
Center for Invasive Plant Management
  http://www.weedcenter.org/inv_plant_info/invasive_info.htm
Centers for Disease Control and Prevention. "Avian Flu"
  http://www.cdc.gov/flu/avian/facts.htm
ChemTox.com (information compiled by Wayne Sinclair, MD, Allergy,
  Asthma & Immunology, and Richard Pressinger, M.Ed., Tampa, FL)
  http://www.chem-tox.com/pesticides/index.htm
Clemson University Entomology Department. "Beneficial Insects"
  http://www.entweb.clemson.edu/cuentres/cesheets/benefici/
Colorado State University Extension. "Beneficial Insects"
  http://www.ext.colostate.edu/pubs/insect/05550.html
Conservation International (conservation suggestions we can do at home)
  http://www.investigate.conservation.org/xp/ib/savingbiodiversity/
  what_you_can_do/anyone_at_home.xm1#2

Cornell Laboratory of Ornithology. "All About Birds"
  http://www.birds.cornell.edu/programs/allaboutbirds/
  "Attracting Birds With Water"
  http://www.birds.cornell.edu/programs/allaboutbirds/
  attractingbirds/otherattractants/water.html
  "Bird Feeding"
  http://www.birds.cornell.edu/pfw/aboutbirdsandfeeding/
  abtbirds_index.html
  "Birdhouse Network"
  http://www.birds.cornell.edu/birdhouse/
  "Birds of North America (subscription)"
  http://www.bna.birds.cornell.edu/bna/
  "Calcium"
  http://www.birds.cornell.edu/publications/birdscope/
  winter1998/bcap98121.htm
  "Calcium"
  http://www.birds.cornell.edu/publications/birdscope/
  autumn1999/calcium99134.html
  "Diseases"
  http://www.birds.cornell.edu/cfw/challenges/birddiseases.html
  "eBird" http://www.ebird.org/content/
  "Feeder Pests and Predators"
  http://www.birds.cornell.edu/programs/allaboutbirds/attracting
  birds/feedingbirds/ feedpestbirds.html
  "Feeding"
  http://www.birds.cornell.edu/programs/allaboutbirds/feedingbirds/
  otherfoods.html
  "Feeding Wild Birds"
  http://www.birds.cornell.edu/programs/allaboutbirds/attracting
  birds/feedingbirds/
  "Great Backyard Bird Count"
  http://www.birdsource.org/gbbc/
  "House Finch Disease Survey"
  http://www.birds.cornelll.edu/hofi/
  "Livestock/Comparative Costs of Crops and Animals"
  http://www.news.cornell.edu/releases/aug97/livestock.hrs.html

"Project Feeder Watch"
http://www.birds.cornell.edu/pfw/
"Project Pigeon Watch"
http://www.birds.cornell.edu/ppw/
"Seed Preference Study Results"
http://www.birds.cornell.edu/publications/birdscope/autumn
1994/spt94084.htm
"Urban Bird Studies"
http://www.birds.cornell.edu/programs/urbanbirds/
"Woodpecker Research"
http://www.birds.cornell.edu/wp_about/
Defenders of Wildlife. "Wild Bird Conservation Act"
http://www.defenders.org/wbcafact.html
Driftwood Wildlife Association. "Providing and Maintaining Nesting
Habitat for Chimney Swifts: A Guide for Homeowners" (Texas Parks
and Wildlife Web site)
http://www.tpwd.state.tx.us/nature/birding/chimnyswift/
chimneyswift-index.htm
EarthRights International. "Burmese Environmental and Human
Rights Abuses"
http://www.earthrights.org/burma.shtml
"Teak and Niger Seed"
http://www.earthrights.org/teak/nigerseeds.shtml
Environmental Defense. "Backyard Habitat"
http://www.environmentaldefense.org/pubs/edf-letter/1999/
jan/h_yardwl.html
"Information About the Overuse of Antibiotics"
http://www.edf.org/pressrelease.cfm?contentid=625
Environmental Working Group. "287 Different Contaminants in Human
Umbilical Cord Blood"
http://www.ewg.org/reports/bodyburden2/execsumm.php
Fatal Lights Awareness Program (FLAP)
http://www.flap.org
Field Museum of Natural History. "Lessons About Chocolate"
http://www.fmnh.org/chocolate/education.html

Florida Fish and Wildlife Conservation Commission.
"Dogs and Vulnerable Birds"
http://www.myfwc.com/viewing/info/disturbance.htm
"Monofilament"
http://www.floridaconservation.org/mrrp/faq.htm
Forest Certification Resource Center
http://www.certifiedwood.org/
Forest Stewardship Council of the United States
http://www.fscus.org/
Forest Stewardship Council International
http://www.fscoax.org/
FuelEconomy.gov
http://www.fueleconomy.gov/
Green Nature. "Making City Skylines More Bird-Friendly"
http://www.greennature.com/article1180.html
Hummingbirds.net
http://www.hummingbirds.net/
Idzikowski, John. "Bird Migration and Movements on NEXRAD
Doppler Radar" http://www.my.execpc.com/CE/5F/idzikoj/
nexrad/nexweb/nexrad.htm
Invasive.org
http://www.invasive.org/
Journey North. "Report About the Whooping Crane Injured by a
Can Top" http://www.learner.org/jnorth/spring2004/crane/update
043004.html#harmed
King County Washington. "Hazardous Waste Site/Beneficial Insects"
http://www.govlink.org/hazwaste/house/yard/problems/
goodbugs.cfm
Klem, Daniel. "Bird-Window Collisions"
http://www.birdscreen.com/Klemcollisions1989.pdf
http://www.birdscreen.com/Klem_afo_collisions1990.pdf
Michigan Environmental Council.
http://www.mecprotects.org/mermapr04/amber.htm
Minnesota Pollution Control Agency.
http://www.mntap.umn.edu/pmp/tipsataglance.pdf
NASA's Earth Observatory. "Deforestation"
http://www.earthobservatory.nasa.gov/library/deforestation/

National Audubon. "Audubon at Home"
   http://www.audubon.org/bird/at_home/
   "Audubon at Home/Beneficial Insects"
   http://www.audubon.org/bird/at_home/plantsforbeneficial
   insects.html
   "Audubon at Home/Pesticides"
   http://www.audubon.org/bird/at_home/reducepesticideuse.html
   "Bird Feeding Basics"
   http://www.audubon.org/bird/at_home/bird_feeding/index.html
   "Birding Trails" http://www.audubon.org/bird_trails/
   "Christmas Bird Count"
   http://www.audubon.org/bird/cbc
   "Cowbird Information"
   http://www.audubon.org/bird/research/
   "Paper Production"
   http://www.magazine.audubon.org/ask/ask0105.html
   "Pesticides"
   http://www.audubon.org/bird/pesticides/index.html
   "Pesticide Guide"
   http://www.audubon.org/bird/pdf/pesticideguide.pdf
   "Population"
   http://www.audubonpopulation.org/why.html
   "West Nile Virus"
   http://www.audubon.org/bird/wnv/
National Parks Conservation Society. "Personal Watercraft"
   http://www.npca.org/media_center/factsheets/pwc.asp
National Wildlife Federation. "Backyard Habitat Program"
   http://www.nwf.org/backyardwildlifehabitat/
   "eNature.com"
   http://www.enature.com/
   "Mercury Products Guide: The Hidden Dangers of Mercury, A
   Resource Guide for Procurement Officers and Consumers About
   Mercury in Products and Their Alternatives"
   http://www.nwf.org/nwfwebadmin/binaryvault/mercury
   products.pdf
   "Motorboats and Pollution"
   http://www.gradewinner.com/p/articles/mi_m0epg/is_n9_v28/
   ai_16817900

"Operation Habitat"
http://www.nwf.org
National Wildlife Refuge Association
http://www.refugenet.org/
North American Bluebird Society
http://www.nabluebirdsociety.org/
North American Bluebird Society. "Mealworms"
http://www.nabluebirdsociety.org/mealworm.htm
Omaha Audubon. "Bluebird Feeding Information"
http://www. audubon-omaha.org/bbbox/bluefood.htm
Operation Hummingbird
http://www.rubythroat.org/
Organic Essentials. "Cotton"
http://www.organicessentials.com/cotton_and_environ.htm
Oraganic Trade Association. "Cotton"
http://www.ota.com/organic/environment/cotton_
environment.html
Pennsylvania Department of Environmental Protection. "Compost Tea"
http://www.dep.state.pa.us/dep/deputate/airwaste/wm/
recycle/tea/teal.htm
Pesticide Action Network North America (PANNA)
http://www.panna.org
PolicyAlmanac.com. "CAFE Standards"
http://www.policyalmanac.org/environment/archive/crs_cafe
_standards.shtml
PopulationAction.org. "Human Population and its Impact on Natural
Resources"
http://www.populationaction.org/resources/factsheets/
factsheet_13.htm
Purple Martin Conservation Association
http://www.purplemartin.org/
Religious Campaign for Forest Conservation
http://www.creationethics.org/index.cfm?fuseaction=
webpage&page_id=1
Ridge to Rivers Trail System. "Recommendations About Enjoying the
Trails with Dogs"
http://www.ridgetorivers.org/trailtip/dogwalks.html

Royal Society for the Protection of Birds. "Climate Change"
    http://www.rspb.org.uk/policy/climatechange/index.asp
Save Our Birds
    http://www.saveourbirds.com
Save Our Seabirds, Inc
    http://www.seabirdrehab.org/indirectcontact.htm
Seattle Audubon Society
    http://www.seattleaudubon.org/
    "Bird Feeding"
    http://www.seattleaudubon.org/natureshop/backyardbirdfeeding.pdf
    "Bird Flu"
    htttp://www.seattleaudubon.org/home/avianflufaq.asp
    "Shade Grown Coffee"
    http://www.seattleaudubon.org/shadecoffee/
    "Urban Habitat"
    htttp://www.seattleaudubon.org/conservation/campaigns
    projects/urbanhabitat.htm
Smithsonian Migratory Bird Center. "Bird Friendly Coffee"
    http://www.nationalzoo.si.edu/conservationandscience/
    migratorybirds/coffee/default.cfm
    "Climate Change"
    http://www.nationalzoo.si.edu/conservationandscience/
    migratorybirds/research/climate_change
Sustainable Forestry Initiative
    http://www.aboutsfi.org/
Sutton Center. "Gallinaceous Birds Hitting Fences"
    http://www.suttoncenter.org/lpch%20newsletter%202004.pdf
    http://www.suttoncenter.org/lpch.html
Tampa Bay Watch. "Monofilament Line"
    http://www.tampabaywatch.org/programbirdisland.htm
Towerkill.com
    http://www.towerkill.com
Tucson's Water Department
    http://www.ci.tucson.az.us/water/>
Union of Concerned Scientists. "Information About the Overuse
    of Antibiotics"http://www.ucsusa.org/publications/nucleus
    .cfm?publicationid=192

United Nations Environment Program
   http://www.unep.org/
United Nations Environment Program. "One Planet Many People"
   http://www.na.unep.net/oneplanetmanypeople/atlas_press
   release.php
U.S. Department of Agriculture. "Aflatoxin Information"
   http://www.usda.gov/gipsa/newsroom/backgrounders/
   b-aflatox.htm
   "BT"
   http://www.nal.usda.gov/bic/bttox/bttoxin.htm
U.S. Department of Energy. "Conservation Tips"
   http://www.eere.energy.gov/consumerinfo/
U.S. Environmental Protection Agency. "Climate Change and Birds"
   http://yosemite.epa.gov/oar/globalwarming.nsf/uniquekeylookup/
   shsu5bnnut/$file/ccandbirds.pdf
   "DDT"
   http://www.epa.gov/history/topics/ddt/01.htm
   "Energy Conservation"
   www.epa.gov/seahome/energy.html
   "Global Warming Impacts Birds"
   http://yosemite.epa.gov/oar/globalwarming.nsf/content/impacts
   birds.html
   "Motorboats and Pollution"
   http://www.epa.nsw.gov.au/stormwater/whatdo/local+councils/
   golf.htm
   "Paper Conservation"
   http://www.epa.gov/epaoswer/osw/conserve/clusters/paper.htm
   "Water-Saving Tips for Residential Water Use"
   http://www.epa.gov/owm/water-efficiency/resitips.htm
   http://www.epa.gov/water/you/chap3.html
U.S. Fish and Wildlife Service. "Loxahatchee National Wildlife Refuge
   (Invasive Exotics)"
   http://loxahatchee.fws.gov/biology/exotics-part-1.asp
   "Pittman-Robertson Act"
   http://federalaid.fws.gov/wr/fawr.html
   "Wild Bird Conservation Act"
   http://laws.fws.gov/lawsdigest/wildbrd.html

U.S. Geological Survey. "Climate Change"
      http://biology.usgs.gov/s=t/snt/noframe/c1110.htm
      "Deer Predation on Wild Birds"
      http://www.npwrc.usgs.gov/resource/2001/deerpred/intro.htm
      "National Wildlife Health Center"
      http://www.nwhc.usgs.gov/
U.S. National Arboretum
      http://www.usna.gov.gov/Gardens/invasives.html
University of Kentucky. "Water Treatment Plants Only Remove a
      Fraction of Pharmaceutically-Active Compounds"
      http://www.uky.edu/waterresources/song.pdf
University of Maine Extension
      http://www.umext.maine.edu/onlinepubs/htmpubs/habitats/
      7150.htm
University of Minnesota. "Locating a Wildlife Rehabber"
      http://www.tc.umn.edu/%7edevo0028/contact.htm
University of Vermont Extension. "Beneficial Insects"
      http://www.ext.vt.edu/departments/entomology/ornamentals/
      beneficials.html
Utah State University. "Landscaping"
      http://www.wildlife.utah.gov/publications/pdf/landscapingfor
      wildlife.pdf>
VegSource.com. "Use of Water to Raise Various Livestock"
      http://www.vegsource.com/articlesd/pimentel_water.htm
Wikipedia. "Nuclear Power and the Price-Anderson Act"
      http://en.wikipedia.org/wiki/Price-Anderson_Act
Wildlife International
      http://wildlife-international.org/en/public/emergency/
      emergencyrehab.html
Wood Wise
      http://www.woodwise.org/guide/goodwood.html
      http://www.woodwise.org/guide/athome.html

Books

Brower, Michael, and Warren Leon. *The Consumer's Guide to Effective Environmental Choices: Practical Advice from the Union of Concerned Scientists.* Three Rivers Press, 1999.

Carson, Rachel. *Silent Spring.* Houghton Mifflin Co., 1962.

Clench, Mary Heimerdinger, and Sally Hoyt Spofford. *Attracting Birds to Your Backyard.* Publications International Limited, 1991.

Dennis, John V. *A Complete Guide to Bird Feeding, Revised Edition.* Castle Books, 2002.

Driftwood Wildlife Association. *Providing and Maintaining Nesting Habitat for Chimney Swifts: A Guide for Homeowners.* Driftwood Wildlife Association.

Dunne, Pete. *Pete Dunne on Bird Watching.* Houghton Mifflin Co., 2003.

Elliott, Lang. *Know Your Bird Sounds Vols. 1 and 2.* Stackpole Books, 2004.

Hatch, J.J., and D.V. Weseloh. "Double-crested Cormorant (Phalacrocorax auritus)," 441. In *The Birds of North America.* Edited by A. Poole and F. Gill. The Birds of America, Inc., 1999.

Henderson, Carrol L. *Lakescaping for Wildlife.* Minnesota Department of Natural Resources, 2000.

Henderson, Carrol L. *Landscaping for Wildlife.* Minnesota Department of Natural Resources, 1987.

Henderson, Carrol L. *Wild About Birds: The DNR Bird Feeding Guide.* Minnesota Department of Natural Resources, 1995.

Henderson, Carrol L. *Woodworking for Wildlife: Homes for Birds and Mammals.* Minnesota Department of Natural Resources, 2004.

Kaufman, Kenn. *Lives of North American Birds.* Houghton Mifflin Co., 1996.

Kyle, Paul D. and Georgean Z. Kyle. *Chimney Swifts: America's Mysterious Birds above the Fireplace.* Texas A&M University Press, 2005.

Kyle, Paul D. and Gerogean Z. Kyle. *Chimney Swift Towers—New Habitat for America's Mysterious Birds: A Construction Guide.* Texas A&M University Press, 2005.

Link, Russell. *Landscaping for Wildlife in the Pacific Northwest.* University of Washington Press, 1999.

Marshall, David B., Matthew G. Hunter, and Alan L. Contreras, Editors. *Birds of Oregon: A General Reference.* Oregon State University Press, 2003.

Newfield, Nancy and Barbara Nielsen. *Hummingbird Gardens: Attracting Nature's Jewels to Your Backyard.* Chapters Publishing, 1996.

Nordstrom, Sue. *Creating Landscapes for Wildlife: A Guide for Backyards in Utah.* Utah Division of Wildlife Resources, 2001.

Schor, Juliet B., and Becky Taylor, Editors. *Sustainable Planet: Solutions for the Twenty-First Century.* Beacon Press, 2002.

Seattle Audubon Society. *Gardening for Life: An Inspirational Guide to Creating Healthy Habitat.* Seattle Audubon Society, 2003.

Skutch, Alexander F. *The Life of the Hummingbird.* Crown Publishers, Inc., 1973.

Stokes, Donald and Lillian. *Stokes Birdfeeder Book: The Complete Guide to Attracting, Identifying, and Understanding Your Feeder Birds.* Alfred A. Knopf, 1980.

Terres, John K. *Audubon Encyclopedia of North American Birds.* Alfred A. Knopf, 1980.

Williamson, Sheri. *Attracting and Feeding Hummingbirds.* T.F.H. Publications, 2000.

Articles in Newspapers, Magazines, and Journals

Ackerman, Dan. "Top Of The News: Autos Should Lighten Up." *Forbes,* July 17, 2001. http://www.forbes.com/2001/07/17/0717 topnews.html.

Eilperin, Juliet. "Pharmaceuticals in Waterways Raise Concern." *Washington Post,* June 23, 2005. http://www.washingtonpost.com/wp-dyn/content/article/2005/06/22/AR2005062201988_pf.html.

Longnecker, M.P., M.A. Klebanoff, H. Zhou, and J.W. Brock. "Association between maternal serum concentration of the DDt metabolite DDE and preterm and small-for-gestational-age babies at birth." *Lancet.* (2001) 358: 110–14.

Longnecker, M.P., W.J. Rogan, and G. Lucier. "The human health effects of DDT and PCBs and an overview of organochlorines in public health." *Annual Review of Public Health.* (1997) 18: 211–44.

McCadams, Steve. "Not Toxic Shot Makes a Difference." *Paris Landing.com.* http://www.parislanding.com/toxic_shot.htm.

Orlando, Laura. "Industry Attacks on Dissent: From Rachel Carson to Oprah." *Dollars & Sense, the Magazine of Economic Justice,* March–April 2002. http://www.dollarsandsense.org/archives/2002/0302 orlando.html.

PBS NOW. "Mercury in Fish," *PBS NOW,* January 21, 2005. http://www.pbs.org/now/science/mercuryinfish.html.

Reynolds, Kelly. "Pharmaceuticals in Drinking Water Supplies." *Water Conditioning and Purification Magazine,* June 2003. http://www.wcp .net/column.cfm?T=T&ID=2199.

Roberts, D.R., S. Manguin, and J. Mouchet. "DDT house spraying and re-emerging malaria." *Lancet.* (2000) 356: 330–32.

Seeman, Bruce T. "Scientists, Communications Industry Struggle with Bird Kills at Towers." *Newhouse News Service,* 2000. http://www.newhousenews.com/archive/story1a051800.html.

Tobin, Mitch. "Delta Beast Rears Its Head: The U.S. Department of Interior May Be Ready To Resurrect The Yuma Desalting Plant." *High Country News,* September 15, 2003, 4.

WorldWatch Institute. "Accelerating Demand for Land, Wood, and Paper Pushing World's Forests to the Brink." *Worldwatch Institute,* April 4, 1998. http://www.worldwatch.org/press/news/1998/04/04/>.

INDEX